Sexual Misbehavior
in the Civil War

Sexual Misbehavior in the Civil War

A Compendium

Thomas P. Lowry

Copyright © 2006 by Thomas P. Lowry.

Library of Congress Control Number: 2006908439
ISBN 10:   Hardcover   1-4257-1950-3
            Softcover   1-4257-1949-X

ISBN 13:   Hardcover   978-1-4257-1950-0
            Softcover   978-1-4257-1949-4

All rights reserved. No part of this book may be reproduced or transmitted in any form or by any means, electronic or mechanical, including photocopying, recording, or by any information storage and retrieval system, without permission in writing from the copyright owner.

This book was printed in the United States of America.

To order additional copies of this book, contact:
Xlibris Corporation
1-888-795-4274
www.Xlibris.com
Orders@Xlibris.com

34522

Contents

Epigraph 7
Acknowledgements 9
Introduction 11

Section I Prostitution

1. Virginia 15
2. Georgia and the Carolinas 44
3. The Deep South 50
4. West Virginia 58
5. Kentucky 64
6. Tennessee 68
7. Missouri 81
8. The Heartland 87
9. Way Out West 94
10. District of Columbia 97
11. The Mid-Atlantic States 105
12. Up North 110

Section II Rape

13. Virginia 114
14. The Carolinas 130
15. The Deep South 141
16. Tennessee, Kentucky, and West Virginia 150
17. The West 161
18. Up North 172
19. Confederate 179

Section III Other Categories

20. Masturbation	183
21. Homosexuality	196
22. Sex at Gettysburg	219
23. Bestiality	226
24. Bad Language	231
25. A Vast Miscellany	248
Appendices	267
Endnotes	271
Index	297

Epigraph

Sexual contact is the harp of a thousand strings.
Abraham Lincoln[1]

The discovery of uncomfortable facts has never been encouraged in armies, who treated their history as a sentimental treasure rather than a field of scientific research.
Captain Sir Basil Liddell Hart[2]

We like our history sanitized and theme-parked and self-congratulatory, not bloody and angry and unflattering.
Jonathan Yardley[3]

---

[1] Wilson, Douglas and Rodney O. Davis: *Herndon's Informants*. University of Illinois Press, Urbana, 2001, page 617.

[2] Tsouras, Peter G.: *The Greenhill Dictionary of Military Quotations*. Greenhill Press, London, 2000, page 233.

[3] Washington Post *Book World,* May 7, 2006.

Acknowledgements

My wife, Beverly A. Lowry, found most of these stories, created the database that made them retrievable, keyed in the manuscript, and proofed it. Without her, the book would not exist. With her, my life is much improved.

The contributions of Michael P. Musick, Robert K. Krick, and Robert E. L. Krick were an ever-flowing font of obscure and hitherto unknown sources. Many other people have helped me along the way. The ones I find in my notes are: Patrice Aillot, E. Susan Barber, John Bradbury, Dennis Brandt, Michael Cavanaugh, John M. Coski, William C. Davis, G. K. Elliott, George C. Esker III, Terry Foenander, David Fraley, James C. Frasca, Larry K. Fryer, Naomi Glass, John Halliday, Jeanne M. Harold, Rob Hodge, Richard W. Hudgens, John M. Jackson, Julie Krick, Michelle Krowl, Patricia M. LaPointe, Leigh Lewis Jr., Rebecca Livingston, Jim Lyons, Benedict Maryniak, Carl Mautz, Marcus S. McLemore, Michael Meier, Emmet V. Mittlebeeler, Dent Myers, Herb Peck, Jr., Joseph Reidy, Patrick Schroeder, Lee Sherrill, Jason S. Stratman, Robert Waitt, Budge Weidman, Russ Weidman, Samuel Whitt, and Jack D. Welsh. To anyone that I may have forgotten, I offer my apologies.

All errors, omissions, or misinterpretations are mine.

A Vice Admiral Edwin P. Hooper grant assisted us in indexing the Union Navy courts-martial. A Gilder-Lehrman Fellowship allowed us to review their manuscript collection at the J. P. Morgan Library.

Introduction

Our ancestors were three-dimensional, warm-blooded human beings. The first two dimensions have been well studied. Their intellects dwelt upon issues of union and secession, states rights and federalism, slavery and abolition. The second dimension was that of character—the courage, endurance and patience that enabled them to carry on in the face of four years of horror and deprivation. The third dimension is the one least studied and least documented: the dimension of passion. This was the fountainhead of a largely overlooked conflict, the war between the sheets, the struggle of the blue, the gray and the pink, and it is this newly found material that forms this book, the first major study of sexual misbehavior in the Civil War.

Passion led men to commit acts that were ill-advised, stupid, dangerous, immoral and/or outright criminal. The boys in uniform might troop into the whorehouse with a whoop and a holler, but retribution was often close behind. When the transcendent moment had passed and the fires of youthful lust had been momentarily slaked, the aftershocks, whether medical, moral, or legal, were often dire. A drunken brawl in a whorehouse would bring the police. A visit to a prostitute might bring disease or a charge of being absent without leave, but sex forced upon an unwilling victim might easily send the offender to the gallows. Sex between two men, especially in the Navy, might put a man in prison for five years. Or more.

How were men in uniform expected to behave? Soldiers and their officers were supposed to be present and accounted for. During the day, they were to rise early, stay sober, perform their military duties, and go quietly to sleep at the appointed hour. Their bodies belonged to the government and, like their weapons, were to be kept in good working order. Soldiers were not supposed to catch a venereal disease nor cavort with prostitutes in public. They were expected to send their pay home to their wives and mothers, rather than to dissipate their monthly thirteen dollars on pornography, whores, and booze. The officers, when their wives visited, were expected to introduce the genuine article, not some tart dressed up with the title of "Missus." All men in uniform were expected to maintain a verbal decorum, and avoid swearing, cursing, and blasphemy.

Out on the muddy expanses of the great rivers and out upon the blue waters of the deep sea, the old sailors were not supposed to molest the young boys. Following the medical beliefs of the time, all men were to refrain from self-stimulation, which was "known" to produce insanity, dementia, and even death. The most ancient Judeo-Christian holy writ forbade sexual congress with the beasts of the field and the fowls of the air.

Forbidden and disgraceful acts were even more unthinkable upon hallowed ground, such as the site of Pickett's immortal charge and Lincoln's "Fourscore and seven years ago," but even the little village of Gettysburg summons up a long written history of fornication, interspersed here and there with bestiality. Yet from coast to coast, every one of these forbidden acts is documented in newly unearthed Civil War records, many of them daily, even hourly, occurrences. How is it that they have lain silent, almost entirely hidden, for 130 years? The great Southern historian, Bell Irvin Wiley, in his classic *Life of Johnny Reb*, cited the reticence of veterans, the Victorian taboo on open discussion of sex, and the intentional destruction of materials of a lewd and lascivious nature. And, until the current generation, he was right—these stories have remained unknown.

There have been at least 50,000 books about the War Between the States and, until quite recently, not a single one focused on the sexual side of the great conflict. In 1994, the author's *The Story the Soldiers Wouldn't Tell—Sex in the Civil War* attempted to fill this gap, and summarized the limited information available at that time, much of which touched on the lighter side of the subject. However, since that time, several developments have opened a carnal cornucopia and moved this subject from a peripheral place in history to a more central one, reflecting more fully the roles that love and lust have always played in human affairs.

The principal source of this new information about Civil War sexuality has been the court-martial records, both the voluminous Union records and the slender remnants of the mostly-destroyed Confederate records. Added to the records of military justice has been a wide variety of sources forwarded by friends and colleagues, mostly letters and diary entries, and primary documents purchased at manuscript auctions. The court-martial records were surveyed by the author and his wife, Beverly, who read and summarized over 90,000 courts-martial, a process involving over 10,000 person-hours of work. Beverly then entered all the summaries into a computer database, a process than filled another year.

So-called *general* courts-martial were held for more serious offenses, while minor infractions were handled by regimental courts-martial. The former were tried by a board of thirteen commissioned officers, operating under the Articles of War. A full discussion of the complex history of military trials will be found in the author's *Abraham Lincoln and Military Justice*.

The records of the surgeon-general shed additional light on sexual behavior, both criminal and consensual. Communicable diseases swept through the armies of both north and south. Among these scourges was venereal disease, with 183,000 reported cases in the Union army alone. (Many of the California regiments had a fifty percent VD rate!) Both the Union and the Confederacy established specialized venereal disease hospitals for cases too severe for the regimental surgeons to treat.

Words themselves have the power to wound, to inflame, or to inspire. Swearing has an undeniable sexual content; consider the widely used "son of a bitch," which designates the recipient as the product of bestiality. Many of the curses flung into the air 140 years ago have been captured in the court-martial records, saved like maledictive flies in amber. Words of prurient intent poured from the presses of the northern pornography industry and were sent through the mails in vast profusion to the boys in uniform. These catalogs and their contents were prohibited by the provost marshals and were frequently destroyed. Enough survived to add to this study.

The battles of the Civil War have been analyzed in thousands of books, enshrined in parks, and reenacted nearly every weekend, but in the 1860's, not every day was filled with flying lead and screaming wounded. In the long days and weeks of training, resting, recuperation and routine duty, men's minds turned from battle's rigors to feats of ardor. While the vast majority of those pelvic encounters went unrecorded, the small fraction that was written down is, indeed, enough to fill a book.

The review of the testimony of tens of thousands of trials, and my years working at San Quentin Prison, very strongly support my belief that the cases here are only a few of the actual events of 1861-1865, and that sexual activity, both overt and hidden, was much greater than the records document. In fact, it seems likely that society in the 1860's was more sexual than the present day "immorality" proclaimed by politicians, mass media religious figures, and other self-appointed guardians of the public weal. Recent discoveries in the field of Civil War-era abortion and contraception may further verify this opinion.

One of the many subjects that emerge in this survey is the lives of the prostitutes. Contrary to the somewhat romantic view portrayed in many films and TV shows, the lives of prostitutes in the 1860s were, to use the words of Thomas Hobbes, "nasty, brutish, and short." Hygienic and sanitary conveniences were nearly absent. Many kept oilcloth across the foot of the bed, since soldiers left their muddy boots on during their devotions to Aphrodite. Most prostitutes were dead by age twenty-five, victims of suicide, syphilis, alcoholism, or morphine overdoses.

People have and have had sexual activity because it is usually pleasurable, often deeply pleasurable. (Rape victims and prostitutes are, of course, exceptions. With rape, the fear, physical pain and threat of death are paramount.

For prostitutes, the work was the antithesis of romance.) The sexual urge is an almost irresistible impulse for most. Ordinary experience, the daily newspapers, and the productions of the great dramatists all teach us that men and women will risk disgrace, embarrassment, lawsuits, unwanted pregnancies, virulent disease, even death itself, in the pursuit of those hours or minutes of transcendental joy. Whether it be termed love, lust, desire, obsession, or infatuation, the pelvic tickle, the small hot coal burning in the groin, the tightness in the chest, the pounding heart, the urge to experience the crescendo and release of sexual fulfillment are all perceived as imperative sensations.

Even with all its hazards, sex was a joy and in the recounting of these tales, the author will let some of that same joy, experienced by our long-ago soldiers, shine through. However, it will be apparent that the joy was often at the expense of others (betrayed wives, infected sweethearts, suicidal prostitutes, broken rules), or at the expense of the soldier, who could suffer disease, prison, remorse, and death.

Many states today have specialized high-security mental hospitals for sexual predators. Prisons hold thousands of men convicted of rape. Although most men and women are well behaved, the daily papers tell us of transgressions by those we trust the most: camp counselors, sports coaches, and members of the clergy.

Sex crimes are prominent in today's outpouring of television dramas and detective stories. Millions of viewers consider themselves minor authorities on the use of DNA in tracing crime scene body fluids, and revel in the arcana of the investigator's bag of tricks. Yet, long before modern forensic science, long before television and tabloid newspapers, the men and women of the Civil War were themselves participants in interdicted sexual behavior, documented here in remarkable detail. It will be apparent that the author has offered little in the way of comment, analysis, or editorializing. This is not a book of analysis, nor would the sheer volume of material allow such pontificating.

What is presented here is direct from our nation's archives, unvarnished, unbleached, in all its living immediacy—the actual words and deeds, uncensored by the dead hand of editors, and free of the meddling of school boards and other self-appointed guardians of morality.

Those who read history of necessity—academicians and graduate students—will find this work a Rosetta Stone, a vast finding aid for future research, a beginning point for monographs, dissertations, and other learned works.

It is my hope that those who read for pleasure will look at this landscape of tumult, where hearts, minds and pelvises intersected, and turn the pages, murmuring, "I didn't know that! It's not what I learned in high school history." And that reader will be correct.

Chapter 1

PROSTITUTION IN VIRGINIA

There is a surprising amount of primary documentation about prostitution during the Civil War, in fact a plethora. A brief history of prostitution will place these documents in perspective. The earliest records of this activity date back to the religious prostitution of Sumer, 5000 years ago. Unlike today's commercial sex, temple prostitutes who offered their services were performing a sacred act, part of the worship of the whore/love goddess, whose attributes remained nearly unchanged for three millennia, as her name evolved: Ishtar, Astarte, and Aphrodite. Twenty-five hundred years after the Sumerians, the temple of Aphrodite at Corinth had sex slaves—sacred prostitutes—whose earnings supported the temple. Xenophon (400 BCE) remarked upon the lack of connection between the wish to have children and the wish for sexual gratification. For the latter, he observed that the streets and brothels of Athens teemed with available women. By Roman times, commercial sex far outweighed any religious intercourse. Paintings unearthed in Pompeii's brothels were a "menu," giving graphic proof of the sexual acts offered for sale. The records of medieval and Renaissance Europe describe swarms of prostitutes in every town and city. Whores and the armies spread the great syphilis epidemic of 1498. Even the Indian chiefs who visited Thomas Jefferson caught syphilis in Philadelphia. With this 5000-year history, it is not surprising to find prostitution during the Civil War. The real surprise has been in how widespread it was.[1]

In the final chapter of this section (Prostitution Up North) I will place Civil War prostitution in its historical perspective, and examine its influence upon military affairs.

Alexandria

Alexandria, Virginia, an ancient port city on the southern bank of the Potomac River, was a major supply and distribution point for the Union Army during the war, but even before the first shot was fired, 1860 census records show at least two establishments that were ready to welcome lonely men. Sarah Billips, age 28, whose business was listed as "House of Prostitution," had living with her Julia Rollings, age 23, and Josephine French, age 19, both of whom listed their occupation as "prostitute." The fourth member of the household was nine-year Thomas, Sarah's son. Next door, living alone, was Mary Murphreys, age 20, also a prostitute. (No euphemisms for these women!) Nearby was Mary Blake, age 32; with Catherine Hutchins and Emma Nelson, both age 22, the threesome formed another "House of Prostitution."[2] With the war, the presence of money and ready transport soon attracted even more women of the evening. Their interaction with the Union Army, not surprisingly, generated difficulties. The courts-martial that are derived from these interactions will be presented in chronological order.

Even with the Union occupation of Alexandria on May 24, 1861, prostitutes were a worry to the nearby Confederate forces. On June 24, 1861, Thomas Jordan, General Pierre G. T. Beauregard's Acting Assistant Adjutant General, wrote to General Milledge Bonham, "The Brigadier General commanding directs that especial care be taken to prevent the passage into an advanced line of women from Alexandria, professing to be wives . . . These women have been the source of much annoyance here, as they are idle and unstable."[3]

Thomas Radcliff, a captain of the 18th New York, from October 1861 to January 1862 "did live with and have the relation of a man and wife with, a person of infamous reputation," according to the charges filed against him. She stayed at Mrs. Catherine Bodkin's boarding house and was accepted as Radcliff's wife until the captain himself told the other officers that she was only his mistress. In spite of his service in McClellan's peninsular campaign and the bloody events at Antietam, he was dismissed for conduct unbecoming an officer and a gentleman.[4]

Lieutenant T. Hamilton Haire of the 31st New York was court-martialed twice. In December 1861, he was dismissed for failing to post sentinels at Little River Turnpike, Virginia, and for sleeping at his post. However, he was still with his regiment in January 1862 and was then charged with being drunk on a reconnaissance to Mason's Hill, with exposing his "person" (penis) while in camp and with keeping a "notorious woman of ill fame" in his tent. Lieutenant William Maitland described Haire as "inclined to be intoxicated," and said that Haire had been drinking beer with the enlisted men. Lieutenant Barnett Sloan had seen "a lady of easy virtue" in Haire's tent, and Captain William Prentiss saw Haire lying asleep in his tent, naked, with the flaps up, on a warm afternoon. Prentiss later heard obscene songs and drunken quarreling in Haire's tent, followed by the emergence of a woman. Haire gave this defense: he could not have been intoxicated, as he drank only beer. He was cashiered, thus sparing him the chance of dying in the swamps of Chickahominy with others of his regiment.[5]

The case of Lieutenant H. D. Davis, of the 16th West Virginia, tried in October 1862, reveals a Hogarthian cast of characters. Davis was charged with calling Lieutenant William H. Poynton (of the same regiment) a "whorehouse pimp." Davis claimed that Poynton (who had held his commission for only a week) lived with the madam of a whorehouse on Prince Street near Pitt Street, and was the proprietor of a "ranch" located "up near the railroad." Sergeant H. Rolin told the Court that Poynton lived in a house of prostitution "on the left side of Henry Street going toward Washington Street." Private Truman Keck, yet another member of the 16th West Virginia, said, "Lieutenant Poynton lives in a house of prostitution on Railroad Street in the alley. There are six nigger wenches there." A citizen, Mathew Paine, was called to testify, but was sent away as being too drunk to be useful.

Davis himself was no saint. Lieutenant Charles F. Howard (apparently of the provost guard) had been sent to find Davis. "I went to four houses in Alexandria looking for the prisoner (Davis) and found traces of him at all of them. I finally found him drunk in his bunk at his King Street headquarters." The mind runs wild as to what these "traces" might have been, but the end result was Davis' being "cashiered" (discharged in disgrace). The entire 16th West Virginia seems to have been of little use to the Union cause. They had been mustered in for three years, but were disbanded after only ten months, deemed incorrigible even by an army desperate for recruits, a record matched only by the 53rd New York Infantry, whose brawling drunks caused the regiment to be disbanded after only six months of service.[6]

The next case found its way into the Executive Mansion and was reviewed by Lincoln himself. Captain Hugh Harkins of the 3rd Pennsylvania Reserves, was convicted of stealing a silver-plated revolver from the sutler, but more relevant to our theme was his theft of $126 ($3700 in today's money) from the pocket of a lieutenant while both were drunk in a "house of ill fame" at 301 King Street. He was ordered dismissed. Although twenty-seven brother officers signed a petition proclaiming Harkins to be a good man, citing his battle service at Fredericksburg and Antietam, the president wrote, "Sentence approved. A. Lincoln July 22, 1863."[7]

In the days before laminated identification cards and soldiers' metal "dog tags," you were whoever you said you were. Even if you were apparently in a four-way sexual situation. In April 1863, Lieutenant Colonel H. H. Wells, Alexandria's provost marshal, wrote to Brigadier General John P. Slough, Military Governor, "I found Lieutenant William Young, 1st Connecticut Battery, in one of the lowest houses of prostitution, with two privates, in bed. The house is known as the Hole in the Wall and is on Prince Street near Pitt. I ordered him to report at your headquarters at 10:00 o'clock." Lieutenant Young never reported, because he had never existed. The man had simply given a false name.[8]

In the same records as the nonexistent lieutenant was another case. "20th of March 1863, a Negro woman, Catherine Ford, a drunken, disorderly prostitute, one of the worst of her class, was arrested and tried by Captain Clark [first name not given], Provost Judge and sent to the Slave Pen [used then as a jail] . . . for her insulting and abusive language—too obscene to be repeated in this report—[and] was ordered to receive a shower bath [buckets of cold water]." Alexandria was under martial law, and the Union army arrested, tried, and convicted civilians.

Few officers could match the remarkable record of the 7th Pennsylvania Reserves Lieutenant George Hopkins. On July 9, 1863, he was the officer in charge of the mounted guard of his regiment, sent to patrol Henry Street "near the railroad." He and his men were on duty for 24 hours. He spent 23 of those hours drinking and carousing at 33 Henry Street, the site of a well-known brothel, called "The First Rhode Island Battery." (Perhaps he misunderstood the concept of a "mounted" guard.) He told the sergeant, "If you need me, I will be at No. 33; enter by way of the alley." On July 18th, he was again on duty and again spent the day drinking, this time at several brothels, returning drunk to his duties. On July 21st, he was back at 33 Henry Street for most of his time while in command. On July 26th, the Sabbath, he walked with two "notorious prostitutes," one on each arm, down the length of dress parade, during family visiting day, and then escorted them along the streets of the city, ending the evening at a "respectable public house," the Continental, where his flouting of his notorious companions caused the proprietor, John Zizeciak, to ask Hopkins to leave. The lieutenant, seemingly a master of the bon mot, responded: "I can whip any Goddamn son of a bitch who says my woman is a prostitute!" Could his behavior be attributed to becoming mentally unhinged during the Battles of Fredericksburg and Antietam? Whatever the cause, he was cashiered.[9]

Hopkins was not the only officer parading with prostitutes. On November 27th, 1863, General John P. Slough issued a circular in which he "regrets to say that certain commissioned officers . . . have on several occasions disgraced themselves and their positions by being found in the public streets and places of amusements of the city of Alexandria in company with public prostitutes." Slough ordered that the provost marshal arrest "all officers guilty of this offense." (Slough, whose "imperious temper" made him unpopular, was appointed Chief Justice of New Mexico Territory in 1865, where he was shot to death during a quarrel in the billiard room of Santa Fe's La Fonda Hotel.)[10]

The same month as Lieutenant Hopkins' transgressions, Private Robert Bright of the 1st District of Columbia Infantry was convicted of desertion, in a plot hatched at "a house of ill fame on Henry Street." He was sentenced to four years at Florida's notorious Dry Tortugas. His penniless and desperately sick wife, burdened with two small children, protested the lengthy sentence.[11]

In December 1863, Lieutenant Eugene Frossard of the 5th New York Veteran Volunteers, was charged with being drunk in an Alexandria house of prostitution and of refusing to pay for the wine he had consumed. He was acquitted of this charge, but was cashiered, after only a few months with his regiment, for threatening two civilians with his pistol.[12]

Fort Lyon was a massive artillery emplacement at the corner of James Drive and King's Highway, using today's landmarks. There, in April 1864, Private George Jeffers of the 10th New York Heavy Artillery, deserted. His first stop was at a saloon, whence he proceeded to "Mrs. Atcherson's" establishment in Uniontown, just across the river, no doubt to the consternation of Mrs. Jeffers, who lived in Sackett's Harbor, New York. George was sent to hard labor for the rest of his enlistment.[13]

Fort Strong was located near the intersection of Lee Highway and Wayne Street. There, in October 1864, Joseph Dudley and John King, both privates in the 1st U.S. Artillery, deserted. Dudley told the Court, "I drank lager beer, then I went to a house [of prostitution] in Alexandria. I intended to stay there until I had spent all my money!" (Carpe diem in action!) King told a more complex story. "We got drunk and went to Alexandria, where bad women persuaded us to put on civilian clothes and shortly thereafter two men came and arrested us and then put us in the Slave Pen [jail] and thence to Prince Street Prison." Both men received three months at hard labor and each forfeited $8 of his $13 monthly pay for three months.[14]

King had fallen victim to a scam reported several times at Alexandria. A prostitute would encourage a soldier to desert and then sell him civilian clothes. After he had dressed, her collaborators would appear and arrest the would-be deserter. She would then retrieve the civilian clothes and keep them for the next victim. There was a $30 bounty ($900 in today's money) that the prostitute would then share with the arresting officers. The soldier and the taxpayer suffered, while the prostitute and the crooked police prospered.

The case of William Greenwood seems to have been another changing-clothes-in-a-brothel scam, combined with an insight into the chaotic state of Union recruitment in November 1864. Greenwood enlisted for a one-year term as a substitute and received a $400 bounty, a small fortune in the mid-19th Century. He first stayed a week at a camp near Trenton, New Jersey, then he and a hundred other recruits were shipped to Harper's Ferry, where they were told that they were now in the 10th New Jersey. "I cannot say which company, since I never saw the regiment." From Harper's Ferry, he was sent to Camp Distribution, Virginia, where he spent one night and was then brought to Alexandria, and put on a boat bound for City Point, no doubt for action in the siege of Petersburg,

Virginia. (It is worth noting that at no time did Greenwood receive any military training.) The boat's departure was delayed, and Greenwood was allowed "to go ashore for refreshment," a serious error by some officer. When he returned, the boat was gone. Surprise! Seizing this self-created opportunity, Greenwood proceeded directly to a brothel, where he told Mary Wilson that he wished to desert. "She told me she would furnish me with citizen's clothing, for which I paid her $25. She told me that she had to take a citizen with her to testify that the clothes in question were for a brother of hers in the hospital. She brought the clothes to the house in a valise. The landlady would not allow me to change my clothes there. Mary Wilson followed me to a colored man's house a little distance [away], where I changed. I then went to another brothel, this on King Street, where I was arrested." He was sentenced to complete his one-year enlistment, forfeiting $10 of his $13 pay each month.[15]

Five additional cases will illustrate the central role that houses of prostitution played in fleecing soldiers—or at least soldiers who were deserting. John Henderson, 14th Connecticut, in May of 1864, had helped bring wounded men to Alexandria. He claims he had left his uniform blouse on the steamboat, and bought a civilian coat from a man who took him to "Mrs. Ryan's, on the railroad." One of his newfound friends then arrested him, and thus collected the bounty offered to those who caught deserters.[16]. Frederick Pebedy, 7th New Jersey, deserted from Camp Distribution and came to Alexandria. Mrs. Fortner, the madam of Philadelphia House on Royal Street sold him civilian clothes for $80 ($2400 in today's money). Once he was dressed, she summoned detectives, who offered to let him go for $100. Pebedy paid the $100—and then they arrested him anyway![17] John Titus, 5th New York Heavy Artillery deserted and went to a "house at 11 Prince Street," where the girls hid him from the provost guard. A Mr. Miller offered to take Titus and two other deserters by small boat to Washington, DC, for $50 each. After they paid the $150, the soldiers were arrested.[18]. William Nolan, 11th New Jersey, left Soldier's Rest in Alexandria and paid a guard $5 to take him to the express office "to send money home." Somehow, he arrived at a house of ill fame where he paid $25 for civilian clothes. "I gave the man two twenty-dollar bills. He went out for change and in about an hour a policeman came and arrested me."[19] William Hammond, 42nd New York, went to the Arcade House at 11 Prince Street, where he paid $70 to a man who promised to take him by boat to Washington, DC. Hammond was told to wait concealed in the attic, where he was arrested.[20] The case of Samuel Proctor, a seventeen-year old boy, and the testimony of prostitute Kate Rivers, illustrate the depth of the corruption in wartime Alexandria. In a collusion between F. Tapley, chief of the military police, and George Wilson, owner of the saloon and whorehouse at 11 Prince Street, a "large number" of soldiers had been urged to desert. Judge Advocate General Holt's investigation showed that the usual charge to the would-be deserter was $150, which was split three ways, Tapley, Wilson and Proctor (who handled the clothing supply) receiving equal shares.[21]

In November 1864, a domestic quarrel shed further light on wartime Alexandria. Private Joseph Pfister was a member of the 2nd Veterans Reserve Corps. His wife was staying at "Mrs. Hamblin's, opposite the Soldier's Rest," with their small son. Private William Hamblin, 117th New York, whose mother ran the boarding house, stated, "Mrs. Pfister came down to my mother's house. The captain or the man who writes passes at Sickles Barracks sent Mrs. Pfister a note [saying] that her husband was down on King Street in a house of ill fame. Pfister came in [to Mrs. Hamblin's] and said to his wife, 'I want you to come home, you damned son of a bitch.' She said she would never live with him again. He was drunk." From here, tensions escalated. Private Pfister began to shout, "This place is nothing but a damned whorehouse." He was ejected twice. On his second return, he stabbed Private Samuel Pillson of the 148th PA, the man who had put him out the first time. For this assault, he received a year in prison.[22]

Private Arthur Connor of the 45th Pennsylvania, was another man who missed the boat at Alexandria. It was January 1865. After the steamer departed, he told the Court, "Instead of going to Soldier's Rest, I got intoxicated and stayed in a house of ill fame that night . . . then I went about town and was arrested in another house of ill fame." He was gone three days. The Court fined him $10 a month for the rest of his enlistment and added three days to that enlistment.[23]

Policing a rowdy army town could be dangerous. Lieutenant William D. Carson, 201st Pennsylvania (a regiment which remained mainly in Alexandria), acting as officer of the patrol, was called to a brothel at No. 6 West Street in February 1865. The madam asked him to eject Private Michael McDonald, a recent recruit of the 79th New York. McDonald was "making a lot of noise" and would not stop. When the lieutenant arrived, the miscreant called him a "son of a bitch" and fired a revolver at him. At the trial, Carson, who had escaped injury, explained his duties. "I visit the houses of prostitution and arrest any soldier who does not have a pass." Apparently, the army was unconcerned about prostitution itself. The important thing was not to be disorderly or without a pass. McDonald, who had just begun his military career, was sent to prison for two years at hard labor.[24]

It was raining heavily the night of April 9, 1865, and two soldiers of the 2nd District of Columbia Infantry, noting that the war was winding down, were less than meticulous in their duty of guarding Alexandria's Salt Hay Wharf. In fact they were quite receptive to companionship when two "colored prostitutes" asked for shelter from the weather. A little later, the night patrol found Private John Lewis and Corporal Noah Hinkley each in bed with one of the women. Both men pled guilty to "conduct prejudicial to good order and military discipline." Lewis said in his defense, "I did not think it was a military offense to stay with a woman." Both men lost three months pay and spent the next 90 days on "police duty" with a ball and chain. In addition, Hinkley lost his corporal's stripes.[25] Hinkley noted that he been arrested and jailed by "Captain [Rufus] Pettit." This officer, the "Beast of St. Asaph's Street," was later dismissed from the army because of his sadistic tortures of many prisoners.[26]

The story of the life and death of Josephine, a young Alexandria prostitute, opens a whole vista of malfeasance in that wartime city. A central actor in that drama was Captain William M. Gwynne of the 66th Ohio, who was age 20 in 1861. In September 1862, Brigadier General Erastus B. Tyler noted that Gwynne, instead of reporting to his regiment at Harpers Ferry, had gone to Alexandria, seeking a position with his uncle, General Slough, military governor of that city. Two months later, on the recommendation of Major General George B. McClellan, Gwynne was dismissed for insubordination.

However, this resilient young man was soon back with his regiment, and was commended for his services at Chancellorsville and Gettysburg. Shortly thereafter, his avuncular connections came to fruition and in November 1863, he became provost marshal of Alexandria, while his comrades in the 66th Ohio marched off to join William T. Sherman in Alabama. In August 1864, Gwynne's affairs became entangled with the above-mentioned Josephine, who at various times used the last names of Bixby, White, Plum and Gwynne. As provost marshal, Captain Gwynne had frequently arrested a Mr. Lewick Palmer, of 127 Cameron Street, for illegal whiskey sales. Palmer, in turn, wrote to Abraham Lincoln, Secretary of War Stanton, Senator William Fessenden, and to the governor of Ohio, asserting that Gwynne had seduced Josephine, introduced her to a life of prostitution, impregnated her, and encouraged her to have an abortion. "She died of the abortion and a broken heart." To answer these charges, Gwynne demanded a court of inquiry, whose witnesses revealed further the inner workings of Alexandria.

Palmer testified first, reasserting his charges and then backed down, bleating, "I have no personal knowledge of any of this." Minnie Schuster, who kept a house of prostitution at 336 King Street, said, "Josephine boarded with me for about two months. She paid her board from the company she kept. She was married and before she came to my place she had been kept at the New York Hotel by Dr. Plum. I never saw any connexion [sexual intercourse] between her and Captain Gwynne. She was sick when she left my place."

Dr. Washington Kilmer, of 212 Prince Street, remembered her. "I first prescribed for her at the City Hotel, then at Minnie Schuster's place, and finally at 210 Prince Street, where she died. When I first saw her, she had hysteria from suppression of the menses. When I saw her at Minnie Schuster's, her menses had reappeared. There was no sign of an abortion or pregnancy, nor do I know of any connection with Captain Gwynne. Josephine was fond of liquor and her habits had a great deal to do with her death. She had a nervous fever and inflammation about the base of the brain."

A Mr. Dunning, keeper of the New York Hotel on King Street, corner of Fayette Street, shed somewhat startling additional light on Alexandria's checkered history. "Josephine stayed at my hotel four times, using three different last names and sometimes the first name of Rosie. When she first came she was kept by Dr. Plum, but Mrs. Plum came to town and he couldn't support Josephine any more. She begged me not to tell my wife as she needed to do some business on the sly and was short of money. I had a crack at her myself and I couldn't go back on her after that. She had half a dozen visitors, then my wife caught a hospital steward coming out of her room, and said, "How many husbands do you have? You've got to go!" The hospital steward took her to a hotel on Fairfax Street but she was back in a few days. My wife let her stay if she'd help with the sewing but that lasted only a few days."

The hotelkeeper's wife remembered Josephine well. "When she first came, she said she was Dr. Plum's wife. I felt sorry for her. She had several letters from her husband. His right name was George Bixby. He was in the 19th Maine. He deserted and reenlisted several time, for the bounty, using different names. His last letter said he was going to California and if she ever wanted to see him, she must go there."

The court of inquiry ruled that Lewick Palmer's accusations were "utterly false and malicious" and ruled in Gwynne's favor.

George Bixby's records are as remarkable as those of his wife. He enlisted in August 1863, spent the next five months in a Union hospital with syphilis, including "open ulcers in the groin," and received a disability discharge. A Los Angeles pension examiner in 1881 noted left-sided paralysis and unequal pupils (the classic "Hutchinson's pupil," often seen in tertiary syphilis). Bixby received a pension for the rest of his life, having never served a day of duty.

Returning to Alexandria, Gwynne, furious at the trouble caused by Palmer, beat him with a riding crop. He was tried for assault and Captain Rollin Gale was tried for not restraining Gwynne. The case was sent to Washington, DC, where no action was taken. Josephine Bixby-White-Plum-Gwynne was buried in an unmarked grave.[27]

The historic district of Alexandria has preserved much of the architecture of the 1860's and even some of the stories. The Il Porto restaurant, at 121 King Street was once a bordello, run by a Madame LeCleaque. After she was murdered by a client in the late 1850s, the building was occupied, during the Civil War, by a pair of Southern ladies selling heirlooms. Their other occupation was revealed when the next tenants found a whisky still in the basement.[28]

The Union steamship *Adolph Hugel*, assigned to patrol the Potomac for smugglers and rebel couriers, was frequently anchored off Alexandria. Numerous complaints that prostitutes were allowed on board resulted in a court of inquiry. Andrew Jamieson, Alexandria's collector of revenue, recalled that, "On several occasions women of known disrepute have been seen to come on the pier, signal the ship, and go aboard in the ship's boat." He noted that frequently the "fun has been so fast and furious" that many people came to the docks to watch. Lieutenant James W. Atwell, of the 1st District of Columbia Infantry told the court of the "Canterberry Girls, known as loose characters, who were pretty lively on board." The captain of the ferry to Washington, DC, asked one of his female passengers if she was going aboard the *Hugel* to fire a salute. She replied, "No, I'm going there to handle a gun [military slang for penis]." The evidence was not enough to convict the *Hugel's* skipper, James Van Boskirk, and he remained with the navy until 1868.[29]

The evidence of the Civil War trials clearly shows that prostitution was tolerated by the Union authorities. The location and function of the houses of ill fame were no secret. At least one effort was made to close a bordello. In May 1863, four women residing at 48 North Henry Street were arrested and told to leave town. (This is the only evidence of such a shutdown discovered in these records.) With the end of the war, the era of martial law wound down, and on May 12, 1865, the civil authorities raided several bawdy houses and locked up "a large number of offenders." These sporadic efforts at discouraging prostitution seem to have had little effect on the widespread and thriving bordello industry found throughout central Alexandria during the Civil War.[30]

Nearly all these cases entered the records because of some hard-to-ignore law-breaking, such as violence, desertion or noisy behavior. These reported cases in Alexandria (and elsewhere) are just the tip of the iceberg. There were, without doubt, thousands of acts of prostitution where money changed hands to the satisfaction of both parties, where officers paid their bar bills, and where the hookers did *not* sell civilian clothes to would be deserters. These Alexandria cases document a thriving sex trade; the full reality was far more pervasive. The soldiers were young, virile, and far from home, with money in their pockets; the "girls" needed and wanted that money. True, many soldiers wrote home denouncing "immorality" and "bad women," but the men who willingly leaped into bed with these scarlet women felt no need to inform the home folks about this part of soldiering.

The Victorian Americans who documented this part of our history used many terms now out of use, a whole vocabulary of sexual euphemisms. Prostitutes were "soiled doves," or "nymphs du pave" (girls of the pavement), or "fair but frail" women, or "Cyprians." The latter added a touch of the classics; Aphrodite was borne ashore on the sands of Cyprus. The workplaces of these women (and a few men) were "bawdy houses," or "houses of ill fame" or "ill repute." Terms less frequently used were "whorehouse" and "bordello." More problematic were "disorderly" or "ill governed" houses. These were usually associated with prostitution, but some were simply the abodes of idle, noisy, drunken, riotous, combative citizens. "Parlor houses," those establishments elegant enough to have a parlor (usually with a piano player) were for the rich and well-connected; such places were rarely raided and even more rarely reported. What ink-stained wretch of the press would wish to annoy a powerful politician or a high-ranking officer? Which brings us to the capital of the Confederacy.

Richmond

Even before the war, the Richmond *Dispatch* had much to say about the ancient trade. On September 7th, 1854, we learn that Willie Ann Smith, a "free black," ran a three-girl brothel on Third Street. The January 17th, 1855, issue described Margaret Connerton, a well-known madam. On July 29th, 1856, the *Dispatch* wrote about the arrest of Frances Waddle for "soliciting sex," and on February 25th, 1857, the readers learned of Alice Hargrove, a cross-dressing "frail" of 12th Street. (She appears to have been a female in men's clothing.) Eager members of the pre-war press informed the public of three red light districts in Richmond: "Solitude," "Sugar Bottom," and "Pink Alley."[31]

Professor E. Susan Barber cast a wider net by searching the 1860 census. She looked for addresses with clusters of young, unmarried women with different surnames, and found four such. Most of the names appeared again in later newspaper reports of scandalous doings, thus confirming that these clusters of young ladies were not some cloistered religious groups or genteel finishing schools, but exactly what had been predicted—whores. The newspapers show us that before the war, prostitution was largely hidden, ignored by the gentry, and firmly segregated by race. By the end of the war, it would be a much different story.

The first capital of the newly-hatched Confederate States of America was at Montgomery, Alabama, but in late May, 1861, the political bureaucracy mounted an armada of railroad cars headed north, and with them went an entourage of fancy ladies, following the money. Soon, one contemporary writer opined that Richmond had more harlots than Paris and New Orleans combined.[32]

The flagship whorehouse of Richmond appears to be that of Josephine DeMerritt, whose establishment catered to the rich and well-connected, offering them a lineup of eight white women and three inmates with male names, who had been listed by the census taker as "female," perhaps the old South's first documented transvestite prostitutes. DeMerritt herself held personal property of $270,000 (in today's money) and seemed nearly immune to police prosecution, most likely from bribing the police and from gently hinting to her better-known clients the virtues of silence.

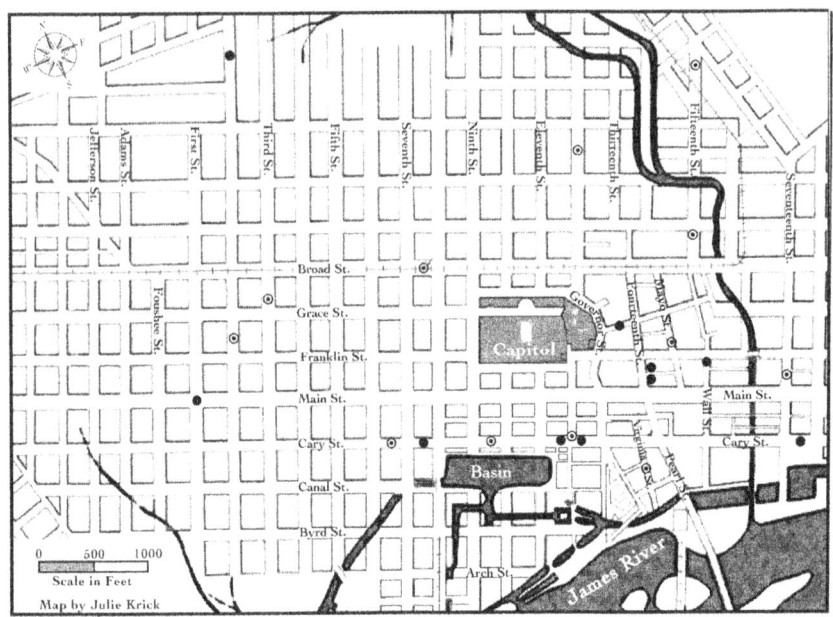

This map of Civil War Richmond houses of prostitution is based on newspaper reports. Exact street addresses were never printed. Locations with cross streets have a solid circle. An open circle indicates where street name alone is given. At least six houses of prostitution were within three blocks of the capitol building. (Map by Julie Krick).

It is not possible to document Richmond prostitution by the use of Confederate courts-martial. When the Confederate government left Richmond in April 1865, the tobacco warehouses and bridges were set afire to deny their use to the approaching Yankees. As the fires spread, the Confederate court-martial records went up in smoke. Luckily for historians, census records and copies of most of the newspapers published in Richmond during the war survived, and their pages tell us much of prostitution in the Confederacy's capital.[33]

Highlights of the ancient trade appeared in each of the five daily wartime Richmond newspapers, the *Dispatch*, the *Sentinel*, the *Daily Whig*, the *Examiner* and the *Enquirer*.

1861

With the records available now, the Richmond *Dispatch* provides the fullest picture of prostitution in the Confederacy's capital during the first year of the war. All the newspaper reports for 1861 cited here are from the *Dispatch*, unless otherwise noted.

April 17th, just five days after the Confederate bombardment of Fort Sumter, Mary Ann Mountcastle, M.C. Jordan and Sarah Sullivan were charged with keeping a disorderly house, as were John Cornett and Mary Riddle. On April 30th, the police raided a "disorderly house" kept by blacks. Among those caught were Ellen Jones (free), Mary Pettus, Lavinia Trent, Ellen (no last name), a slave belonging to C.A. Hall, and Ellen James. June 3rd, Thomas and Ann Dobson were accused of keeping a disorderly house. June 8th, Mary Wilson was arrested for being the proprietor of a house of "evil fame." June 18th, Mary Gleason was charged with keeping a disorderly house, with much drinking and fighting therein. The following day, she was sentenced to jail.

The second half of 1861 was just as busy, according to the *Dispatch*. On July 29th, Ann T. Hughes was charged with keeping a disorderly house, but was acquitted the next day. August 7th, Mike and Catherine Needham were jailed for keeping a disorderly house, as was Emma Wittenham. August 17th, Patsey Winne was accused of keeping a disorderly house.

On September 11th, the *Daily Whig* reported that Lizzie Winn was accused of keeping an "ill governed and disorderly house on Mayo Street, where persons assemble for purposes of lewdness." The next day, the jury wrangled over a verdict and on the 13th, she was discharged on the basis of a hung jury.

Continuing the reportage of the *Dispatch*, on September 18th, James Moore and his wife were charged with keeping "an ill governed and disorderly house," and on the following day Michael Shannahan and Ann Dobson were fined for keeping their own "disorderly house." On October 10th, John Sullivan was jailed for keeping "a disorderly and ill governed house where the night was made hideous by brawlings and contentions." October 12th, Delia Williams was arrested, warned and released "for arraying herself in man's apparel and making herself extremely ridiculous." (In the 1860s, cross-dressing was clearly unacceptable, and probably unsettling to male authorities.)

On October 16th, 1861, the *Enquirer* reported "Blanche Martin, a nymph du pave [a beauty of the streets], who appeared in court, "in the exquisite language of a western poet 'as smiling as a basket of chips,' was arraigned upon the charge of threatening the existence of Kate Robinson, a nymph more frail than fair, and required to give security that she would refrain from interfering with the corporeal ease and comfort of the 'Bonnie Kate.'"

Returning again to the contributions of the *Dispatch*, on October 25th, a similar event was reported under the headline, "Extraordinary Freak." The reader learned that "Considerable excitement was occasioned on 12th Street, below Main, yesterday afternoon, by the appearance of a man dressed in woman's clothing. He soon made himself scarce and the police did not succeed in tracing him to his hiding place." While the police were worried about a cross-dresser, a soldier was being robbed in a whorehouse On October 29th, Private James Johnson, Company H, 9th Alabama, had his money stolen at a house of ill fame on Locust Alley. Witnesses said that he had already been in a fight in the same house. (Locust Alley ran between Franklin and Main streets, southeast of the capitol.)

On November 14th, the *Dispatch* waxed lyrical, under the heading of "Another Foray." "The work of moral reform has commenced in earnest. Modest virtue may now lift its eyes and smile sweetly at the coming of the long-promised millennium. Richmond is to be purged of vices that have started forth at night, from dark and lonely hiding places, and sailed 'on obscene wings athwart the moon.' Following close upon the proceedings against the exhibitors of unlawful games, comes a demonstration against the Cyprian dames, which happened in this way. Officers Quarles, Davis, Wicks and Blackburn, armed with a warrant issued by the mayor, at the instance of certain parties, proceeded yesterday to a house on Virginia Street, kept by Clara Coleman, and took her into custody, together with Jenny Read, Ella Willard, Anna Willet, Mildred Coleman and Ann Beasly, and conducted them all to the station house. The charge against the first is for keeping a disorderly, ill-governed establishment, of evil fame and reputation, and against the others for participating in the vicious works there carried on. The party will be arraigned before the mayor hereafter. It has been suggested that the Divine Example furnished in the Advice to the Penitent Magdalene will be imitated in this instance—'go and sin no more.'" On November 15th, the *Dispatch* published a follow-up. "Cyprians in Court—the mayor yesterday investigated the charge against Clara Coleman which reads as follows, 'keeping an ill governed and disorderly house of evil name and fame and reputation, where diverse men as well as lewd women assemble to get drunk and fire pistols and make a great noise, to the disturbance of all the good people in the neighborhood then and there passing and residing.' Several citizens testified to the facts, and the mayor sent the case to the grand jury, requiring the accused to give security in $300 for her future good behavior. Five boarders at the establishment were held to bail in $150 each, to appear before the grand jury."

Clara Coleman's troubles were not over. November 18th, she was indicted by the Hustings Court for keeping a house of ill fame, and on December 17th was indicted again for keeping an "ill governed house" and was assessed $100. On Christmas Day, in another probable prostitution case, Margaret Phelan and Amanda Ferguson were reported arrested as "vagrant white women," in company with five "unlawfully assembled Negroes," thus completing the *Dispatch*'s 1861 coverage of the flesh trade.

1862

The *Dispatch* continued its reporting, with Ann Carter being jailed January 3rd, for keeping the traditional "disorderly house." On January 18th, the *Dispatch* reported a "Bloody Affray," in which James Keller had received a severe wound to his face, allegedly at the hands of Virginia McFaden in a bagnio "at the Northern extremity of 15th Street, in the Valley." February 10th, John Taylor was charged with exposing his "person," and on the 24th, Sally Pendergast was jailed for keeping a "house" on New Market Alley. The *Dispatch*'s supply of stories seemed endless. March 10th, William Carson and Ann Beazley were in conflict at a "house of ill fame" in Butchertown. March 13th, soldier James Phillips was acquitted of making a "lascivious attack" on Martha Jane Miller, "a white girl under 21 years of age." April 7th, prostitute Charlotte Gilman, a witness in a counterfeiting case, was arrested in Memphis, whence she had fled. May 6th, a brothel next door to the YMCA hospital was causing trouble. May 12th, Alice Hargrove and Julia Selden were keeping a "disorderly house" at 15th and Poplar. May 20th, three "battered up and trifling looking females," Elizabeth Miller, Frances Taylor, and Delia Byrd were jailed for prostitution, as was Louisa Buchannon on June 21st.

The *Dispatch* continued its efforts for the second half of 1862. July 14, Martha Morgan was arrested for keeping a house of ill fame. August 15, Lucy Smith, a "free negro," was sentenced to twenty-five lashes for keeping a "disorderly house." August 29, Nora Enright and her mother, Honora, were jailed for keeping a disorderly house. September 3, Mary Horne was arraigned for keeping a house "where various men and women of various colors assembled in an unlawful manner." September 22, Josephine DeMerritt, Anna Lewis, Kate Clinton, Mary Brown, and Agnes Richardson were charged with keeping a house of evil fame. September 27, Elizabeth Palmiter, a Mrs. Haskins, and others were charged with keeping a disorderly house. Earlier in September, Emma Marsh rated the front page. Not only was this inmate of "Mulberry Grove," on Cary Street, a person of ill fame, but on September 8, she was reported to have been riding in the streets with a young lieutenant, "to the disgust of decent people, and against the peace and dignity of the Commonwealth." Off she went to jail and the necessity of a $150 bond.

The *Dispatch* continued its coverage. October 1, page 2, Mary Walder was fined $150 for keeping a disorderly house of bad name. The same day, we read that Ella Bram, Rose Fitzpatrick, and Maria Cam, keepers of a disorderly house at the corner of 19th and Main, were released on their promise to leave the area. On October 3, Margaret Poffy was noted to be in court for "being drunk, using indecent language in Jail Alley, and keeping a disorderly house." Appearing the same day as Poffy was Louisa Espey (Espy), arrested for keeping a disorderly house in Jail Alley. Louisa was released the next day on payment of $200 security.

The *Dispatch* reported on page 2 of the October 23rd issue that James J. Cox, proprietor of a boarding house on 9th between Main and Cary, was arrested for keeping a "house of ill fame." However, the inhabitants were all men of military age and heavily armed, including a lieutenant from a Louisiana regiment. The police jailed everyone in the house. Three "mulatto women" made the front page on November 17: Willianna Tyree, Lucy Boasman, and Mudgy Manson, all arrested for keeping "a disorderly house of ill fame" in Adams Valley near the old ink factory. The police also arrested three men found in the house: Richard Nantz, William Hardley and James B. Shook. The latter was a member of the Richmond Fayette Artillery, who, in 1865, was under treatment for syphilis at Chimborazo Hospital. Also on the front page were Belle Jones and Josephine DeMerritt, "indicted for keeping disorderly and ill-governed houses, where lewd persons of both sexes congregated."

In 1862, there were ten references to prostitution in the *Daily Whig*. On February 7th, Cecillia Smith was arrested for that offense. On the 12th, Elizabeth Hardeman was also arrested, and on the 22nd, Susan Pendergrast and Mary Driscoll were arrested, the latter at a house on Cary Street between 17th and 18th Streets. On March 7th, Mary Waldron was arrested on 15th Street. There were no more sexual references for seven months in the *Whig*, but the *Dispatch* added three April items. On April 1st, a white man was brought before the mayor for exposure of his "person" on the street, and a black man also appeared for using vulgar language in public. "As the particulars would only minister to a morbid appetite, our readers must content themselves with this brief mention." Eighteen days later, Jane Jones, "a white person," appeared in the mayor's court as the proprietor of a big yellow house called Noah's Ark, on Second Street, between Duval and Jackson Streets, a place resorted to by "lewd characters." She posted a good behavior bond of $150. A story published April 28th told of two women, "having the appearance of Cyprians," who loitered at the Confederate States Military Prison (better known as Libby Prison), "making signs to the inmates, smiling, bowing and smirking." The women were jailed for the night.

On November 17th, the *Whig* resumed reporting on the doings of the soiled doves. Ann Thomas was arrested at Mulberry House on Cary Street. Two days later, there was a follow-up to the story. On the 20th, Alice Ashley was arrested at 12th Street and Cary Street. December the 5th, Ann Thompson, a madam who employed ten prostitutes, was arrested, again at 12th and Cary Street. December 12th found Mary Stevens being arrested.

Private John A. Smith, Co. G, 57th North Carolina, wrote to his sister from camp six miles north of Richmond, along the (Brook) Turnpike Road. In a letter dated September 28, 1862., he told her, "We have more dogs [promiscuous men] in the service than anybody else. Just as soon as we get to a town old married men and young go right to the hore houses." He advised his sister not to let any "old people" see the letter.[34]

1863

In 1863, the war was entering its second year. That year, the *Daily Whig* reported only one prostitution item: Ann Thomas was arrested once more, this time on April 20th. Further research may discover more *Whig* items, but from what is available thus far, the *Sentinel* had more to offer, and the following items appeared in that newspaper. June 1st, Delia Novel and Martha Edwards were arrested for being of "evil fame." September 17th, Martha and Lucy Melton were fined $150 for keeping a "disorderly house." September 18th, Mary O'Donnell and Patrick and Ann Brannon were cited for keeping a disorderly house. September 21st, William Leiber and Martin Murphy were sent to the chain gang, charged with "evil fame and name." (Were they male prostitutes? Pimps? Proprietors?) September 23rd, Charles Langford was also charged with "evil fame and name." October 22nd, Lucy Timmons, Fanny Vincent and Maggie McCabe were cited for keeping a house of "evil fame, name, and report," the evidence given in this case was of such a nature as to preclude publication.

Maggie McCabe had posted a bond for good behavior, but having failed in her attempt at reform, was sentenced to jail, according to the *Sentinel*'s October 24th issue. On November 2nd, Ann Brennan and Mary Donahoe were cited for keeping a disorderly house. November 27th, Augustus Simcoe was cited for shooting Ella Johnson, "a woman of ill fame." December 8th, Mary J. Smith and Catharine Hall were whipped for "behaving in a disorderly manner in the public streets." December 28th, Isabella Rix was fined for dressing as a man.

A third newspaper, the *Examiner*, also awaits full exploration but has yielded one 1863 item. The reportage for September 1st included "Mayor's Court—Ann Thompson, well-known citizen, charged with being a person of ill fame and reputation, and being in a disorderly room of evil fame, name and reputation, on Broad Street. Ann came up gowned in a plaid silk dress as checkered as her life has been. It is her first time." Another 1863 commentary came from Treasury Department employee, W.S. Bassford, who in his diary described Richmond as "a second Sodom . . . gamblers, thieves and murderers," adding that it was not safe for a man to go out at night.[35]

1864

The years 1864 and 1865 continued the saga of the flesh trade in the capital of the Confederacy. The *Sentinel* has yielded reports particularly descriptive of the temper of the times, dispelling the glamour sometimes attributed to the courtesan's life. On July 1st, 1864, the following article saw the light of day. "Mayor's Court—not for a long time has the Mayor's Court been so crowded with prisoners as on yesterday. Still amongst them all, there was no case of importance or even of ordinary interest. Most of the prisoners were either women or negroes. [Hardly a politically correct statement today.] Fourteen white women, of different ages, whose names we omit as of no earthly interest to our readers, were charged with keeping a house of ill fame, to the great annoyance of all the people of their neighborhood. The women occupy the house on Wall Street near Franklin, known as [illegible] Stable. It is a large new brick house, containing at least a dozen rooms which are rented out separately. It has always been tenanted by persons of the lowest character or of the most destitute description. More thieves and burglars have had their local habitation in it and been captured under its roof than in any other house of its age in the city . . . recently, its inmates having become peculiarly disagreeable to the neighbors, complaint was made to the mayor, who issued a warrant for the arrest of every person found in it.

"The warrant was executed by the police at a late hour, Wednesday night, when the police found their 14 women and three men. Ten of the women were under 30 and were of the vilest character, the dirtiest person and the most brazen face. The other four were between 45 and 60 and it was clear that only extreme poverty had driven them into such disreputable associations. Among the captive females, we noticed Amanda Logan, who is now under indictment for receiving a quantity of stolen goods. The young women were impudent, but the old folks were much distressed at their situation. The whole party having been called to the bar, Mr. Bradford and a number of other persons residing in the neighborhood, were examined as witnesses. It appeared that this was the most disorderly house in town. The women, during the day, expose their persons [naked bodies] in the windows and hallooed at, threw at and spat upon all passers-by. But when the sun went down, arrived the time for the exercise of their most disagreeable practices. They got drunk and made the night hideous with their maudlin reverie, which was varied by fights and shrieks and cries of murder. Persons living on Franklin Street a whole square off, could not sleep for the wild hurly-burly."

The second *Sentinel* item, dated July 7th, 1864, included two soldiers who were apparently patients from the huge Confederate military hospital at Chimborazo in the suburbs of Richmond. "Mayor's Court—We notice some of the most important cases disposed of by the mayor yesterday. Mary E. Vanderlip and Sarah E. Jones, charged with keeping a disorderly house at Rockett's were committed to jail in default of security to keep the peace. John C. Dawson, a recently-released penitentiary bird, found in the above house, was committed to jail and J. M. Boykin and R. Holesworth, soldiers from Chimborazo [Hospital], caught in the same, were sent to the Provost Marshal." (Confederate records show two J. M. Boykins, one from the 4th Alabama Reserves, Co. D, and another from the North Carolina Home Guards, Co. C., but no Holesworth. The miscreants may have given false names.)

In addition to these longer stories, the 1864 *Sentinel* carried many brief items related to the ancient trade. April 19, James Hardy and Pat Garrick were charged with vagrancy. They "do nothing but hang around houses of ill-fame and consort with thieves." May 26th, Mary Davenport and Emma Woodward were cited for having a "disorderly and ill governed house." June 9, Pocahontas Kyper was arrested for assaulting Mildred Bohannon. "Both are white women and reside in that delightful locality near the Old Market known as Baker's Alley." On the 28th of July, Abbey Howard, "of ill fame" was in court as a victim of theft. August 17th, Alice Hardgrove, "a woman of ill fame," was in court for assault. August 18th, Delia McCarthy appeared, charged with being "a woman of ill fame." August 22nd, the court considered details of a shooting at Catherine Blankenship's brothel. September 3rd, in an event a little different from the usual, Private William O'Brien (possibly of the 10th Battalion, Virginia Heavy Artillery), was arrested for being drunk and "exposing his person on the street." September 22nd, Maggie Andrews was in court for being "a woman of ill fame," and "of squalid appearance." September 24th, the participants of a fight at Alice Thomas' house of prostitution were in court. Four days later, there was a hearing about Ann's injuries. October 4th, Elizabeth Loyd, "age about 19," was arrested for associating with Negroes and with keeping a brothel. November 12th, Mary Jane Bayne, a native of North Carolina, was sent to Castle Thunder (a Richmond prison) for prostitution.

The *Daily Whig* had much to say about the events of 1864. On February 22nd, there was a murder in a whorehouse at the corner of Cary Street and 23rd/24th. On March 28th, a masked ball, attended by many women of dubious reputation, was broken up by the police. On April 8th, the *Whig* reported a murder in a whorehouse on Lombardy Alley; Elizabeth Liggon had stabbed Albertine Cephas. April 11th saw Anna Jackson arrested for dressing in drag. April 14th, there was more on the Cephas murder. June 7th, Florence Rivers was identified as a woman of "ill fame," as was Georgianna King on June 23rd. July 1st brought a mass arrest: Fourteen women living on Wall Street were in court for "drinking whisky, fiddling and dancing, fighting, screaming, yelling, swearing, using obscene language [and] indecently exposing their persons." July 7th, Mary E. Vanderlip and Sara Jane Rose were in court, charged with keeping a house of ill repute on Main Street at Rockett's Landing.

The final four months of 1864 kept alive the spirit of carnal activity, as reported in the *Whig*. September 6th, Fanny Gray was reported to be keeping a house of ill fame between 14th and Governor Streets. September 24th, Ann Thomas was keeping a house on Cary Street, and on the 28th, Miss Thomas is mentioned again. October 13th, Emma Cummings and Moll Wood were in court for plying their ancient trade on Cary Street. November 19th, Alice Hardgrove was said to be operating a house of prostitution on 17th Street. The year ended on December 15th for Ella Fisher, a prostitute living on Cary Street between

7th and 8th Streets, when she killed herself with an overdose of laudanum (an opium derivative).

The *Examiner* had one contribution to the subject during the year 1864. On July 19th, under the heading "Caged Camp Followers," the *Examiner* told its readers, "A department is devoted at Castle Thunder to the detention of a number of depraved and abandoned women, to prevent their following the army and contributing by their pestilential presence to the destruction of the morale of the soldiers. Some of them [presumably the women] are yet good looking and may at one time have been beautiful. It has been found necessary to keep them in constant confinement, as once at liberty, they follow and hover in the tract of an army, like carrion crows that snuff a field of slaughter."

1865

The last year of the war brought three relevant entries in the *Daily Whig*. January 18th, Catherine Blankenship was charged with keeping a house of prostitution on Main Street at First Street. January 20th brought more on Catherine's girls—Mary Taylor, Mary Blankenship and Anne Williams. Finally, on February 15th, Virginia Boisseaux of Second Street was identified as a prostitute.

The 1865 issues of the *Sentinel* reported three more events of a sexual nature. January 20th, Annie Williams, Mary Taylor and Mary Blankenship were charged with keeping a disorderly house of ill fame on 21st near Cary. March 21st, Pocahontas Lee was "indicted as a woman of ill fame." March 24th, "half-breed Ann Edwards" and six white girls were arrested for keeping a disorderly house on Main Street, below 22nd Street. A few weeks after "half-breed Ann" had her moment of fame, the offices and presses of three of Richmond's newspapers were destroyed by fire. Only the *Sentinel* and the *Whig* escaped the flames.

In July 1865, three months after the Union occupation began, an army doctor used oaths which were far from Hippocratic. Assistant Surgeon John H. Sayler of the 62nd Ohio visited the Dew Drop Inn on Locust Alley. This establishment had a saloon downstairs and Cyprians upstairs. Sayler went up into one of the girl's rooms and sat down on a sofa. He later told the Court, "Being in a high state of frustration [did he mean sexual tension?], I requested that the window shutters be closed." His partner said she needed the madam's permission to close the shutters. Sayler cursed her, went into the hallway and pushed open the madam's door. She, being "partially undressed" spoke to him harshly. The ensuing brouhaha brought the police. At the trial, Captain Henry Hitchcock, also of the 62nd Ohio, appeared as a character witness: "Dr. Sayler is an excellent surgeon—when sober."[36]

Another, more fragmentary, revelation about the Cyprian trade in Richmond is from a badly-faded letter that tells us, "Lieutenant Colonel Frank [Francis] P. Anderson of the 59th Virginia consorted with abandoned women in Richmond . . .

beastly intoxicated . . . a shame to his command . . . a habitual drunkard . . . a New York tough." Another source also cited his "fondness for abandoned women."[37]

Norfolk and Portsmouth

History was made on March 9th, 1862, when the first clash between ironclad ships changed the future shape of the world's navies. The Union's *Monitor* and the Confederacy's *Merrimack* (renamed the CSS *Virginia*) fought their prolonged duel on a body of water called Hampton Roads, a spot where the James River, Chesapeake Bay and Atlantic Ocean mingle. Four cities lie on the banks of this confluence: Norfolk, Portsmouth, Newport News and Hampton. The first two had been navy and maritime cities long before the Civil War.

A letter of Sergeant George W. Tillotson of the 89th New York sets the scene. "Getty's Point, Virginia. June 14th, 1863. My dear wife . . . the principal excitement here . . . is on account [of] the feat, fandango, dance, flare-up, festival . . . of the 89th [New York] for next Wednesday. Our company has subscribed $32.00 for it. The committee . . . are now gone to Norfolk to procure the knick knacks and invite the ladies to such an affair. I hope it will be respectable ones, but from the bad name Norfolk has for bad women (there being . . . over 500 in the place that are registered professionally bad) I have my doubts."[38]

Three officers of the 20th New York Cavalry contributed to the dissolute quality of Norfolk. Captain Frederick Stewart was court-martialed on many charges in July 1864, including embezzlement, lending government horses to prostitutes, and being accompanied on the streets by a woman in male attire, riding astride her horse, not sidesaddle like a proper lady.[39] Lieutenant H. Clay Stewart loaned a Federal horse to a "woman of the town" and rode through the public streets with her. His inamorata was Lucy Ripon, who lived at 12 Bermuda Street in Mrs. Banks' house of prostitution.[40] Lieutenant William Trout was drunk and raising a fuss on August 24, 1864, at the corner of Church and Main Streets, where he was beating his horse across the head with a two-foot board. The same morning he was violent at Eliza Thomas' house of prostitution at 107 Church Street, where he was slapping Lissie Burnham. Anna Harrington, one of the "boarders," and a witness in the trial, had known Lieutenant Trout for five years, although the nature of the relationship remained unclear. In the whorehouse altercation, Lieutenant Trout knocked Eliza Thomas to the floor after she threw a pitcher at him.[41] All three officers were sentenced to be dismissed in disgrace, a sentence approved by Major General Ben Butler.

Private John McGill of the 99th New York was accused of stealing $52 from a sleeping civilian, William Van Dorn. The location was a whorehouse on Norfolk's Broad Water Street, kept by Sally Ann Herbert, "a colored woman." Van Dorn said he was asleep on the floor of the house at 9:00 in the morning, but was quite unclear as to why he was thus sleeping or what sort of establishment he thought it was. Although Patsy James ("colored") testified that she saw McGill take Van Dorn's pocketbook, the Court acquitted McGill. None of the witnesses would concede that this house was a place of prostitution.[42]

"He is the worst man in the company," testified a witness at the trial of Private Thomas Jackson of the 11th Pennsylvania Cavalry. Jackson had been absent without leave seven times and at the time of his final arrest, on February 20th, 1863, was drunk at "a house of bad repute" in Norfolk. He was drummed out of the army, clad only in his underwear.[43]

Captain Thomas Champlin, Commissary of Subsistence in Norfolk in September 1863, sold 30 tons of government coal to a Church Street prostitute named Fanny. He also sold government coal to a prostitute named Jenny at 102 Church Street. Of course, Champlin kept the money. He was dismissed in disgrace.[44]

The court-martial system was not the only judicial arm in Norfolk during the Civil War. The city was under martial law and provost courts enforced civil order. The usual offenses tried were robbery and the sale of whisky to soldiers, but lawbreaking in the sexual sphere was far from absent. In the six-week period of June 23, 1864 to August 11th, 1864, fifty-four people were convicted of such offenses.

The offense of "being a common prostitute" was charged against Jenny Francis, Emma Lewis, Lucy Chase, Chancey Jones, Jenny Copeland, Nancy Archey, Indiana Wilcox, Clara Cooper, Dollie Ann Trout, Ann Singleton and Kate Greenwood, all designated as "colored." Undesignated women, probably white, who were charged with "being a common prostitute," included Nellie Howard, Lily Bryant, Mary Marshal, Maria Shields, Catharine Martin, Sarah Oakley, Emma Williams, Eliza Bordan, Fannie Stewart, Lizzie Johnson, Charlotte Parker, Sara Beal, Sarah Oakley, Ella Hutchinson, Eliza Myers, Lydia Morse, Hannah Harris, Martha Miller, Martha Beals, Georgianna Smith, Hannah Stanford, Amanda Lynch, Mary Meyers, Mary Ann Godford, Mary Etheredge, Hanna Barston and Lavinia Lynch. A typical sentence was that the woman pay a fine of $20 or spend 30 days in jail, although some of the African American women were sent to prison "until discharged by the Superintendent of Negro Affairs."

Most of the trial records are extremely brief, but a few give details or different designations. Frances Williams, "colored," paid a $25 fine for "lewd and lascivious cohabitation." A few days later, George Sparks, also "colored," was fined for the same offense, as was a soldier (whose name is illegible) of the 13th New York Heavy Artillery. Other citizens enjoying "lasciviously cohabiting" were G. F. Morrison, "civilian," and Martha Keeling, "colored."

After Ann Butt was convicted of "keeping a house of ill fame on Rhea's Lane, Norfolk," she was fined $250 ($7,500 in today's money) and ordered to leave the military department encompassing Norfolk within 30 days. Elizabeth Waterfield, also convicted of keeping a house of ill fame, was fined only $50 and was not required to move. Others caught in the Federal net were Evert Wingold, "civilian," fined $25 for "fornication," Mary Stewart, who was fined $20 for "lewd and lascivious conduct," and Caroline Berry, whose trial for "keeping a disorderly house" was postponed. It is clear from even a brief glimpse into Norfolk's wartime affairs that forbidden sexual conduct was widespread.[45]

In the city of Portsmouth, Private Eli Carter of the 27th Massachusetts seemed to be a rival of the legendary Sergeant Bilko. Although he was a patient at the Balfour Army Hospital, Carter had rented a house on nearby High Street, where he sold liquor on the first floor and had "lewd women" on the second floor, women including Marcellus Jones, Bessa Jones and a Mrs. Saunders. Carter, whose household included his wife, a school-age child and a cook named Sophia Phillips, was fined $100.[46]

Privates Robert Day (55th Pennsylvania) and Edward McGee (4th New Jersey Light Battery) were passengers on the steamer *Escort* in April 1865. When their ship touched at Portsmouth, both men deserted. When they were caught, each man used the same excuse: "A man gave me whisky and took me to a house of prostitution." Both men were convicted of being absent without leave and fined $8 a month for the next three months.[47]

Military justice was not consistent in the 1860's. Private Charles Collins also deserted at Portsmouth and also went to a "bawdy house." This 21-year-old private with the 8th Connecticut, was sentenced to six years in prison at hard labor.[48]

What is now Hampton County was once Elizabeth City County. The Register of Proceedings of Freedman's Court, for February 6, 1867, gives the case of "Brevet Major George E. Head vs. Frances White, Timpy Liggins and Mary Wilson," all "colored," charged with prostitution and vagrancy. "The defendants were discovered by Major Head in an outbuilding of the military prison, acting with open and gross lewdness in the company of enlisted men. On being ordered to leave the premises, defendants refused. They were identified by six witnesses as public prostitutes and vagrants. The defendants pled guilty and were ordered confined for three months at military prison, Fort Monroe."[49]

In January 1866, during a quarrel over cutting firewood in Elizabeth City County, William Brittingham shot and killed a "colored man." Of thematic relevance, the location of the murder was Sugar Hill, also known as Slabtown, both synonyms for neighborhoods of African American prostitution. Based on the testimony of black witnesses, Brittingham was sent to prison for three years. (Before the war blacks did not testify against whites.)[50]

A Virginia Miscellany

Good fiction can be more than "facts," a case in point being F. Scott Fitzgerald's short story, "The Night Before Chancellorsville." In it, a trainload of Baltimore whores displays a wondrously self-centered lack of comprehension of the gunfire and bloodshed surrounding them.[51] Our documented prostitution cases contain no Chancellorsville episodes, but stories from nearby Fredericksburg can tell us much.

Captain Joseph Williams of the 16th New York Heavy Artillery was tried in February 1864 for conduct unbecoming an officer and a gentleman. He told several brother officers of his business, running a Fredericksburg house of prostitution. "I had seven girls. I made $80 a night, but the bitches beat me out of some of it. I lost wines and furniture when Old Patrick [Provost Marshal General Marsena Patrick] closed me down." Captain Williams carried photographs of his girls, happy to pimp for the ladies that filled his house. He was convicted and dismissed in spite of his claiming that his boasts were meant as jests. Major General Ben Butler reviewed the case and concluded, "A more utterly worthless scoundrel never disgraced the service of the United States." For the next 30 years, Williams pestered the War Department for reinstatement or absolution.[52]

On June 16, 1862, Major Charles E. Livingstone of the 76th New York wrote to department headquarters from Fredericksburg, "A report has gained ground in our regiment that a man named C.B. Young has been appointed colonel of our regiment . . . he is one of the partners keeping a . . . 'Shakespeare house' in the city, a place of low repute and infamous character . . . he kept prostitutes imported from Northern cities who paid bed money and who openly practiced their vocation . . . I sent five prostitutes from his house to Washington, some of them terribly diseased." Whoever C.B. Young was, he never joined that regiment.[53]

On Valentine's Day 1863 a member of the 8th Georgia, who signed himself "Tivoli," wrote to the Atlanta *Southern Confederacy*, which published the letter on February 19th. "Camp near Fredericksburg. In the vicinity of camp there are many houses of ill fame and in one of these, a man named Owens was concealed evading the conscript law. A young man named Earle S. Lewis, a private in the [South Carolina] Palmetto Sharpshooters . . . attempted to arrest him . . . and was struck over the head with a hatchet and . . . seriously injured."

The siege of Petersburg generated three stories. A Union provost marshal report, dated January 7, 1865, tells us: "Baltimore House—outside of cavalry picket line—a house used for assignation—or rather as a whorehouse—by soldiers just within our lines who steal through the picket line at night—this house is beyond the Poor House—in that direction—called by the Rebels, Petersburg House—near the telegraph road to Fort Powhatan—three girls named Emma, Lizzie and Jane were brought from Petersburg by some Rebel officers and soldiers."[54]

An October 29, 1864 inspection report for Lane's Brigade (Confederate North Carolina troops) states: "There is more to be feared from the men's visiting the degraded 'houses of ill fame' at and near Petersburg than any other danger. The surgeons at whose suggestion the allusion is made report a number already diseased from frequenting these abandoned places of resort and express the opinion that unless these houses are broken into, the army will be deprived of the services of many this winter . . . besides their constitutions shattered for life and morals forever corrupted."[55]

In March 1865, Captain Wilson Strickler of the 21st Pennsylvania Cavalry was at Gregg's Station, Major General Philip Sheridan's headquarters, about 1,000 yards east of Fort Stevens in the defenses of Petersburg. In the evening, the provost guard visited a house on the Jerusalem Plank Road, to arrest men who were there without passes. The guard found the house "occupied with ladies and soldiers" and tried to arrest Strickler, who was not only drunk and without a pass, but very belligerent. Strickler was reprimanded for his behavior. As to the nature of the "house," it is unlikely that ordinary civilian women would do social entertaining in a battle zone.[56]

Drewry's Bluff, on the James River, almost ten miles downstream from Richmond, was the site of a major Confederate fort that guarded the capital from Union ships. Sightseers and wicked women posed a threat to this crucial battery, as described in the July 17th, 1863 Richmond *Examiner*. "We understand that no more passports will be issued to parties of pleasure-seekers to visit the Bluff for the present. The commandant, Captain Lee, has been compelled to protest against these excursions from the fact that among a great many respectable people who visited the Bluff, a few were found disreputable enough to introduce lewd women and whisky, to the danger of demoralization among the soldiers. Again, it is adjudged no time, when an attack from the enemy may occur any day, for all sorts of people to be poking about the batteries, noting their strength, counting the guns, et cetera. Visits are now confined until further order to persons having business there."

Drummondtown, in Virginia's Accomack County, was the site of two relevant episodes. Lieutenant Thomas J. Moore of the 2nd District of Columbia Volunteers was raising hell on December 13th, 1861. First, he was "so drunk as to be incapable of performing any duty." But of more serious import, he left camp without permission, hired a carriage, drove it so hard that it required repairs and, when he arrived at Lizzie Beloit's house of prostitution, about four miles distant from Camp Wilkes, he threatened her with a pistol (She told the Court, "I cried; I thought I was going to die!"), burned her bonnet and returned to camp with one of her dresses, a "fancy flounced black dress with red trim." Lieutenant Moore escaped with a reprimand.[57] [II679]

With the coming of Reconstruction, a new judicial forum was added to the old: the Freedman's Court of Accomack County. There, on May 4th, 1865, Maria Handy, Nancy Bundy, Sally Bundy and Leah Colburn were charged with "keeping a house of prostitution and not having any visible means of obtaining a livelihood." Each woman was fined [an amount now illegible] and since they were unable to pay that, each was sent to the Drummondtown Jail. Agnes Ann Gunter, also of Drummondtown, was charged with "attempting to entice enlisted men from the camp for purposes of prostitution." She was jailed for a week.[58]

Brigadier General John. F. Reynolds presided over the May 1862 trial of a Union captain, accused of keeping a white woman "of bad repute" under guard near Bristoe, Virginia. The first witness was Private John Monagan, Company A, 5th Pennsylvania Reserves, who described the activities of his superior, Captain Hezekiah C. Ulman. "It was when we came to guard the Railroad from Bristoe to Manassas. I saw a girl on the railroad in company with Captain Ulman . . . there were colored people living in the house he took her to, he came back and got some of the men to go on guard . . . Captain Ulman had a lantern. He walked up to me and asked me what I was doing there. I told him I was on duty at the Railroad Bridge. He said that I was to guard . . . the house. I told him that I had stood my time and guessed that was all that would be required of me. He said, 'A Secesh colonel was to be there [at the house] that night and I will Court Martial every damn son of a bitch that disobeys an order.'"

A second witness testified the woman was a Miss Layman, come from Manassas "looking for her brother." (This explanation was used by many prostitutes to gain entry to a camp.) "Captain Ulman sat on her bed, but her limbs were not exposed." This was contradicted by another witness: "Her overclothes were off, nothing on her arms or neck and her breasts partly bare." Another Union soldier, a little more skeptical than the others (and perhaps a voyeur), climbed a tree and saw, "the girl, nude from the waist up, lying on her back on the bed. The captain was sitting on the bed and another captain was sitting in a nearby chair." After much contradictory testimony on the subjects of underwear and nudity, Captain Ulman was acquitted.[59]

The 6th New York Cavalry was camped at Cloud's Mill, just south of Alexandria, in July 1862. There, Captain Robert E. Ellenbeck was charged with bringing a prostitute into camp and "entertaining" her for six hours. He later used the countersign (password) to pass her buggy through the lines as she returned to Alexandria. When queried about her character, one witness said, "I have known men to have criminal connexion with her for a sum of money." Another soldier verified this, adding that he, himself, had had such "connexion" with the young lady. Ellenbeck was acquitted, just in time to join his regiment in the Peninsular campaign. He was acquitted a year later, in a second court-martial, on charges of throwing away the regimental forge and anvil (crucial for shoeing horses) near Dumfries.[60]

The steam transport *Jenny Lind* ran between Washington D.C. and Aquia Creek in August 1862. There were orders that only persons with a pass were to be allowed aboard. Colonel Lafayette C. Baker, head of the U.S. Secret Service, testified that his detectives had found eighty-three persons on board with no pass, including sutlers, speculators, gamblers, "army thieves," camp followers and prostitutes, including Emma Bates and Eliza Shoemaker. One of the unauthorized passengers was described as "a graduate of the Mississippi River, a fast man who keeps posted on fast women." The ship's commander, Captain E.J. Savage, was acquitted of the charges of allowing notorious miscreants aboard his vessel.[61]

In May 1863, a boatload of civilian prisoners sent from Washington D.C.'s Old Capitol Prison to City Point, Virginia, included "two notorious prostitutes," which much annoyed Lieutenant Colonel William H. Ludlow, Assistant Inspector General at City Point.[62]

In August 1863, Oscar Hinrichs, a great-grandfather of "Muppets" creator Jim Henson, and an engineering officer on the staff of Confederate general Edward Johnson, noted that along Orange Court House Plank Road, officer's wives had come to visit and those officers who had no wives were enjoying "the questionable pleasure of public women."[63]

At Culpeper in October 1863, two captains of the 118th Pennsylvania, Frank A. Donaldson and Lemuel C. Crocker, received an invitation to "visit an abode of opulence" maintained by a member of Culpeper's "aristocratic society," as described in Donaldson's rather facetious memoirs. While there, they drank heavily and paid undue attention to a lovely "dark-eyed mulatto," who wore "an exceedingly low-necked dress." Crocker and Donaldson contributed to a drunken brawl and escaped into the night with a purloined bottle of brandy. Reading the convoluted Victorian euphemisms of the narrator's prose, it seems almost certain that this was a melee in a whorehouse.[64]

Stevensburg is a little village just east of Culpeper. There in April 1864 Corporal John O'Conner of the 39th New York had been placed on picket, but he didn't stay long. In pleading guilty to being AWOL, he told the court, "I heard the boys say there was a house with some young girls, so I went to see them." O'Conner was reduced to the ranks and fined $4 (31 percent of his pay) a month for four months.[65]

Yorktown plays a vital role in American history, perhaps even in the little contribution of Private Owen Daly of the 148th New York when, in December 1863, he was tried for firing his pistol at provost marshal Capt. Joseph Brooks of the 9th Vermont. The venue? A whorehouse, of course, located "in the hollow, this side of our quarters . . . 50 rods from camp . . . it was a bad house, a house of ill fame . . . 20 or 30 Negro women were in and around the place. The boys said it was a house of ill fame." Daly had knocked on the door and the women told him to go away. Brooks told Daly to go to camp; the reply was surly and aggressive. The dark of night seems to have shielded Daly from being positively identified, and he was thus acquitted.[66]

In October 1863, Major George Thistleton of the 1st Maryland Cavalry (Union) was tried for abducting Miss Sarah Bussey of Orlean and conveying her eastward seven miles to Warrenton for purposes of "criminal intercourse." (His regiment had fought at Bristoe and Warrenton in the preceding weeks.) The badly faded records reveal no statement by Miss Bussey. One witness recalled, "She said she wanted to go if she had to put on soldier's clothes." This apparent willingness may be why he received only a reprimand. A year later, he was court-martialed again, this time for theft, falsifying records, and frequent public association with prostitutes. He was dismissed in disgrace. In 1941, Thistleton's daughter wrote to the War Department, hoping to use his service record to join the Daughters of Union Veterans.[67]

Captain David Thompson of the 2nd District of Columbia Volunteers was another officer with a portable woman. At Edsall's Station, he kept a "woman of disreputable character" in his tent on the nights of June 12th and 13 and July 7th and 8, 1864. Witnesses said that Thompson had found her in a whorehouse on 12th Street in Washington, D.C. and brought her south with him. Sergeant George E. Moore did concede to the Court that during the woman's visit to Edsall's Station, her conduct was "very ladylike." Thompson was cashiered.[68]

Private Emsa Jusco of the 5th Veteran Reserve Corps was absent without leave two months at Charleston. During his October 1864 trial, he pled guilty and in his plea for mitigation added, "Me and some boys got tight and went up on the hill, where there were some women, and the regiment was gone when we got back." Jusco might have been shot, but he got off with six months hard labor.[69]

A native of Switzerland hiding in a whorehouse? Private Hermann Falkenberg of the 1st New Jersey Artillery deserted at Fairfax Seminary, Virginia, in July 1863 and was discovered 16 months later, concealed in "house of bad character" in Washington, D.C. He was sentenced to complete his enlistment doing hard labor in prison. He spent much of that time trying to involve the Swiss Consul-General in his problems.[70]

A few miles south of the campus of Virginia Tech is the old town of Christiansburg. There, in September 1865, Lieutenant Robert Thompson of the 11th Connecticut "associated with women of known lewd character." Testimony showed that Mary, Jenney, Julia, Cornelia and Virginia all lived in a brick house near the central depot, and that Lieutenant Thompson went riding with some or all of them during the day and stayed with them during the night. These escapades, plus the theft of a few gold watches, resulted in his being cashiered and his crimes being published in his hometown newspaper.[71]

The 11th Connecticut was popular with the unattached young ladies who gathered at Christiansburg. Two more lieutenants, Charles Parker and Charles Simmons, spent many intimate moments with the Mitchell sisters, Belle and Emma, described as "women of ill-fame." The details are obscure, because all the testimony was about a horse stolen by Parker. Both men were dismissed.[72]

Women continued to be of ongoing concern to Union authorities. On May 20th, 1864, Major General Benjamin Butler issued a "circular" from the headquarters of the Department of Virginia and North Carolina. "All women now in camp, that have followed the Army in the field, will at once be sent to the Provost Marshal at Bermuda Hundreds, to be forwarded to Fort Monroe." Many women followed the armies: laundresses, vivandieres, family members, nurses—and some prostitutes. The phrase "all women" solved the problem of distinguishing one from the other.

The war ended, but not the oldest profession. The Staunton *Spectator*, on December 8, 1886, ran this obituary: "An abandoned woman about twenty-one years of age who called herself Eva Wilson, but whose real name was Lana Farara . . . died yesterday morning . . . came here from Richmond last August. Her mother, whose name is Bullock, resides in Richmond."

This brings us to the end of Virginia's documented contributions to the industry of paid sex, but there are many states yet to be heard from.

Chapter 2

PROSTITUTION IN GEORGIA AND THE CAROLINAS

North Carolina

"Ada Belle is rather small with a nice figure. She has light hair and blue eyes." Thus spoke witness Private E.V. Anthony of the 120th Indiana at the trial of his superior, Captain Henry Stephens. The defendant was being tried at Raleigh, North Carolina in November 1865. He had been drunk and disorderly on the public streets, where he punched an officer of the 25th Michigan and proclaimed the Michiganders "a lot of rascals." Further, Stephens, who had a wife and four children back in Dover Hill, Indiana, had been keeping 28-year-old Ada Bell Benton in his quarters, introducing her as his wife. Witnesses claimed that she had been kept by a different captain the year before and that she was well known at the "Little Hotel" in Indianapolis. Stephens left North Carolina with a dishonorable discharge. The reaction of his wife back home is unknown.[1]

John Boyden claimed that the madam of a Raleigh whorehouse had overcharged him for liquor. This private, a member of Light Company E, Third U.S. Artillery, had visited the establishment when he was supposed to be on stable call. Since the date was May 1866, Boyden seems to have lost any wartime sense of urgency. His AWOL and abusive language to the madam earned him a $6 fine.[2]

Wilmington was the downfall of two men. Charles F. Brown, a captain in the 37th U.S. Colored Troops, was Officer of the Day in August 1865. Instead of visiting the various military posts on his beat, he went with "two lewd females of the worst character" to the bar at the Palmetto Hotel, where they drank Stone

Fences (bourbon whisky, sweet cider, and ice), and "reveled to excess." Brown was docked three months pay and received a severe reprimand.[3]

Private James Johnson of the 28th Michigan was in Wilmington in the spring of 1866. It would seem that enforcing Reconstruction still left much time for play. He was accused of beating and robbing a civilian, and the testimony was devoted to determining his whereabouts on the night of March 14th. The victim, Civilian James H. Ellis, claimed that he had been hit behind the ear with a "slung shot," knocked senseless, and robbed of $60 in cash and his pistol, while playing cards at a whorehouse run by Mrs. Anna Kennedy, located "over past the railroad." Johnson assembled a bevy of witnesses to show that he was not even there at the time of the crime—11:00 p.m.

Anna Kennedy said that Ellis had borrowed $5 from her around 8:00 p.m. that night and then went into the room of Frances Clark, who recalled him as drunk and belligerent—"He paid me $5, but he knocked me down with the butt of his pistol." Mrs. Kennedy continued: "Ellis told me he had quit going to another house because of Yankees there and if he caught any damn Yankees in my place, he'd blow their brains out. When I told him not to make a row, he drew his pistol and fired it into the house. One of the gentlemen with Ellis then knocked him down. As for the defendant, he was never there that evening. I have known Ellis for three years and know him well."

Rooth (sic) Ann Stubbs, who lived "between Eighth and Ninth Streets," recalled that Ellis had asked to see Mrs. Kennedy around 8:00 p.m. that night. "I told him that she was in her room nursing her baby; when she came out of her room, Ellis grabbed her around the waist and she pushed off from him." Frances Walden, another "boarder" at Mrs. Kennedy's, recalled there being a "fuss on the piazza," but had nothing further to add.

Sergeant George M. Cook, of the 28th Michigan, stationed at the jail, told his version of the evening. "I asked Lieutenant [Chauncey] Declute if I might go out and see the folks. Johnson and Pete Orchard and I drank at Sue Thompson's, then at Joe Turner's house. Around midnight, we went to the City Hotel and about 1:00 a.m. Leonard [Johnson's nickname] said he was going up to Anna [AKA "Tall Anna"] Yance's place; he didn't want to go to Anna Kennedy's place because he'd had a fuss with the police and thought that they would look for him there." Elizabeth Piner, an inmate at Tall Anna's place on Chestnut Street, testified that Johnson arrived at her room around midnight and stayed all night.

Emma Parker, who lived at Joe Turner's house on Fourth Street, testified that Johnson was at her place from 10:00 p.m. until midnight. She recalled the exact date, because "it was Miss Josephine's birthday."

The evidence seemed convincing that the defendant was not the man who had knocked Ellis unconscious, and Johnson was acquitted. Their recorded words paint a picture of a world now long gone and almost forgotten.[4]

One of the early Union successes was the capture of New Bern. It was there, in June 1862, that Private Albert Humphrey of the 23rd Massachusetts was charged with the 45th Article of War—being drunk on duty. Lieutenant J.R. Drew of the same regiment, who was Officer of the Guard that day, recalled that Humphrey was too drunk to stand guard. "I was hunting him up and found him about 100 rods [1600 feet] from the guard house, with two other members of the guard, trying to get into a house of ill fame. He breathed right in my face and I smelt whisky." When the lieutenant brought him back to the guardhouse, Humphrey "was inclined to be a little ugly." At the guardhouse, "he threw off his cartridge box and went to sleep . . . dropped off as if he had no control over his body." An hour later, Drew tried to put the man on duty, but when Humphrey put his cartridge box on upside down, gave up. Two privates testified that Humphrey had only taken "a glass of Stomach Bitters" and was cold sober. The Court disagreed and gave the defendant thirty days of hard labor.[5]

David Mullins was a long ways from home when the 23rd Missouri served in Harnett County in April 1865. He and Lafayette Millsparr of the same regiment, in company with Eliza Kennedy, a "woman of very bad reputation," were authors of a small crime wave, stealing bacon, silver, gloves and a silk dress and attempting to hang a civilian. Mullins got a year in prison; Millsparr's record is missing the verdict page. We found no trial record for the "woman of very bad reputation."[6]

The citizens of Morganton were probably unfavorably impressed with Captain John Bowles of the 5th Ohio Cavalry, who commanded the occupation there in September 1865. With enlisted men, he visited "a house of ill fame," kept by Clara Pearson, "between the Ashville and Rutherford Roads, about nine miles from Morganton." A few days later, he received "a notorious prostitute" in his tent and told his men that he had had "carnal intercourse" with her. He was acquitted of demanding sex from Sarah Ann Denton as the price of releasing her father from jail (perhaps because one witness described Sarah Ann as the worst whore in the county and a known liar), but was convicted of the other charges and sentenced to be reprimanded.[7]

South Carolina

As the war drew to a close, navy as well as army men left their marks in the records, including three officers from the USS *Squando*. Thomas A. Looby, an acting assistant engineer, was raising hell in Charleston in August 1865. He was a frequent customer at a whorehouse at No. 6 West Street. He was drunk and in a quarrelsome mood during one visit, claiming he was from headquarters, sent to examine prostitutes' licenses. When Millie McGiven did not cooperate, he began to choke her. She jumped out of a window; he jumped out on top of her. He dragged her back in the room and "used her roughly for about half an hour, violating her person." When she asked him what he was doing, Looby replied, "I am trying to kill you, you damned bitch, and if you were dead, I would do what I am doing now." (Threats of necrophilia are rare in Civil War records.) This story was confirmed by Delia Morris and Gertrude Charles of the same address. The defendant had been offensive at other locales as well. A house of ill fame on Princess Street had felt his wrath, and at 11 Beresford Street he terrified Grace Piexotto and chased Jeannie Steward up the stairs and tried to whip her.[8]

Acting ensign R. M. Lamphier was present during Looby's rampage, and was charged with conduct unbecoming an officer. Delia Morris testified that Lamphier was "very gentlemanly" during his visit, but failed to save her while *she* was being raped by Looby. Instead, he watched the event through a window. Lamphier was acquitted.[9] The third officer from the *Squando*, acting assistant engineer William Finnegan, was also charged with "conduct unbecoming." Miss Delia Mims and Miss Gertrude Charles, both of 6 West Street, told the court that Finnegan was "gentlemanly," as did Grace Peixotto. Finnegan was also acquitted. Looby was dismissed in disgrace.[10]

Navy carpenter David A. Waterbury, stationed at Port Royal in May 1865, was accused of stealing money at the Naval Carpenter Shop. In the testimony, there is an extensive discussion of trollops in Charleston. Waterbury had made the acquaintance of two women, Molly and "Scroot" who worked at 6 West Street. Waterbury asked them, "Did I treat you badly on Saturday?" and one of them replied, "Not very and you made it all right by giving me $20."[11]

Lieutenant Christian Noell of the 54th New York Veteran Volunteers was in Orangeburg in October 1865, when he was tried for being "beastly drunk" in the streets, and with being in a house of ill fame, run by "a mulatto," Harriet Douglas. After much contradictory testimony, he was acquitted.[12]

Captain Edwin J. Scranton of the 128th U.S. Colored Troops was stationed at Beaufort in the late summer of 1865. There, he allowed "a colored woman of bad repute" to enter camp and allowed her to sleep in his bed. He was ordered not to have anything further to do with her, but a few weeks later he married the woman. Scranton was dismissed from the army.[13]

Georgia

A Civil War history of prostitution in the Peach State might start with the 1850 Federal census of the "free inhabitants" of Dodd County. There, four women, Sara Doyle, Mary Doyle, Lucinda Killian, and Susan Killian, listed their occupation as "Fucking."

A decade later, the 1860 census of Atlanta told more. In Ward 1, nineteen women listed their occupation as prostitute. In an age before convenient contraception, many prostitutes bore children. Deborah Banks reported her children, Mary and James. Sarah Kingston had two-year-old John and Mary Paine had a seven-year-old daughter, apparently born when Mary was age 12.

The reported ages of the prostitutes in 1860 ranged from 18-year-old Mary Simpson to 52-year-old Mary Berny.

In Ward 2, Matilda Shadix lived alone, while three young women resided at T.A. Oglesby's "boarding house." In Ward 3, eighteen women, all in their twenties, lived in one house, presided over by 59-year-old Elizabeth Robinson. As with the others, they all listed their occupations as "prostitute." Six more women in Ward 3 listed their occupations as prostitute, as did seven women in Ward 4 and four women in Ward 5. In all neighborhoods, most prostitutes reported their birthplace as Georgia.

Private William Burson of the 29th Pennsylvania had been placed in the reserve of the guards at Atlanta, but left his place and went 300 yards to "a house of ill fame." Soldiers on guard duty in October 1864 had been ordered not to go to that establishment—"but were in the habit of doing so anyway." Burson was convicted of disobedience and sentenced to four months of hard labor. However, the Court petitioned the reviewing general for clemency because of Burson's "extreme youth." (He was age 18 and 5 foot 3 inches tall.) [14]

William McDonald seemed to live by scheming and scamming. This private, of the 149th Illinois, was at Atlanta in October 1865, when he stole a pair of pants and a razor from a freedman, and had organized a plot to take discharged colored soldiers (who had just received their final pay) to a house of ill fame and there rob them. His plan was detected before its completion and he was sent to jail for six months. [15]

An Illinois private decided at Savannah that it might be more fun to live in a whorehouse as an officer than be on campaign as a private. Consequently, George Govro of the 52nd Illinois bought a pair of shoulder straps and went to the bagnio run by Mrs. Elliott, at the corner of South Broad and Huston Streets, where he passed himself off as Lieutenant William Hale. He had been there several weeks when the provost guard pulled him out from under a bed. He got ten years in prison at hard labor. [16]

Joseph McNutt also awarded himself a promotion. This captain of the 159th New York not only allowed his troops to pillage plantations, but pinned major's oak leaves upon himself. Then, accompanied by three prostitutes, he took command of the steamer *Jeff Davis* on the route from Savannah to Augusta. During this refreshing sea voyage, he "promoted" one of the hookers, pinning gold leaves on her. The court-martial board was not amused. McNutt was docked three months pay and was dishonorably discharged. [17]

Lizzie Wright's Savannah house of ill fame, at the corner of Harrison and Ann Streets, was the scene of near-deadly violence. On June 4, 1865, eight drunken soldiers of the 6th US Infantry had been refused entrance. As they attempted to break down the door, Sergeant Samuel Wood, working as a policeman, complete with badge, asked them to stop. The drunks turned on him. Two men held each arm, while men in front of and behind him beat him with bricks. As he was losing consciousness, members of the 8th Indiana poured from Lizzie's front door and attacked the attackers. Wood rose to his knees and shot a man who was about to crush his head with a rock.[18]

Augusta generated two trials involving prostitutes. Captain Thomas Sheldon of the 18th Ohio was tried twice. In his first trial, he was acquitted of beating and robbing a "colored citizen." His second trial, in September 1865, was for breach of arrest. Instead of remaining in his quarters as ordered, he had left and gone to a house of ill fame. Here, he pushed his luck too far. The Court ordered him cashiered.[19]

Corporal Alexander Stableford of the 19th US Infantry was tried the following month for being absent without leave. He was gone several hours, and was found in "a house of ill fame." He pled guilty, offered no defense and was reduced to a private, with a reprimand.[20]

At Cuthbert, Elizabeth Neely kept a house of ill fame "south of the courthouse and across the creek from camp," presumably the camp of the 145th Indiana, which, in October 1865, was part of the Union occupation. Major Henry Winter, then commanding the regiment, took a fancy to Elizabeth. Using a government ambulance, he carried her seventy miles to Bainbridge, where they stayed for eight days of bliss, registered as husband and wife. Then the honeymoon was over; Major Winter was reprimanded and suspended for a month from rank and pay.[21]

At Resaca, in August 1864, Private John M. Rebestok of the 10th Missouri went beyond the picket lines to a "house of ill fame," where he attracted attention to himself by being drunk, noisy, and belligerent. Since he had no pass and the house was off limits, his plea of "too drunk to remember" was of little use. He was docked three months pay, plus three months of hard labor.[22]

At East Macon, Second Lieutenant Jacob Hommes of the 137th US Colored Troops was in double trouble. It was near Christmas 1865. He had gotten very drunk and attacked a sergeant and several privates with his saber, for no obvious reason, but it was his domestic life that concerns us. He had in his tent Lizzie Mathews, whom he claimed he had married in 1852. Several witnesses disagreed. Lieutenant Terrence O'Hanlon had seen her earlier at a house of ill fame in Macon, "near the railroad bridge over the river. She lived there with three other women. When I passed by, she beckoned to me. Lieutenant Hommes told me he had taken her from a house of ill fame and married her and now he wanted nothing to do with her. She is of medium height, with sallow complexion, regular features and dark hair, about 30 years of age." Thomas Knight of the Macon City Police knew her well. "Last September, she was living on Mulberry Street near the gas house and kept a house of ill fame there. She had with her three or four girls of bad character. She has lived in Macon about two years." The army had had enough of Lieutenant Hommes. By New Years 1866, he was a civilian.[23]

Chapter 3

PROSTITUTION IN THE DEEP SOUTH

In the early years of the war, the Union had no jurisdiction over the Deep South and thus generated no Federal records there. As Union forces penetrated deeper into the Confederacy, the martial law of occupation and Reconstruction gave birth to records, the foundation of any history. The capture of New Orleans in April 1862 and the long occupation of that city marked the beginning of searchable court-martial documents.

In January 1863, Private Barrent Sherriger of the 128th New York was cursing his captain at New Orleans' St. Charles Hotel. Sherriger's defense: "I left to get drunk; I stayed at a disorderly house all night and drank rum." His captain said, "He is non compos mentis." The court gave him five years in prison, reconsidered their verdict and gave him ten years instead.[1]

That September, Private Patrick Gray of the 9th Connecticut was convicted of desertion at New Orleans. "I had gone on a spree, was drunk for three days and left my uniform at the house of a woman on Phillippa Street." Gray got a year in prison with a 24-pound ball and chain.[2]

Private Daniel Woods of the 31st Massachusetts had a wild night in Baton Rouge in October 1863. He was accused of assaulting an officer. Woods told the court: "When I first met the gentleman who proved to be Lieutenant [Alexander] Elting [156th New York] it was in a house of ill fame in Baton Rouge. I was quiet, peaceful and sober. I was ordered to leave by this gentleman and did so." Another witness added this recollection: "We'd gone up the stairs of the brick house. The old lady asked what we wanted. We said we wanted to see the girls. She said her girls were all sick and a captain ordered us out. He ordered the provost guard to shoot the defendant." After much conflicting testimony, Woods was given three months in the county jail with half of each month in solitary confinement.[3]

William Coleman of the 2nd Louisiana Cavalry (Union) had the instincts of an entrepreneur. He deserted on Christmas Day in New Orleans and was arrested two weeks later, keeping a "drinking, dancing, and disorderly house." He got six months hard labor with a ball and chain and lost $10 a month for the rest of his enlistment.[4]

Eight men were sent to get Private Ananias Woods of the 14th Rhode Island Colored Heavy Artillery, "dead or alive." Woods was AWOL from Camp Parapet, an artillery post on the east bank of the Mississippi River near New Orleans. When Woods was discovered—"drunk, in a house with a woman"—he attacked the guard with his fists and a bayonet. Woods went to prison for the rest of his enlistment.[5]

In September 1864, Lieutenant Edward H. Dunning of the 7th US Colored Heavy Artillery, set out on a boat trip across Lake Pontchartrain. His craft, the picket boat *La Reine Hortense*, carried two guests, cigar smoking "Negro prostitutes," escaping arrest. The prostitutes had been using "profane and obscene language in the presence of ladies and gentlemen." Not surprisingly, Dunning was drunk. The surprise came when he was acquitted. The reviewing general, Stephen Hurlbut, disagreed with the acquittal and ordered Dunning dismissed from the army. Perhaps Hurlbut had been influenced by Dunning's previous arrest for being drunk and disorderly aboard the US Schooner *Corypheus*, and with challenging a Navy officer to a duel.[6]

There are many long-forgotten units in the Civil War. One of these was the First Company of Sappers, Miners, and Pontoniers, of the US Volunteers. A private from this company, Thomas Burns, deserted in New Orleans and was arrested three months later, in November 1864, in a house of prostitution on Barracks Street. Burns had deserted three days after his enlistment, taking with him his $100 enlistment bounty. When arrested by policeman Henry Swellenhas, Burns claimed to be "Tom Cork, of General Bank's bodyguard." Whoever he was, the court gave him a year at hard labor.[7]

The 10th Illinois Cavalry was stationed in New Orleans in May 1865. Private John Kiser and a friend, "Jack," entered Lizzie Reice's house at 119 Philippi Street. Mrs. Reice said she was the only woman present, and that she was already "engaged for the night" by a sergeant. Jack refused to leave, proclaiming, "I'll be damned to hell if I leave; I'm as good as any man here." Predictably, Jack and the sergeant were soon fighting; Kiser joined in the fray and stabbed the sergeant, which earned Kiser four months at hard labor. "Jack" turned out to be Private John Lyons of the 16th Ohio Light Artillery. Why he used the alias of "John Arnett" was not explained. Lyons was also tried for stabbing the sergeant, now revealed to be John Capron of the 1st US Infantry. The confusion deepened when we learned that Mrs. Reice was not the only woman present. Miss Lucy Parker, also of 119 Philippi Street, told the court that Lyons dragged Capron out of the door and into the ditch, where Kiser cut the sergeant with "a long butcher knife." In his testimony, Capron confirmed 119 Philippi as "a house of ill fame." Lyons was sentenced to three months at hard labor.[8]

Private James Williams of the 20th US Colored Troops was escorting a prisoner along the streets of New Orleans. At a crib (small house of prostitution) located "right up above Rampart Street," Williams allowed the prisoner to deliver a bundle of clothes and to kiss the woman who received them. Sgt. Joseph Carson, also of the 20th USCT, threatened to shoot Williams for neglecting his duties. In May 1865, Carson was court-martialed for this threat and acquitted.[9]

Peter Williamson, a private with the 46th USCT, demanded admission to a "house of ill fame" at 55 Burgundy Street in New Orleans in May 1865. Miss Lena Smith testified that when she refused him admission, he drew his bayonet and shouted, "I will kill the damned bitch." Williamson was docked one-month's pay.[10]

Private Eli Dennis of the 93rd USCT was raising hell at 127 Conte Street in the early summer of 1865. Prostitute Mary Lee told the court, "I live in a common house, a public house . . . Dennis stayed in another girl's room all night and gave her $10 . . . He threw up on the sheets . . . in the morning he went out through my room, where he stole two dresses, a pin and three dollars in cash." Conflicting testimony led to Dennis' acquittal.[11]

Dr. Henry A. Murray was not a credit to his lofty profession. This assistant surgeon of the 84th USCT, in March 1866, was arrested, "beastly drunk," in bed, in "a colored woman's house of prostitution," at 200 St. Louis Street. He was ordered to report himself to the office of the New Orleans provost marshal. Instead, he went to Bianca Robinson's house on Union Street, where, still drunk, he was arrested again. Murray was dismissed in disgrace.[12]

Two privates of the 2nd VRC were convicted of a brutal assault in the foyer of a house of prostitution at 144 Toulouse Street. The madam, Mrs. Annie Brown, testified. The victim was a Private Gross of the 16th Illinois Cavalry. He was stabbed by James Robinson and beaten with a "loaded cane" by Samuel Bell. Robinson, whose alias was "Yankee," got six months at hard labor, while Bell was sentenced to three months of the same.[13]

At a small whorehouse on the corner of Burgundy and Toulouse Streets, Mrs. John Frisby sold a half pint of whiskey to Sergeant Alonzo Alcorn of the 19th Iowa. The price was two dollars; the date was a week before Robert E. Lee's surrender at Appomattox. Mrs. Frisby suspected a police "sting," and asked Alcorn, "Are you one of those men sent to entice and entrap me?" He replied, "Oh, no. Not me!" At the trial, he proudly described how he had entrapped her. She was acquitted; the reviewing general wrote a note denouncing the practice of entrapment.[14]

New Orleans, the "Big Easy," continues its long history of involvement in prostitution. In 2002, the FBI assigned ten agents to tap the phone line of madam Jeanette Maier, with the stated purpose of catching mob bosses. The 5000 monitored calls yielded not a single mobster, but did reveal the bedroom preferences of many of New Orleans' elite: politicians, judges, bankers, and football heroes. With the possible revelation of the madam's client list, one attorney remarked, "These men are more afraid of their own wives than they are of the Federal government."[15] While our court-martialed Civil War soldiers were hardly New Orleans' elite, they were part of a long chain of lonely men and desperate women dating back to the year that Louis XIV cleaned out the brothels of Paris and shipped the girls to the New World.[16]

Mississippi

The state of Mississippi was the scene of further evidence of prostitution, seen first in the trial of a man of the cloth: Paul Wald, hospital chaplain, USA, who served at the officers' hospital at Natchez. His relevant offense occurred on February 1, 1865, when he proposed to Hospital Steward F. J. Mead that they visit "houses of ill fame for the purpose of having illicit intercourse with their inmates." Wald was also found guilty of drinking in a saloon with enlisted men, of telling hospital steward O. Bloomfield, "You are a hellish scoundrel, and I will blow your brains out," and of being drunk on duty. Chaplain Wald was convicted and dismissed.[17]

Prewar Natchez had been two cities. Natchez-on-the-Hill held the glorious mansions of the plantation owners and the commercial firms that served them. Natchez—Under-the-Hill was a long sand spit at the base of the bluffs. Its population was saloon keepers, gamblers, and prostitutes, who served visitors both from the river and from the Natchez citizens willing to risk being cheated or murdered. The Mississippi River has swept away most of the lower town, leaving only a few saloons, often visited by tourists from steamboats like the *Delta Queen*.[18] Natchez-Under-the-Hill appears in an unusual Civil War document. Private Fieldings Gordon, 6th US Colored Heavy Artillery, deserted in July 1865, at Vidalia, Louisiana. He was captured, convicted and sentenced to 30 days in a military prison. Testimony showed that he had been mustered in at Natchez-Under-the-Hill. Did the army have a recruiting office amidst the thieves, murderers, card sharks, and whores of that sordid neighborhood?[19]

One of the most remarkable documents of wartime Mississippi life is the report of Federal Detective Edward Betty. He took passage on the steamer *Luminary*, traveling in disguise as an ordinary businessman. While much of his report is devoted to corruption in the cotton trade and Union profiteers, who "abused the Negroes as bad as did the prior owners," he had much to say about the skin trade.

Whoring and drunkenness are common among officers of the army at Vicksburg . . . while coming up to Memphis . . . I saw two gunboats, sending women on board of our steamer . . . It was not difficult to determine they were harlots . . . A little steamer called the *Self* . . . at Vicksburg, she had a number of harlots aboard, and it was her custom to land near [army] posts or alongside naval vessels to allow the women to ply their vocation. Officers drive out in hacks and attend the theater in Memphis with harlots . . . venereal diseases are common among the soldiers at Memphis and the worst feature of the evil is that rather than run the risk of exposure or punishment, the unfortunate ones patronize Quack Doctors who cheat them out of their money and in a majority of cases aggravate the disease by malpractice. Women exercise a great and baleful influence . . . all along the river from Cairo down. At the offices of Provost Marshal's they are always to be found . . . smiling, simmering, sentimentalizing, and exercising those cunning little arts used by women to beguile men . . . Rebel women sacrifice their honor to obtain favors of U. S. officers at Memphis. The hotels harbor prostitutes who generally represent themselves as the wives of Colonel this or Captain that . . . Whores are in constant transit from points on the Ohio River . . . to points below and it is safe to say that nine out of 10 women traveling on the Mississippi River are prostitutes . . . Cairo is the best point for observation along the river . . . The harlot who could not sleep with her paramour on the [railroad] cars takes the same stateroom with him as his wife on the boat from Cairo.

After further ruminations on gamblers, corrupt boat captains, quinine smugglers and crooked cotton brokers, the detective concluded his report: "The Government seems to have no friend except the poor private soldier, who is lying on the hurricane deck, sweltering in the sun, because he is not allowed in the cabins."[20]

After Grant's brilliant capture of Vicksburg, with its calamitous disruption of Texas grain and livestock destined for the eastern Confederacy, the city settled down to the usual vices of an occupation. But even before the Yankees arrived, there were public events with painted ladies. Molly Bunch, Vicksburg's most prominent madam, was hosting her annual Washington's Birthday Ball on February 22, 1861, when the fire department arrived and hosed (literally) both the guests and the tarts. The moralists and their fire engine then proceeded to Madam Bunch's residence, where they sprayed and smashed her furniture.[21]

Further investigation showed a political flaw in Ms. Bunch's party arrangements. In the past, she had invited only the more dissolute Vicksburgians. In 1861, her invitation list included the ministers of the city's churches. The men of the Gospel, forgetful of the Savior's admonition about casting the first stone, arranged the baptism by fire hose of the revelers. Bunch asked the city to reimburse her for the property destroyed by the mob (and the firemen), but the city council denied her request.[22]

During the occupation of Vicksburg, the records suggest that officers were worse behaved than the enlisted men. Miss Hattie Lee (AKA Emma Williams) was a twenty-six-year old madam with a house at the northeast corner of Randolph and Locust Streets. On a February evening in 1866, Lieutenant Colonel George L. Simpson of the 66th USCT showed up drunk and noisy at Miss Lee's doorstep. When she refused him admission, he kicked the door down. Somewhat confused about female anatomy, he "placed his pistol at her breast and threatened to shoot her brains out." She called the police. Simpson shouted, "I will shoot the first Goddamn son of a bitch of a policeman who dares to enter." At Simpson's court martial, Mrs. Lee testified demurely that she had four "lady boarders," who sometimes received "gentleman callers." Colonel Simpson was booted out of the army.[23]

First Lieutenant Charles Stopples of the 58th Ohio obtained a pass for four officers "and party" to leave camp and proceed into Vicksburg. Apparently exceeding his mandate, Stopples took ten officers and two women to "an all-night pleasure party at Shirley House." Some technicality acquitted him of "conduct unbecoming an officer and a gentleman."[24]

Mrs. Sarah Allison was the madam of a Vicksburg house at the corner of China and Washington Streets. In early December 1865, Second Lieutenant David F. Jenkins of the 33rd Illinois Veteran Volunteers was thrown out of Allison's house for being drunk and disorderly. Jenkins, drunk again and apparently enamored of inmate Eliza Kirby, returned to see her. When he was informed that she was not at home, having gone to the "circus show," he broke the window of the house and assaulted "a Negro provost guard" posted there to maintain order, severely wounding the man's head with a brick. Jenkins was cashiered, but the sentence was remitted because of his "four years of honorable service." Miss Kirby, when called to testify, exhibited a memory defect that would have done justice to a mobster before a Senate committee. "I am unaware that this was a house of ill fame. I do not know the reputation of this house. I know nothing of the other girls living there. I, myself, have no occupation."[25]

The steamer *Maria Denning* was bound for Vicksburg in January 1866. Major Andrew J. Krause of the 108th USCT set a poor example for his men when he addressed Mrs. Krause, his loving spouse, thusly: "You may go home as soon as you please, God damn you, I'll lick you if you don't behave yourself." Perhaps the missus was upset with Major Krause's two prostitutes, which he had brought on board at Rock Island, Illinois, one of whom was seen in the major's bunk, nude, with her clothing on the floor. Or perhaps it was Major Krause's escorting the two harlots to the officers' elegant dining table, while neglecting his wife. The army sided with Mrs. Krause and dismissed her husband in disgrace.[26]

"He was with girls of pleasure . . . at a house of ill fame in Nashville." This was Captain William Fisher of the 12th Illinois, as described in court-martial testimony. And where did Fisher get the money for his prolonged sojourn in the unnamed bordello? By gambling with enlisted men. He had won $800 ($24,000 in today's money) from "the Indiana boys," and told his friends, "As long as I can get privates to skin, I'm okay." The card shark was not tried until his regiment reached Corinth, Mississippi, where he was also charged with being AWOL while officer of the day. This predatory officer received a reprimand and lost six month's pay.[27]

The Christmas Whorehouse Riot

In late December, 1863, a large Union force was resting and recuperating at Bovina, two miles west of the Big Black River bridge. One of the few local attractions was a whorehouse. About 9 P.M. on December twenty-fifth, a man rushed into the camp of the 20th Illinois, shouting that the much despised Jayhawkers (1st Kansas Infantry) had invaded the whorehouse, killed two members of the 20th Illinois, and wounded four more. Three members of the 20th Illinois, Sergeants Edward Williams and John McLaughlin, with Private Josiah Kent and dozen others, rushed to the scene of the combat to avenge their comrades. When they arrived, the house was ptotected by the provost guard, men of the 124th Illinois. Williams and his friends demanded entrance to see if any Jayhawkers remained. The guards told them to go away. There was tussling and curses. A shot was fired. A woman screamed. Finally, calm prevailed. The Jayhawkers were gone. No one was dead; no one was wounded. In the sober light of day, the cries of murder and vengeance were only faint echoes.[28]

Alabama

The first Confederate capital was at Montgomery, Alabama, and that city appears in several of these prostitution cases. A Confederate soldier confirmed the presence of shady ladies there. "My dear wife," wrote Benjamin C. Giddens, Company G, 3rd Tennessee Mounted Infantry, "I am anxious to get away from this place [Montgomery], for I never saw so many strumpets and their audacity and vulgarity is beyond all reason. I think that my company has spent not less than $200 after the nasty whores. Some of our company that I thought were decent strange to say have turned from the path of virtue, have lost all that is virtuous and good. Just now while I am writing I received an invitation from an officer to go to one of these houses of ill fame. There was two strumpets in camp today, in their fine carriage and dressed in their silk. [One] invited the whole company to come to her house tonight."[29]

Union soldiers also left a record of Montgomery's tarts. A drunken brawl at Jenny Yarbrough's "house," landed Sergeant James Whitbeck, 58th Illinois, in jail. He had fired a weapon at one of Jenny's girls, Catherine Ray, and was convicted of assault with intent to kill. He was reduced to the rank of private and sent to military prison for six months.[30]

Private Gloucester Hatfield, also of the 58th Illinois, violated a sacred trust. The army owed $213.50 in back pay to a soldier who was sick in a smallpox hospital. Hatfield was given the money and told to deliver it to his ailing comrade. Instead, he hurried to Molly Dunn's whorehouse in Montgomery, where the money was "stolen." "As God is my witness, I am not guilty of any intent to wrong [Private] Walker or to steal or purloin from any person." Hatfield claimed he was robbed while he was passed out drunk on the sidewalk outside of Ms. Dunn's place. Hatfield was given a dishonorable discharge.[31]

Anderson Redford was a Confederate guerrilla, roaming the hills that surround Huntsville, Alabama. He boasted of murdering two Union soldiers and killed many cattle and swine belonging to civilians. When he was captured and tried, Elizabeth Fowler of Huntsville testified against him. Redford said her testimony was not believable, because "she keeps a house of ill fame."[32]

On April 9, 1861, Confederate soldier W. L. Martin wrote from Warrenton, Florida, of his adventures in Mobile, Alabama. "We got to Mobile, Ala . . . located ourselves in some barracks on Congress Street . . . The boys indulged to a considerable extent with public "Ladies" of St. Michael St. of course they were some of the prettiest women I ever saw anywhere much less in a whorehouse . . . Direct your answer . . . in care of Capt. W. H. Kilpatrick." (possibly Major W. H. Kilpatrick, 5th Mississippi Infantry Battalion).[33]

Florida is our final stop in the Deep South. In May 1864, the 35th USCT was camped on the Volusia Road, "across the Sebastian River," near St. Augustine, and 200 yards from the Hartshorne home. There, Sergeant Lewis Bryant offered money to Mr. Hartshorne's daughter-in-law, if she would "accommodate" him. Although witnesses testified that Bryant had muttered, "The Colonel had no right to put a guard over a Damned Secesh Whorehouse," no one had heard any improper offer to Sarah Hanam. Bryant was acquitted.[34]

Captain John W. Migrath of the 25th USCT was accused of many transgressions near Pensacola, in the autumn of 1864. He had transported "disreputable women of color," to Santa Rosa Island, where he "promenaded" with them. He also stayed out of camp without permission and cursed the regimental surgeon. Migrath was dismissed.[35]

The contradictions between ideal behavior and forbidden pleasure have not diminished over the decades. At Tallahassee, Florida, State Representative Marvin Couch (Republican), a devout member of the "God Squad," and recipient of a "perfect" rating by the Christian Coalition, was arrested at noon in a shopping center parking lot and was charged with receiving oral sex from a prostitute, unnatural acts, and exposure of his sexual organs.[36]

Chapter 4

PROSTITUTION IN WEST VIRGINIA

Libby Bastide, a "woman of notoriously bad character," forms the centerpiece of West Virginia's most heavily documented case of prostitution. Her partner in sin was Captain Henry W. Scott of the 1st New York Cavalry Veteran Volunteers. The locale: Camp Piatt in Kanawha County. At his December 1864 trial, he was charged with bringing a "Mrs. Scott," alias Libby Bastide, into camp and "did openly live and cohabit with said woman as his lawful wife; and when expostulated with by the colonel commanding the regiment, did endeavor to justify and defend his conduct and afterward did continue to live with said Mrs. Scott . . . thereby bringing disgrace upon the good name of the regiment."

In sixty pages of testimony, several points stand out. Colonel Robert F. Taylor reported a conversation he had had with Scott months before. "He stated to me that while the regiment was away from Camp Stoneman [Maryland], his wife had been guilty of improper conduct with both officers and men, that he now believed that she was a notorious whore, that she had deceived him, and that he never intended to live with her again. This conversation occupied two hours, during which Captain Scott gave me the names of some of the officers who had cohabitated with her. Later, when she arrived at Camp Piatt, I asked Captain Scott if he still claimed her as his wife. He replied that he had written to several families in Rochester [New York] and that he had decided that she was a good woman and that he had slandered her. I told him I was a different opinion and that she must go. At Camp Stoneman, her character was very bad indeed, the lowest of the low. Her actions were not those of a married lady, improperly addressing officers and flirting."

In March 1864, Scott had submitted his resignation "for the purpose of attending to my domestic affairs." The resignation was rejected for lack of a certificate of non-indebtedness.

Lieutenant E. H. Brady recalled that at the cavalry camp at Giesboro Point [Camp Stoneman, now the site of Bolling Air Force Base], Mrs. Scott had occupied the tent of Major James E. Williams for four nights while Captain Scott was away. "But I never saw her undressed."

Lieutenant Alfred L. Bancroft had known her in Rochester three years earlier. "She was supposed to do things outside the family that she ought not to do, and she has told me that herself. At Rochester, she told me, 'I have never thrown a good thing over my shoulder and never would do so, as long as I can fool Mr. Scott. I got drunk and had intercourse with a gentleman.' At Camp Stoneman, she once had her legs across mine and allowed me to feel of her very freely, and invited me to come see her at the brick house. I declined the offer."

Lieutenant Allen Vanderbogart told the Court: "Captain Scott told me that his wife had had improper intercourse with Major Williams, but that she must have been under the influence of some drug when she did that. He also told me that his wife had diseased him at Camp Stoneman."

Lieutenant Orlando Bacon recalled an episode at Bolivar Heights [above Harpers Ferry], at a private home. "I exchanged cards with her there. Her card said Libby Bastide. She told me it was her right name. There were four officers of the Sixth Corps there, including Captain Samuel Urquhart. She introduced me to him. Three of the officers left; Urquhart gave her a kiss, whispered to her and then he left. I remarked to her that she must be doing a pretty heavy business in the Sixth Corps. She said she'd left the cavalry and joined the Sixth Corps. She showed me a badge of the Second Division, Sixth Corps and said, 'My Sammy gave it to me. He is my true and only love.' She also told me that she had her husband right under her thumb." The Court inquired of Lieutenant Bacon if she had been improper at Camp Piatt. "Yes, she allowed me to look down her stockinged legs."

Lieutenant John T. Clague had seen a love note that she wrote to Captain A.T. Pickett, in which she said she loved him better than she did her own husband, and signed herself "Libby." Clague had also seen her out riding with Captain Urquhart, who he said was "a gay young man," and Captain Scott himself had told Clague, "I have positive proof of her infidelity with Urquhart." The defense produced six witnesses, who all said that Mrs. Scott was of good character and ladylike at all times. Throughout the trial, Captain Scott asked witnesses if they knew of Colonel Taylor's hostility towards him. All the witnesses dodged the question.

Scott was acquitted of bringing a notorious woman to Camp Piatt, but was found guilty of not recognizing his wife's infidelity. He was ordered dismissed. The case was reviewed by Major General George Crook, who noted that the proceedings were "fatally flawed," and forwarded the case to Lincoln with a recommendation of summary dismissal. Lincoln sent the papers to his Judge Advocate General, Joseph Holt, who viewed Mrs. Scott as "of infamous character," and concluded that Captain Scott's blindness to his wife's deceptions was hardly grounds to make Scott "unworthy of the military service." Holt disagreed with Crook's recommendation. Apparently, Lincoln agreed with Holt. Scott remained with his regiment. His apparent nemesis, Colonel Taylor, was himself dismissed from the army just two months after Scott's trial. The regiment fought dozens of engagements throughout West Virginia, but its most vicious fighting may have been among its own officers.[1]

A very strange case was that of Private Rezin Ravencraft of the 11th West Virginia. At Parkersburg, he was ordered to take Virginia Robinson, "a woman of degraded character," to headquarters. He shot her in the left thigh, causing her to bleed to death. He was tried for murder in February 1864, and claimed he was ordered to shoot her. One witness testified, "Ravencraft has been deranged since 1854 and was in the lunatic asylum. I feared he might kill my own children." He was found not guilty, but insane. The reviewer disapproved the proceedings and returned him to duty.[2]

Lieutenant Jacob Johnson's quarrel with the government went on for a decade after his death. After brief service with the 6th West Virginia in 1862, he was charged with conduct unbecoming and officer and a gentleman, with nine separate specifications: He lay in bed with Mary Somers, a lewd woman, in the presence of his enlisted men. At Webster, he took his noncommissioned officers to a house of ill fame. He sent one of his men to buy whisky, went on a picnic, drinking with his men and "had connexion with a lewd woman in the presence of his men." A few weeks later, when he was supposed to be hunting for "secesh mail," he lay in bed with a prostitute. On a different occasion, he took Lidia Williams, "a notorious prostitute," into a private room and kept her there for half an hour. At Phillipi, he "tampered with a colored woman," and wrote notes to her urging her to come to his bedroom in the night. He took part of his men's rations to a house of ill fame and bartered the food for sex. He neglected his duty, "being absent from his men, visiting profligate women." Finally, he used "insulting language toward ladies of good character, calling them damned liars and damned bitches." The setting of his public tryst with Mary Somers was a "meeting house," in other words, a church. This satanic scene was lit by a candle on the pulpit. Private Nixon Potts, age 56, painted a word picture for the court. "Mary Somers' character was very bad in respect to whoring. Sergeant Jerome Mortars went to Trussels to fetch her. We were supposed to take her to the guardhouse at Grafton. The sergeant and Lieutenant Johnson shared a bed. When Mary got in, the sergeant got out. We were all quartered in the same room. The soldier who slept next to them said that she took foul hold of the lieutenant."

Sergeant Mortars added his memories. "When she fell in between us, I left and slept on a bench. In the morning, the lieutenant said I might do as I pleased with her. I told her to leave Webster and Trussels, to take her bonnet and go and if she came back I'd shoot her. She replied, 'You're just mad because you couldn't screw me as Lieutenant Johnson did.'"

Twenty-four-year-old James E. Jones of Company B spoke next. "I saw the lieutenant go into a room with Lidia Williams. She is what is called in plain Lattin [sic] a whore."

After much similar testimony, the prosecution rested and Lieutenant Johnson submitted a 1500-word defense, a marvel of obfuscation, which read in part: "It is not merely indecorous conduct, meaned by the continued rules of the society in any community nor by the standard of moral that any number of a court martial or were a court martial, shall have such setup for official conduct as gentlemen behaving. If so, there could be no uniform rule to determine it and no uniformity or certainty in effacing observance of the article in question." In spite of this novel (or merely incoherent) defense, he was convicted and dismissed. But the story isn't over.

In the 1890's, he made application for a pension, asserting that he had received an honorable discharge and claiming the following disabilities: "Sore eyes for 35 years, hands and feet swollen for 35 years, tetters [a sort of chronic scabby pustule] over the hands and feet and trouble urinating," all suggestive of long-term advanced syphilis. A pension examiner, Dr. W. Degarmov, noted: "Urinary retention, epidermis comes off, hands cracked and bleeding, fingernails look like black nuts." His application was rejected because he had been discharged in disgrace. He died in 1897. Eleven years later, his family members prevailed upon their congressman to intercede in a request that they receive the dead lieutenant's pension, but this, too, was rejected.[3]

Captain Levi Bryte was the terror of Sutton, firing his revolver out of a whorehouse window at his own troops, and generally bringing disgrace upon the 3rd West Virginia. Bryte, it seems, was stricken with the charms of the Widow Strader, a resident of Linton. She, in turn, displayed near-miraculous parthenogenesis, having produced four children since the death of her husband, and the daughters were now old enough to be "of loose character." The prosecution witnesses were a cornucopia of facts. A private had seen Bryte with his arms around the woman, and the sergeant major, who had seen the captain and his inamorata "laying down together, having sexual intercourse in a 'holler,'" confirmed the nature of the Strader bagnio, telling the Court he had been there fifty times himself. For these offenses and for selling government ammunition to his troops, Bryte was dismissed in May 1863. Eight years later, he was still writing to the War Department, asking for compensation.[4]

Captain William Woodward of the 28th Pennsylvania may have been the victim of false charges when, in February 1863, he stood trial for "introducing whores into camp, entertaining them in his tent, taking them to officer's quarters at Harper's Ferry, and entertaining whores between tattoo and taps." Testimony showed that the two women in question were Mrs. Woodward and her cousin. He was acquitted.[5]

Private Martin B. Smith of the 12th West Virginia was hardly a credit to his uniform. At Maryland Heights, he tried to shoot his captain. He cursed his sergeant at Bloody Run and threw a bottle at the man. At Martinsburg, he evaded the guard and went to visit prostitutes, a venture made easy by its location: "There is a house of ill fame right close to the post." These offenses, plus intentionally breaking his rifle, earned him ten years in the penitentiary and a dishonorable discharge at his March 1864 trial.[6]

Lieutenant John S. McDonald of the 17th West Virginia failed to provide moral leadership when he spent the night with "a woman of ill fame" at Bulltown, and the next day carried her behind him on his horse. At Weston, he was absent without leave with another woman of ill fame, and with her, was captured by rebel guerillas. These offenses, plus encouraging two sutlers to sell whisky to his troops, and his selling two government mules, led to his February 1865 trial, where he was dishonorably dismissed, with his crimes to be published in his home town newspaper. In 1906, he was still seeking reconsideration of his case.[7]

Lieutenant James McGill of the 11th West Virginia kept Elizabeth Stewart, "a notorious whore," in his tent at Parkersburg. Not only that, but he ordered the guards not to arrest her and he had her "dressed in male clothing." This tryst "in the woods" lasted two weeks, but his behavior was no better in town, where he was arrested in a saloon, drunk, throwing oysters and butter. He was dismissed. Ninety years later, his heirs submitted affidavits from two sergeants, who asserted that it had all been a practical joke. The War Department refused to overturn the conviction.[8]

A West Virginia historian has illuminated the Civil War skin trade at Parkersburg. The upper class courtesans trolled at the Swann House on Ann Street, while the less elegant women worked in the cribs on Kanawha [First] Street and along the riverbank east of Market Street. Even the police feared to venture there at night.[9] An undated clipping from *The Lubricator,* a newspaper published in the oil town of Volcano, in eastern Wood County, criticized "our young gentlemen who take prostitutes to church and stand in the porch while the soiled doves walk in."[10]

Captain Horatio Tibbals of the 12th Ohio, in October 1863, was so drunk he fell off his horse at Fayetteville. A little later, he neglected his duties as Officer of the Day by visiting the Killingsworth House of ill repute, seven miles from camp, "near the Raleigh Road." There, he insulted an old woman and, was also seen sitting on one of the prostitute's beds. The hygienic standards of the house were defined by one of Tibbals' men, who caught "a bad disease there." Tibbals was cashiered (discharged in disgrace).[11]

Francis Cordrey was age 24 with blue eyes and dark hair in 1862, when he was mustered into the 126th Ohio. In his diary, he mentions arresting women in Martinsburg for "whoring," arresting a soldier for having "connexion with a Negro wench," and being present when a Negro man was hanged for "fornycaboogry." Cordrey was wounded in the thigh at Monocacy, and received a medical discharge in May 1865.[12]

Brigadier General Francis P. Fessenden was stationed at Grafton in May 1865, when he wrote to his friend, Colonel Thomas Hubbard of the 30th Maine. Fessenden detested Grafton ("a hole, a collection of hovels"), and hoped to be transferred to Clarksburg, "a better place, where you can do horizontal things . . . without people being inquisitive."[13]

In April 1863, Private Amos Hackenberry of Company D, 74th Pennsylvania, was in Randolph County, when he wrote to "Dear and Beloved Wife," describing nighttime picket duty in a field of dead horses. "It smelled midlin strong." Then he added a curious note. "You would better not send your picture it is not very safe to send and another thing is whenever I want to see some ladies I just go to Cerely [sic]. There are 12 in one house."[14]

In April 1863, John Moon of the 2nd West Virginia was on a scouting party between Brawley and Huttonsville. The group was very tired and its commander called for a halt. Moon asked permission to go ahead a quarter of a mile and meet his party the next morning. He was not seen again for four days. Witnesses testified that Moon had been at the Stoerker House, whose inmates were "people of loose character." When Moon returned, he had lost his shoes; perhaps he had bartered them for a companion of loose character. Moon was given fiften days at hard labor and lost a month's pay.[15]

Lieutenant John W. Smith of Stewart's Cavalry (Indiana) was quite a handful in February 1862, while stationed at Wheeling. He was convicted of hitting a sergeant with a saber and of being AWOL twice; more relevantly, he "has frequently told the privates about his having venereal disease and has kept them posted as to its various stages. He is also a habitual attendant at houses of ill fame." Witnesses said that he been "doctoring himself" for venereal disease and had been displaying his genital lesions to the men in his company. Smith was dismissed.[16]

Throughout the Civil War, men were arrested in and around houses of prostitution, but rarely for simply being there. If they were disorderly, or there after 9:00 p.m., or there without a pass, they might be arrested, but the visit itself was unremarkable. Our West Virginia men, presented here, not only saw prostitutes, but added some other malfeasance to the event. It is highly probable that these cases reflect only a tiny fraction of the industry of prostitution in Civil War West Virginia.

Chapter 5

PROSTITUTION IN KENTUCKY

"I hope to have God on my side, but I must have Kentucky!" Whether Lincoln said those exact words, expressing the strategic location of the Bluegrass State, is unclear, but such thoughts were certainly in his September 22nd, 1861 letter to Orville H. Browning: "I think to lose Kentucky is nearly the same as to lose the whole game."[1] Many of the soldiers in wartime Kentucky had their own passionate thoughts, not all of them political.

Louisville, a major port on the Ohio River, was, quite naturally, a center of concupiscence. Lieutenant Gideon H. Dunham of the 59th Ohio was so ill-behaved that he was dismissed by direct order of Major General Rosecrans, thus bypassing the usual court-martial path. In General Orders No. 44, dated Christmas Day, 1862, Dunham was sent away in disgrace "for being found in a state of beastly intoxication in a house of ill fame at Louisville." He was age 23. In February 1864, Sergeant William Knight, 20th Kentucky, was accused of stealing $50 from a discharged soldier, at a house of ill fame kept by Mollie Clark, but was found not guilty. Mollie does not appear in the 1864 Louisville city directory; perhaps Clark was not her real name.[2]

Private Philip E. Sergeant of the 21st Illinois was excited over receiving his veteran's furlough. Too excited. He got drunk at a house of ill fame on Louisville's Lafayette Street and threatened a sergeant with a revolver. He was fined two month's pay.[3] The trial of Private James M. Thompson of the 123rd US Colored Troops tells of Martha Bodine's "colored whorehouse," which catered to both black and white men. One witness referred to it as a "house of assignation." (Witness Elizabeth Shuck ran a beer cellar on Water Street, between Second and Third Streets.) Thompson was charged with murder, for shooting a white man in the alley between Second and Third Streets; he was convicted of manslaughter and sentenced to a dishonorable discharge and five years in the penitentiary.[4]

Lieutenant Thomas F. Fouts of the 8th Iowa Cavalry was in town, having his horse shod. Did he wait patiently on that February day in 1864? Hardly. Taking an enlisted man with him, he proceeded to a "house of ill fame" on Lafayette Street, where they spent the night. Fouts was fined three months pay, reprimanded, and ordered to sing to his company "The Song of the Fall of Fort Sumter."[5]

Our final Louisville case took place at Park Barracks. Lieutenant Edward P. Pitkins of the 20th Michigan was in command that August in 1863, when he decided to take action regarding an outbreak of venereal disease attributed to two German women who slept under the "whorehouse tree" in camp. He had them arrested, tied to an iron grating with their dresses pulled up to reveal their "persons" [genitals], and then had them hosed down with a "force pump." This went on until the enlisted men who had gathered to watch became "sick and disgusted with the sight [and] began to slip away." Pitkins was "severely reprimanded."[6]

Camp Nelson, near Nicholasville in Jessamine County, was a major assembly point for Union soldiers, and 3000 of them are still there, in neat rows, deep under the grass. In April 1865, at least two men at Camp Nelson were more lively than the current inhabitants. The first was Daniel Meeker, a surgeon of US Volunteers. There were many charges filed against him—falsifying employee records, selling a government horse, embezzlement, and accepting bribes from the sutler—but what concerns us here is his employment of a prostitute, Georgia Anderson, as a nurse. Not only that, but one witness said, "I saw Dr. Meeker and that woman together at church!" After 130 pages of testimony, the stories amounted to nothing, and Meeker was acquitted.[7]

Near the "lower end" of Camp Nelson, lived a man who tended bar and sold pies. W.H. Hall was a widower who lived with his daughters, Mary Elizabeth Pate (whose husband was in the 7th Ohio Cavalry), Ellen (age 18), Martha (age 17), Rachel (age 16), Ruth Ann (age 10), Sarah (age seven), and two young sons. On an April evening in 1865, near midnight, Captain Samuel Fitch of the 6th US Colored Cavalry broke down the Hall's door and announced, "This is a damned whorehouse. I intend to fuck one of you women before I leave." He drove Mr. Hall out, using fists and a club, and shouted, "I'm going to stay here all night." Mrs. Pate, not easily intimidated, retorted, "In that case, I'll have to kill you." The trial ended with a long written defense by Fitch's counsel, the gist of it being that if some people thought the Hall girls were whores, then Fitch's actions were excusable. This novel defense failed and Fitch was dismissed in disgrace.[8]

Two men from the 2nd Illinois Cavalry had a wild night at Columbus in March 1863. Sergeant John C. Cox and Private George Bywater were at a "house of ill fame" and violently resisted the provost guard when ordered to return to camp. Cox lost a month's pay; his companion got twenty days at hard labor.[9]

Two lieutenants of the 40th Kentucky Mounted Infantry were tried for "conduct unbecoming" for "attending dances at houses of ill fame" at Grayson, in May 1864. The defendants were Warren Devore and Henry Evans. Witness James Jordan of Company C, said he knew of no house of ill fame in Grayson, and Lieutenant J.W. Frazer was equally ignorant of any whorehouses, but he had seen Devore play his fiddle at a dance held at the house of Mary Ann James. The end result of the trial was two acquittals.[10]

At Elizabethtown, the elegantly named Fountain B. Hawkins, a captain in the 48th Kentucky, was far more sportive than the two preceding lieutenants. Not only did Hawkins fail to pursue guerilas, robbing loyal citizens instead, but he had considerable contact with disreputable women. In April 1864, while wearing his uniform, Hawkins visited houses of ill fame, including "Mrs. Johnson's place," and was seen on the streets embracing "Fanny Wright, a public prostitute, who had come to his office in the Eagle House, and of conducting her to his room." Later in May, he made an inspection visit to the army post at Nolin, taking with him "a well-known prostitute." All this was a bit much; he was cashiered.[11]

The army was clearly opposed to walking or riding with prostitutes. At Lexington, in the summer of 1864, Sergeant Daniel E. Grover of the 11th Michigan Cavalry was in a carriage that had stopped at Elliott's Dry Goods Store. Into the carriage climbed Anna Rayburn and a second woman, both residents of "a public place opposite the Phoenix Hotel." For the crime of riding in a carriage up the main street with two prostitutes, he was reduced to the rank of private.[12]

Albert Archer offered no defense at Bowling Green, in May 1863. This captain of the 111th Ohio was Field Officer of the Day. He was found drunk, in a house of ill fame, clearly not attending to his duties, and was cashiered.[13]

For cheek, brass, and sheer unadulterated chutzpah, it would be hard to beat Harry W. Barry, who came close to the beau ideal of Major General Harry Flashman, whose insouciance marks the greatest novels of George MacDonald Fraser. The fictitious Flashman began his career as a bully, expelled from prep school. Through a series of misunderstandings, he became a decorated war hero in spite of his cowardice, a favorite of Queen Victoria in spite of his extraordinarily lewd private life, and a wealthy man in spite of being a spendthrift. His American adventures include *Flash for Freedom*, in which he is both a slave trader and a confidant of John Brown and Abraham Lincoln.

Flashman's real life counterpart, Harry Barry, had been a first lieutenant in the 10th Kentucky, but was booted out as being "wholly inefficient as an officer and absent without leave." He soon heard about America's first officer candidate school, conducted in Philadelphia by Colonel John H. Taggart. Fourteen months after being discharged in disgrace, Barry was back in the service, this time as Colonel Barry of the 8th US Colored Heavy Artillery, commanding the post at Paducah. Nine months after assuming command, he was charged with consorting with a Mrs. Kerr, a "lewd and disreputable character," and with assisting her in extorting gold from a local bank. Barry was still awaiting trial when he was mustered out. Within months, he was promoted to brevet brigadier general, based on forged letters from Rutherford B. Hayes, James A. Garfield, George H. Thomas and other Civil War luminaries. The newly-minted one-star general then used the same tactics to become a brevet major general. From this elevated status, he was elected to congress, only to die at age thirty-five, after a prolonged drunk.[14]

The font of Kentucky stories never goes dry. Near Danville, John Sewell of the 6th Kentucky Cavalry insisted on leaving the march, to visit a house of prostitution. His sergeant told him, "No." Sewell attacked his sergeant with a saber; the sergeant shot Sewell, who died two months later. Sgt. George H. Smith of the 2nd New York Cavalry had just been commissioned a captain and Commissary of Subsistence. En route to his new duties, he spent several nights in Louisville houses of prostitution, but was foolish enough to write a *very* detailed letter home about his adventures. The letter came into the hands of Secretary of War Stanton. A few weeks later, Smith was dismissed in disgrace and fled to Europe.

Thirty years after the guns fell silent at Appomattox, soldiers returned to Louisville, at the Grand Army of the Republic annual national encampment. Presiding over the 1,134 delegates was Commander in Chief Thomas G. Lawler of Illinois. For the convenience of the delegates, the Wentworth Publishing House issued the "GAR Souvenir Sporting Guide." The veterans, now in their fifties and sixties, were offered the chance to see Bradt's National War Museum, bicycle champion Sid Black, balloon ascensions at Riverside Park, and Field's Minstrels at Macauley's Theater. However, the majority of the pamphlet was devoted to ads placed by twenty-eight whorehouse madams. A typical one might be this full-page come-on from Daisy Mills of 711 West Street: "To the many visitors to the city during the Encampment and Races the writer desires to call their especial attention to the delightful little cottage owned and personally managed by Miss Daisy ... She has four of her most intimate friends from Chicago to assist her in receiving her callers, and as they are all beautiful and accomplished, it is unnecessary to add they are the swellest of swell entertainers." Bessie Dean of Green Street offered fourteen girls, and Jew Louie had twelve young ladies to receive callers in "Oriental splendor." The other two-dozen houses followed a similar format. One can only guess the balance of victory and defeat, as these veterans of a pre-Viagra era stormed the masked batteries of hundreds of Louisville lovelies.[15]

A century and a half after the war, the last veterans were gone, but the association of Kentucky, prostitution, and the army continues. Fort Campbell, home to the famous 101 Airborne Division, is the principal source of income for the little town of Oak Grove, a patchwork of mobile homes, massage parlors, strip joints, and pornography shops. In 1997, the local sex trade rose briefly to national prominence, with a sex, murder, and extortion scandal involving the police, the city council, and two dead prostitutes.[16]

Chapter 6

PROSTITUTION IN TENNESSEE

Memphis

"Country matters," as Shakespeare termed them, were well under way in pre-war Memphis. The 1859 City Directory had such advertisements as "Dr. Brooks Celebrated Compound—There is no [menstrual] obstruction [i.e., unwanted pregnancy] which will not yield under its use," or "Bell's Golden Wafers, the great English remedy for gonorrhea, gleet, stricture . . . and seminal weakness."

Dr. H. J. Holmes announced his Infirmary for Ladies, "now at the Navy Yard's Commandant's house," where "all the diseases of the womb and bladder might be cured." Dr. Butt's Dispensary at the corner of Fifth and Market Streets offered "scientific treatment of chronic, virulent and special diseases—with special attention to diseases peculiar to females." Dr. Whittier, who also treated "special diseases," had his office in St. Louis, but told Memphis readers that "every case can be successfully treated by mail." (In the 1860s, diseases labeled "special" or "private" were venereal.)

The police booking ledger for January 1859, in addition to dozens of drunken Irishmen and slaves without passes, had this entry for the 11th day of the year: "Mary Williams, a drunken whore, put up for drunkenness by Butler and Myer."

Memphis was ready to greet the new decade. The 1860 City Directory listed 81 saloons (Arata's through Zanone's), and the reader was directed to lager beer saloons and oyster saloons for additional listings. (There were two German newspapers and six slave dealers.)

Even more informative was the 1860 census. In the Fifth Ward, near the river, there was 42-year-old Mary Maguire, a native of Ireland; at her "boarding house" lived six young women, ages 12 to 23. In the same ward, 24-year-old "bagnio keeper" Lizzie Whitias (or Whitress) had nine girls at her place, including her older sister Jennie, all of whom gave the census taker their occupation as "prostitute." At the same address were two female servants. Lizzie declared property worth $5,000, a considerable sum in 1860. The Fifth Ward, which occupied the area between Beale and Union Streets, had further offerings for the lonely traveler. Eliza Goodrich, age 30, also a "bagnio keeper," had five girls, all declared as "prostitute." Priscilla Petty, net worth $6,000, headed a household of nine women in their twenties, who declined to give their occupations. Most were from Tennessee or Louisiana, but Madeline Sinclair claimed Scotland as her birthplace and Jeanie Hathaway hailed from Wisconsin.

Josephine Brown, age nineteen, headed a small house of two other teenage girls, concluding the data from Ward Five. No prostitutes were listed in Ward Six, and no City Directories were published during the Civil War. It is clear that Memphis was ready to meet the occupying Union forces—at least in bed.

The Iron Clad seems to have been Memphis' best-known house of prostitution, and appears in the testimony of at least five courts-martial. One of these trials calls to mind an old, rather tasteless, aphorism for describing a man with limited social skills: "He couldn't get laid in a whorehouse with a hundred dollar bill in his hand." Alexander Grimes, a private of Company K, 12th Iowa, on September 13th, 1864, presented his hundred-dollar bill at the store of Ferdinand Englebrecht, who refused to honor it. Grimes then proceeded to the Iron Clad, where he tried to use the same bill for a bottle of wine and a night with a girl. At his trial for passing counterfeit money, one witness was Captain Harry Lee of the 7th Wisconsin Battery, who said, "I have experience in detecting counterfeit money, and I know that the bill numbered 62608 is counterfeit." The bill is still in Grimes' court-martial in the National Archives. Grimes himself got three years in prison and a dishonorable discharge.[1]

Captain Ormsby H. Huston set some sort of record for malfeasance. He commanded Company H, 53rd Indiana, described in his March 1863 trial as "ill-disciplined, many of the men are without guns." He had also told the regiment's colonel, "Kiss my ass, you damned old fool, you damned son of a bitch." Surgeon Madison Rose told the Court, "Captain Huston has required medicine three times for clap; gonorrhea has rendered him unfit for duty for two months." Lieutenant Henry Perkins recalled, "He told me he has had three whores in one night, and is well known at many houses of ill fame, including the Iron Clad." Huston was dismissed.

Service and pension files show a richly textured life. Huston had gonorrhea as a boy, but said, "I cured it myself." (Since physicians in the 1850s had little success in curing such diseases, it is highly unlikely that Huston actually cured himself.) At age 17, he enlisted in the 4th US Artillery and served from 1856 to 1861, acquiring malaria in Florida and frozen ears in Nebraska Territory. In 1868, he spent three months in the Louisville, Kentucky Insane Asylum. In

1895, he applied for a pension. A supporting letter from his Grand Army of the Republic post told the Pension Bureau that Huston was "a brave and worthy soldier, enfeebled and broken down by disease contracted in the service, utterly helpless, supported by an aged mother." In 1899, his pension application was rejected.[2]

Colonel John F. Ritter was the highest-ranking officer recorded as an Iron Clad customer. In June 1863, he commanded the 1st Missouri Cavalry, and in this position, he allowed his men to beat and rob African Americans civilians and told an officer commanding US Colored Troops, "You're a damned son of a bitch, I wish I'd gone with the South." As to his nocturnal career, testimony showed his activities with prostitutes Annie Wilson and Kate Richmond. One of his officers testified that he had gone to the Iron Clad with Colonel Ritter several times. The defense mounted by the colonel's lawyer was long and spirited, including this key observation: "If every officer of the army guilty of fornication was considered unworthy . . . few would escape censure." Ritter was suspended from rank and pay for six months.[3]

Lieutenant James S. Risley of the 32nd Illinois was tried for "conduct unbecoming an officer and a gentleman," for an act committed at high noon. Risley went to the Iron Clad, helped a prostitute out of a window, and rode off with her. Corporal Samuel Temple told the Court, "I saw him in a hack with the top down with a whore from the Iron Clad. The Iron Clad is 75 yards off Main Street. I know it is a whorehouse—I have been there myself." Risley was dismissed.[4]

Memphis was under martial law in April 1863, and military courts tried civilians, such as William O'Brian, accused of robbery and attempted murder. Sims Lane, a wealthy tobacco farmer, came to town for the nightlife and soon met four new "best friends" in a bar. They admired Lane's wit—and his bankroll. After a tour of saloons and bordellos, O'Brian garroted Lane, then hit him on the head with a brick and ran off with $1000 in cash ($30,000 in today's money). Lane survived and O'Brian was brought to trial. The testimony shed further light on Memphis' bordellos. The robbery occurred at 11:00 p.m. on Beale Street. In tracing the progress of the drinking party, the court called upon the testimony of Anna Belsford, madam of the Iron Clad; she recalled the party well. "They were too drunk to admit to my house. I don't admit drunk groups unless one is sober enough to care for the others. I know Mr. Lane; he is here frequently." (Ms. Belsford gave the address of the Iron Clad: Winchester Street between Front Row and Main Street.) The same party that had been excluded from the Iron Clad also visited "Miss Lizzie Whitress' place on Shelby Street." O'Brian got three years in prison and students of Memphis history got yet more pieces to the puzzle of life in that city.[5]

The court-martial transcripts give us the names of three more establishments. Maggie Moodie's house, at the corner of Washington Street and Centre Alley, housed Millie Glenn, Mary E. McDonald and Kate Woods, all of whom testified in the murder trial of Thomas Martin of the 1st Mississippi Mounted Rifles, a Union colored regiment organized in March 1864. He had shot and killed another soldier, while both were at Maggie's place. Martin's lawyer asked the court to ignore McDonald: "The frail [i.e., immoral] witness, Mary McDonald, unblushingly admits that he slept with her that night, but the veracity of a bawd . . ." His attempt to discredit her testimony, simply because she was a prostitute, failed. Martin was sentenced to be hanged.[6]

Private John W. Lamond of the 2nd New Jersey Cavalry disappeared from his regiment for a month and was arrested in bed at the Señora Saloon on Winchester Street. He was sentenced to be shot, but was saved by a technicality.[7]

Private George Matthew of the 7th Illinois Cavalry, absent for ten months, was found in August 1864 at the "Union House," at the corner of Second and Beale Streets. His defense: "My purpose was to loaf and carouse." He got "prison until the end of the war, at hard labor."[8]

Daniel Mytinger had an upward-bound career until 1864. He was a corporal in the 22nd Ohio, then quartermaster sergeant and finally first lieutenant. At Duvall's Bluff, Arkansas, when his request for leave was not approved, he told friends, "I'm going anyway." Sixty days later, he was arrested in Memphis, where he had spent his time "going to the theatre and to the houses." He was dismissed May 9, 1864. His 1905 request for a pension was rejected.[9]

Most women, including prostitutes, aspired to be "ladies," which included riding sidesaddle. Thus it was with the "wife" of Lieutenant James A. Price of the 7th Indiana Cavalry at Memphis in April 1864. She was riding sidesaddle, but Price himself gave away the charade by his noisy drunkenness, which led to the discovery that she was, in fact, a prostitute. He was dismissed.[10]

Captain Joshua Bourne, 7th Missouri, had 24 separate specifications charged against him, most of them concerning conflicting factions among the officers, but one charge claimed that at Memphis he had visited houses of prostitution and there contracted syphilis and gonorrhea. However, as the actual trial unfolded, the charges evaporated like the morning dew. The one witness who was queried about Bourne's sexual life answered, "I don't know anything about the affair." Bourne was acquitted.[11]

In a mass trial of a dozen prostitutes who had violated an order closing their Beale Street house, the testimony degenerated into low farce. Two detectives were assigned to survey the establishment. One spent three hours in bed with one of the girls, and the other eloped with a second prostitute. Eventually, all the women were ordered to leave Memphis, but not before the authorities had looked foolish.[12]

In September 1864, the Federal authorities changed tactics and instituted a system of mandatory licensure and medical inspections of all the prostitutes in Memphis.[13] This innovation invoked a long response 2000 miles away in

California's gold country: "This official recognition of prostitution marks the downward testimony of the American people." This was the conclusion of a long article describing the Memphis system of licensure.[14]

One of the more puzzling trials in the Federal records is the September 1864 Memphis court-martial of Lieutenant Colonel William P. Hepburn, 2nd Iowa Cavalry. He had been the judge advocate of a trial of Lizzie Booth, accused of smuggling. On the night between the testimony and the court's deliberation, he went to her room and offered to trade sex for a favorable verdict. "He thrust his hand into my bosom!" Hepburn denied the charges and produced many witnesses who said that Lizzie was an ordinary prostitute and a liar; he was acquitted. However, Lizzie was the widow of the deceased Union commander at Fort Pillow, and she, herself, had recently enjoyed an audience with Abraham Lincoln. Only Demosthenes could sort out the truth in these two cases.[15]

An assortment of sources shed further light on the Memphis carnalcopia. A letter from Private George Gee, 32nd Wisconsin, in May 1863, gave his opinion that many of the prostitutes were the impoverished wives of Confederate soldiers and anxious to even the score: "One morning a lieutenant and two privates were found in a cistern with their throats cut from ear to ear." The same series of letters described searching whorehouses for deserters, finding revolvers under a girl's body in bed, and seeing "unmentionable" sights.[16]

Doctors continued to thrive on disease. An 1862 ad by Dr. Whittier (offices in St. Louis, but steamboats were swift and frequent) promised to cure "syphilis, gonorrhea, gleet, the effects of solitary habits, impotency, weakness, and [!] evil foreboding."

Memphis figured prominently in the aforementioned report by Detective Edward Betty, who wrote at length about "harlots" and "debauchery," noting that all along the river, both army and navy units received whores that were delivered right to their doorsteps, not unlike pizza today.[17]

In 1865, the final year of the war, the medical business continued to prosper, judging by the published ads. Dr. Butts continued to promise "the scientific treatment of all private diseases of whatever nature, in both male and female, and guarantees a perfect and radical cure . . . without the use of mercury or noxious drugs." Dr. Butts' Pocket Medical Adviser, a bargain at three cents, offered "remedies of excessive and perverted sexuality and self-abuse," as well as cure of all venereal diseases.

The chief of police, in the 1872 Memphis Municipal Report, listed 18 houses of prostitution, containing a total of 150 women. Since the Federal system of licensure and inspection was long gone, it seems likely that venereal disease was still epidemic.

These same issues have been studied by other historians, using other sources of information. Darla Brock focused on the prostitutes of Memphis.[18] Lawrence Murphy studied venereal disease in Union troops west of the Mississippi River and found a far higher rate of infection than troops in the east. The California troops reached an astonishing level: In 1862, 43 percent of the California troops had some form of reported venereal disease.[19]

Nashville

Nashville's Civil War prostitutes even made the front page of the New York *Tribune*. On June 6, 1863, this item appeared: "General Granger has ordered all houses of ill fame to be vacated by the 8th instant. There is great excitement among the 'fancy.'" The failure of Granger's order was soon apparent, and it was replaced by a successful program of medically-supervised, legalized prostitution.

The sex trade in mid-19th Century Nashville has been the subject of several studies. An analysis of the 1860 census showed that most houses of prostitution were located in an eight-block area along Church Street, between today's First and Fourth Avenues, all conveniently close to the steamboat landing. (These streets bore different names in 1860.) Two hundred seven women gave their occupation as "prostitute."[20]

The wartime difficulties with venereal disease and the successful efforts to control this epidemic form a positive story in the dismal history of Civil War infections. Licensure and frequent inspections, as well as kindly treatment of the prostitutes by the doctor in charge, all contributed to a remarkable success.[21]

Recent research has fleshed out our knowledge of Nashville's bawdy houses and their clientele. Corporal Hibbard Ridgely of the 102nd Ohio, while absent without leave, got into a drunken quarrel and was stabbed by prostitute Ida Ewing, "rendering him unfit for duty." At the trial, most witnesses professed to remember nothing, and Ridgely was let off with fourteen days in the stockade and reduction to the ranks.[22]

Prostitution was such a public event that the bordellos were used as landmarks. On the Fourth of July 1864, Private James C. Richards of the 12th Indiana Artillery robbed another soldier at gunpoint, "50 yards from the house of ill fame kept by Mrs. Wright." It is clear from the transcript that all present at the trial knew exactly where Mrs. Wright's place was.[23]

Captain Gideon Ayres of the 17th US Colored Troops was drunk as Officer of the Day, left his post and proceeded to the Railroad House, a house of ill fame, as noted by Lieutenant Charles Earnshaw, who was also there. Ayres was fined a month's pay. Three months later, he was killed in action near Nashville.[24]

"I command the whole city of Nashville, whores and all!" This somewhat expansive declaration was made by Captain Richard Bladen of the 1st Tennessee when he was Officer of the Day—and very drunk—on September 24, 1862. At a whorehouse, he took off his sword (a military protocol no-no) and gave it to one of the prostitutes (even more outrageous!) and then danced with several of the Cyprians, while still wearing his sash of authority. When an officer of the patrol guard, Lieutenant R.M. Cunningham, of the 19th Illinois, arrived at a Bladen-authored disturbance, the captain hit Cunningham with his pistol, inflicting severe facial wounds. Bladen capped his night by ordering Tennessee troops to fall in and fire on Illinois troops. He was dismissed in disgrace.[25]

Private Charles Smith of the 10th Ohio left his regiment as it passed through Nashville and was found, four months later, "residing in a house of ill repute." He was put to hard labor for the rest of his enlistment, wearing a ball and chain.[26]

The legendary Sergeant Bilko would have admired Captain William Fisher of the 12th Illinois, who said, "I hate the service and its pay, but as long as I can get damned privates to skin [cheat], I am satisfied." He won $800 from the "Indiana boys," and gambled with other enlisted men, a strictly prohibited act. At Nashville, he was also absent without leave, in August 1862, time that he spent "for pleasure . . . at a house of ill fame." Fisher was reprimanded and fined six months pay.[27]

Fisher's financial gains were nothing compared to Paymaster Major Adam Freeman, who stole $25, 941.31 intended to pay Union troops. How did he spend his money? "From the first day of October, 1863, [he was] notoriously in the habit of visiting houses of ill fame [in Nashville] for the purpose of prostitution, and associating with females of bad repute, and committing acts of adultery with these, and particularly on the 31st day of October, notoriously guilty of lewd and lascivious conduct . . . with notorious and public prostitutes." Just what particular act or acts of lewd behavior occupied him on Halloween is not recorded, but his theft, whoring and a substantial amount of drunkenness earned him five years in prison and a fine identical with the amount stolen. A year later, Andrew Johnson remitted most of the sentence.[28]

Was Henry Johnson really in a Nashville whorehouse in April 1865, or was he just being insolent? This private in the 13th US Infantry was absent without leave for twenty-four hours. When his major asked him where he had been, Johnson replied, "I was in a whorehouse." True or not, he was fined $10.[29]

Private Joseph Elking of the 13th Tennessee Cavalry was tried for murder in June 1864. The charge alleged that he had shot and killed a prostitute ["a sporting girl"] at Martha Carson's house on Criddle Street, between College and Cherry Streets. The victim, Elizabeth Stevens, died within 15 minutes of being shot. Prostitute Mary Douglas recalled that Elking had been drinking heavily and had handed the pistol to her, then suddenly grabbed it back, causing the shot that killed Elizabeth. Mary "saw no expression of intent." Private John Crow of Elking's regiment confirmed Mary's observations and the defendant was acquitted.[30]

Civilian Isaac Hoyt was charged with clubbing a lieutenant over the head and robbing him of $1000 at Mrs. Dora Pucket's house of ill fame at 59 North Vine Street. The victim was Lieutenant William Ward of the 2nd Tennessee

Mounted Infantry, who had slapped Mattie Hurley across the face. After hearing all sides, the Court acquitted Hoyt.[31]

When Rosine Klimmer was asked, "Do you not sell whisky to soldiers at your home and are not soldiers frequently there?," she refused to answer. The issue was John Smith's trial for desertion and theft. He had come to Klimmer's, saying he was sick and she gave him a bed. While she was out of the room, he stole a child's winter cloak. Smith was given three years in prison. After Lincoln's death, Smith wrote to Andrew Johnson, reminding him that he had served in the bodyguard when Johnson was governor of Tennessee. But was Smith's crime at a house of ill fame? The best answer is "probably."[32]

Thomas Kerr joined the army at age fifteen and by age seventeen was so disabled that he was transferred to the Veteran's Reserve Corps. During his service at Nashville with the 2nd VRC, he was court-martialed for sleeping on sentry duty and for taking a "public prostitute" from the refugee camp and keeping her in his bed. A witness recalled, "I saw them in bed, but I did not see the actual cohabitation." Lieutenant John Kerr (probably his brother) pleaded for clemency: "He is a good soldier and a severe sentence would greatly trouble his mother." Young Kerr was sent to sixty days hard labor with a ball and chain and fourten days on bread and water.[33]

Wagonmaster William Nye was tried for kicking a Corporal Eise in the face, disabling him for a week. The reason for the Christmas Day assault is unclear, but the nature of the College Street location seems certain. Military policeman C.D. Harmon of the 24th Wisconsin said, "I saw him [Nye] take a girl and go upstairs and when the guards came to arrest him, he was asleep." Some confusion about the actual assault led to an acquittal.[34]

"I know he was drunk. I went through his pockets and couldn't find a cent." This eager opportunist was nineteen-year-old Lucy Sanderson, a whore living at 131 College Street. The man with the empty pockets was Private George Prossen, of the 16th US Infantry, charged in March 1866 with stealing $500 by means of force and violence from "a colored soldier." Why did Prossen introduce Sanderson as his defense witness? To prove he was too drunk to rob the colored man. It didn't work. Prossen got drummed out with his head shaved, a dishonorable discharge and seven years in prison.[35]

Patrick Kane was a new recruit in the 5th US Cavalry in January 1866. He was absent without leave overnight. His excuse: "The corporal gave us permission to go down a little ways to a certain house. There were some women down there, and he gave us permission to see them. He did not say how long we were to stay." Whether his naïveté was real or feigned, Kane got three months at hard labor.[36]

William H. Githens, a surgeon with the 78th Illinois, wrote in a January 8, 1863 letter, "I don't suppose there is another city in the United States that has more villainy and meanness than this . . . the worse class, I think, are the prostitutes. They swarm here by thousands and many a hard-earned greenback goes into their clutches . . . murder and robbery is quite common."[37]

Private Joseph M. Steele of the 16th US Infantry was a determined man. He was already in the guardhouse in April 1866 when he escaped and walked to Cherry Street, where "he went into a house to see some girls." He seems to have been uncooperative when arrested, since he was "wounded in the head." His sentence was six months at hard labor and six months loss of pay.[38]

Steele had a kindred spirit in Henry Jones of the 13th US Infantry. Jones was absent without leave from his regiment at suburban Edgefield. When he was arrested at Nashville, in a whorehouse, he escaped from the Nashville guardhouse and was soon arrested—in another whorehouse, where he violently resisted capture. He pled guilty and got ninety days at hard labor.[39]

"I done it to a woman nine times that night." Was this reality or merely idle boasting on the part of Captain William G. Ritchey of the 16th Illinois? He had a habit of being out all night when assigned to guard duty, both at Stone's River and at Nashville. His "nine times" speech was on the morning of September 19th, 1862, as he returned to his guard post and asked his men, "Why don't you go and get some?" One wonders why his regiment had kept him so long, since "for the past three years, he has proved himself entirely incapable of commanding, drilling or disciplining his company." Ritchey was dishonorably dismissed.[40]

Nancy King was another prostitute called as a witness. Two men were quarreling on College Street over money to buy whisky. One man drew a knife; the other man produced a pistol and fired. Anthony Metta of the 18th Michigan was tried for murder. Miss King, of "Smokey Row," told the Court that they had asked her for whisky, and described their condition to the court.[41]

Today, cab drivers hesitate to enter parts of many cities. Such dangers also existed during the Civil War, such as the 1864 case of Musician Thomas O'Neil of the 10th Tennessee. His victim, "a colored man," told the court that O'Neil forced him to drive to Mrs. Overbeal's place, then to Mrs. Wright's on Jefferson Street, both "bad houses," then knocked him down and stabbed him "on the Jefferson Street Pike near Squire Creighton's place." O'Neil got three years in prison at hard labor.[42]

An intriguing letter, dated February 6, 1866, from V. A. White to Mrs. Jane Trail, was mailed from Au Sable, Michigan. The writer, who had been in some domestic difficulty, told her correspondent, "I first left home without telling anyone where I was going. I went to Decatur. There I sold my horse and saddle. From there, I went to Pulaski, Tennessee. There I bought me some clothing, stayed until I made them up, and from there I went to Nashville. I got off the train, ordered the omnibus driver to take me to the best fancy houses. He done so. I stayed at 154 College Street. Asked what the terms of board was, I was told $30 per week. I thought that steep, but supposed I could make it easy as any of the other girls and so I stopped there. Well, I made money. Lots of it, and I lived in splendor. I made sometimes $75 a day." After four months in the trade, she tired of it, cut her hair, bought a uniform and joined Company D of the 1st Michigan Engineers and Mechanics. Diligent search has failed to identify her in the ranks of that regiment, but the letter appears genuine and the insights into Nashville's sporting life are valuable.[43]

As with Memphis, when the war ended, civilian administration returned, the system of licensure, inspections and treatment disappeared and Nashville, like Memphis, reverted to its usual rapid spread of venereal disease.

Elsewhere In Tennessee

Cumberland Gap, the historic passage through the mountains, was the scene of two episodes of carnal malfeasance. Lieutenant Thomas Craycroft of the 11th Tennessee left camp on October 28th, 1864, "and did remain so absent until on or about the 30th day of October, when he was found drunk and in the company of a woman of ill fame." He pled guilty (hence there is no testimony) and was dismissed.[44]

Another lieutenant of the 11th Tennessee, Richard Gresham, had been absent without leave for three months. When he rejoined his regiment at Cumberland Gap, he was up to fresh mischief, described in a letter that he sent to his brother: "I taken too men of my company and run the blockade one night and played hell generally . . . we all got drunk and went to a hoare house and tore it down and run the wiman off and some of them come the next day and reported it to the general." In a postscript, Gresham added, "I have to do something to be cashiered . . . wee get plenty to eat and nothing to do." The devil continued to find work for idle hands.[45]

There was much military activity around Murfreesboro and, not surprisingly, much chance for mischief. Private Albert Weatherby of the 1st Michigan Light Artillery was at Fort Rosecrans, just west of today's city limits, when he left his sentry post to visit a "house of ill fame." His guilty plea precluded any testimony, and he was sentenced to a month at hard labor without pay.[46] Private Franklin Beck of the same regiment left the same fort and "visited the quarters of colored women of bad character." He, too, pled guilty, but was fined two months pay without the hard labor.[47]

Private Charles Carter, 35th Indiana, was more boisterous at Murfreesboro. While drunk, he seized his lieutenant by the throat, incited other men to mutiny and told a picket guard, "Come with me and I'll take you to a whorehouse!" Carter got fifteen days at hard labor with a 24-pound ball and chain and lost three months pay.[48]

The 155th Illinois served only seven months, but one wild day and night at Tullahoma filled many pages of testimony. Lieutenant Colonel Joseph Berry, quarreled with his superior, Colonel Gustavus Smith, at parade, and threw out his tent mate, Major John Lacy, calling him a "damned dog." Near camp was the establishment of Mrs. Prince, also known as "The Land Shark." Several of the officers—Berry, Captain John Lowber and Surgeon Russell Collins—were hiding in the bushes, watching the premises. The enlisted men could see them and were amused at the officers' feeble attempts at concealment. As one private approached Mrs. Prince's place, Berry called out, "What are you doing here?" The reply: "We are here for the same purpose you are." Berry continued the dialogue: "I want nothing to do with her, but you go ahead and fuck her." Berry was fined two months pay. The reviewing officer, Brigadier General Richard W. Johnson, recommended dismissal.[49]

A shoot-out at Fagan's house of ill fame! John McAdams of the 5th Tennessee Cavalry was drunk in the streets of Shelbyville and in a "boisterous row" in a whorehouse. When threatened with arrest, he fired at the provost guard, who returned fire. When the smoke cleared, "McAdams was not there, so we arrested the women." However, he was soon found, and two months at hard labor with a ball and chain gave McAdams time to sober up.[50]

Another Shelbyville case is more puzzling. In June 1864, the provost marshal had received orders from Nashville to remove "all lewd women" to Lincoln County, and leave them there, with instructions that if they returned, they would be arrested and sent to the military prison at Nashville. The group that was sent south contained eight women. Telegraph Operator John W. Rockwell took Mary Scott off of one of the wagons and "laid her in the shade," as the records tell us. After much confusing testimony, Rockwell was acquitted.[51]

Private Martin Crosier "kept a woman of lewd character at Clarksville," according to the February 1864 trial records of this member of the 83rd Illinois. His enlisted compatriots knew "nothing" when queried, but Lieutenants B.W. Perkins and D.M. Clark both said they had seen Crosier "walking or riding with a woman who was generally considered to be of lewd character . . . and he said that she was his woman and it was nobody's business." Crosier was reprimanded and fined one months pay.[52]

The second Clarksville case was that of David Huston, like Crosier, a member of the 83rd Illinois. On a warm July night in 1864, he was corporal of the picket guard. He allowed two prostitutes to visit his post and he and another private had "carnal knowledge" of the women. He was docked four months pay, spent fourteen days in solitary and was reprimanded.[53]

The few surviving Confederate records include Lieutenant Reuben Y. Ausbon of the 9th Alabama, who commanded the train guard on the railroad from Chattanooga to Wartrace. During the journey, he allegedly "hugged, kissed and otherwise fondled, a harlot." In spite of these inflammatory charges, evidence was slim and he was acquitted.[54]

Three more Confederate records relate to Tennessee. Private P. J. Sparks, Company G, 1st Arkansas Riflemen, "kept company with whores" on the march from Loudon, Tennessee to Barboursville, Kentucky. Sparks had his head shaved, forfeited all his pay, and received a dishonorable discharge.[55]

Long after the war, a clergyman recalled his service with the 13th Arkansas [CSA] at Fort Pillow. A wicked old man, "bent and decrepit," used to bring his daughter to camp. The future parson, "innocent and modest as a girl," failed at the time to comprehend the nature of these visits.[56]

Another innocent man of the cloth, the Reverend Brother Mac, was traveling with the 6th South Carolina, near Lenoir Station. A scout came riding back to the regiment, shouting that "Some—[dashes in original] were at the next town." The term he used, "an obscenity totally unfamiliar to the ecclesiastic mind," kept Brother Mac unaware of the den of harlots just ahead.[57]

Lieutenant Peter Gepner of the 10th Ohio faced several charges for his activities near Chattanooga, including the shooting of a soldier. The trial centered on the nature of his visits to a "house on the hill near the camp of the Tenth Ohio, near where General Wood's headquarters used to be." The occupants were a Mrs. Richardson and her unmarried sister, Delilah Shadrick. One soldier testified, "One hundred men at camp say it is a whorehouse," and another recalled, "I knocked on the door, but she said she was full." The most unusual contribution was that of Private John Rape, Company G, 10th Ohio: "I went there to see women of doubtful reputation . . . I had reason to suppose that Mrs. Richardson had a private disease . . . I gave her medicine at her solicitation." The Court asked, "How do you know that Mrs. Richardson is not a virtuous woman?" The answer: "Because I have screwed her, that is how I know." Lieutenant Gepner was found innocent of murder and of visiting prostitutes, but was convicted of an earlier and different offense at Nashville, and was fined two months pay.[58]

Near Cheatham's Mills in Robertson County, in August 1864, Private Commodore Workman of the 8th Tennessee Cavalry was at a "house of ill fame kept by one Mary Williams," when he shot and killed Private Joshua Wilson of the same regiment. Workman was convicted of manslaughter and given three years at hard labor.[59]

Abram McCurdy may have been the worst cavalry officer in the Civil War. He was the major of the 10th Ohio Cavalry and witnesses said, "It was impossible to proceed on a secret expedition with him along," due to his loud, drunken singing and tendency to fall off his horse. He called the colonel a "God damned son of a bitch" and incited his men to plunder, while encamped near "the Widow Morgan's in east Tennessee on the Little Tennessee River." McCurdy, Lieutenant Elias Gregg and another officer, with a "Negro guide," proceeded to a nearby house. When asked by the Court why the witness thought it was a house of ill repute, he said, "If a couple of strangers would go in a house and kiss the women and feel their breasts, I should think it was a house of that kind!" The group visited three houses of ill repute that evening, including one run by Sally Jenkins, a white woman. McCurdy asked the witness, "Did you see me take improper liberties with the women that night?" Answer: "Nothing more than kissing them and feeling their breasts." Then another question: "Do you know if any of the houses that we visited were houses of ill fame?" Answer: "One of the houses I am positive was. The woman said that if I had greenbacks [Union currency], I could stay with her." McCurdy was not only cashiered, but was to have his crime published in his hometown newspaper.[60]

Private William Ingram of the 28th Illinois was absent without leave at "the Widow Brooks' place near Colliersville." It is highly likely that his hostess accepted money for the visit. Ingram was fined a month's pay.[61] On the Fourth of July 1865, at Cowan, a government employee asked two "bad women" to go for a walk with him to "the spring." Civilian Reuben Short knifed the man and was sent to prison for three years.[62]

Sergeant Samuel White of the 9th Kentucky, in July 1863, went absent without leave one night to visit a house of ill fame "on the road from McMinnville to Woodbury." When arrested by the patrol, he said he had to urinate and then escaped into the woods. When caught, he was reduced to private and docked two months pay.[63]

Highway robbery earned Thomas Sheppard nine years in prison. This soldier of the 3rd Ohio Cavalry was drinking at "Miss Elizabeth Pinion's house" in Columbia, when he saw a man with money. Moments later, he had the victim out in the back alley where he beat him and robbed him of $175.[64]

William H. Boone, a Second Lieutenant with the 33rd Indiana, was stationed at Christiana. In January 1864, he went twelve miles out of camp to a "house of disreputable women," and engaged in a brawl in which one man was killed and two were wounded. A soldier witness asserted, "I saw no disreputable women," but a neighbor of the women took quite the opposite view. For being AWOL and for having lost several weapons, Boone was dismissed from the service, but reinstated by order of General George Thomas.[65]

On September 4, 1865, President Andrew Johnson wrote to Major General G. H. Thomas, complaining of the misbehavior of colored troops in Greenville. "The Negro soldiery take possession of and occupy property in the town at discretion and have even gone so far as to have taken my own house and inverted it into a rendezvous for male and female Negroes, who have been congregated there, in fact, making it a common Negro brothel. It was bad enough to be taken by traitors and converted into a Rebel hospital, but a Negro whorehouse is infinitely worse."[66]

War in Tennessee, as it has done in all places and at all times, had torn the fabric of society and loosened the moral restraints of more peaceful and settled eras.

Chapter 7

PROSTITUTION IN MISSOURI

Civil War Missouri was, in reality, two different cultures. One was St. Louis, a cosmopolitan metropolis, with centuries-old roots planted by early Spanish and French entrepreneurs. The other ninety-five percent of the state was largely rural, and deeply troubled by bushwhackers, bandits, and violent counter-insurgency efforts.

St. Louis generated thirteen prostitution-related courts-martial and a cluster of records related to control of the trade. In the trial of Private John Morris of the 10th Kansas (in June 1864 he left his guard post to visit a whorehouse), we learn that "being in a house of ill fame was a violation of the post headquarters order." While the actual order has not been located, it seems clear that in St. Louis, the army discouraged visits to such establishments.[1]

On Christmas morning, 1863, James Andrews went out the back door of a saloon and into the attached whorehouse, violating the above-mentioned order. This corporal of the 11th Missouri Cavalry angrily resisted arrest, saying, "I'll jerk piss out of you!" The guard insisted on taking Andrews out through the alley; Andrews insisted: "I came in through the saloon and I'll go out the same way!" He was reduced to the ranks and fined $13.[2]

In March 1865, Private John M. Lamper of the 41st Missouri, left his guard post, stole ten pairs of boots from a shop on Market Street, and then went to Rose's house of ill fame on Sixth Street, where he spent the night. His sentence of a dishonorable discharge and five years of hard labor was later remitted, following a letter written on his behalf by Ulysses S. Grant.[3]

New recruit Elijah Van Auken of the 2nd Illinois Cavalry made a poor beginning to his military career. At Seventh and Morgan Street, there was a combination beer saloon and house of prostitution. A witness informed the Court, "They is all connected. There is a door from the saloon into the house where the girls stay, and through which they come into the saloon." In the saloon, Van Auken beat up a sergeant and was shot while trying to escape. He was sentenced to a month in prison.[4]

Private Henry B. Jones of the 10th Minnesota was on guard duty in March 1864. And where did his commanding officer find him? In bed with a prostitute at the Missouri Hotel, corner of Main and Morgan Streets. Jones' excuse: "It's not my fault. She followed me to the hotel room." He was fined $25.[5]

Two more men of the 10th Minnesota were found in St. Louis whorehouses, "in violation of existing orders from Post Headquarters." M. Dixon and James Riley. Their April 1864 guilty pleas precluded testimony, thus we have no details. Dixon spent ten days at hard labor with a ball and chain, while Riley got a week in solitary.[6]

William Conine, a private in the 155th Company, First Battalion, IC, was assigned to escort a squad of recruits from Benton Barracks into St. Louis. Instead, Conine and his buddy Elza Wolferton of the same unit, went first to Madame Cooper's house of ill fame, and then to a similar establishment, the Lindell Gardens. At both places, they created quite a fuss, and both men got a month at hard labor.[7]

Federal Detective T.C. Tomlinson was assigned to escort a prisoner (Edward W. Wilson, alias Colonel Edwards) to jail in St. Louis, one evening in June 1864. Instead of proceeding as directed, he and his prisoner drank their way through several saloons and then stopped at Madame Henry's house of prostitution, where he and Colonel Edwards drank wine with the Cyprians. They ended the evening at the residence of a Dr. Steiger, where Tomlinson's prisoner escaped. The detective was sent to be a prisoner himself at the Myrtle Street military prison, for a month, and lost his job.[8]

Being found in a whorehouse affected three more men. Private William Bergoon of the 10th Kansas, left his guard post in June 1864 and went to a house of ill fame, where he was arrested. Edward B. Levison, an unassigned recruit, left Benton Barracks in February 1865, and was missing for a week. He was found in a house of ill fame on Poplar Street and received three years at hard labor and a dishonorable discharge. Sergeant W.C. Watkins of the 12th Missouri Cavalry, said he was just looking for a missing corporal when he was found sitting on a lounge at a whorehouse. His 40-minute absence earned him a $5 fine (ten days pay in the 1860's) and a reprimand.[9]

Lieutenant John Miller, Company D, 14th Illinois Cavalry, seemed to neglect his military duties. On the last day of February 1863, he left his camp at Peoria and traveled to St. Louis where, a month later, he was found ". . . selling liquors and keeping and attending bar in a house of prostitution and ill-fame; and this in the uniform, and while wearing the emblems of his rank and position as an officer of the volunteer services of the United States." The witnesses were clear in their testimony. "The house of ill fame [232 Second Street] is a very low, contemptible place, probably the most miserable in St. Louis . . . [Miller] had been acting as a pimp for the house." The court asked, "How could you tell he was serving liquor?" The detective replied, "When I see a man serving liquor, that's proof enough for me." Miller was not only dismissed, but had his crimes published in the St. Louis and Peoria newspapers.[10]

Buried in the millions of cubic feet of paper at the National Archives is a handwritten "list of houses of ill repute closed," in the first two months of 1863. All these houses were in St. Louis. The scribe those many years ago wrote the following, "January 27, Sixth Street between Franklin Avenue and Washington Street. Reopened January 28th; January 27, Madame Cooper, 89.91 Morgan Street, reopened January 30; January 30, house between Eighth and Ninth Street; January 30, Jenny Scott's Bower of Beauty, No. 193, between Carr and Biddle Streets; January 31, No. 101 North Fifth Street; February 12, Mrs. Baldwin, on the levee, between Greene and Morgan Streets, reopened; February 13, Madame Frost, Sixth Street, second door from Cam [bridge?] Street; and February 18, two houses, No. 44 Cam [?] Street, one on first and one on second floor."[11]

The 10th Kansas spent most of their three-year enlistment chasing bushwhackers, but, shortly before they were mustered out, several companies did provost duty, as reported by the St. Louis *Democrat* on August 18, 1864. The previous week, they had been sent to evict several floors full of prostitutes from a five-story building on Fifth Street, between Pine and Chestnut, on Harrolson Alley. The eviction was based on "Nuisances Committed," not just prostitution itself.

Just six years after the Civil War, the St. Louis city fathers passed the Social Evil Registration Law, legalizing prostitution, with a program of examinations and treatment similar to the army's wartime program in Nashville. The St. Louis program was funded by fees collected from the women themselves. The following year, the Missouri General Assembly put an end to this brief social experiment.[12]

Rolla

Rolla, the home today of the University of Missouri-Rolla, was the end of the railroad line during the Civil War, and therefore busy with military commerce, which attracted the usual number of camp followers.

John Sears of the 13th Missouri Cavalry was on patrol guard in May 1865, when he was found in a house of ill fame, "in the lower end of town." Sears claimed that it was not a whorehouse, but a prosecution witness thought otherwise. "I have heard these women using language that no decent woman would use, obscene, vulgar and profane language, and I've found soldiers in bed with them." The defense retorted, "How did you know but what these women might be the wives of the soldiers you found them with?" The answer: "Because women don't generally have more than one husband. I arrested six different men in bed with one of them, during one night, three of them she claimed as husbands and the others she said were cousins." Sears lost his case and two month's pay, as well as spending thirty days at hard labor.[13]

Lieutenant Alfred H. Blake of the 20th Wisconsin, provost marshal at Rolla, was accused of demanding sex in return for political favors. Jane McMannus testified that Blake came to her home and said that if she "went to bed" with him, her husband, Robert McMannus, would be released from jail. When Jane refused to go to bed with him, Blake asked if he could have Jane's hired girl instead. The widow Pauline Dietz claimed that Blake asked her to go to bed with him and "do it," otherwise he would revoke her liquor license. Many witnesses said that the two women were whores and not to be believed. After 95 pages of testimony, Blake was acquitted.[14]

An unnamed officer in Wood's Battalion of Missouri Cavalry, recruited at Rolla, was released from arrest in 1862, but was warned, "Do not again outrage the whole camp and insult decent women by bringing hoors into camp."[15]

In June, 1864, a corporal and three guards, all of the 9th Missouri State Militia Cavalry, were ordered to take charge of prostitutes Sarah Tweety, Sarah Price, Elizabeth Lee, Nellie Dixon and Catherine Yokum, and "proceed with them to St. Louis and turn them over to police at the Seventh Street Depot."[16]

On August 25, 1862, Privates Timothy Hickey and Henry Millman of the 37th Illinois were convicted of having sexual intercourse with "a woman of the town in the presence of a large number of witnesses." The two men's sentence was to walk in front of the guardhouse for thirty days with placards reading "Blackguard" in large letters, then to be drummed out of camp. The reviewing officer described the men as too "brutalized" and "degraded" to associate with other soldiers.[17]

It was common for prostitutes looking for customers to enter army camps, claiming to be looking for lost brothers or cousins. Mary Ann Day had been in Rolla for ten days, when she was arrested on May 2, 1863. She claimed to be a "good Union girl," looking for her brother, who she said was in the 1st Iowa Cavalry. The judge advocate ruled that she was a "notorious prostitute," and she was confined at Rolla's Fort Wyman until placed on the train to St. Louis.[18]

The 49th Wisconsin had two surgeons with the same last name: O.W. Blanchard and P.W. Blanchard. One of them, with several other officers, was arrested in a house of ill repute at Rolla, in March 1865. Apparently they were not prosecuted, as there is no court-martial record.[19]

Springfield

Rural Missouri in the 1860's was not a locus of actuarial sophistication. Private Rufus Merricle of the 23rd Missouri, told his court-martial that he was unsure of his age, but thought he might be 16 or maybe 17. (He also signed his statement with an "X.") He enlisted at Stockton and was marched to Springfield. "I was taken prisoner eight miles from Springfield at a house of ill fame, together with 25 more men." His captors were part of Coffee's band of Confederate guerilas. Merricle was convicted of later serving in two Confederate units:

Blanton's Arkansas Infantry and Perkin's Guerillas, recruited at Rolla. His comrade, Private William Capps, was captured in the same whorehouse raid and convicted of the same charges. Both got ten years in prison.[20]

In May 1865, at Springfield, a Mrs. Whitstine and a Mrs. Rogers were declared to be "public nuisances" who "seriously interfered with military service and impaired its efficiency." They were both ordered out of the district. Two weeks later, a similar case was reported. A Mr. J. H. Balyou swore an affidavit that four women, camped in a cave two and a half miles north of Springfield, were frequently drunk and by their conduct attracted soldiers, who also became drunk and disorderly, firing their rifles at passers-by. General John Sanborn ordered the women transported "at least 40 miles from Springfield."[21]

At Jefferson City, in February 1865, Corporal James D. Whaley of the 4th Missouri Militia Cavalry was guarding supplies. He was convicted of leaving his post and going to a house of ill fame. His written defense told a different story. "I started to get my supper and as I went along up the railroad, I was passing this house of ill fame and there was some soldiers in there fussing and quarreling and I stopped to put down the fuss as I thought it my duty for it was in hearing of my post and I had orders to put down all fussing." The court had a different view of things. Whaley lost his corporal's stripes and spent four months at hard labor.[22]

Private Columbus Brittian of Whaley's regiment made threats of murder "at a house of ill fame out west of Jefferson City," and spent fifteen days in the guardhouse, with a ball and chain, for his July 1864 intemperance.[23]

Few things are lower than shooting a pet dog. But Remus McBain was indeed the bane of a peaceful June night in 1864, at Versailles, Missouri. This private, in the 9th Missouri Cavalry, was supposed to be wide-awake on night guard duty. He was not. After an abrupt whisky-fueled nap, he awoke, left his post and went to "a low part of town," where four drunken whores joined him in a rampage of broken windows. Remus shot the dog that was defending the female owner of the vandalized house. For this, he spent eight months at hard labor, padlocked to a ball and chain and receiving no pay.[24]

At 9:00 p.m., a good soldier was supposed to be in bed—his own bed. Private Charles D. Wright, also of the 9th Missouri Militia Cavalry, spent several nights cruising the town of Macon, visiting the Whaley Hotel, the Concordia Grocery [in 1864, a "grocery" was a liquor store], and the Eagle Bar Room, as well as various houses of ill fame. For his nocturnal rambling, he received thirty days at hard labor with a ten-pound iron ball chained to his ankle.[25]

A. C. Smith liked literary clarity. This private in the 9th Missouri Militia Cavalry freely admitted to being drunk and absent without leave in Versailles on a May 1864, night. He admitted, too, that he had climbed through a citizen's window, but he balked at the charge of "insulting ladies." He wrote in his defense, "The accused declares the name 'ladies' a misnomer. The word 'fancy' should have been prefixed to the word 'ladies' and the proper idea would have been conveyed." In brief, his insulting words had been addressed to prostitutes, not decent ladies. This somewhat rarified defense may account for his light sentence: a fine of $10 a month for two months.[26]

Captain James R. Van Zant said that he had fought in the Mexican War and later had turned down a Confederate commission, in order to fight for the Union. Judging by his performance at Iron Mountain with the 24th Missouri, he had done the Union no favor. In addition to numerous problems with missing oxen and mules, Van Zant came late into camp one afternoon, bringing with him several women of doubtful reputation. He had been drinking. Like many drunks, Van Zant liked his companions to be equally drunk, and so succeeded. In an hour of pressing whisky upon his enlisted men, he soon succeeded in having the camp in a quarrelsome uproar, further confused by Van Zant firing his pistol into the air—while still in his tent. But, returning to our theme, Sergeant Jerome Smart told the Court, "There was with him in his tent two women that I know to be notorious characters, following the army around and letting any soldier associate with them." Although Van Zant made a show of sending the women away at dark, as soon as the men went to bed, he gave a whistle, and a witness recalled, "I heard someone coming into his tent, talking . . . I judged that there was two or three and that they were women." Another witness said that they were "common strumpets." The court-martial decided that Van Zant's services were no longer required by the Union.[27]

William Clarke Quantrill was a feared man in the states of Missouri, Kansas, and Arkansas and in Indian Territory. His war on Unionists, both military and civilian, has spawned dozens of books, many of them wildly sensational, some of them purely products of the writer's imagination, and a few reliable histories, the best of those being the biographies by Connelley and by Castel.

Quantrill had a mistress, Kate King, who is said to have taken his middle name out of her love for him. Others say that he kidnapped her in 1863 and forced her into being his mistress and that later on she formed an affection for him. Quantrill was mortally wounded in late May 1865. Prior to his death, he gave a Catholic priest $800, half to be used for a gravestone and the rest to be sent to Kate. Connelley says that the total sum was $2,000, not $800. According to Castel, "Kate used her share to establish a famous St. Louis brothel." In 1879, Charles F. "Fletch" Taylor, a retired bushwhacker, wrote that "she keeps a fancy house in St. Louis now." A search through St. Louis' City Directories turned up only one possible reference, that in 1872: "Clarke, Kate, boarding, 112 South Sixth." The houses of prostitution were often listed as "boarding houses" in the 1800's. Castel tells us, "Quantrill never told the truth about his life," so finding the true Quantrill story may be an exercise in futility. Whether his mistress really received a large sum of money, and whether she really opened a bagnio with it, remains to be discovered by some other and more persistent researcher.[29]

Chapter 8

PROSTITUTION IN THE HEARTLAND

At Indianapolis, Indiana, a Second Lieutenant of the 153rd Indiana was celebrating the capture of Charleston, South Carolina. While this was a major Union victory, the army objected to his way of honoring the occasion. Lorenzo McAllister became drunk and was arrested in a whorehouse. The actual testimony paints a more complex picture. Corporal W. H. Shirley, 17th VRC, a member of the provost guard, said that Lorenzo was found ". . . at the house of ill fame kept by a woman they call Molly Green at the east end of the city, on the north side of E. Washington St. There were four women there, perhaps more. We had orders to take all soldiers out of such houses when we went there. [McAllister] told me he had gone to the house of ill fame to get his pocketbook. He was in a bedroom. . . . with a girl . . . she had on a regular day dress . . . he was in his uniform. I don't know if he was drunk. He seemed to walk straight."

Captain Hugh Middleton, 17th VRC and provost marshal of Indianapolis, told the court, "When officers are taken in houses of ill fame in the city their names are taken and they are ordered to report to me the next morning." Witnesses for the defense stated that McAllister had been of good character since at least age ten, that he had served honorably for three years with the 8th Indiana, had risen to the rank of captain, and had been in charge of Union entrenchments during the siege of Vicksburg. He was newly appointed as recruiting officer for the 153rd Indiana. In spite of his excellent record and the seemingly minor infraction, on February 21, 1865, McAllister was dishonorably dismissed, leaving us only with this glimpse into wartime prostitution in the Hoosier State.[1]

Our other six Indiana cases are also from Indianapolis. Private Lewis M. White of the 5th VRC was not a very clever thief. He stole some jewelry from Mrs. Catherine Morris of 331 Blake Street and was later arrested in a whorehouse directly across the street from Mrs. Morris' home! His May 1865 court-martial awarded White a month at hard labor.[2]

Officers are supposed to set a good example for their men. Further, officers do not socialize with enlisted men. First Lieutenant Johnson J. Vaughn, 90th Indiana, violated both those rules. On May 10, 1862, he went to a house of ill fame with "a group of privates." On October 21, 1862, he visited a house of ill fame with Private Samuel A. Simms. Four days later, he asked Sergeant Andrew Neil to accompany him to a house of ill fame. On November 24, 1862, he visited a house of ill fame with Private Charles H. Brown, and made five such visits with Private John Ferguson. The records tell us a bit about these houses: "Molly Green's, on the eastside, is one of the most popular . . . Jenny Davis' is on the southeast side . . . Sue Williams is on the northeast." A fourth house, the Red Gate, was favored by Lieutenant Vaughn who was quoted as saying, "I'm going to the Red Gate to get a fuck." Colonel Henry Carrington had ordered that any officer found in a house of ill fame would be dismissed. Vaughn was, indeed, dismissed.[3]

In December 1864, Private Franklin Spurgeon of Company A, 5th VRC, was convicted of stealing $365 and was sentenced to three years at hard labor and a dishonorable discharge. But there was more to the story. On January 30, 1865, fifteen members of Spurgeon's company signed a petition to Abraham Lincoln, shining more light on the crime. On the night of October 13, 1864, Sturgeon and four others decided to "raid" the whorehouse kept by Milton W. Perdue. There, they found several men in bed with women. They hauled the men out of bed, making a nuisance of themselves, but causing no injury. One victim, Private William Adams, "of some Indiana regiment," was in bed with Elizabeth Ann Perdue, a daughter of the proprietor. She testified that some man other than Spurgeon had taken Adams' money. In view of Spurgeon's loyal service since age sixteen, the petitioners, who signed themselves "the broken relics of many a battle fought in defense of our national unity," urged mercy. The reply, dated May 4, 1865, which recommended remittance of the remaining prison time, was signed by Major A. A. Hosmer, Judge Advocate, "in the absence of Judge Advocate General Holt." Lincoln was dead and Holt was pursuing the conspirators.[4]

William E. Scott, blacksmith of the 13th Indiana Cavalry, was convicted of "conduct prejudicial" in April 1864. He had arranged the enlistment of his female lover. She was "determined" to be with Scott and had been enlisted, mustered, and issued a uniform. Some described her as his loyal and loving lady friend, while others said she was a prostitute. Sadly, for students of women's history, her name is not in the record. Scott was reprimanded.[5]

The rank of sergeant major is an extremely responsible one among the enlisted ranks. Sergeant Major J. A. Ross, 19th US Infantry, had much to lose when the urge of Eros caused him to go AWOL, enter the bordello of James

Smith on Liberty Street, and climb naked into the bed of one of Smith's girls. Captain T. A. Newman, 11th US Infantry, had gone to Smith's one night to arrest soldiers. There, he found Ross, whose clothes were under the bed. Ross claimed that Newman asked the prostitute, "Has he had all he wants; has he stayed long enough?" While Newman waited downstairs for Ross to dress and join him, Ross did dress, but went out the back of the house and hid in the cellar. Ross lost not only his exalted rank, but was branded with a hot iron with the letter "D", and after four months of hard labor had his head shaved and was dishonorably discharged.[6]

At Indianapolis' Burnside Barracks, John Raper of the 71st Indiana was a very demoralizing force. He was a habitual drunk. He had "a loathsome disease, to wit, the pock," and he brought a "woman of lewd habits" into camp. Raper induced another soldier to have intercourse with her, which gave him six weeks of debilitating syphilis. The June 1863 court-martial had Raper drummed out with a dishonorable discharge.[7]

Illinois

Illinois contributed two Navy trials to this study. Cairo, at the confluence of the Ohio and Mississippi Rivers, was a major port for the US Navy's "brown water" sailors and Marines. In December 1864, John H. Jones, a seaman on the USS *Great Western* was tried for desertion. "I wasn't deserting . . . I was just trying to get to a house of ill fame for a little sport with some women." This defense did not save him from five years at hard labor. Patrick Baker, a private in the US Marine Corps, was convicted of "highway robbery" at Cairo. He had stolen "a purse and other articles" from Captain T. J. Lambert of the 68th Ohio. During his day of crime, Baker stayed two hours at "an old lady's house near the International Hotel." The term "old lady" often referred to the madam of a house of prostitution. In May 1864, Baker was sentenced to hard labor for the rest of his enlistment, wearing a ball and chain for the first six months. This was followed with a dishonorable discharge.[8]

The steamer *Olive Branch*, carrying a load of recruits south to Port Hudson, Louisiana, stopped at Cairo. Captain Henry Snow of the 28th USCT collected $72 from the recruits, allowed them to buy him a hat, and then looked the other way as the men visited a house of ill fame. The end result of Snow's neglect was the escape of fifteen recruits. He was dismissed in disgrace.[9]

Camp Butler, six miles east of Springfield, Illinois, was the scene of an indiscretion by Second Lieutenant George R. Stoddard, 146th Illinois. When a serious fire broke out, Stoddard, who was serving as officer of the guard, could not be found. A search discovered him at "a house" near the camp, dancing "with women." He was fortunate to escape with only a reprimand and loss of a month's pay.[10]

Corporal Edwin Milgate, 146th Illinois, was corporal of the guard at Peoria in February 1865. His chief duty was to confine new recruits to their barracks. The army's worst fears were confirmed when Milgate "did permit recruits under his charge . . . to go to grog shops and a house of prostitution." Six of these men never returned. Milgate's witnesses showed it was the malfeasance of the recruits, not Milgate's neglect that caused the escape. He was acquitted.[11]

Camp Douglas was close to Chicago, close enough so that Private James M. Cooney, 15th VRC, who was on picket duty in February 1865, went there. A cold wind often blows off Lake Michigan in winter. Perhaps it was fear of frostbite that caused him to leave his chilly post and seek the all-night warmth of a woman at a Chicago "house of ill fame." Cooney was sentenced to be shot by a firing squad, a high price for an evening with a lady in the leisure profession. His sentence of death was remitted by General Joseph Hooker.[12]

A letter by Corporal Franklin Carpenter, Company K, 3rd Vermont, written at Freeport, Illinois, on March 27, 1864, to "Friend Fred" in Brattleboro, indicated an interest in running his own whorehouse, earning money instead of spending it. Both he and Fred sound like scoundrels. "How did you get out of that scrape you was in when I was there? I have had a good time since I got away and have jumped two bounties and when that plays out I'm going to keeping whorehouse. I wish you was here. We have some gay times you can bet your life on it. Captain Dunashee [spelling?] came to Chicago after me . . . but when he got there I was somewhere else. They can kiss my ass. I am now traveling with Brock's Minstrels." Carpenter was not as clever as he thought. He was captured, convicted, and sentenced to be shot on February 10, 1865. In a perhaps misguided moment of compassion, Lincoln spared Carpenter's life.[13]

At Detroit, Michigan, William Nesbitt of the 5th Michigan, whose prior three years of service had been spotless, came to grief. He was escorting new recruits to Washington, DC in July 1864. When the steamer *City of Cleveland* stopped at Detroit, Nesbitt was ordered to take two substitutes, the brothers Davis, to the Cass Hotel, feed them supper and then hurry back to the steamer for an early departure. Where this simple plan went wrong was described by Private A. F. Day, 4th Michigan. "I know he took two men off the boat and took them to the Cass House for supper . . . from there he went up Jefferson Avenue to the corner of Woodward Avenue and then took a hack to the corner of St. Catherine's and Russell streets. There we went into a house of ill fame. The two men that the accused had in charge went upstairs with women. The accused went up with them. I stayed in the parlor. The accused came down alone. The accused said, 'It was time for them to come down.' But they had gone out the back door and could not be found." Nesbitt got three months at hard labor.[14]

In another Detroit case, James Collins, a Michigan soldier with the provost guard, was a sentry at the recruiting barracks, keeping out undesirable persons. One such person, perhaps more attractive than the rest, approached Collins and soon they were coitally engaged. Collins was not only drunk and distracted from his duties, but made threats of violence to the corporal, to the sergeant and to the captain, all of whom tried to put him under arrest. Collins escaped with a reprimand. William Core, a private with the 2nd Michigan Cavalry, deserted and was found at a house of ill fame in Jackson, Michigan. He was found not guilty.[15]

Ohio

In 1860, Ohio seemed off to an exuberant start, based on the census records from Darke County, Greenville Township. In addition to the tireless fifty-six-year-old Sarah James and forty-three-year-old Ellen Bishop, both of whose occupation was "Prostitution," there was William McCormic, "Drinking Whisky," William Michael, "Hoaring and Drinking Whisky," Samuel Woods, "Screwing in [the] Woods," and Elizabeth Henning, whose occupation was the same as Samuel. This colorful record was called into question, when a little research showed that all the respondents were inmates of a mental hospital.

Otherwise, Ohio produced a relative paucity of cases. A board of examination, convened November 7, 1861, considered the case of Captain Joseph C. Grannan of the 4th Battalion, Ohio Cavalry. (He may have also served in other regiments.) He had been charged with being too familiar with the enlisted men, having gone with some of them to a house of ill repute in Cincinnati. Grannan acknowledged the visit but said it was before he had received his commission. The board recommended that he be discharged.[16]

Private David C. Gates of Company G, 1st Ohio, lost his right arm in an 1861 skirmish at Vienna, Virginia. In September 1879, he married Martha Mear at Covington, Kentucky. He died two years later at Portsmouth, Ohio, of heart disease. Three years after his death, she opened a house of prostitution at 17 W. 5th Street in Portsmouth. Years later, this became an issue in her widow's pension. In 1894, the mayor and chief of police of Portsmouth deposed that she had kept a "notorious house of prostitution" for the past thirteen years. Town Marshal Frederick Schmidt stated, "I have visited this house at various times—in my official capacity." Other witnesses said she was living in sin with one Herbert Vail, "of no occupation." The widow Gates lost her pension because of "open and notorious adulterous cohabitation since the death of the soldier."[17]

Minnesota troops fought in two wars: the Civil War down south and the conflicts with Indians in Minnesota. Fort Snelling is now in the suburbs of Minneapolis and was also the location of the "Reserve House" saloon. There, in March 1865, Captain Peter B. Davy, 2nd Minnesota Cavalry, was with a prostitute, drunk. He also had bad words for his major, his colonel, and his commanding general, Henry Hastings Sibley, about whom he remarked, "God damn him, he may kiss my arse." Davy was also drunk with enlisted men and defrauded the government with his purchases of hay and horses. The court ordered him dismissed.[18]

Wildly conflicting testimony involving a priest, a pimp, a whore, and an officer marked a trial at Fort Ridgely, near New Ulm, Minnesota, in April 1864. Captain Rudolph Schoenemann of the 6th Minnesota was accused of entering the bedroom of Corporal and Mrs. Smith at 1:00 in the morning. The captain was wearing only a shirt and drawers and was bent on rape. One witness said Mrs. Smith was a whore who prostituted at "The Cave," while a Catholic priest told the court that she was "a good woman." Corporal Smith said that he used to buy whiskey for Schoenemann, when the 6th Minnesota was campaigning against the Indians. Witness Alexander Sipes, of "no occupation," testified for the prosecution; he, in turn, was denounced as a "whorehouse pimp," by Captain Harry J. Gillham. The court asked Gillham how he knew that Sipes was associated with a whorehouse. "Because I have visited there." The court acquitted Schoenemann, a decision approved by General John Pope.[19]

St. Paul, one of Minnesota's twin cities, contributed its share to the history of fornication. The St. Paul *Pioneer*, March 9, 1865, told its readers: "A Fancy Row—Lottie Lyons, Fanny Maxwell, Lizzie Mason, and Belle Moore, four fast young women from one of the houses of ill fame in the city, indulged in a field fight on Tuesday evening on Wabashaw Street near the Market House." They all worked at Madame Robinson's house, had a quarrel with a girl who had left the establishment, and pursued her with bludgeons, while uttering "a hot fire of not very choice words." The police intervened and the four lovelies were locked up for a few hours. At court, Fanny was fined $5, Lizzie $10, and the other two girls each $15.

The same newspaper, on July 12, 1865, published a rather facetious essay on the newly-enacted ordinance Number Ten. After expanding upon the hopelessness of eliminating vice—because where there is "demand" there will always be "supply"—the author described the "use tax" levied by the city council upon each and every instance of commercial carnal connection. The town fathers published a tariff of rates, based upon the economic principle of "the consumer pays the duty." Since the tax fell upon the customers, not the whores, it was a tax upon men, and thus commendably self-sacrificing, since the city council was all male. In its first year, the tax brought in $4000.[20]

Passed out drunk in a St. Paul whorehouse! That was Private Samuel Quinn of the 23rd VRC. On January 23, 1865, he was given a gun in order to escort prisoner Jackson Moore to the office of the provost marshal. He never got there. Two men were sent to find Quinn and located him unconscious in the foyer of Mrs. Turner's house of prostitution. Prisoner Moore was long gone. It took Quinn 48 hours to become sober enough to converse. His defense had two parts: first,

"I remember nothing," and secondly "I support my aged mother." He was fined two months pay and put to hard labor for the same length of time.[21]

Arkansas is at the border of the heartland and the mid-south, and will be examined with the former region. At Little Rock, Sergeant Henry Schroeder of the 43rd Illinois was sergeant of the patrol guard on the night of November 2, 1864. He got drunk, and "did forcibly break open the door of a house of ill fame and otherwise behave in a disgraceful manner." Since he pleaded guilty, there was no testimony and thus no details. Schroeder was sentenced to have his chevrons cut off at dress parade and to lose three months pay.[22]

Even worse behaved was Second Lieutenant William Bradford of the 1st Missouri Cavalry. At Little Rock, in July 1865, while provost marshal, he embezzled $2425 and was grossly drunk at several houses of prostitution, including one run by Mrs. Boyd. He was cashiered and ordered to refund the stolen money.[23]

At Washington, Arkansas, Private Doras Lewis of the 12th Michigan Veteran Volunteers, a 20-year old former farmer who had received a $300 enlistment bounty six months earlier, stabbed a sergeant while both were at a "colored house of ill fame." Army records tell us that Lewis was 5'6" tall with blue eyes and dark hair. He was sentenced to five years of hard labor, but after only three months he died of typhoid fever.[24]

Private N. Shoe was another guard who was overkindly to a prisoner. Shoe was a soldier with the 12th Michigan, stationed at Devall's Bluff, in June 1865. He was ordered to convey a prisoner from the guardhouse to a barbershop and then return him. However, after the haircut, Shoe took the prisoner to Mr. Whitty's saloon and then to a house of ill fame "in the rear of Ball Alley." Of course, the prisoner escaped. Shoe himself became a prisoner for a month.[25]

Even though Isaac Clickner of the 3rd Missouri Cavalry was illiterate, he should have known better than to give his horse to two "women of bad character." This ill—advised equestrian romp, in March 1864, at Searcey, Arkansas, earned Clickner four months at hard labor.[26]

Throughout Mid-America, Venus was willing to accommodate Mars—for a price.

Chapter 9

PROSTITUTION WAY OUT WEST

Today, the Civil War seems to be a Virginia affair, with brief excursions to Antietam and Gettysburg, but there was indeed Union and Confederate activity out West. Not the Mississippi West, but way out West. California provided 15,725 men in blue, with about a thousand each from Oregon, Washington, and Nevada. Their major duty was to replace the regular army units that had been fighting Indians in the 1850s. The discoveries of gold and silver insured a rowdy and unsettled society in the far west and attracted, even in those sparsely populated states, a predictable bevy of ladies for hire. Texas, which is neither Deep South nor Heartland, had been an independent republic and, in the 1860s, as it is today, was a world unto itself. For our purposes, it will be included in the Far West.

In 1861, the entire population of Sacramento, the capital of California, was 15,000. Imagine the impact of the 5000 men who trained at Camp Union. This vast depot occupied the land now known as William Land Park. Was the capital of the Golden State ready to receive 5000 virile young men? A study of Sacramento prostitution in 1860 says "yes."[1]

Sacramento was a river town, and like its sister cities on the Mississippi River, prostitution thrived along the levee where the steamboats tied up. The ancient trade in Sacramento was partly segregated by ethnic origin, within an area bounded on the west and east by Front and Sixth Streets and on the north and south by H and L Streets. The Chinese lived along I street, the French congregated along 2nd Street between L and K Streets. Anglo, African-American, and Mexican prostitutes mingled throughout the riverfront neighborhood.

E. Clampus Vitus is an unusual historical society, which places bronze markers throughout the West, especially at sites of less than glorious activities: murder, prostitution, and heavy drinking. Their plaque on the Lady Adams

Building in Old Sacramento notes that it was once used as a "rooming house," a common euphemism for bordello.

In San Francisco, the regular army artillery units stood ready to repeal a Confederate Navy that never arrived. Years of boredom can lead to many problems. Chinatown had whole blocks devoted to prostitution. Chinese men were arriving to work on the newly authorized transcontinental railroad. They could not bring their wives with them, but San Francisco entrepreneurs filled the need by importing enslaved Chinese girls. They didn't last long; most of them died within five years of arriving in California. If the Union soldiers visited these sad Asian beauties, the encounters did not generate courts-martial. (It was not until 1895 that crusader Donaldina Cameron began rescuing these sex slaves. History repeats itself: California police recently freed dozens of South Korean women, smuggled in to work in massage parlors.)[2]

Camp Floyd, in Utah territory, was in Cedar Valley, west of Utah Lake. There, Lieutenant Colonel Marshall Howe of the 2nd Dragoons was accused of hiring an 83-year old destitute woman as a laundress in order to have access to her 12-year old granddaughter, for purposes of "carnal knowledge." After the initial hearing in this 1860s trial, the case was continued. Howe later served as Colonel of the 3rd US Cavalry and retired in 1866, so it would seem that nothing came of this dramatic charge.[3]

Two men of the 7th Iowa Cavalry found ways to get in trouble at Omaha, Nebraska Territory, in the autumn of 1863. Private George R. Clark was accused of stealing two revolvers and taking them to a "house of ill fame." He was acquitted. Private David Davis had been sent to get some water. Instead, he got drunk and was arrested in a brawl at a whorehouse, which cost him two months of hard labor.[4]

Fort McRae, New Mexico, was on a bluff overlooking today's Elephant Butte Reservoir. There, in December 1863, Private Thomas Johnson of the 1st California was charged with molesting laundress Monica Salazar. His defense: "I played with her in a manner very common, having often done so before. She had been drinking rather freely, and as we were playing, she caught hold of my privates and I pushed her away. In a word, she is a common prostitute." The court saw on the matter differently and gave Johnson three months at hard labor.[5]

Fort Bayard, New Mexico, near today's Silver City, was the site of a post-Civil War offence that suggests that some things never change. Lieutenant John Little of the 15th US Infantry was accused of engaging "in a noisy and disorderly altercation with a woman of lewd character, one Clementina Shearrer, alias Gentle Annie." A month later, Little was drunk at a "low and disreputable dance hall, kept by one William Johnson, in Central City, New Mexico, and frequented by soldiers and notorious Mexican women, and did then and there engage in dancing together with said women and enlisted men." For these and other infractions, Little was dismissed in December 1875.[6]

The story of modern Texas begins with the fight against General Antonio Lopez de Santa Anna. (Essential to the story is the concept of a "yellow girl"—a mulatto.) At the Battle of San Jacinto, the Texans attacked while the general and his men were taking a siesta. Santa Anna was dozing in his silken tent with a mulatto girl—Emily Morgan. Distracted by her lovely presence, Santa Anna was slow to repel the attack and thus lost Texas. Emily is immortalized in the song, "The Yellow Rose of Texas." While many historians doubt the evidence for the story, there seems good reason to believe its essential truth. If indeed true, Texas owes its very existence to the charms of the "yellow girl," Miss Emily Morgan.[7]

A somewhat better documented free spirit was the "Great Western," Sarah Bowman, who during her many years with the army carried a whole series of soldiers' last names. During the Mexican war, she brought coffee and soup during the 160-hour artillery bombardment of Fort Brown, Texas. Standing 6 foot 2 inches tall, with red hair and blue eyes, she was hard to miss. Four decades of army travels took her halfway across the continent. She was buried in Yuma, Arizona in 1866, at the age of 53 and, with the remains of dozens of men in the old post cemetery, was moved to the San Francisco National Cemetery in 1890.[8]

On December 6, 1864, Michael Harslett, recently discharged from Company I, 3rd California Infantry, wrote a letter to Major General Irvin McDowell, then commanding the Department of the Pacific. Harslett described several of his previous officers, in particular Captain Samuel P. Smith, Company K, 2nd California Cavalry, as abusing their position. Smith, and other officers, brought prostitutes with them to Fort Churchill, Nevada, ordered enlisted men to put up and take down the tents for these women, and to pack and transport the baggage of the prostitutes, all in government wagons, with government teams. "If a traveling brothel in this command, coupled with drunkenness [is] recommended by the US military, I know not, but one thing I do know, respected sir, and that is the scenes of riot and drunkenness I have witnessed at Ragtown and other places in Nevada beggar description."[9]

The Union's minimal presence in Texas may account for the paucity of trials. In May 1864 Private George Gaffney of the 20th Wisconsin was tried for being arrested twice while drunk and noisy at a Brownsville bordello. He was sentenced to march in front of his regiment wearing a sign reading "For Having Intercourse with a Lewd Woman." In October 1865, Private William Munro of the 3rd Michigan Cavalry was arrested in a "crib" without a pass. The crib, the sort of little shanty used by the poorest and most desperate prostitutes, was conveniently located just behind the Brownsville jail. Munro was sentenced to four months of hard labor.[10]

Chapter 10

PROSTITUTION IN THE DISTRICT OF COLUMBIA

A few items from the capital's newspapers may foretell what will be found in other records. On October 25, 1863, the Washington *Star* reported a scene in the criminal court of Judge Fisher, "This morning, Anna Maria Branson and Ann Cavano, two well-known characters from 'Fighting Alley,' South Washington, were indicted for grand larceny." They had stolen a coat and a pair of pants from the store of Waldheimer and Grossmayer. While the clerk was reading the indictment, one woman loudly asked the other, "I don't know what the hell he's talking about, do you?" The answer: "No, dammit, no." When asked to plead, Anna responded for both. "I'm guilty and when I get out of this fix I will steal the clothes again and set fire to the store!" The judge questioned the women and learned that Anna, age eighteen, was born in Ireland but had lived in DC since age two, while nineteen-year old Ann was a native of the capital.

Events took a nasty turn when the judge asked what they had been doing for a living, and the reply, boldly, was "We have been***." What the reporter put in asterisks can be easily guessed. The judge ordered them each to serve three years in the Albany County Penitentiary, to which they replied with a "gross exclamation."

The Washington *Daily Constitutional Union* on April 28, 1865, told its readers, "Ann Morris, who keeps a house of bad repute on Water Street, Georgetown, together with four of her 'girls,' have been sent to the workhouse, to afford time for penitence and future correction of morals." Dozens of other reports of Washington, DC wartime prostitution have appeared in print, including the official Federal list of bordellos in the capital.[1]

The careers of two prominent Washington madams can be followed in the annual city directories (forerunners of today's telephone books). Sarah "Sal" Austin was listed as running a "boarding house" at 500 6th St W. in the years 1860-1865. Julia Dean, "widow of William," had her establishment at number 12 Marble Alley (where the National Gallery of Art stands today) over the same span of years. Newspaper reports confirmed not only the nature of their professions but the rivalry between the two women.

The area now called the Federal Triangle was, in 1861-1865, a nest of saloons and houses of prostitution, dubbed by the newspapers, "Hooker's Division." William Holmes, a young private in the 14th New Hampshire, served in the deep South and as a provost guard in DC. He wrote, "I am tired of seeing officers chasing whores . . . sick of officers horing drunk in DC . . . they should be shot . . . they pay six dollars [two weeks pay for a soldier] for a girl."[2]

Even John Wilkes Booth was in on the action. In addition to courting a daughter of New Hampshire Senator John Parker, Booth had a torrid relationship with Ellen "Nellie" Star, an attractive prostitute who turned tricks at 62 Ohio Ave. where her sister was the madam.[3]

In this sordid and lawless society it is not surprising that records show at least 35 Washington, DC prostitution-related court-martials, including some related to remarkable events in hospitals. Private Benjamin Culp of the 11th VRC (and formerly of the 56th Pennsylvania) was in Stanton General Hospital recovering from "intermittent tertian fever," (malaria) in June 1864. Apparently, his strength was returning. When arrested, he was drunk, in bed, smoking a cigar, with two prostitutes, who were also drunk and also smoking cigars. When arrested, the threesome made "gestures prejudicial to good order and military discipline." Culp was fined eight months pay and recovered enough to die in 1899 of "miner's asthma," acquired in the coal mines of his native state.[4]

Another but different threesome involved John W. Brown (4th New York Cavalry) and George G. Cummings (9th New York) who at one in the morning at Lincoln General Hospital were found in bed with a "disreputable woman." Their acquittal was angrily disapproved by General John Martindale, whose West Point years may not have prepared him for such configurations.[5]

The provost marshal in each town was the head of the military police. On July 13, 1864, the office of the assistant provost marshal at Forrest Hall prison forwarded several prisoners, including "Mrs. Eliza Taylor (fourth arrest of late) government clothes taken from her house a short time ago, sells liquor to enlisted men, very disorderly house, very filthy, et cetera." This memo was found in the trial records of James Veitch.[6]

Peter Strauss had been a captain in the 12th New York. He quickly adapted to civilian life, helping soldiers to desert, at Siegel's Restaurant on 7th St. He was caught when a servant girl denounced him after he suggested that he, she, and a prostitute have a three-way sexual encounter.[7]

Frank Willard had his eye on the main chance. His good eye. The other eye, a false one, was his ticket to bounties: he would put the eye in, enlist, collect his money, take the eye out and get a medical discharge. He pressed his luck too far. His "mother" wrote to the colonel of the regiment, claiming that the soldier's father was dying, and begged for a furlough for the soldier. The "mother" turned out to be a prostitute, Fidelia Stearns, Willard's conspirator. The army was not amused. Willard got ten years in prison, more than many murderers.[8]

Two wounded Irishmen still had strength enough for a wild Christmas Eve at a whorehouse on 11th St, between D and E streets. Both were unassigned recruits in the Veterans Reserve Corps. Twenty-five-year old James Hotey arrived at the house with a $350 and had spent $305 ($9,000 in today's money) by the time he was arrested. His friend, Patrick McCarthy, age 21, was wearing only his pants when arrested. He and his woman for the evening "were preparing to go to bed," when the police arrived. Both men were convicted of AWOL and fined $10 a month for four months.[9]

Another man, whose name also suggests a Hibernian heritage, was Captain Patrick O'Murphy of the 115th Pennsylvania. He was found in his full uniform in a house of ill fame on 12th St. His defense? "I was too drunk to know where I was." O'Murphy was "dishonorably dismissed."[10]

Big Annie was a bartender in Philadelphia; her domain was on "Chestnut Street below 4th St." She reappeared as the "wife" of Lieutenant Henry Leo when the 30th Pennsylvania was at Camp Moore in the District of Columbia. Although her behavior was "ladylike," the deception was uncovered; she was sent away and, in February 1862, Leo was dismissed.[11]

Many of the trials named the madams. We encountered Sarah Austin earlier. Private Robert J. Doe of the 5th New Jersey Artillery forged a pass into town and in September 1863 registered at a hotel as "Lt. Perry." From there, he went to Sarah's place, where a detective asked for his papers. Doe told him, "I've come into town to visit houses of prostitution and to play Faro. My parents are rich and I can afford to play. I'll give you this valuable watch if you let me go." We note that the detective did his duty because Doe was convicted and sent to prison for year, with a fine of $10 a month.[12]

Another "name brand" house was Madame Duprey's, which shared Marble Alley with the bagnio of Julia Dean. Two young lieutenants of the 1st Michigan Cavalry, Jabez Daniels and Charles Snyder, left their camp on Capitol Hill and walked west, "to buy some socks." They entered the Duprey establishment, "not knowing what sort of place it was," around midnight and were joined shortly thereafter by Lieutenant William H. Penrose, then officer of the patrol. He asked for passes. Snyder produced an outdated one with a new date scribbled in lead pencil. Daniels claimed to be a Captain Brewer. Penrose arrested twenty-eight mostly drunk privates and the two lieutenants. "The women of the House were in a partial state of nudity, which could leave no doubt in any person's mind of the character of the women and the house." It was February 1862; the war was over for both Daniels and Snyder. Their alibi of buying socks at midnight made little impression on the court; both men were dismissed from the service.[13]

Private George Hemhoffer of the 7th VRC was ordered to take a prisoner to the sinks (toilet facilities). Instead, the two of them went to "Mrs. Buckley's." Hemhoffer was tried in February 1865. The city directory for that year lists, "Mary Buckley, widow, bds, Third West n Virginia Ave." The term "bds" indicates a "boarding house". It is highly likely that the widow's boarders were, like Hemhoffer, also in "a partial state of nudity." Hemhoffer got a month at hard labor.[14]

Another disabled soldier was Lieutenant George W. Arndt, of the 19th VRC. His disability did not preclude his being absent without leave, drunk, disorderly, and in a house of ill fame at "540 Twelfth St., above C Street." The provost marshal's list of bordellos shows Louisa Koerner at that address. Defense witness Lieutenant William Coddington, 6th VRC, was in the house nightly as part of his patrol duties. He told the court, "Lt. Arndt was drunk, but not disorderly. His uniform looked like he had been lying in the mud." Arndt's defense was, "My absence was caused by some old friends I hadn't seen for some time . . . I took several drinks but was neither drunk nor disorderly." He was docked three months pay.[15]

Private Joseph Lowry of the 2nd Pennsylvania Heavy Artillery was acquitted of stealing a horse in April 1861. One witness had seen Lowry at "Bates Alley on 6th St, near the post office, in a dissipated house kept by a colored woman." Bates Alley ran from G Street North to H Street North, between 6th and 7th Streets West.[16]

P. T. Barnum said, "There is a sucker born every minute." Three French-Canadians proved his point. They bought passes "good for all night" (of sexual pleasure) from one Eugène Houache, who had forged these utterly worthless documents. The three victims told the court, "$100 to amuse ourselves . . . at one of the houses of the town . . . was a fair price." Houache got a year in prison. The court seemed brighter than the victims.[17]

In May 1865, Lieutenant James W. Doxie of the 27th Michigan had a wild night with some of his enlisted men. They left Tenleytown and proceeded to downtown DC. Doxie pled guilty to "conduct unbecoming an officer and a gentleman" and apologized to the court for his ignorance of DC geography (His regiment had just arrived from Appomattox and service at Petersburg.), but he was able to recall some of his night's ramblings. "We drank at a saloon under Willard's Hotel then went to at least two houses of ill fame—several houses near the corner of C and 14th streets." His sentence of dismissal was remitted.[18]

Lieutenant John W. Tiffany of the same regiment was also raising hell in Tenleytown. He allowed his men to break into a private's house and beat up the soldier's wife, who suffered facial injuries. Tiffany defended his actions: "This woman was a notorious character and as she has been with the army some time, I presume that she had become somewhat demoralized." This defense of blaming the victim was unsuccessful and Tiffany was dismissed. In 1904 a special bill was passed in Congress, overturning his conviction.[19]

Private Michael Fletcher of the 7th VRC was celebrating the end of hostilities by being AWOL for three nights in May 1865 and creating his own hostilities when he assaulted his sergeant, whom he called a "lowlife dog." When arrested, Fletcher was naked and sound asleep in a DC brothel. A witness said, "When drunk, which is often, he is outrageous." Fletcher had six months in prison to sober up.[20]

Twenty-one year-old Private John Eustace, of the "First Army Corps" was arrested in February 1865 as a house of ill repute at 13th and C streets. "The woman charged me $10 to spend the night." Eustace, of course, was drunk. His night on the town cost him five dollars a month for the next two months, 38% of his salary.[21]

Private Thomas Boyd of the 9th New York Artillery seems to have been a common criminal, a thug. At DC's Georgetown, he invited a more innocent soldier to join him on "Cherry Alley ... to have some fun with the girls." As soon as they were alone, Boyd beat the victim nearly to death and stole his $15. Two and a half years in prison showed that the court considered this to be a grave offense.[22]

In August 1863, the 157th Pennsylvania was busy guarding the Union's capital. Captain Aldus Hawthorne's contribution to this noble effort was taking two prostitutes to the Crystal Springs racetrack—on horseback. The effect was enhanced by his appearance: dirty shirt, jacket unbuttoned and sword missing. He also gambled and drank with enlisted men, both prohibited activities. Surprisingly, Hawthorne's only punishment was the loss of a month's pay.[23]

Albert H. Ridebok, a private in the 1st New Hampshire Cavalry, deserted from the huge equestrian depot at Camp Stoneman and went directly to a brothel on 14th Street, where he was arrested. After a $10 fine, he returned to duty. It was the last Christmas of the war; perhaps he wanted to spend it in friendly company. Private John Robinson of the 3rd Massachusetts Heavy Artillery, when charged with desertion, portrayed himself as an unwilling victim. "At Washington, DC, a stranger came up to me and took me to a house of ill fame, where he got me drunk and took me prisoner." The charge was reduced to AWOL and Robinson was fined $10 and had 24 hours added to his enlistment time.[24]

Hugh McClune was probably the most outspoken lieutenant in the 135th Pennsylvania. He was convicted of saying that the South was right and that the Union was waging an illegal war. His somewhat testy language to some of his troops was considered conduct unbecoming an officer: "Go to hell, you are a set of hell hounds and ought to sink to the bottommost pit of hell ... you are too mean to be among dogs. There is Gilbert: he is rotten with the pox [syphilis] because it can be seen in his [illegible]; there is Murr, he don't run to those whorehouses, but fucks his fist until his face is full of boils and pimples." (Urban myth links acne and masturbation.) A third charge—placing a guard over a house of prostitution on Capitol Hill—was dismissed. McClune was not only cashiered and prohibited from any future federal employment, but was sent to Old Capitol Prison to the end of the war. Further, his crimes were to be published in newspapers "throughout the United States." In 1886, 24 years after his conviction, McClune wrote to President Grover Cleveland, asking to have his sentence overturned.[25]

The 50th New York Engineers was noted for its unruly members. Private John Dole of Company D was no exception. In the spring of 1864, he was arrested many times for being AWOL. In March, he left his unit at the Washington Navy Yard and proceeded to a combination saloon and whorehouse on Garrison Street, across the street from the Marine Corps barracks. A witness told the court, "Dole's character is bad . . . disrespectful . . . frequently drunk." Dole got 60 days hard labor wearing a 24-pound ball and chain.[26]

Lieutenant Max Sievers of the 1st West Virginia Light Artillery, in October 1863, was arrested in a brothel at 540 11th St, where he had gone using a forged pass. (The provost marshal's list of whorehouses shows establishments at numbers 531, 533, and 595 on that street, so this may be a new one for the records.) Sievers, who spoke mostly German, was dismissed. General Samuel Heintzelman denied a request for leniency.[27]

In September 1865, Robert Foster, a private in the 194th Ohio, was accused of threatening his captain with a knife. His defense was most unusual. "These two citizens that come over there, were keeping a sporting house; I went into the house and there was a lots of men out of my Company in there. I told some of the boys in the Company not to have anything to do with these women, for they were all diseased. This citizen told me to get out of the house or he would blow my heart out, and as I walked out of the door, he pulled a pistol, fired at and struck me in the left arm; two or three days afterward, they came to the Company, to pay damages done to me. I told them I did not want money for satisfaction; and at the time these two men were standing by Captain Wolverton, one of them had his hand on the revolver, as I had my knife out, and as I stepped toward Lieutenant Brown, he caught my arm." The court did not believe him and sent him to six months at hard labor, at no pay, with a 30-pound ball and chain.[28]

Camp Barry, in the District of Columbia, was located one mile northeast of the Capitol building. There, the military career of Lieutenant George Warner came to an end. This stalwart of the 5th New York Independent Battery was court-martialed for failing to join his regiment in the field. What was he doing instead? Witness James T. Brownson, a hack driver, said Warner had sent him for a woman, to be brought to his barracks. Her reputation? "All the hack drivers say that she is a third class whore. I understand she keeps a little house and some girls. She was laughing the other day at the driver, because she had beat him out of his hack hire." Warner, sensing that further such testimony would quickly condemn him, withdrew his plea of "not guilty." He was dishonorably dismissed.[29]

The war was not very old when two officers of the 58th New York got themselves into trouble. One evening in November 1861, First Lieutenant Abram Nussbaum and Major Theodore Lichtenheim occupied a theater box with two women. The theater manager noted that they were "notorious harlots" and requested that the provost guard remove all four of the party. Both officers failed to cooperate with the arresting officer, claiming they had just met the women and had no idea of their scarlet reputation. The court was not swayed; both officers were dismissed.[30]

In September 1863, Dr. George Fossard of the 146th New York, wrote to a friend: "I had an exceedingly pleasant journey to Washington, DC. In New York, Dr. Duane introduced me to a lady of easy virtue, whom I brought on to Washington, stopping overnight at Philadelphia and Baltimore. She is a young boss whore, keeping a house in Washington. She took a great fancy to me and would hardly let me leave her." This little escapade does not seem to have damaged Fossard's career. On November 5, 1864 he was promoted to full surgeon, assigned to the 56th New York.[31]

Military justice applied to civilians as well as to soldiers. Military commissions, in the news again in regards to terrorist detainees, tried two such cases. Maria Kelly and Rebecca Smith, prostitutes residing at 540-12th St. were both convicted of buying civilian clothes for soldiers trying to desert. Both women were sentenced to spend six months in prison.[32]

The end of the war did not signal the end of prostitution in DC, and it continues in the news even today. The latest addition to the Smithsonian Institution is the Museum of the American Indian. On that same location, from 1864 to 1878, the elegant "parlor house" of Mary Ann Hall served congressman, lobbyists, and other notables. The buried remains of champagne bottles and fine chinaware, discovered during the archaeological survey for the new museum, gave silent testimony to nights of well-heeled and well-connected revelry. Ms. Hall was the soul of discretion; no scandals, no court appearances, and no black book. This policy assured both the privacy of her clients and the growing wealth of the madam herself. She is buried in the Congressional Cemetery, near J. Edgar Hoover.[33]

Remarkably, a president of United States personally intervened on behalf of a notorious whore and thief. On June 21, 1866, Andrew Johnson granted Mary Blake, convicted of keeping a bawdy house, "a full and unconditional pardon." Since she was not only under suspicion of receiving stolen goods and awaiting trial for larceny, in addition to her recent fine of $500 ($15,000 in today's money), one must wonder if some unreported deal had been struck.[34]

Even small boys were part of the trade in the late 19th century in Washington, DC. Not as prostitutes, as in some cultures, but as steerers. Downtown Washington swarmed with boys delivering telegrams (the so-called "night messengers"), selling newspapers, hawking gum. They could also earn extra money by directing visitors to the brothels that still flourished in Murder Bay, also dubbed Hooker's Division.[35]

In 1997, prostitution was frequently reported in the *Washington Post*. Between March 7 and April 22, seventy-one women were arrested for prostitution. At Thomas Circle, a wreath-laying memorialized twenty-two streetwalkers murdered in the course of their occupation. Pimp Benjamin Gerard pleaded guilty to transporting young girls from Canada to work as prostitutes in DC. His employees mostly worked "the track," an area near the corner of 13th St and New York Ave. Northwest.

A colleague reported the action at 11th and K streets Northwest on May 31, 1997. At 2 AM, fifteen prostitutes in bikinis and Lucite heels were parading around the intersection. Eight were white; seven were black. Three pimps in white suits were in evidence. A police car with a bullhorn told passersby; "These girls all have diseases which have put men in the hospital." The girls screamed back, "Don't listen. It's all lies!"

District of Columbia Police Detective John Mehalic III, described by a witness as a "overweight white man in polyester pants," went on trial for demanding oral sex from prostitutes, in return for not arresting them.[36]

One of President Clinton's advisers, Dick Morris, regularly used the services of call girl Sherry Rowlands, who used "kinky sex," including toe sucking, to keep her client happy. He was less happy when she sold the story to a tabloid newspaper. (Even $200 an hour doesn't buy silence in the nation's capital.) Much of the story evolved in the tax evasion trial of Rowland's madam, Chanida Tungkahotara. Police estimated that eighty percent of the prostitutes in this country work through "escort" services.[37]

A wholly different merger of government and prostitution is seen in the career of Matild Manokyan, Turkey's best-known madam, and owner of thirty-two brothels and dozens of shopping malls. The Turkish government honored her five years in a row for being Istanbul's top taxpayer and for her honesty in reporting her income.[38]

It seems obvious that Civil War prostitution never went away, it just morphed into new economic and administrative forms, propelled by man's least reflective organ and woman's ability to make money by reducing the priapic to non-tumescence.

Chapter 11

PROSTITUTION IN THE MID-ATLANTIC STATES

Maryland, the Old Line State, was a southern state kept in the Union by force. The turmoil inherent in such tension generated many trials, few as dramatic as that of Colonel William S. Fish, Provost of the Middle Department, commander of the 1st Connecticut Cavalry, thief, liar, whoremaster, and, finally, convict. His customs inspectors in Baltimore confiscated many silk dresses, which Fish kept for himself. His officers confiscated $20,000 in Confederate cotton bonds; Fish sold them in London and kept the money. He kept the cash found in the pockets of deserters

More central to our theme were his relationships with the most prominent madams of Baltimore. The bill of indictment notes that he "habitually visits a house of prostitution kept by Emma Morton." He was also a frequent visitor at the elegant bagnio run by Annette Travers, and instructed the provost marshal not to enter the Travers establishment. Fish attended a ball at the house of prostitution run by Nancy Thomas wearing his uniform. (Poems describing Fish's misdeeds were circulated among Baltimore's secessionist elite.) For these, and a wide variety of other offenses, he was fined $5000 ($150,000 in today's money), and sent to the prison at Auburn New York. His many appeals were reviewed by Secretary of War Stanton and by President Lincoln.[1]

Second Lieutenant George Fielding, of the 11th Veterans Reserve Corps, was stationed at Baltimore's Fort McHenry. On May 29, 1865, he commanded the provost guard, and was sent to a tavern called The Vineyard to preserve order. While there, he "became drunk . . . . incapable of performing his duties . . . and ended in dancing with the lowest class of prostitutes." Although witnesses described him dancing with "a woman," and having a "staggering gait and inflamed eyes," he was acquitted. The reviewing officer disagreed with this decision and admonished Fielding to "be careful not to place himself in like danger the second time." Part of Fielding's defense hinged on the nature of The Vineyard, and he submitted a copy of an order issued by his superior, a Captain Meagrew, which stated, "take the second relief and proceed to The Vineyard . . . and arrest all persons, soldiers, citizens, or women who attempt to raise any disturbance . . . Should there be a big row, arrest the proprietor, close his house, and send him to me . . . under guard, and if that won't do it, smash his damned bar to pieces."[2]

Baltimore produced four additional cases. Edward Hawkins joined the 2nd Massachusetts Cavalry in January 1865 and received a bounty of $193. A few weeks later, he was at Fort Federal Hill in Baltimore. He got a pass to visit town. When he did not come back and was arrested, he gave this excuse: "I got on a spree and got tight in a house of ill fame, were I remained until the following night, when I was arrested by a detective." He seems to have left his $193 in the whorehouse. He was fined $10 a month for six months.[3]

Private William Hall was also with the 2nd Massachusetts Cavalry. Around Valentine's Day, 1865, he took his $500 in enlistment bounty and headed for downtown Baltimore. Eight days later, when he was arrested, he said, "I had my bounty and wanted to go on a spree. I stayed in a drinking house and brothel." His bounty, the equivalent of forty months of a soldier's pay, was not accounted for. He was fined $10 a month for six months. Riches to rags in seven nights.[4]

"How did I get to Philadelphia?" Private Michael Graham of the 1st Michigan went into "a certain house in Baltimore that had a bad reputation and I was drugged and stupified and I don't know how I got to Philadelphia." His April 1862 odyssey also included enlisting in another company. He was convicted of desertion, but the order of sentence is illegible.[5]

Private Henry R. Williams of the 1st Maine Veteran Volunteers had received a $400 reenlistment bounty. He told his sad story. "On or about the 22nd day of February 1865, in the evening, I went from camp with some of the men belonging to the fort. (Baltimore's Fort Federal Hill). I being an entire stranger to the city was conducted by them to a house of ill fame, where I became intoxicated and was robbed of about $16 and my overcoat, blouse, military vest, were stolen and in their place left an old hat and an old citizen's coat. I had about me $60 besides, which they did not find. I was aroused up and forced to go out on to the street where I fell helpless until arrested . . . I was temporarily insane from liquor." Williams was fined $10 a month for six months.[6]

The 1st Indiana Heavy Artillery had been in Baltimore six months when, on February 7, 1872, J. M. Boller wrote home to a friend, describing the light duty, which left him time for recreation with the "patriotic young ladies" who devoted themselves to gratifying "the passions of the soldiers." He paid them visits "every few nights." Two weeks later his regiment left for New Orleans.[7]

Elsewhere in Maryland, trollops, tarts, and trulls made their further mark in military history. At Relay House, First Lieutenant John Smith of the 213th Pennsylvania was convicted of "conduct unbecoming," after he brought a "notorious whore" to camp and introduced her as his wife. His three episodes of being AWOL and his history of horse theft did not help his case. In November 1865 he was dismissed from the service.[8]

At Annapolis in November 1864, Captain Morris Hazard of the 51st New York was drunk at eleven in the evening when he appeared at the door of a 39-year old widow, Eliza Mason, and asserted, "You are a whore. Are all your whores full?" When she replied that she was a decent woman who took in sewing, he called her "a goddamn bitch." In spite of the many witnesses who testified against him, Hazard was acquitted.[9]

Nobility is rare in war, but a few gentlemanly acts are in the record. At Havre de Grace, Private Julius McCreary was in bed with a woman upstairs at the widow McCabe's liquor store. The arresting officer told the court: "I told him it was time he was back in camp, he asked 10 minutes indulgence and I gave it to him." It was charity wasted on this soldier of the 10th New York Cavalry. After receiving his ten minutes, McCreary was foul-mouthed and violent; when he arrived at the guardhouse, he tore the grating off the window and escaped. When he was captured, he received a sentence of hard labor for the rest of his enlistment, the court noting his "systematic defiance of all military government," and they "failed to discover anything of a redeeming nature in the character of the prisoner . . . Even his conduct upon his trial was reckless and intemperate." In June 1862, McCreary went off to prison.[10]

At Salisbury, four drunken soldiers of the 194th Pennsylvania seemed to have escaped just punishment. In August 1864, Daniel Matthews, William Powell, David Nicholas, and John Dudley, were riding through the streets with three "lewd women," when they stopped to rob a store of whiskey and tobacco. All four men were acquitted.[11]

In the early spring of 1865, the provost guard at Cumberland posted orders that all soldiers and officers were to be out of the whorehouses by 9 p.m. and in their quarters by Taps. Second Lieutenant William J. Mulby of the 2nd West Virginia Veteran Volunteers disregarded this order and appeared at the door of Annie Wheeler's house around 11 p.m., demanding entrance and threatening to break down the door. Annie called the provost guard (who had experienced problems with Mulby two hours earlier) and they ordered him to the office of the provost guard. His reply? He attacked the guard with a "slung shot," severely wounding the heads of Privates Joseph Maguire and Daniel Jenkins. McGuire, who had been knocked unconscious, recovered by the time of the trial and testified, "We were ordered to shut up all whorehouses, saloons and groceries . . . I know Annie Wheeler's was a whorehouse. I have seen men and women in bed together and on the floor together . . . having illegal intercourse." Mulby was dismissed in disgrace.[12]

Frederick, the site of Barbara Fritchie's immortal—if never spoken—words, "Shoot if you must, this old gray head," was also the workplace of some of Frederick's younger women, three of whom were entertaining First Lieutenant William R. Thomas of the 46th Pennsylvania, in February 1862. Sadly, Thomas was not content to merely luxuriate in the sensuous and sybaritic pressing of lush female flesh; he became drunk—ugly drunk—in this "fancy house." He was soon in conflict with a corporal, who later told the court, "I was having a little sport of my own and was making a little noise." The corporal lost a tooth and the lieutenant lost his commission.[13]

This Frederick tradition of naked hospitality remains unbroken. A 1999 police investigation of Angelika Potter's prostitution service produced allegedly inflammatory evidence. Her list of "clients," filling several large three-ring binders, was apparently returned to her for shredding. Charges of police "cover-up" filled the newspapers. Meanwhile, the principal of Frederick's Thomas Johnson High School, was arrested for soliciting sex from a voluptuous young woman, who turned out to be an undercover police officer. The ghost of Lieutenant Thomas would feel right at home in today's Frederick.[14]

Pennsylvania, the Keystone State, which contributed 337,000 men to the Union cause, was also the site of many events involving the exchange of cold cash for carnal connection. One of the most remarkable documents of the era was a charitable function advertised by six Philadelphia madams. They planned to contribute to the "Committee for a Day's Labor," sponsored by the Great Central Fair for the Sanitary Commission. Were they truly the legendary "whores with a heart of gold," or was there a disclaimer in the fine print? The text of their broadside stated that the undersigned would open their "respective places of amusement," on the dates printed and all the receipts for that day would be donated to the Sanitary Fair—"provided that there is anything left after treating the party." (!). The ladies taunted "pimps, reporters, and editors," to all "spend a days labor," and as a reminder of "safe sex," as practiced today, "None of the visitors will be allowed to come to tea without French Kid Gloves [condoms]." These six madams signed their names and added the dates of their "Charity Day."[15]

Sergeant E. B. English believed firmly in the gracious treatment of prisoners. Aboard the train, in March 1865, while escorting prisoners to Philadelphia, he provided whiskey for them and allowed one prisoner to wear his sword and belt. On arrival at the City of Brotherly Love, Sergeant English took another prisoner to a "house of ill fame." Soon Sergeant English was a private again, owing the government $10 a month for six months.[16]

Deeply religious Private James Wood of Company G, 199th Pennsylvania, was offended by what he saw in Philadelphia, and in his letter penned October 2, 1864, he wrote, "Sabbath morning. Very rainy and muddy got our rations . . . Read of [St.] Paul's shipwreck and then read in Psalms felt comforted . . . O how different from Sunday at home swearing and all sorts of wickedness going on . . . Plenty of bad women in camp O the wickedness from the private up to the Commanding General."[17]

Wood had been in the army only one month. What might he have seen during his brief basic training? Nearly all Pennsylvania recruits began their career at Camp Curtin at Harrisburg, on the banks of the Susquehanna River. As soon as the camp opened, prostitutes flocked to Harrisburg. The pious citizens were deeply shocked by the sudden profusion of bordellos, many of which were in houses rented from the same pious merchants.[18]

At McConnellsburg, the court had to decide whether Mrs. Margaret Henry was a decent widow woman or the proprietress of a bordello. On October 6, 1865, Captain Felix Boyle of the 3rd Provisional Pennsylvania Cavalry visited her house at "early candlelight." She told the court, "He took a hold of me and pulled me behind the door. At first he talked good to me—he offered me $10 to let him stay all night. I told him I wasn't that kind of women. He says to me, 'the nicest ladies in the country takes men.' I told him, 'ladies dressed in silk that walk the streets, their insides is as black as the stove." Boyle tried to lift up her dress without success. He left, promising to return at 11 p.m. When he did, she threatened to put a bullet in him. Earlier that month she had boarded four soldiers, which raised the issue of possible improper activities. One witness said, "The women who frequent Mrs. Henry's house were of ill fame . . . I have been with ladies myself . . . I have had actual contact with them myself." The court seems to have believed Mrs. Henry's version of events and ordered Boyle to be dismissed.[19]

Delaware contributed one case. At Wilmington, Second Lieutenant John D. Hart of the 1st Delaware, was admitted to the US General Hospital for treatment (His ailment is unnamed.) He left the hospital on July 10, 1863, without permission and stayed away thirty days. Surgeon E. J. Daley took this as proof of Hart's restored vigor and ordered him to return to his regiment. Instead, Hart went on a two-week drunk, which culminated in a pistol-waving invasion of Mrs. Getty's whorehouse, in which he drove all the girls, dressed or not, into the street. He was dishonorably discharged, sent to prison for a year, and was "to be forever prohibited from holding any office of honor, trust or profit under the United States Government."[20]

Chapter 12

PROSTITUTION UP NORTH

Since the North was not under martial law, it generated few military cases involving prostitution. This is not to say that the ancient trade did not exist. Indeed, whole books have been written about sin and vice in New York, the east coast's major metropolis, but this discussion is largely limited to prostitution documented in military records.[1]

One prostitution case involved the President himself. Private Charles H. Boirs, 8th US Infantry, serving with the provost guard for New York City, was sentenced to be shot for desertion. His wife wrote to Lincoln, "He was lured into a house of ill fame and then had been druged (sic) and while in that state was persuaded to desert . . . I am now entirely destitute, but manage to get along." General E.R.S. Canby recommended mitigation to hard labor for the rest of Boirs' enlistment. Lincoln agreed.[2]

Private Edward J. Ford of the 13th VRC was guarding recruits (they tended to run away) in February 1865, in New York City. Instead of tending to his duty, he left his guard post and went to visit a house of ill fame, taking one recruit with him. Ford was fined most of his pay for six months. At Albany, New York, Private Lemuel Owens, another member of the VRC, allowed a confined soldier to escape. The deserter was found in a "bawdy house" on Franklin Street, and Owens got three months at hard labor with a 24-pound ball and chain.[3]

Congregationalist minister Thomas K. Beecher, chaplain of the 141st New York, was concerned about Elmira's numerous brothels. The usual political response in the 1860's was to arrest the prostitutes. Beecher, in contrast, noted that the "disorderly houses" were "neat, quiet, homelike and attractive," and that any disorder was caused by the male customers, not the girls. Beecher suggested that the male patrons have their names published in the *Daily Advertiser*. He did not disclose how he knew so much about the "homelike" atmosphere.[4]

Corporal Emory F. Pratt, a member of the Invalid Corps' 16th Regiment, on guard duty at Dunkirk, New York, was supposed to be taking care of deserter Till Clark. A recruiting officer, Second Lieutenant Charles Kimberly of the 112th New York, told the rest of the story. "I met them about half past 10:00 at a saloon. I ordered Pratt to take the deserter to the barracks immediately. While I was searching for another man at a house of ill fame, Pratt and the deserter came in. I then took the two to the barracks." Pratt's efforts to be a genial host cost him $10 a month for four months and his corporal's stripes.[5]

The New England states made their contributions to the ancient trade. Commander Frederick A. Neville, a 35-year veteran of the Union Navy, had charge of the receiving ship *Ohio*, tied up in Boston's harbor. Neville had not appeared in his office for four days. The police sent to search for the missing officer found him drunk in a "house of ill fame at 100 Charleston Street, with a madam and six whores and a colored kitchen girl. He owed the madam $30 for wine." The evidence was presented to a court of inquiry. No decision about a court-martial appears in these records.[6]

Private Clarence Howard of the 13th VRC was yet another guard happy to accommodate men who wished to see women. At Springfield, Massachusetts, in December 1864, Howard collected $20 from recruits Daniel Dowd and Edward Fitzgerald and allowed them to visit a nearby bordello. Dowd lingered with the ladies and was caught, but Fitzgerald cut short his carnal capers and escaped into the night.[7]

Silas Swift is listed as serving with the 95th New York, the 96th New York, and the 57th Massachusetts. In February 1863, he was stationed at Great Barrington in the latter state and wrote to his brother about the easily available girls of that town. He had gone to a party, where "I got a little whore hitched onto me and I could not get rid of her until . . . ."[8]

New Hampshire contributed two cases. At Concord, Private Richard Ross of the 13th VRC was missing for two weeks in November 1863. When he was located at "the Yellow House," a place of prostitution, he sent word that he would return to camp "soon." This casual attitude did not sit well with his superiors, and Ross went to prison for the rest of his enlistment.[9]

"It wasn't my fault! A man took me to a house of ill fame in Manchester and got me to drink twelve glasses of liquor and then I went to bed. Also, I lost my hat." This story was told by Private Edward C. Burnap of the 8th New Hampshire, regarding his overnight absence in October 1864. He spent the next six months at hard labor, during which time he received no pay.[10]

The 14th US Infantry was stationed at New London, Connecticut in the late spring of 1865, where at least three of its members came to grief. Corporal John Houston deserted and was found in a house of ill fame. His punishment? First, the letter "D" was branded on his right cheek with a hot iron, then he was sent to hard labor for the rest of his enlistment. When his incarceration was over, his head was to be shaved and he was to be drummed out. Of course, his corporal's stripes were long gone. Private William Campbell had also been arrested in a New London whorehouse, but he received only a fine—$10 a month for six months. A month later, Private Eli Cerow had been denied a pass, but went into town anyway. He was arrested at "Alonzo Spooner's house of ill fame." Cerow lost $10 a month for ten months.[11]

Was George A. Hall trying to defend two ladies at Hartford, Connecticut, or was he interfering with an officer in the performance of his duty? The officer in this case was a captain trying to arrest a hack driver who was conveying two "women of ill repute." "They were whores," the captain informed the court. For reasons best known to himself, the drunken Private Hall, a member of the 5th VRC, cursed the captain and assaulted him with fists and rocks. Hall was given six months of hard labor for his defense of the hookers; his sentence approved by General Hooker himself.[12]

Did prostitution affect military efficiency? The best documented answer lies in Nashville, where venereal disease was so rampant that many regiments were under strength even before they left town for the war zone. The commanding general made at least three major efforts to combat the problem, finding most success with a mandatory program of medical examinations, detailed in the author's earlier book.

A Summing Up of Prostitution

Two major observations emerge from these 304 prostitution-related trials, and from the many other primary sources cited. The first observation is the ubiquity of prostitution. Whorehouses were in every town, in every village; in the cities, they were in every neighborhood. In reading the full transcripts of the trials, it became clear that both the witnesses and the trial boards were fully aware of the location and nature of these "houses of ill repute," in fact, many witnesses had visited them—many times—and not just as observers. Overt, publicly acknowledged prostitution was far more a fact of life in the 1860s than in our own era. Not today's midnight pedestrians in their mini skirts and high heels, with their grinning overdressed pimps, not the desperate crack whores, but, instead, young women gathered under the relative safety of the same roof, and in the close company of other "girls." True, venereal disease and violence were ever-present threats, but the established whorehouse and its clients had a sociology with many overlooked advantages.

The second observation is the house of prostitution as a locus of conflict and riot. Most likely, the vast majority of exchanges of sex for money were peaceful, but hundreds of soldiers utilized the location and occasion to become quarrelsome, unpleasant, and violent, most often while intoxicated. For some men, the greater gratification seemed to come from exercising foul temper and evil intentions; for them the comfort of a warm bed and a willing partner (even one willing for pay) were lesser pleasures.

The swift passage of the years has erased the corporeal bodies so vividly portrayed in these records. It has been, as always, ashes to ashes and dust to dust. Yet we see written on these yellowed pages that the protagonists were not necessarily satanic Jezebels, nor were their clients necessarily moral dissolutes, but all were trying to survive amongst the vast disruption of a nation at war with itself.

Chapter 13

RAPE IN VIRGINIA

Rape has long been associated with war. Genghis Khan is reputed to have said, "The greatest joy a man can know is to conquer his enemies and drive them before him. To ride their horses and take away their possessions. To see the faces of those who were dear to him bedewed with tears, and to clasp their wives and daughters in his arms."

Long before the Great Khan's armies swept out of Mongolia, other records tell us of rape in antiquity. The law code of Hammurabi (1,800 BCE) prescribed death for the man who raped another man's wife, and held the wife blameless. The Hittite penalties for sexual crimes (1,500 BCE) varied by the location of the offense. For rape in the mountains, where the woman's cries could not be heard, the man must die. For rape in the house, where help was nearby, the woman was the one to be executed. We will see this same pattern, 800 years later, in the Old Testament.[1]

In the same era as the Hittites, the inhabitants of the Egyptian village of Deir el Medina recorded their fear of Paneb and his son, Aapahty, who raped and murdered with impunity.[2]

The Old Testament has much to say about rape. Judges 21:10, around 800 BCE, tells us how the Israelites kidnapped and raped 400 virginal girls of Jabesh-Gilead, after murdering the parents and brothers of the girls. The Israelites then encouraged the Benjaminites to kidnap and rape the girls of Shiloh.

Our modern concepts of rape are far different from the Biblical tradition. Today, we view rape as a crime of violence, in which the unwilling victim is subjected to an unwanted violation, a clear criminal assault upon her legal and personal rights. Twenty-five hundred years ago a woman (or girl) was property, to be disposed of as seen fit by her father, or her husband, or her military captor. Forced sexual intercourse was the right of the conqueror, or an act that impaired her value for an arranged marriage, but the personal opinions (which would include pain, fear, and lack of pleasure) of the raped woman seem to have been of little consequence. It would be many centuries before this changed.

Deuteronomy 20:10 describes the divinely approved course of action after successfully besieging a city: kill all the men and use the women any way that pleases you. On the smaller scale of the individual victim, we are advised in 22:28 that if a man rapes a girl, he must pay the girl's father fifty pieces of silver, marry the girl, and never divorce her. Whether she wishes to marry her assailant is not in the text. In 22:23, we see the echoes of Hittite law. If a man rapes a betrothed girl out in the country, he shall die, but she has committed no sin. However, if he has intercourse with a betrothed girl in the city, where her cries could be heard, both shall be put to death. There is no mention of the presence or absence of force during the intercourse.

In the same era, Exodus 21:7 laid out the rules for selling one's own daughter as a sex slave. We are told what the new owner may do if she does not please him; there is no mention of what may be done if he does not please her.

The concept of blaming the victim is seen vividly in 2 Samuel 13:12. Amnon, having enticed his virgin sister Tamar into his bedroom, rapes her. With his lust slaked, he then "hated her with intense hatred."

A few centuries later, the Hellenic Greeks pondered rape. In Athenian moral discourse, *hubris* was a key concept. It was more than pride or arrogance; *hubris* was any deliberate act intended to dishonor another person, in order to give the aggressor a sense of superiority. Since *hubris* angered the gods, an act of *hubris* could endanger the whole city, and the penalty for *hubris* could be death. Classical Greek legal codes had little to say about rape itself, but if the rapist stood accused of *hubris*, he was in grave peril.[3]

To be an Athenian citizen, one had to be of "pure blood," with both parents being Athenian citizens. The raped woman was not of primary concern, but her child, who could not be proven to be eligible for citizenship, was a major problem. This potential disturbance in the harmony of Athenianship applied to seduction as well; again, the issue was one of offspring whose blood "purity" was suspect. The Greeks were very precise in their definitions. Lucian wrote: "The adulterer must be caught . . . in the very act of copulation, plug in socket."[4]

Teachers of Latin revel in cases and declensions. They rarely mention the central theme in Roman history—rape. "The rape of the vestal virgin Rhea Silvia . . . resulted in the birth of Romulus, Rome's founder. The rape of the Sabine maidens results in the assurance of a continuing population for the city." In similar fashion, the monarchy falls as a result of the rape of Lucretia, and the attempted rape of Verginia leads to the re-establishment of the Republic.[5]

Even by the time of Chaucer, our current definitions of rape had not emerged. Anglo-Norman law centered on *raptus*, a term which covered abduction, elopement, seduction, ravishment, and forced intercourse. Simple rape did not interest the courts as much as abduction and seduction, which could raise questions of property and inheritance. Aquinas and other theologians labored mightily on the issue of the rape of virgins. In theory, while the girl was no longer a physical virgin, she could still be a spiritual virgin. But how to verify a state of spiritual virginity? What if the experience had piqued her interest—even a little bit? Thus the theological heavyweights edged closer once again to blaming the victim.[6]

Leaping ahead three centuries, we arrive at the American Revolution, where the most vicious rapists were the New Jersey loyalists. Nathanael Green noted, ". . . The brutes often ravish the mothers and daughters and compel the fathers and sons to behold their brutality." A leading British officer, Lord Rawdon, had this to say about his troops:

> The fair nymphs of this isle are in wonderful tribulation, as the fresh meat our men have got here has made them as riotous as satyrs. A girl cannot step into the bushes to pluck a rose without running the most imminent risk of being ravished, and they are so little accustomed to these vigorous methods that they don't bear them with the proper resignation, and of consequence we have the most entertaining courts-martial every day.[7]

In 1779, British troops raided New Haven, Connecticut, and brutally raped many women. Three years earlier, the King's men had kidnapped women on Staten Island and held them for days in army camps, where their pleas for help went unanswered.[8]

In 1813, the world was ablaze with war. And rape. In Spain, after Wellington's bloody siege of Badajoz, the British victors engaged in a three-day orgy of pillage, murder and rape. At Hampton, Virginia, Admiral George Cockburn's sailors committed robbery and rape. At Craney Island, Virginia, French and Swiss mercenaries under the British flag, ran riot, raping, robbing and burning. The writings of the early 1800s suggest a historic shift in the meaning of rape; the injury to the victim became primary, and issues of citizenship, property, inheritance, and virginity diminished. But even at the time of the American Civil War there were striking exceptions to this modern trend. The rape of a slave woman could not, technically, be a crime, since she was property, not a person, and, as we will see in the Civil War military justice records, rape was often assumed to be the woman's fault.

Long after the Civil War, rape continued to part of warfare. During the conquest of Germany, nearly ten million German girls and women were raped by Soviet soldiers. In a decade of Liberia's brutal civil war, about sixty percent of the population was raped—men and boys, as well as women.[9] What level of brutality do the records of the American Civil War demonstrate?

Sexual Misbehavior in the Civil War | 117

We will first present all the data discovered in the records of military justice and then, in the final chapter in this section, Rape up North, place that data into a historical perspective, both in this nation's story and in the context of other wars across the span of history.

Alexandria

Private Asa G. Smith, 97th New York, was charged with attempted rape. After being noisy drunk on the streets on April 3, 1863, he entered the home of Levi Bentheim at 74 Prince Street. Caroline Bentheim, Levi's wife, testified that they had moved from Baltimore three days previously. She found Smith in her kitchen. He grabbed her dress. She screamed. Private Henry Smith, 26th Michigan, was being shaved next door. He answered the screams and found the defendant with one hand over Caroline's mouth and the other "trying to raise her clothes." After a violent struggle, the rescuer choked Asa Smith and dragged him into the street. "The defendant had his pants unbuttoned and half way down." Caroline herself recalled no dress raising or attempt to cover her mouth. (The house had very recently been a whorehouse, which may have led Asa to expect a warmer reception.) Henry Smith was recalled as a witness. He said Caroline was too hysterical to clearly remember the events of the sexual assault. He had seen the defendant's penis and it was "quite rigid." Asa Smith was fined $12 a month for six months.[10]

Private William Devlin of the 5th Pennsylvania Heavy Artillery came into the house of Rachel Johnston, "a colored woman," and ordered her to lie down on the bed with him. When she refused, he chased her into the street threatening her with an ax. His June 1865 court-martial sentenced him to a year in prison and the loss of $12 a month for four months.[11]

On April 10, 1862, Sarah Ann Compton, who lived on Duke Street, was walking across a field with some friends. Private James Hickman of the 7th Pennsylvania and some companions approached the women. "The prisoner asked if we had anything to sell. They commenced to follow us. The accused caught the old lady by the mouth and set her bleeding. I hollered. He ran up and pushed me down with violence. He kept my face in the snow for 20 minutes, telling me what he would do. I cannot say the words . . . They were of the most vulgar character. He said he would take my life if I did not do those things. He picked me up to carry me into the swamp when the guard arrived. My nose was bleeding. My dress was torn. He pulled out some of my hair." Hickman got three years in prison.[12]

City of Richmond

On the night of April 11, 1865 on Deep Run Road near Richmond, three men of the 38th USCT entered a private home. John Sheppard, an illiterate 20-year old, raped Mrs. Fanny Crawford and fourteen-year old Eliza H. Woodson. Back at camp, he bragged, "I fucked the old one and the young one too." Dandridge Brooks also raped Eliza, after threatening to kill her. William Jackson, age 24, raped both Fanny and Eliza. The men also stole eight pounds of butter and a silver thimble, which were found in Sheppard's knapsack at camp. In July the regiment was transferred to Texas; on July 30, 1865, all three men were hanged at Brownsville.[13]

On September 21, 1865, Mrs. Catherine Sharp was sewing in her room at the United States Hotel in Richmond; with her was her "colored servant," Emeline Christian. Pvt. Dennis McGill, 4th Massachusetts Cavalry, entered the room, uninvited, called Mrs. Sharp a "damned whore," threw her on the bed and attempted to have "carnal intercourse" with her. In this turmoil, he also kicked and knocked down Emeline. Mrs. Sharp recalled, "He used dreadful language, which I don't care about repeating." McGill asserted that she had beckoned to him from her window and had sent a little girl down to fetch him. "Did you do not take hold of some paper and plug up the keyhole of the room?" She denied any such acts. In prewar Virginia, colored people did not testify against whites. Now it was different. Emeline recalled, "He tried to take advantage of her . . . tried to throw her onto the bed. She told him to close the door. When he got off the bed she ran into the kitchen and picked up a hatchet and said he she would split his brains open. Then he kicked me and struck at my head with his saber. Mrs. Sharp's husband is at Norfolk. She does not receive visits from other gentlemen." McGill asked the court for mercy, adding he had just been released from a prisoner of war camp. "Mrs. Sharp kissed me. If I had money, none of this would have happened." He got two years in prison.[14]

Private Michael Shehan, 8th Maine, was charged with rape and with attempted murder. He was tried by a military commission, although he had demanded the right to a court-martial. The victim, Mrs. Maria Wade, a widow, told the court, "I ain't got much learning . . . I reckon I am about age fifty." She claimed that on a moonlit night in August 1865, Shehan, without provocation, suddenly picked her up and threw her into Haxall's Millrace Canal, near the steel works on the James River. Another man, identity unknown, pulled her out. Then Shehan "ravaged me . . . took me on the ground like a hog . . . said he'd cut my throat and tear me in half if I hollered . . . After he was done, he ravaged me again." The commission was deeply skeptical. They asked her many times why she did not defend herself better, asked why she did not cry out, asked how a big woman like her could be so "easily tossed into the canal." The two sides of the equation seemed equally balanced: her somewhat implausible recollections, and the court's determination to blame the victim. In the end, they sentenced Shehan to nine months at hard labor.[15]

Elsewhere in Virginia

Richmond County is on the Northern Neck, downstream from Fredericksburg and far from the city of Richmond. In that county, at Union Wharf, George Hill of the 2nd New Hampshire, terrorized a household of "colored citizens," who testified. Mr. and Mrs. Jerry Croxen told the court, "He took $15, all the money that we possessed in the world." Susan Jackson said that he had pulled her into a back room, exclaiming, "I want to ride you. You ought to be ashamed to let a Yankee go around with a hard cock in his britches." Hill's tent mate said he never left the tent that night. Hill was found not guilty. Tried with him were Peter Malloy and William Ryan of the same regiment. Malloy was convicted of threatening the Croxens with a bayonet and was sentenced to a year in prison. Ryan was also given a year in prison for the same offense.[16]

Cloud's Mill, now long forgotten, was near Annandale in Northern Virginia. There, in July 1865, four members of the 1st Pennsylvania Provisional Cavalry were court-martialed for attempted murder and for the rape of "Miss Judah Lewis, spinster." In the cases of Privates John E. Riley and George W. Ulch there was no testimony and both were acquitted. Privates John Price and John D. Kane were convicted of beating their captain with clubs; there was little testimony about a rape. Both Price and Kane were given dishonorable discharges.[17]

Near Prince George's Courthouse, two men had a fatal encounter—but were they guilty? One evening in June 1864, Daniel Geary and Gordon Ransom, both of the 72nd New York, came to the isolated home of Mrs. Mary Stiles and her 48-year-old cousin, Miss Lucy William. The two men offered to guard the house. During the night, they seized Mrs. Stiles. One man held her down, while the other raped her, then the two men traded places. Geary, aged, 18 had a long history of desertions and had been hospitalized for syphilis. Gordon, aged 23, had a better record. Both men were convicted. After reviews by Lincoln, both men were hanged on July 15, 1864. In Burke Davis' book, *The Civil War: Strange and Fascinating Facts*, he wrote that "Mrs. Stiles . . . confessed on her deathbed . . . that she swore the lives of these men away in order to contribute her mite toward the extermination of the Yankee army."[18]

Langley, in Fairfax County, is currently the location of CIA headquarters. In October 1863, it was also the home of James K. Nelson, his wife, his fifteen-year-old daughter, and several small children. Sergeant Charles Sperry of the 13th New York Cavalry got drunk, left his post, and got it into his head that the Nelsons were harboring rebels. Taking with him Privates John Martin and John Tully, Sperry arrived on the Nelson's front porch about midnight. When Mr. Nelson opened the front door, they seated him, half naked, on the front porch. Sperry posted Tully on the porch and told him, "If the old man moves, shoot him." Then Sperry whacked Nelson on the head with his pistol and he and Martin entered the house. The daughter, Annie Nelson, recalled that when Sperry grabbed her arm her mother began screaming. Sperry hit the mother on the head with his pistol and dragged her into the next room. He then turned to Annie and attempted to rape her. She fought him furiously. When she tried to flee, Sperry punched her twice in the face and hit her on the head with his pistol. "He said that I must surrender to him. I told him I would die first. Then he hit me on the head twice more and attempted to put his hands under my clothes." He did lift her dress and exposed her body, but she resisted penetration. During a brief distraction, Mrs. Nelson escaped and ran out into the dark. Sperry was convicted and sentenced to death. An appeal to Lincoln was unsuccessful. Sperry was shot at Old Capitol Prison on March 3, 1865. Martin was given three months at hard labor and Tully was acquitted.[19]

At Cedar Creek in July 1863, Privates Patrick Noonan and Samuel Clark of the 62nd Pennsylvania were in a field belonging to a Mrs. Brown. These two soldiers, and several others, made a "violent assault and attempted rape" upon "a colored woman," causing her to breed bleed profusely from the nose and mouth. When their captain told the men to stop, Noonan cursed him and Clark cried out, "We are old soldiers and will protect each other. This is none of your Goddamn business, so go away or I'll kill you." Noonan was fined $10 a month for two months. Clark was fined $10 a month for the rest of his enlistment and ordered to do three months of fatigue duty.[20]

William Newton's career with the 5th Vermont was all downhill. In November 1862, he was a first lieutenant and was reprimanded for being AWOL. Three months later, he left at the Battle of Fredericksburg and went to Vermont. He was court-martialed and dismissed, but was reinstated at the rank of sergeant major because of his sterling qualities, qualities not readily evident in the record. In December 1864, he was court-martialed again, this time for attempting to rape Mrs. Amanda Boyce. He entered her home at Round Hill. "He asked if I would accommodate a soldier for greenbacks. I refused. Then he asked me if I'd accommodate him for sugar and coffee. He put his arms around me. I told him no gentleman would treat a married woman in that manner." Newton was reduced to the rank of private, fined $10 a month for the rest of his enlistment and was made to march before his regiment with a placard reading, "Robber and Maltreater of Citizens."[21]

Private James Maley of the 16th Michigan Veteran Volunteers was at Amelia County in May 1865. At the home of Peter Clay, he obtained brandy by threatening to burn the house and told Mr. Clay, "I will return and sleep with your daughter." At the house of Richard D. Mills, he was charged with raping two "colored servant girls," Anna and Eliza. Anna told the court, "He said nothing out of the way to me. He did nothing to me." Eliza had a different story: "I was coming up to the house. He asked me if I wouldn't give him a little fuck. I told him I couldn't give it to him now, but wait until I went in the house and came back and I would give it to him then. He told me to go down behind the barn." When asked by the court, "Did you allow him to have intercourse, did you give him a little fuck?" She answered, "Yes, and he offered to give me a ring and some greenbacks . . . He did not offer me violence or throw me down." The court asked, "Did you lie down?" "Yes, sir." "Did he give you the greenbacks?" "No, sir, he did not." (The colored girls testified over defense objections that colored persons could not know the nature of an oath.) Maley was convicted of robbery, but not of rape. He was fined $10 a month for two months.[22]

At Lighthouse Point in June 1864, Horatio Gates, 2nd New York Cavalry, was accused of raping Mrs. Clorinda Taylor, "colored." He admitted that he had sent her husband on an errand and had then pulled her towards the bedroom, but without success. Several men testified that in exchange for bread, meat, or coffee that she had quite willingly had sex with them. Mr. Taylor was aware of these arrangements. When asked if his wife was "crazy," he replied that she had been so for seven years. Gates was acquitted.[23]

At Manchester, Private Robert L. Merrill of the 1st District of Columbia Cavalry was tried for the attempted rape of Virginia Quatles, "colored woman." She said, "I was walking up the hill, near the Petersburg railroad. He come up behind me and throwed me down. I holloed and he told me to hush holloing, if I didn't stop, he'd hit me with a piece of wood. He pulled my clothes up and one of the soldiers from Belle Isle came here and told him to get ready to go under arrest." Corporal Alex Smith, 8th Connecticut, said, "I saw him with a girl down in the weeds. She was struggling, trying to get away from him. He had her clothes up. The girl made an appeal to me. I didn't stop. I didn't consider it any of my business." In October 1865, while Merrill was preparing his written defense, he escaped and was not seen again.[24]

At Burkesville, Private George McCullough of the 7th Michigan was charged with raping Mrs. Louisa Fears. "He walked into my house. My mother was there. He ordered her to leave. He drew his pistol and threatened her if she didn't leave. After she left, he threw me down on the bed; he stripped my clothes up and then he did just as he wished to." The mother confirmed the story: "I heard her begging and pleading." At the trial, in April 1865, Lieutenant Colonel George LaPointe, 7th Michigan, testified that Mrs. Fears had been given $50, "On account of the accused, as compensation for any damages alleged." The transaction is documented, in a note signed by Louisa A. Fears: "In consideration of $50 received from Lt. Col. G. W. La Point, 7th Mich Inft, would rather that the case of rape between George McCullough and myself be dropped." The prosecution halted.[25]

Fort Monroe was so crowded that an annex, Camp Hamilton, was opened just north of the fortress itself. There, in September 1863, Maurice Miller, 3rd Pennsylvania Heavy Artillery, was tried for the rape of Harriet Ann Foster, "colored." She told the court, "I and another girl were going down to Slabtown.

We saw three men; the prisoner was one of them. One of the men went on one side of me and the prisoner on the other. He placed one hand on my face and the other on the back of my head. The other man took hold of my legs and they threw me down. The prisoner got on top of me . . . pulled my clothes up, exposing my person and he unbuttoned his breeches and took out his privates; he then fucked me." Her friend, Catherine Thomas, "colored," said the man who was on top of Harriet Ann was not the prisoner. "The one who was on her was taller than the prisoner and of a different complexion." Miller was acquitted.[26]

Thomas Mitchell had been in the service for seventeen years. In 1865, he was serving with the 1st New York Engineers and was charged with raping a ten-year old "colored girl," America Virginia Pierman, at Fort Harrison, just south of Richmond. The first witness was Brevet Brigadier General James F. Hall, Mitchell's commander. He had left Mitchell holding his horse. When the Hall returned, he found a crying child, a distressed father, and Mitchell absent on a preposterous mission to "find a spring." The girl testified: "I live near Chapin's Farm. The man said I could have a gray jacket if I went with him to the rebel huts. He pulled me inside, covered my face with oilcloth. I pushed it off. He pulled my clothes up and touched me. He unbuttoned his pantaloons and took his thing out." The court asked, "Did any part of his person enter you?" "Yes, sir, the thing he took out. Afterwards I was bleeding real hard. I know him by his talk. He didn't talk like Virginians."

Surgeon Robert Loughran, 20th New York State Militia, had examined her. "The usual evidence of virginity was gone. The hymen had been ruptured so recently that it had not yet had time to heal. There was a black and blue spot near the entrance of the vagina . . . . I should think that rape committed upon the person of a child of that age would produce the same result." Mitchell was sent to prison for three years.[27]

Ben Butler and Abraham Lincoln both reviewed the case of Lieutenant Andrew Smith, 11th Pennsylvania Cavalry, who raped Jenny Green, "colored," at City Point. "He threw me on the floor, pulled up my dress. He held my hands with one hand, held part of himself with the other hand and went into me. It hurt. He did what married people do. I am but a child." (Her age is not given.) Smith was dismissed and sent to prison for ten years. Smith's attorney blamed it all on the girl. General Butler's review denounced the practice of raping former slaves, and Lincoln, on December 31, 1864, wrote to Stanton, "I concluded . . . to let him [Smith] suffer for a while and then discharge him."[28]

Private Peter Raucher of the 5th Pennsylvania Cavalry tried to rape Mrs. Sarah Hanvey, at her home, known as "Goods," near New Market Mills. He seems to have committed this outrage as he attempted to desert to the Confederacy on the Darbytown Road, nine miles from Richmond. She said that he entered the house at 4 a.m., claiming to be looking for rebels. Then he put his arms around her neck and kissed her until she began screaming. She recalled that he spoke mostly German. On cross-examination, she had no recall of his facial appearance and relied on his voice as the only identification. The court found the evidence too thin and acquitted Raucher.[29]

At Warrenton, 82-year old Pricey McCoy was assaulted by Charles C. Rogers of the 3rd Vermont. The court met in July 1863 in the victim's own home. Rogers was convicted of beating and bruising her, but his attempt at rape had been unsuccessful. Lincoln approved the sentence: Rogers was drummed through his regiment with his head shaved and went off to serve five years in prison.[30]

At Sperryville, three men of the 1st New York Light Artillery terrorized the household of a Mrs. Swindler. Private Lewis Trost and "Negro servant" Jerry Spades were convicted of raping the Swindler's "colored servant," Polly Walker. Lewis Sorg was not a rapist, but did destroy Mrs. Swindler's quilts and drank her brandy. Spades got five years at hard labor, to be fed on bread and water one week of each month; Trost got hard labor for the rest of his enlistment with the same bread and water regime and then a "disgraceful discharge." Sorg got a year at hard labor.[31]

Some officers were dismissed by direct order, without a court-martial. At Upperville, First Lieutenant Thomas Sullivan, 10th New Hampshire, and several other men appeared at the door of Miss Taliaferro, searching for "rebel arms." Sullivan instructed his companions to stay in the parlor and play the piano while he and Miss Taliaferro, who may have been related to Brigadier General William Booth Taliaferro, went upstairs to search. "[Sullivan] closed the door and threw his arms around me, trying to hold me. I escaped from his arms and rushed downstairs." The 35-year old officer was dismissed by General Orders 195, in November 1862.[32]

Today's city of Virginia Beach was once Princess Anne County. There, in December 1864, Private Levi Lemon, 20th New York Cavalry, used language astonishingly vulgar even for a drunken cavalryman. Miss Lydia Hanley recalled his words: "You have got a cunt and I am going to suck you; you are a damn mean woman and I am going to fuck you." While he did not actually touch her, his intrusive words earned him six months at hard labor.[33]

William Lightfoot, "a free colored man and camp retainer," was tried for rapes committed at Crab Neck, York County, in May 1862, upon the persons of Mrs. Lucy E. Thomas and Mrs. Mahaly Wright. Nineteen-year old Lucy recalled that Lightfoot appeared at daybreak and said he had orders from General McClellan to bring the two women to Union headquarters. "When we started off, we thought he [Lightfoot] was a white man. He kept the cape of his overcoat over his head. He led us about three miles into a swamp, water up to our knees. He tied my aunt to a tree, led me about 100 yards and then treated me as mean as a man could treat a woman. He said if I did not give up to him, he would blow my brains out." The judge advocate asked, "Did he succeed in having sexual intercourse with you? Did or did you not resist him? Did he use force?" She replied that there had been sexual intercourse and that she had tried to resist him. "Did you lie down?" "I did." "Did you lift your clothing?" "No, he lifted it himself." Mrs. Wright's testimony confirmed that of her niece. Lightfoot claimed he had been cleaning his captain's tent at the time of the crime. He was hanged May 13, 1862.[34]

Private Abner Young, 5th New York Cavalry, was at Petersburg in July 1864 when he was charged with raping Sarah Gilchrist, "mulatto," and with inciting four other men "to commit rape upon the person of said Sarah Gilchrist, and while said four soldiers did then and there ravish and carnally know her person by force and violence . . . did remain present, encouraging, aiding, and abetting therein." Seventeen-year-old Sarah, AKA Sukey, testified that she was in bed when Young and his friends arrived. She saw his face when he lit a match. There was but one room; "I slept there with five other colored people. The three soldiers each came into my bed and had connexion [the Victorian spelling] with me. I was afraid to holler; they had guns. He gave me one old, no-account dollar. I didn't want it." The court asked if she had ever had "connexion" before. "Yes, that was a long time ago, with someone I liked very well. It was a colored person."

One of Sarah's male roommates was closely examined as to how he could tell, in the dark, when intercourse occurred. "I stood near enough to hear. It makes a noise that every man makes in that operation. I am a man and I know just what noise the man makes in that exercise." Many pages of defense testimony included the assertion that the "colored house" was a site of carousal. Young was acquitted.[35]

At Sandy Point, Charles Atwater, 33rd New York Battery, was charged with raping Mrs. Mary Jane Kottman, "colored." She told the court that Atwater told her to get in bed. When she resisted, he dragged her towards the bed and told her if she didn't stop shouting he would shoot her. "He pulled out his revolver and bursted two caps at me." When she screamed louder, he ordered her out, kicking her as she passed him. Atwater's comrades, George Allenberg and William Geoghean, testified that no such event had occurred. In his written defense, Atwater asserted, "This woman is known to our garrison to sell herself to the highest bidder, but although [I am] an enlisted man, I have honor of enough about me not to get in any sexual relation with a colored individual." He was acquitted.[36]

Occoquan Creek, in Prince William County, near Manassas Junction, was the site of the April 12, 1864, crime of Thomas B. Bond, a soldier in the 9th Pennsylvania Reserves. Miss Sara Jane Ledman told the court: "I was on my way home. He stopped me on the road, with a knife in his hand. At first he spoke very politely but then he told Miss Fairfax [who was with Sarah Jane] that he had to arrest her and that the only thing that would save her would be if she consented. He then clinched Lizzie and me both but Lizzie got away in. He threw me down and said if I hollered he'd cut my throat. He done just as he pleased with me." The court asked, "Did he have connection with you?" "Yes." "Did he penetrate your person?" "Yes." "Did you resist him all you could?" "Yes." Nineteen-year old Lizzie confirmed the story. Bond's attorney, in relentless cross-examination, tried to discredit both women. The court convicted Bond and sent him to prison for fifteen years.[37]

Charles Clark, 20th New York Cavalry, was charged with raping Mrs. Laura Ennis, "colored," at Pocahontas. "He came across the field at Wilson's Landing; he had a gun and an ax. He pulled me out of the cart. James Carey, a colored man, was with me. The accused offered to shoot him if he went for help. I begged the accused to let me alone, then he ravaged me. He said, 'Lay down, you haven't been *** yet.' When he was finished, he said if I told, he'd shoot me and skin me." The court asked if she had raised her own dress. She replied that he had done it. The court asked if the connection was with her consent. "No." In the same event, she was also raped by a Joseph Redmond. Clark was found guilty and sentenced to five years at Norfolk's Hard Labor Prison; Redmond seems to have escaped.[38]

White Oak Church was a Union hospital during the first Battle of Fredericksburg. Four months later, it was the site of two rapes alleged against Lot Edwards, 5th Vermont, specifically that he had ravaged Irene Ann Sadawhite, "a colored girl age 12," as well as Mrs. Fanton Frazier, "a colored woman." He also beat up John Frazier, Fanton's husband. William Kane, 104th New York, was the first witness. He sent for help when a soldier came out of the Frazier's house and said, "Stay and get some screwing; that's what we're after." Irene Ann told the court that a dozen men wanted to come into their small house. "Uncle John said it was too many. They cursed him and said what they wanted was the women. Aunt Fanton threw water on them and drove them out." The men came back and threw Irene Ann on the bed. One man held her and the other tried to put his "private parts" into her. He did not succeed but did make her very sore. She was not able to identify the man.

Fanton told the court: "The men told my husband, 'We came here to fuck the women,' then they dragged him out. I threw hot water on them and drove them out, but they broke down the door. They dragged me into a gully. Four held my hands and feet until three had been served with what they wanted." However, she, too, could not identify the rapists. Edwards was acquitted of rape, but found guilty of being AWOL and was fined $10.[39]

Sergeant Lawson Perkins, also of the 5th Vermont, also raped Irene Ann Sadawhite. The same witnesses testified. Perkins was sentenced to have the chevrons torn off his sleeves at dress parade, to be drummed out with a dishonorable discharge, and to serve five years in prison. Eight months later, a petition for his release reached Washington, DC. The final record entry reads, "Pardon for unexecuted part of sentence. A. Lincoln Dec. 7, 1864."[40]

At Mechanicsville, William Fitzgerald, 105th Pennsylvania, was tried for the attempted rape of Mrs. Mary McCue. "He came into the house, sat on the edge of my bed, held my shoulders and began pulling off my clothes. I sent the colored girl for the guard. I remember that the prisoner had a blue line worked in the skin around his neck." Fitzgerald got a year in prison.[41]

Sergeant Henry Snow and Private John Gray, both of the 2nd New York, were stationed at Camp Butler near Newport News. Both men were charged with throwing down, ravishing, and injuring "an old Negro woman, Harriet Lane." The trial, held in January 1862, was quickly terminated. The only witness, Harriet Lane, had died.[42]

The trial of George Hakes is a classic in hostile cross-examination. This corporal in the 6th Michigan Cavalry was charged with rape of Mrs. Cornelius Robinson, wife of "a loyal colored citizen," at her home about two miles from Winchester. Hakes came there about one in the afternoon and sent Mr. Robinson on an errand to buy some sheepskin. Mrs. Robinson, who had given birth five days earlier, remained at home. Hakes pushed her into the bedroom. "He said if I did not give up to him that he would shoot me. I said, 'Then you'll have to shoot me.' He put one hand on my mouth and drew out his privates with the other hand. He pulled up my clothes. I shut my legs. I tried to resist him but I was not well. He had one hand on my mouth and one hand on his contrivances."

During the Civil War, it was common for the defendant to conduct his own cross-examination, referring to himself in the third person. Hakes: "Why did you not bite him [i.e., me] when he had his hand on your mouth?" Robinson: "I did not think of it. I was halloeing." "Could you not prevent him from entering you if you had tried?" "I was trying to push him [i.e., you] off me. He told me if I didn't put my legs back on the bed he would kill me." "When he had gained entrance, did you try to throw him off?" "Yes I did, and threw him off two or three times." "How long was he on you before he finished?" "About five or ten minutes" "Did he have an emission while having connection with you?" "Yes!" "Was the sensation pleasant or otherwise to you?" "No, it was not pleasant." After several such bizarre exchanges, the trial closed. Hakes was reduced to the ranks, given a dishonorable discharge, and was sent to serve two years in prison.[43]

In the case of Union Navy quartergunner James Hogden, rape was an afterthought. At White House, on the Pamunkey River, he had attempted to desert to the enemy using a small boat. When captured, he was sentenced to seven years in prison for desertion. The records mention that he "ravaged a colored woman" while ashore, but no charges were filed in regards to the rape.[44]

Thomas Dawson, seems to have been a braggart, confidence man, and rapist. When he joined the 20th Massachusetts, he regaled his new comrades with his exploits during his service with the British Army in the Crimea, including his winning the Cross of Honor, a medal that did not exist. At Morrisville, while he was AWOL, he raped 60-year old Frances West, first in her bed and then in her yard as she fled his assault. A search of her bedroom revealed his suspenders and a wet spot on the mattress. Lincoln refused to mitigate the sentence of death and Dawson was hanged April 20, 1864.[45]

Camp Sheridan was near Stevenson's Depot, about four miles from Winchester. In January 1865, Frederick B. Wells, Company D, 90th Battalion, New York Veteran Volunteers, went AWOL from camp, entered the house of Mary Harvey, and attempted to rape her. Mrs. Harvey said that he threw her down on the bed and choked her, but that no actual sexual activity occurred. There was contradictory testimony as to whether she was married, and as to whether she was a "woman whose character for truth and veracity is very poor." The court decided in favor of Mrs. Harvey and sent Wells to three years at hard labor with a 24-pound ball and chain attached to one ankle.[46]

At Lynchburg, Sergeant Major Alfred Waxey of the 8th Pennsylvania Cavalry was AWOL one night in June 1865. He went to the home of a colored couple living between Sixth and Seventh Streets and drove the man out, in order to rape his wife. The events in the dark were unclear, but the activity was sufficient that Waxey was reduced to the rank of private.[47]

"Being made an example," is usually not a good thing; it was certainly true in the case of Robert H. Hughes, a "colored teamster" with the quartermaster depot. In June 1864, in Kent County, Hughes entered the home of Lucy Atkins, "a white woman," threatened her with a bayonet, stole her butter, threw her down, and tried to "take her clothing up." The following day, he was convicted and sentenced to die. General George Meade endorsed the sentence, writing, "The discipline of this Army requires that an example be made of offenders of this class." Three days later came a final note: "Sentence approved. A. Lincoln June 15, 1864."[48]

Did a guilty man escape? Did the reliability of an eyewitness once more come into question? Captain William Hart, 4th New York Cavalry, was stationed in Frederick County. Margaret Schulenberg's husband was in custody. Captain Hart offered to escort Mrs. Schulenberg to her home. In a wooded area, he pushed her down. "He began by trying to kiss me . . . I resisted . . . I told him I was pregnant . . . He violated my person . . . He had full sexual intercourse with me and satisfied his desires." She distinctly remembered that "he had stripes on his sleeves." As a captain, Hart would have had shoulder straps, not sleeve stripes. He was acquitted. Four months later, Hart was killed in action at Raccoon Ford.[49]

Dr. E. G. Elwell, "veterinary surgeon and horse doctor," was witness to a possible sexual assault at the main sally port of Fort Monroe. In July 1865, Julia Thomas, "colored," threw a brick at William W. Walters, 3rd Pennsylvania Artillery. Walters "threw up her clothes and exposed her person." Whoever was at fault, Walters got fifteen days hard labor and a $5 fine.[50]

Five men were up to mischief one May night in 1863 at Fletcher's Chapel. Four men from the 5th US Artillery (John Southwick, Peter Stone, Charles V. Wells, and Owen Cooper), and Henry Surriver of the 107th Pennsylvania, left camp without permission and came to the house of David and Julia Underwood, "colored." Surriver told the couple, "I have come to have some screwing done." He ordered David to fetch oysters and put his arm around Julia. She threatened: "If you don't stop, I'll cut you with a knife." Stone and Cooper offered some money but did not touch her. Southwick and Wells just stood there silently. Each of the five men was fined one month's pay.[51]

The North Landing River connects the sounds of North Carolina with Hampton Roads and is part of today's Intracoastal Waterway. Five miles southeast of the US Navy's Fentress Field is Pungo (Pongo) Bridge, site of the gang rape of Grace Barnes, on April 28, 1864. The six men involved were all members of the 20th New York Cavalry. James Hallion, Nicholas Kane, Edward Pickett, Thomas Hunt, William Cahill, and John Brennan were on the road near the bridge when they met Grace, who was carrying a bundle of laundry. "They asked me to give them a diddle ... I said no ... they drived me into the woods and threw me down ... five of them had connection with me ... I said, 'For God's sake, let me go home' ... one of them held a stick over my head ... the sweat was pouring off me like water. They never let me rise up my head but twice ... They kept me there for near two hours and a half." Kane said, "I don't know if she laid down for all of us ... but she did for me. I was present when the other four ... had connexion with her. We did not pay her anything. She prostituted herself willing to all the men. I did hear her beg to be let up." The prolonged testimony established varying degrees of guilt. Hallion, whose previous crimes included slicing a guard with his saber, beating up a commissary sergeant, and threatening to kill his lieutenant, was sentenced to be shot, a decision reviewed twice by Lincoln. In the end, Ben Butler commuted the penalty to three years in prison.

Kane, Pickett, and Brennan received dishonorable discharges and five years in prison. Hunt received only three years, in view of his "extreme youth." Several witnesses verified that Cahill did not have intercourse with Grace; he was acquitted. Just as the four rapists were buttoning their pants, Sergeant Owen Curren arrived. Grace recalled, "I prayed him, I begged of him, for God's sake let me go home. I am near about dead. I was standing then and he [Curren] threw me down again, right hard. Then he had connexion with me, but didn't but one time. He was the last man who had connexion with me. I still can't hold my water." Curren also got five years in prison and a dishonorable discharge.[52]

A soldier of the 17th Maine noted in his diary that on December 10, 1864, Colonel Edwin R. Biles, 99th Pennsylvania and his adjutant were "perpetrating one of the vilest outrages upon two defenseless women." According to diarist John W. Haley, the two men offered to burn the women's house down unless they submitted to "infamous proposals." Haley noted that private soldiers would be hanged for such a crime, but "Old Byles is an officer." At the end of the war, Biles was brevetted brigadier general, for "gallant and meritorious service."[53]

Chapter 14

RAPE IN THE CAROLINAS

North Carolina

At New Bern, Second Lieutenant Hugh Gallagher of the 158th New York was on a drunken rampage. While claiming he was officer of the guard, he slashed the face of a sentry, drove a 70-year-old woman out of her house, and tore off her clothes. "He put his hand on my hip." (In Victorian terms, this usually meant buttock.) Gallagher claimed she was in a house of prostitution, an idea induced by whiskey, not reality. The March 1863 trial dismissed him from the army.[1]

Hospital Steward Eugène Hannel of the 2nd Maryland was stationed at New Bern in September 1863. He was charged with raping Rebecca Ann Cradle, a "colored girl" employed at the hospital. Witnesses said he fed her Spanish fly, locked her in his room and beat her. A surgeon told the court: "She was admitted to the hospital in a state of mild mania, sometimes insane, sometimes lucid . . . her private parts were lacerated and swollen, her hymen was intact but lacerated, scratches were on her legs . . . her insanity was caused by a concussion of the brain from the stoppage of her menstrual flow, which she had at the time of the violence." Hannel was given two years in prison.[2]

The trial transcript of Robert Ireland, 5th US Colored Troops, is missing. He was convicted of rape at New Bern in August 1865 and sentenced to ten years in prison. His service record says he enlisted in July 1863 at Cincinnati. At that time he was a 44-year-old boatman, 5'8", with black hair. In November 1865 his sentence was overturned by Holt, and Ireland was returned to his regiment. Further details seem lost forever.[3]

There was a camp for white refugees at New Bern. On June 4, 1864, Frank Failey, US Army Signal Corps, was another man on a drunken rampage. Not only did he assault a sentinel and steal clothing, but he allegedly attacked two women. Mrs. Matilda Kither, in bed with a very sick child, was awakened by a man "kissing me and fooling with me . . . I cried and talked good and bad and asked him to get off me . . . He did not leave . . . He ravaged me . . . It was dark . . . I cannot be sure who it was." Witness William Schiffer of Company F, 3rd New York Cavalry, asleep in the next room, was awakened by the noises in Mrs. Kither's room. "I saw one man lying on the floor. I saw him have connexion with her . . . there have been a good many other such circumstances but this is the only one I have seen so well. She did not object to his 'sparking' her." Mrs. Bretty Tolson, the other victim listed in the charges, and her family occupied three nearby rooms in the refugee barracks. She said nothing happened to her that night. The charge of rape was dropped, but for drunk and disorderly behavior, Failey was fined six months pay.[4]

In Mecklenburg County, "colored citizen" Emanuel Baxter was charged with the rape of Mrs. Elizabeth Russell. Investigation showed that Baxter had lived in the house for four years (probably as a slave) and that Mrs. Russell had moved into what had been Baxter's room. It appeared that he had not been notified of the change. "It used to be Baxter's room . . . I screamed . . . he did not touch me." Baxter was acquitted.[5]

The extremely faded records of Private John Cornish, 30th US Colored Troops, tell us that he was convicted of attempted rape in April 1865, at Raleigh. He was sentenced to hang, but this was commuted by President Andrew Johnson.[6]

At Raleigh, Mrs. Dilsey Jones, a "colored freedwoman," former slave of a Mr. Haywood, and more recently an employee of Mrs. Ann Bagwell, was shopping for a basket at the store of Cook and Upchurch on Hargett (?) Street. Charles Cook invited her upstairs to see his stock of baskets. Upstairs, "He caught hold of me by the right arm and also by the throat and threw me on the bed, and continued choking me, and put his knee on my chest . . . He unbuttoned his breeches, then he pulled up my clothes and threw my legs apart. Then he got on me. He did what he wanted to and ravaged me. I said I'd tell my husband, and he said, 'Go ahead, tell him, Goddamn you.'" The court asked, "What attempt, if any, did you make to prevent the prisoner doing what he wanted to?" "He had me so tight I couldn't do anything." The court also asked if she could read or write (she could not) and about her knowledge of the calendar. "I know there are twelve months in the year, but I don't know what this date is today." The date of the trial was early April 1866. They acquitted Charles Cook, the white defendant.[7]

On the road running northeast from Wilmington, one mile from Smith's Creek Bridge, five men pushed a nameless 16-year-old "colored girl" into the bushes. When they emerged, the men were laughing and the girl told a nearby witness, "They tried to take my maidenhead." Only one man was tried for this crime. John Murray, 117th New York, was court-martialed in May 1865 and acquitted. The victim did not testify.[8]

There was a "Camp of Contrabands" on the south side of the Cape Fear River, opposite Wilmington. There, on the evening of April 22, 1865, William McManus, 33rd New Jersey, attempted to rape Julia Jennison, "colored." "I was in Lieutenant O'Brien's room making the bed. It was dark; I had a candle lit. The defendant and another man come in. The defendant lit his pipe and ask if I'd sleep with him. I told him no. He said I got to do it. I told him I wouldn't. He knocked me down with a chair. Before he hit me, he catched me under my dress and commenced after me there and I commenced knocking after him. He knocked me in the eye, and said, 'Jeff Davis had but one eye and why couldn't I have.' I had the other man down on the floor." The sergeant who arrested McManus (the other man escaped) said he knew nothing of any attempted rape. McManus was sentenced to have his head shaved and to receive a dishonorable discharge. Brigadier General Joseph R. Hawley, a native North Carolinian, disapproved the sentence, "the evidence being deemed insufficient."[9]

At Smithfield, James Lee, 4th US Colored Troops, left his regiment in April 1865, stole an ox, shot at the ox's owner, molested three women—from whom Lee stole socks and gloves—and used "low and coarse language" to 15-year-old Miss Alice Michener, whom he attempted to violate. Lee was sentenced to hang. Holt commuted the sentence to ten years in prison because the rape was not completed.[10]

Also at Smithfield, "colored citizen" Aston Beckwith was charged with the attempted rape of "a girl named Fanny (col'd)." Fanny Simpson testified: "I was walking alone when I met him at Buffalo Hill. He told me he was going to carry me over into the bushes and get on me. He then carried me into the bushes. I try to get away and he hit me. He then flung me down and got on me. He threw my clothes over my head and hurt me right here [points to her stomach]. He unbuttoned his pants. He tried to have connection with me and hurt me badly." Nancy York, "colored citizen," testified. "The white people sent her to be to be examined. I am a midwife. I took the girl and stripped her and examined her. I saw no signs whatever of her having been ravaged or any attempt to ravage." Aston was acquitted.[11]

Sixteen-year-old Willson Dosier, an illiterate former slave, was tried in September 1865 for the attempted rape of 14-year-old Elizabeth Miller, in Currituck County. "I was passing along a lane some distance from my home. He was in a field and came to the fence and said, 'If you don't lie down and let me put my prick in your cock [female genitalia in 1860s slang], I will whip you,' and he began to cut a whip. There was a boy and a girl with me and we all started and ran. The defendant ran after me a little way." Dosier got a month in jail. Miller's race was not specified.[12]

At Kinston, James Preble, a 22-year-old former railroad brakeman and member of the 12th New York, raped Miss Letitia Craft and attempted to rape Mrs. Rebecca Drake and Miss Louise Bedard, on March 16, 1865. He was shot by a firing squad two weeks later, at Goldsboro. At Goldsboro, in April 1865, Corporal A. C. Warner, 9th Illinois Mounted Infantry, was tried and acquitted of attempted rape upon Nicy Allen, "colored woman."[13]

At Trenton, in May 1865, "colored citizen" John Korneday stole from three different citizens a wide assortment of items: meat, eggs, lard, cornmeal, peas, and an ox. He also raped Eliza Betts. "He laid me down on the floor and committed a rape in front of the children." Korneday was sentenced to ten years in prison, the first five years with a 24-pound ball and chain.[14]

Forced sex with a small boy seems to constitute a form of rape. Charles Manly, age eleven and a small Negro boy named Myatt were driving a steer-drawn cart near Raleigh. Patrick Hickey, 3rd New York, climbed into the cart and told Myatt to walk next to the steer. The three proceeded slowly along the tree-shaded country road. Charles described what happened next: "The man said he belonged to Lee's army and had killed four Yankees. After we were about two miles from the city he unbuttoned his pants and made me rub his privates. After we had passed 200 yards he made me rub his privates again. When we had passed 2 miles further he made me put his privates into my mouth and rub them. I then commenced crying. I asked him to let me alone and he said yes. He promised to return the next day and bring me some candy." The court asked:

"How often did you rub his privates?" "The first time in the cart, the second time in the woods, and once after that time. He said if I didn't stop crying he'd shoot me." The court asked if anything happened during the rubbing. "Some white stuff came out each time."

Myatt, age eleven, lived with the Manly family. He remembered the defendant: "Yes, sir, I saw him with Dr. Manley's little son Charles. Mr. Hickey made him suck his privates." The defendant got a dishonorable discharge and a year in prison.[15]

The Caswell Wood family lived on the Neuse Road, fourteen miles from New Bern. One night in January 1863, Farrier Germain Goodrich and a Corporal Wheedon, both of the 3rd New York Cavalry, drank two or three bottles of whiskey and began to think about women. Wheedon said he knew of a house of prostitution a few miles up the road. When they arrived, they tied the head of the household, Caswell Wood, to a tree and confined Mrs. Wood to the kitchen. Goodrich dragged their daughter, Penelope, into a different room and closed the door. "He said he'd like to marry me for an hour. I did not agree. He stripped off everything but a little short flannel shirt. He asked if I was going to strip. I made no reply. He came to me, broke my apron string, unfastened my dress and stripped off everything I had on but my shift. Then he forced me down. He worked until he found he could not succeed in his wishes. He offered me three dollars which I refused. Then, he seemed to realize he was not in a house of prostitution and he fell asleep. I got dressed and sat by the window until day. Then the chickens came and crowed and woke up the corporal who was asleep on the piazza." The court gave Goodrich eighteen months of prison at hard labor and a dishonorable discharge. "The court is thus lenient on account of the impression in the mind of the accused that he was in a house of ill fame."[16]

Enoch George, 5th Ohio Veteran Volunteers, was convicted of raping Mrs. Nisa Grimes, a married colored woman, at Raleigh. The trial was held eighteen hours after the event. A surgeon testified that Mrs. Grimes was distressed and physically sick. George was sentenced to life imprisonment. General Henry W. Slocum reviewed the case and noticed that George had fastened the door with her consent and that she had "heated water and taken a bath preparatory to being ravaged [that] does not indicate such a degree of resistance on her part." While Slocum noted the need to "punish all outrages" in this case, he released the prisoner and returned him to duty.[17]

Thomas Ennis of the 6th Iowa was charged with the rape of 27-year-old Mrs. Caroline Neal, who told the court, "I haven't seen my husband in two years; I don't know if he is dead or alive." She and her mother lived in a small house a mile from Grove Hill, in Warren County. Ennis rode up and hitched his horse. "Mom told him she hoped he would have pity on us poor folks. He went in the house and took the priming out of our gun. He demanded our revolvers, but we had none. He said he'd kill us, but if we would supply what he wanted he would save us. Ma said he could not want anything of her, and she was an old woman with a heap of children. He looked at me and said that young woman will do. I said I was 27 and no young woman and married, but he said that made no difference." Ennis grabbed Caroline's neck with one arm while holding his gun in the other, threw her on the bed and had connection. The court asked, "Did the flesh of the prisoner enter your person—was there actual penetration?" She said yes. The court convicted Ennis and gave him two years at hard labor.[18]

At Rocky Run, Charles Alberts, 12th New York Cavalry, beat up Emeline Tucker and her husband. Mr. Tucker said, "The defendant raped my wife." She told the court, "He put his pecker right into me." Contradictory testimony led the court to acquit Alberts.[19]

On the march to Cox's Bridge, James White, 37th US Colored Troops, stopped at a household of two women and several children. He grabbed one woman around the neck, tried to kiss her, held a pistol to her head and said he'd kill her unless she would let him go to bed with her. In spite of White's surprisingly literate written defense, he was convicted of "insulting a woman," and was given two years at hard labor.[20]

In the case of Patrick Tully, 12th New York Cavalry, was the court particularly obtuse or just meticulous in their search for the truth, or perhaps even voyeuristic? Tully raped Casey Ransom, "colored," at Newport Barracks. "This man came to the house . . . said he was officer of the night . . . offered me two dollars . . . I told him I did not want it . . . he threw me on the floor . . . said if I hollered he'd hit me on the head with his pistol . . . he pulled up my clothing and took out his 'what's his name' . . . he put it in me . . . I did not like it." The court asked: "What did this man put into you?" "He put his pecker into me." "What do you mean by the word pecker?" "The thing he calls his prick." "In what part of your body did he put his prick?" "He put it in my cunt." The court was finally satisfied. They gave Tully two years in prison and a dishonorable discharge.[21]

Alabama was a Confederate state, but, starting in 1862, the Union raised six Alabama regiments. Sergeant James Lee of the 1st Alabama Cavalry was at Granville County, where he was charged with the theft of money, flour, dried apples, cornmeal, ham, and horses, as well as killing a man's dog. He was also charged with the rape of Martha Taber, "colored." (The extensive records are badly stained, but much is legible.) She told the court: "He drew his pistol and told me if I did not do as he asked he would kill me. He made me go to the house with him, shut the door and told me to spread myself . . . or die . . . then he ravaged me."

Sergeant Lee's defense took two avenues. The first was race. "She is not competent to testify because she is a free person of color within the fourth degree. A mulatto, the product of a black and a white is in the first degree. The product of a mulatto and a white is in the second degree. A product of that person and a white is in the third degree and the product of that and a white is in the fourth degree. That is one-sixteenth Negro blood. It is only in the fifth degree that a Negro may testify. That is the rule of evidence in North Carolina." Lee's other line of defense was character. He produced five witnesses who swore that Martha Tabor was a liar, a drunk, and a public whore. Lee was acquitted.[22]

George P. Lawton, 5th Ohio Cavalry, was in Franklin County in June 1865. He was charged with stealing a large bay horse belonging to a Mrs. Foster, and with the attempted rape of Martha Jones, "colored." There was no evidence presented regarding the rape. The court focused entirely upon the horse. Lawson was fined $20 for his theft.[23]

At Asheville, in early May 1865, four men of Company E, 1st US Colored Heavy Artillery, raped Miss O. Garrison. The perpetrators were Privates Alexander Caldwell, Alfred Cutlett, Washington Jackson, and Musician Charles Turner. They were tried by drumhead court-martial and shot the next day in front of their regiment.[24]

South Carolina

Charleston was the site of several sexual offenses. On February 6, 1866, Betsey Jones, "colored," age fourteen, was in the kitchen of a home at 66 Wentworth Street. R. H. Vanderhorst, "colored," entered the room. "He caught me around my neck. I got away from him. I told him to let me alone. He said if

I moved again he would stick me with his pocketknife . . . also that he would cut my throat. He scared me and I stood still. He pulled up my frock. I stood up until another woman came . . . and he ran away." She added that he had entered her and that it was against her will. Vanderhorst said that she had "played with him" and had asked for money. "I had not time to commit the offense . . . It was impossible that I could commit a rape upon the girl of her age." The court disagreed and sentenced him to "be hung by the neck until he is dead." General Dan Sickles thought the evidence insufficient to hang a man and disapproved the sentence.[25]

Luckey Glass, "colored citizen," was charged with raping a white child, Geraldine Ann Jarcke, age eight, at Charleston. The date was February 24, 1866. "My mother left the house and left me at home. The prisoner came into my room, threw me on the floor, threw a blanket over my head, stuffed it in my mouth, took out his privates and pushed them inside my privates." Glass was an employee of Mrs. Jarcke. Dr. Alfred Raoul was summoned. "I found the little girl very much excited and trembling." He made a physical examination. "I found the parts very sensitive to the touch, contused, engorged, bruised, and intensely inflamed." Glass denied the crime but was sentenced to be hanged. General Sickles reduced the penalty to five years at Sing Sing Prison, citing Glass's "youth." From prison, Glass wrote to General U. S. Grant, complaining that he had been tried without counsel. The appeal was referred to Holt, who was unsympathetic. "The proof of his guilt was complete . . . his sentence was commuted to confinement . . . for five years, of which he has served sixteen months. The crime was one of unmitigated atrocity, for which death was probably the appropriate penalty."[26]

Was thirteen-year-old Ellen Collins the victim of rape and abduction or was she a willing celebrant at a two-day party? White citizen Hamilton Woolf was charged with keeping Ellen prisoner at Charleston's Tivoli Gardens for two days in July of 1865. "I was going to school with my books, to Mrs. Bingley's in Mill Street. I met Mary Millar. She asked me if I would go with her to a house opposite Woolf's bar room in Ring Street. We went into the house and Clarence Woolf came in with a bottle of whiskey. He offered me some but I did not take it. Mary got so drunk she could hardly stand, and asked me to stay with her until she was sober and we would go on to school. It was about quarter to nine when we came to the house and about one o'clock she had got over." From this point the story became tangled and contradictory. Ellen, Mary Millar, Sissy Cambridge, Mary Beamer, a Miss Sigwald, Mary Jane Griffiths and Mary Lee were all involved. The witnesses disagreed about whose undergarments were torn, who slept with whom, who was bleeding, and who might have pressed charges in order to force a marriage. Out of these 65 pages of youth run wild came the court's decision: Hamilton Woolf was not guilty. This unusual transcript, with its detailed addresses, lurid stories of young delinquent white girls, and loss of parental control, is a unique glimpse into Charleston life after four years of war.[27]

Beaufort was also a scene of carnal misdeeds. Four men of the 56th New York were particularly disgraceful, abusing the very persons whose sufferings had aroused the sympathy of the abolitionists. In April 1864, all four men were AWOL for two hours, between 9 A.M. and 11 A.M. John Davis broke into Betsy Gladson's house with an axe, and hit her with a stick. She testified: "He held my feet down for Private [Robert] Corey." James Jackson was charged with aiding in the rape by Corey, who himself was charged with attempted rape. Captain H. P. Killain testified that he had interviewed Betsy Gladson, who was "crying very loud." Betsy recalled Corey breaking down her door and hitting her. "Then he turned my clothes over my head and went in on me, the other man holding my feet." The court asked, "Did the prisoner have connection with you?" She replied, "I don't understand what you mean." After some clarification, she continued. "He choked me half to death to hinder me from hollowing. After that he took his prick out and I felt it on my right leg." Corey denied the rape, the assault, and the charge of being absent without leave. Davis, Corey, and Jackson were given brief sentences for being AWOL, and acquitted of both rape and assault. Richard Kennedy was cleared by a 13-year-old "colored boy" who said, "He's not the one who did it." Although the victim testified, her opinion was ignored.[28]

Three men of the 79th New York, James Meoliff, John Cowing, and Robert Crozier, were charged with maltreating a Negro family at Beaufort. Corporal Thomas Gallagher of the provost guard recalled, "A colored man came running up and said some men were misusing the women. He showed me the way. As we went upstairs in the back piazza, Crozier knocked the Negro down. Meoliff was in the garden having a tussle with a Negro woman. She was trying to get away. He told me to clear out. My opinion was a he was trying to force the woman and have connection with her. She was Tina, a slave." Meoliff was fined six dollars a month for two months and put in solitary for ten days. The other two soldiers were acquitted.[29]

Peter McGuire of the 55th Pennsylvania was accused of trying to rape the women in the household of Jesse Barnwell, "colored," near Beaufort. Jesse told the court, "The prisoner said, 'I will lie with them or I will kill you.'" The women fled the house and hid in the underbrush. In the December 1864 verdict, McGuire was given a month at hard labor for being AWOL, but acquitted of his threats of rape and murder.[30]

The final Beaufort case was an assault upon an "old Negro woman." (She was forty years old.) George W. Collins of the 8th Maine, a man of "good character," was the defendant. The principal witness was Second Lieutenant C. S. Doubleday of the 2nd Battalion, Invalid Corps. "I had been up at the parade ground watching the colored regiment drill. I was coming down the street and

I saw this man had a Negro woman down on the ground rolling her around the street. She was crying out for help. She said he was trying to feel her." The location was "A" street, "between No. 11 and No. 5 hospitals. No one bothered to ask the victim's name, nor was she asked to testify. Collins was given a year at hard labor and fined $10 a month for 12 months.[31]

McPhersonville was the scene of an attack by five members of the 104th US Colored Troops: Benjamin Redding, James Grippen, Henry Davis, Gabriel Richardson, and Howard Dixon. At night in late August 1865, a group led by Redding burned the house of Mrs. Mary Heape, beat her son, and raped her young daughter, Euselia. The same group attacked the house of Mrs. Emily Mew, raping her and Mrs. Mary McTier. The men also threatened other citizens with bayonets and stole various household items. Redding and Grippen were both convicted of multiple rapes and were hanged, "in the presence of their regiment," at Hilton Head in late November 1865. Davis and Richardson were convicted of assisting in the rapes. Both men were put to hard labor until the end of their enlistments and given dishonorable discharges. Dixon was acquitted.[32]

In October 1865, a "colored girl," Sarah, who worked at Murray Robinson's plantation, was beaten and raped at Rowe's Pump. Her assailant was Oscar Mendelsohn of the 54th New York Veteran Volunteers. He chased the sixteen-year-old victim and threatened to kill a "colored man" who tried to protect her. "He caught me by the breast, threw me down and ravaged me for a quarter of an hour." Mendelsohn got five years at hard labor and a dishonorable discharge.[33]

Near Benettsville, on March 6, 1865, a party of foragers from the 10th Illinois heard crying coming from an isolated house in the woods. William Walker recalled, "We approached quietly, thinking there might be a rebel in there. We found a man [Sergeant Arthur McCarty, 78th Ohio Veteran Volunteers] on top of a girl about age eighteen. She was down on a pile of corn sacks and her clothes were up, exposing her person. She was crying for her mother. The man rose up, buttoned his pants and remarked, 'If you want any fucking . . . there was an easy-going thing to pitch in.' We did not arrest him because he said he had paid money." A witness for the defense, Corporal Jacob Madsen, 78th Ohio, said that the girl, Martha Clowell, had been named as a prostitute by a twelve-year-old boy in town. "I gave her a dollar in greenbacks and had connection with her." McCarty told the court, "I gave her a quarter of a dollar in silver." The girl did not testify. McCarty was convicted, drummed out, and sent to prison for two years, but was released by President Andrew Johnson before serving the entire sentence.[34]

An ancient medical adage is *primum non nocerum*—first of all, do no harm. This precept was violated by Assistant Surgeon Charles F. Lauer of the 55th Pennsylvania, charged with multiple rapes at the Milne Plantation on Port Royal Island. The doctor began the trial with a long legal quibble about precision in the charges. Once the trial began, he objected to the testimony of colored people (the witnesses against him) on grounds that they could not comprehend the nature of an oath. All his objections were overruled. Testimony began with Rebecca Smith.

> I was sitting on a bench. The doctor came along and sat along side of me and asked me if I would do it. I said no. He asked me why. I told him because I didn't want to do it and then I went into the house. He followed me. When I said again I wouldn't do it, he slapped me. When I called my Aunt Sarah, he picked up a chair by the leg—it had no back—and struck me over the eye. He kicked me twice in the stomach and boxed me on the face. I went out the door and told Captain Nesbitt, who said he didn't think the doctor would do such a thing.

The defendant cross-examined Rebecca. "Did you fall over a chair and cut your face?" "No." "Did you fall against the door and cut your face?" "No." The next woman to testify was Sarah Allen. "I am well acquainted with him [Dr. Lauer]. I used to do his laundry. I heard him trying to get her to go to his tent. She didn't want to. He slapped her and I said to him, 'Doctor . . . when a woman did not give up to him, he should leave her alone instead of striking her.' He told me to go back to bed."

The next witnesses was Eda "colored," who said that he came to her house on three nights, wanting to "knock" her. She finally took to sleeping in the cotton fields so he would not bother her. He punched her with his fist when she refused. The court tested her for general knowledge, to clarify her suitability as a witness. Eda was certain that it was July, because it was "watermelon time."

Sixty more pages of testimony included allegations that Rebecca was promiscuous, that his assault upon "Jane, colored" was a medical examination, and many comments upon the details of Union administration of a plantation. In the end, the doctor was convicted of attempted rape, reprimanded, and suspended from rank and pay for two months. In the reprimand, published in General Orders No. 67, General Rufus Saxton exclaimed, "It is his [i.e., my] duty to express his regret that any officer wearing the uniform of the United States Army should have so dishonored the service and [his] honorable profession."[35]

Colonel Richard White, commanding the 55th Pennsylvania, was charged with running after "a Negro woman," throwing her on the ground, and attempting to violate her person at Edisto Island, on June 26, 1862. He was acquitted of this charge, along with two charges of being drunk and disorderly.[36]

At Tripp's Plantation on St. Helena Island, Prince Chaplin, "colored citizen," was charged with the rape of Rosina Pinckney. "He often asked me to do it with him but I never did. This time, he threw me down on the road and raised my clothes. He choked me. He connected with me." Chaplin was given nine months at hard labor.[37]

At Summerville, on March 19, 1866, a woman named President Miller was raped by Musician Frank Harrison of the 35th US Colored Troops. "It was between midnight and day. Harrison and a man named Kelly Clark kicked in our door. The prisoner forced me to have connection with him. I never saw him before that night." Miller's sister, Sarah Lee, confirmed the story. Harrison received a dishonorable discharge and was sent off to five years of hard labor, part of the time with a ball and chain. Another member of the 35th US Colored Troops, Captain Edward S. Daniels, came close to a rape charge. At Brown's Hotel in Summerville, he was drunk, tried to force his way into women's rooms, and said, "They are a parcel of whores . . . this nothing but a damned whorehouse." He was dismissed.[38]

The final South Carolina rape case was set at Folly Island. The New York Independent Battery was stationed there in the summer of 1863. Second Lieutenant François Wallenus was very drunk when he forced himself into the quarters of several soldiers. He took hold of one of the wives, who resisted him. He told several enlisted men, "If you will hold her down, I will force her." She recalled, "He told me what he wanted to do, in words too indecent even to tell my husband. He held my arms. He put his hands up my clothes." General Israel Vogdes was disturbed by the verdict of acquittal and sent the case to Holt, who replied, "Upon what grounds the court based their decision it is difficult to conceive. The proof is positive, the testimony of the lady is uncontradicted and unimpeached. Besides this outrage, the conduct of the accused in drinking with enlisted men . . . is sufficient of itself to demand his summary dismissal by order of the President." Under Holt's note is the following, in a familiar hand: "This officer is dishonorably dismissed. A. Lincoln."[39]

Chapter 15

RAPE IN THE DEEP SOUTH

Mississippi

At Natchez, in the summer of 1865, Patrick Manning, 8th New Hampshire Veteran Volunteers, was on guard duty. He neglected his duty by getting drunk and attempting to rape Clara Greer, "a lady." She told the court, "I live on Maine Street, between Union and Rankin Streets. He tried to throw me down. I hollered and he kicked me. He offered me five dollars, which I refused. He wanted to take advantage of me." Manning got three years at hard labor and a dishonorable discharge.[1]

Mrs. Caroline Andrews of Biloxi was visiting Ship Island in May 1865. Peter Small, 74th US Colored Troops, was charged with raping her. At the trial, she testified that he had not been anywhere near her, nor had any assault of any sort occurred. The records do not clarify why he was charged. Small was acquitted.[2]

Alabama

At Montgomery, four men of the 52nd Indiana broke down the door of Penny Robinson just before daybreak in May 1865. "They knocked me down and all four men had connexion with me." She and the colored woman in the next room identified the men as Josh Childers, Mark Tulley, Lewis Sappington, and G. Hoopengamer; the latter was the fourth and last man to rape her. Tulley claimed he was too drunk to remember anything. All four men were sentenced to five years in prison.[3]

Also at Montgomery, two men of the 1st Louisiana Cavalry (Union) were charged with the rape of Louise, a 14-year-old "colored girl." The first man charged was James Deery. "He and two others grabbed me on Jerusalem Street, right in front of Mr. Crawford's Bible House, at ten in the morning. They dragged me into an empty blacksmith shop. He hit me with his fist and said, 'I'm going to have you if it costs my life.' He smelled of whiskey . . . when he unbuttoned his pantaloons, his person was exposed. Then the guards came and took him off." A second man, Augustus Morrison, stood by as a lookout, waiting his turn at rape. Deery asked for clemency, declaring "an officer gave the whiskey and I remembered nothing. Besides my widowed mother is dependent upon me." Geary got five years in prison, Morrison only three.[4]

Twelve miles from Selma, in Perry County, 30-year-old Mrs. Mary A. Cummings was raped by one of her former slaves, Green Cummings, on April 4, 1865. "In the house was me, my daughter and a nigger girl. Green came in the room and said if I didn't submit that me and my little girl and the house would be destroyed instantly, the Yankees would throw sky balls over the house. Then he forced me and had intercourse with me. He injured me. I was in no fix whatever for no such person . . . . He also said that the Federals had ordered him to do this and that I must go and live in the black folks house." (Mary's husband, who had been captured while fighting with the Confederate militia, was not at the trial.) The defendant was sentenced to be hanged.[5]

Citizen John Riley of Cahawba was tried for manslaughter and rape in the summer of 1865. The dead woman was Jane, a slave of the defendant. Jane, a crippled woman, "over 50 years old," had been ordered to "spin six cuts of cotton per day." When she failed in meeting her quota, Riley beat her with a buggy whip, a handsaw, and a club and left her bleeding from the mouth and nose. She died. Martha, a younger slave, resisted his sexual advances. He told her, "Goddamn you, I've bought you for my own use." He raped her often and beat her each time she refused him. He had recently tied her across a log and given her 500 lashes for resisting him. Riley was convicted of assault, was fined $10, and was given a week in jail.[6]

German-speaking Captain Louis Heizer of the 9th Ohio was tried for conduct unbecoming an officer and a gentleman. At Tuscumbia, in February 1863, he went to a private home and addressed the lady of the house thusly: "Is your husband not in the house? I fuck you once if it must be." Heizer was acquitted.[7]

Paul, a "Negro cook" with the 80th Ohio Veteran Volunteers, was at Jackson County in the spring of 1864 when he was tried for the attempted rape of a thirteen-year-old white girl, Sarah Williamson. "I am almost 14. I live near Larkinsville. Paul often came to our well for water. One day in May he came in the house, sat in a chair and tried to pull me onto his lap. I hollered and he went out. Then he came back and threw me on the bed and pulled up my clothes. I began to scream and he ran out and over to the railroad." Her father, J. H. Williamson, said he could clearly see finger marks on her neck. Paul got six months in the Huntsville jail.[8]

Ishmael, a "colored citizen" of Madison County, was charged with the rape of Miss Sylvester Johnson, a sixteen-year-old girl of Huntsville. It was a dark night and identification was difficult. "I could tell he was a nigger by feeling his head. It was wooley. His privates entered my private parts." Without a positive identification Ishmael was acquitted.[9]

William H. Wood, 21st Wisconsin, was raising hell at Camp Dawson in July 1863. He went to the home of a 50-year-old widow and threatened to play "Hail, Columbia" with her house. He trapped a 24-year old girl in a springhouse and refused to release her "until I get my way with you." Wood was fined a year's pay and put in jail for sixty days.[10]

Henry B. Kerone, a lieutenant in the 40th Missouri, was frequently drunk and disorderly in the spring of 1865. At Greenville, by the use of force, he made a "colored woman, name unknown" lie down and submit to sexual intercourse. He told her: "We have set you free and we intend to do as we please with you." Several witnesses said they saw Kerone "ravish" her. He was acquitted.[11]

At Holyoke, Mary Bankister was raped by two soldiers of the 1st Louisiana Cavalry (Union): Frank Enger and Joseph Holroyed. "I am aged 21 and live six miles from Blakely on the Blakely and Pensacola Road. I was at home at my father-in-law's house at night on the fifth day of April 1865. The two men came to the house. Enger took his pistol and said if I did not submit he would shoot me. He took me down on the floor and said if I resisted he'd kill me and set the house afire. His member entered my body only a little—not as bad as the other one." The court asked, "How many inches did his member penetrate your body?" She answered, "I suppose two inches." After Enger raped her, he passed out drunk. Then Holroyed made her remove all her clothes and get into bed. She pleaded the need to attend to her small child, but he ignored her. "He had sexual intercourse with me five times and he penetrated my body as far as it was possible each time. He caused me very much pain." Both men were given dishonorable discharges and ten years in prison at Dry Tortugas.[12]

Florida

Three men of the 55th Massachusetts (colored) were tried for a rape committed near Jacksonville on February 17, 1864. Mrs. Sarah Hammond, who lived near Cedar Creek, said, "I screamed and begged for mercy, but they threw me on the ground. One violated me while the other three held me. Then they took turns." John M. Smith was age 21, with light complexion, born at Old Towne, Maine. Lloyd Spencer was also age 21, born in Delaware and could not read or write. John Cook was 23. All three men were hanged the day after the crime. A fourth man, Wallace Baker, escaped but was later shot for mutiny.[13]

Thomas Little, a private in the US Marine Corps was tried for attempted rape near Pensacola. He left his guard post at the Navy Yard and tried to rape

Martha Woodham in her own home at the refugee camp at Warrington. Woodham did not testify, but her roommate, Mary Rice, had this to say: "Mr. Little tore off all Miss Woodham's clothes and exposed his person." When arrested, Little persuaded the guard to let him stop at a saloon for a drink. There he escaped, ran to another saloon, and ordered seven glasses of ale, which he drank until violently subdued. At the trial, Little's commander described his character as "bad." Another witness noted, "It is common for a Marine to be drunk and disorderly." A defense witness said that both women were "common prostitutes . . . I know . . . I have had carnal intercourse with both of them." Little was sent to prison for five years.[14]

James Bernard, a frequently drunk "old man," was a native of France and a stevedore by trade, living alone near the beach at Warrington. He was charged with the January 1865 rape of Sarah Allison, age eleven. The victim was "subject to fits and is of unsound mind." Other records described her "mental imbecility." Her mother heard Sarah crying as she emerged from a nearby house, saying, "The old man hurt me." The mother promptly entered Bernard's house and found him lying in a "very much tumbled bed," with blood on his face. Sarah, also, was bleeding from facial injuries. A US Navy report noted that Sarah was "too ill to be interrogated," and Surgeon J. R. Tryon certified that a rape had been attempted, verifying the mother's report that Sarah's "Private parts were rubbed raw." Bernard denied any wrongdoing, but was sentenced to a year of hard labor.[15]

Some court decisions are puzzling. Such is the case with John Doyle, 15th Maine. One night in June 1863, he broke into the Pensacola home of the wife of Captain James Williams. "I was asleep. Mr. Doyle broke the door down. He said he was with the secret police, to see if white people had Negroes hidden in their homes. With his strength, he overpowered me in spite of everything I could do to resist him. I was forced to do as he willed. He said if I had him arrested he would blow my brains out. He threatened me with his bayonet." Doyle presented quite a different story. "I have witnesses who will testify that she has loose morals, but I can't produce them just now. Mrs. Williams liked it [intercourse] and asked me for money." He was acquitted.[16]

At Tampa, Mate Benjamin P. Hale of the USS *Sagamore* was tried for attempted rape. It was autumn of 1865. Fifteen-year-old-Martha Delia Roland ("colored") had gone down to the beach to see the boats come in. "Mr. Hale threw me on the ground under a tree and tried to pull up my clothes. He unbuttoned his pantaloons. I yelled for help and my mother came. He offered me money to make it right." Hale was convicted and dismissed. Another puzzling record is seen in the case of Landsman Michael F. Gavican of the USS *Cimarron*. In June 1864, he was charged with the "brutal rape of a Negro woman, Ritter Connors," at Lighthouse Point. The record shows no prosecution, no testimony and no defense.[17]

The farm of Hampton Smith was in Levy County. There, in July 1865, "colored citizen" Calvin Brown "entered the sleeping room of Mrs. Nancy Ann Smith, seized her by the throat and used threatening language, with intent to violate her person, while she was in bed." The pages of testimony are missing but they were apparently convincing enough to send Brown to prison for fifteen years.[18]

Citizen Joseph Stafford was charged with the attempted rape of Alvina Ann Hancock at St. Marks, in the autumn of 1865. Their stories are remarkably different. "I stopped along the road to talk to a citizen. Mr. Stafford came up and said, 'Goddamn you. Didn't you know that I was your friend. Come out here in the bushes. If you don't give me what I ask for, I'll stab you, you Goddamned bitch.' Then he patted me on the shoulder and offered me money. He was still holding a cocked gun. Then he hit me on the head with a gun and split my hip with a Bowie knife. When he offered me money he asked me to give him some cock. He said I looked so sweet he wanted to taste me." Dr. G. H. Kittler described a 1 1/2 inch cut on the right side of her psoas muscle. The defense witness painted a different picture. William I. Moore, a farmer, said, "I know nothing to his character contrary to being good. I know he is a member of the Free Will Baptist Church. I also know Alvina Ann Hancock. She stopped at my place a few days. I had some colored men hired. She got to be so troublesome with the men that I was compelled to turn her off. Her general reputation was bad. My family says she is a strumpet and that she uses awful language." I. G. Skipper, who had known Stafford since he was a little boy, described him as "harmless and inoffensive." Stafford was found guilty and sent to Dry Tortugas for five years.[19]

The Commodore's Pump was located in Wolsey, near Barrancas. Mary Jones, her sister Elizabeth Cohron, and their children occupied a tent near the pump. Around midnight on December 10, 1864, Lewis Williams, 82nd US Colored Troops, entered the tent. They asked him to leave, and he began to curse them. Several nearby colored men asked Williams to calm down, which only inflamed him. The two women picked up their children and ran toward a nearby house, hoping for protection. Williams overtook Mary, threw her down, jerked her child from her arms, and tried to pull up her skirt. Elizabeth came up behind him and struck him with "a hickory club as big as an arm." Lewis wrested the club from her and struck Elizabeth twice on the head. Surgeon Clark Mason said she had two severe wounds on the top of her head. He was familiar with the sisters and their illnesses, and "I have understood that the husband of Elizabeth Cohron kept both of them and that Mary has children by Mr. Cohron." Williams was sentenced to hard labor for the rest of his life.[20]

Edward Hurley was a private in the US Marine Corps, stationed on the USS *Muscoota*. He was at the circus at Key West in the late 1864, which resulted in a charge of trying to rape ten-year-old Dora Angus. "Outside the circus tent, he asked me to come with him. I said no. He pulled me round the corner, pitched me down, tore my hat and the waist of my dress. He also tore my pantalettes trying to pull them off. He said if I wouldn't sleep with him he'd cut my throat." A male witness told the court that Hurley had said, "I was going to fuck her and I will fuck you too if you will let me." Hurley pleaded drunkenness as an excuse. The court gave him a year in prison.[21]

Georgia

At Atlanta, in September 1864, Lieutenant John Arbuckle of the 61st Ohio behaved disgracefully. At night, while intoxicated, he went into the home of Mrs. Sarah Bucklew and Mrs. Sarah Grogan, on Ivey Street. They asked him to leave. He replied, "I'm a gay old boy from the country, here to have a little fun." In a five-day trial, the convoluted events of the evening became somewhat clearer. After Arbuckle would not leave, they locked themselves in Mrs. Bucklew's bedroom. He banged on the door and pledged by his "solemn word of honor," that if they let him in, he'd just chat and then go away. They opened the door. He entered, cursing and saying that he had the full authority of Generals Sherman and Thomas. Grogan tired of this and went to her room and Bucklew hid under her bed covers. Arbuckle undressed and slid in beside her. "I told him I had the clap, to make him go away, but he had connexion with me anyway, against my will." A guard appeared and Arbuckle shouted, "This is nothing but a Goddamn whorehouse." Then Lieutenant Colonel Edward Solomon, 82nd Illinois, arrived and told him to be quiet, go to his camp, sober up, and report under arrest in the morning. Arbuckle was not cooperative. Much of the testimony centered around the nature of the house. Lieutenant William H. Smith, 61st Ohio, said, "We asked a nigger whether he knew of a house of ill fame. He showed us a house, but it was empty. Then we saw some cavalrymen at Mrs. Bucklew's house, so we went in. The women did not object." Arbuckle was dishonorably dismissed with the loss of four months pay.[22]

On Augusta's Woodlawn Avenue, Richard Clary, 4th US Cavalry, was charged with stealing a horse, a wagon, and two mules, and with the rape of a "colored girl, in a field near the depot." The evidence was found insufficient and in October 1865, he was acquitted. Also at Augusta, in the early spring of 1866, John Cotzenberger of the 16th US Infantry was charged with being absent without leave and with raping "a colored woman." There were three soldier witnesses to the rape. At the trial, none could remember a thing. The victim did not testify. Cotzenberger was acquitted of rape but was fined five dollars for being AWOL.[23]

In a third Augusta case, Saphio, a "colored citizen" and former slave, was tried for the attempted rape of Annie Hooker. The first witness was Annie's mother, Catherine, Saphio's previous owner. Catherine had been away shopping. "When I came home, a servant told me that Saphio had twice tried to pull Annie's dress over her head. We found no fault with him until recently when he became impertinent." Annie told the court that when she was at home with her baby brother and "the servant girl, Tilly," that Saphio locked the door, threw her on the sofa, pulled her dress up, and undid his pants. At this point Tilly screamed and interrupted them. Saphio was given five years in prison at hard labor.[24]

At Savannah, Bunkum P. Osborne, "colored citizen," was tried for the rape of Elizabeth Webster, "colored." Osborne and several other men invited her to go to a ball with them. Other men joined them at the corner of State and Whitaker Streets. They drove a while into the country, where they stopped on the Ogeechee Road. Osborne asked her for sex. When she refused, he called her a "goddamn white man's hoarish [whorish] bitch." He threw her on the ground. She got up and hit him. With the assistance of five other men, he held her down, put sand in her mouth, and raped her. When she protested that she was pregnant ("in a estate of indifferent health") Osborne said, "It's just a white man's bastard and we will kick it out of you." All six men raped her and then "they threw sand on my private parts." Dr. William Charters examined her and found hoarseness and severe bruises on her throat. He was unable to confirm rape, as she was maritally experienced. Captain Samuel Cowdrey, 162nd New York, the local provost marshal, said Osborne had confessed to the crime. A baker who had employed Osborne for three years at the corner of Taylor and Whitaker Street said Osborne was of "excellent character." Osborne was given seven years in prison.[25]

At Sandtown, three men of the 2nd Kentucky Cavalry went on a drunken rampage at the home of a Mrs. Campbell, which she shared with her mother and with Sylvia Campbell, apparently a servant, variously described in the records as "a mulatto," and "a yellow girl." The three men were Elijah Sergeant, Joseph Hunter, and John Goodwin. Sylvia said that Sergeant held a gun to her head and raped her four times, and that Hunter had dragged her into the woods, but not raped her. Goodwin hit Sylvia so hard that blood ran from her ears, nose, and mouth. The senior Mrs. Campbell told the court, "Yes, they dragged the nigger into the woods. She has not been able to do a lick of work since, but lies around useless. Her mistress has to wash all her own clothes." Sergeant got two years hard labor, Hunter three months, and Goodwin hard labor with the ball and chain for the rest of his enlistment.[26]

At Madison, Julia Ann Autry was in the woods, cutting bark. With her were her seven-year-old brother and her dog. Austin Starks, "colored citizen," seized her around the waist and covered her mouth with his other hand, which he then moved to her bosoms and then to her legs and then "up my clothes as far as he could." She screamed. Her brother screamed. Her nearby mother screamed. The dog jumped up. Starks ran. "He put his hand right on my private parts . . . he did not expose his person." 1865 trial that he had been drunk and was very sorry. The court gave him five years in prison.[27]

In the words of mid-Victorian jurisprudence, "The said Albert Lane, Company B, 100th Regiment Ohio Volunteers did on or about the 11th day of July, 1864 at the house of Mr. John Dickerson, in Cobb County, Georgia, upon one Miss Louisa Dickerson, violently and feloniously did make an assault and did . . . then and there forcibly and against her will, feloniously did ravish and carnally know her." Miss Dickerson testified for the prosecution. Lane went to prison for ten years.[28]

The charge of attempted rape in the case of Mrs. Nancy Newsom of Newman seems to have been a bit extreme. The defendant in this June 1865 trial was Jerry Galloupe, 3rd Iowa Cavalry. Nancy did not testify, but at least three witnesses who were in the same room at the time of the alleged assault had much to say. "He was lying drunk in her bed, pulling her by the hand . . . she is said to be of bad character . . . they were standing together . . . she had her clothes partially up . . . after he was arrested, she asked the captain to release him . . . [Nancy and Jerry] sat together on the bed . . . she smiled at him . . . she told me that he was a mighty purty man." Galloupe received twenty days at hard labor for being disorderly.[29]

In Catoosa County, near blockhouse No. 10 on the Chattanooga Railroad, 35-year-old widow Nancy Yarbroth, was at home with her eight-year-old son. James Bradburn, 145th Indiana, showed up drunk and asked for supper. She started to cook when he said, "Never mind cooking. I want a diddle." She left the house. When she returned, he was asleep. "He never laid a hand on me and apologized when he left." Bradburn got two weeks of hard labor for being absent without leave.[30]

The stories of Charles Billingsly and William Cutsinger, 7th Indiana Light Artillery, ended in an unusual manner. The regiment was camped near Burnt Hickory. At night, on May 28, 1864, the two men left camp and went to the home of James Smith. Claiming military authority, they arrested him and took him away. Then the two artillerymen returned looking for his wife, Louisa. Billingsly, using a false story, lured her into the woods. "He throwed me down on my back and held my hands. I told him to stop. He said he intended to frig me right there or kill me." After he was done with her, Cutsinger showed up and both men raped her. Then they all returned to the house, where both men raped her again. Back at camp, Billingsly told Private Joseph McCloskey, "We had a good time last night. We arrested a man and told his wife that we would release him if she gave us a diddle." Billingsly was given ten years in prison, with "food and water only as absolutely necessary." Cutsinger also got ten years with "food and clothing only as absolutely necessary." Neither man served time. Both men escaped and deserted to the South. Neither man appears in the roster of Confederate soldiers.[31]

At Flat Rock, Gabriel Ballard, 143rd New York, entered the home of two white women. The younger one told a sergeant who had come later to investigate, "He pushed me onto the bed and tried to crawl on top of me." At his November 1864 trial, Ballard was acquitted.[32]

John Bass, 48th Illinois, was arrested for trying to rape "an old lady," in Chatham County. The victim, Mrs. Mary E. Dugger said, "I was sitting down at the fireplace when he came in. He drew a pistol and said I must give up to him." The court asked, "By give up to him did he mean to commit a rape?" "Of course he did. He said he wanted to fuck me!" The court requested no further clarification. In December 1864, Bass had his head shaved and was drummed out of his regiment.[33]

Civil War Georgia is poignantly remembered as the site of Sherman's "March to the Sea." The stories of theft, arson and destruction are legion—and sometimes debated. In the late 1800s, a dedicated Southerner, Clarence Poe, set about collecting personal reminiscences. He advertised widely, inviting former citizens of the Confederacy to send him their stories. When the book was published, he told his readers, ". . . it is interesting to note that out of hundreds of letters sent the writer on the Civil War, not once is rape mentioned."[34]

Chapter 16

RAPE IN TENNESSEE, KENTUCKY, AND WEST VIRGINIA

Tennessee

Although Tennessee had two major urban centers, Memphis and Nashville, almost all the documented rapes occurred in rural areas. A knowledge of Civil War railroads is helpful in identifying the locations of some offenses.

James Sibley, 13th US Colored Troops, was charged with attempted rape and attempted murder at "Section 6, Nashville and Northwest RR." Forty-nine-year old Susan Houlihan said, "It was dark. I can't swear that is him. They used the utmost endeavor to accomplish their ends with my daughter. One man hit me on the head and one choked me." Her daughter, Margaret, age sixteen, escaped twice and was dragged back twice. Several women lived in the house and a soldier said, "We come to Spicer's to see the girls." Sibley was given six months in prison with a ball and chain. Samuel Keith, George Fowler, and Robert Clark, all from Sibley's regiment, seem to have been part of the same of event. Although all were charged with attempted rape, there is no testimony about rape. All three were given six months in prison for AWOL and assault.[1]

John G. Price, 2nd Tennessee Mounted Infantry, approached the wife of a Captain Chambers, in front of her tent "near the N & NW RR." Price was rather drunk, mumbled a sexual invitation and fumbled with her clothing. He was hauled away and after a brief trial in August 1864, fined one month's pay.[2]

Abner Stevens and Leander Banister, both of the 145th Indiana, were AWOL overnight at "Blockhouse No. 10, Chattanooga RR." They were tried for the attempted rape of a Mrs. Yarbroth, but no testimony was introduced about the subject of rape. For being AWOL, both men got two weeks of hard labor. There were three rape cases at Pocahontas. Private Lawson Camp, 55th US Colored Troops, a nineteen-year-old native of Mississippi, described as "a desperate villain," was convicted of "raping a white girl" on November 18, 1863. He was shot by a firing squad the following day. Private Zeno Cliff, 12th Illinois, went into "the Negro quarters" at Pocahontas. When arrested, he was attempting the rape of Harriet Ragan, who testified against him. He was acquitted.[3]

While on patrol near Pocahontas, Francis Bruss, 12th Illinois, put his gun down, entered "the Negro quarters" (which were tents) and attempted the rape of a colored woman employed by the quartermaster. She did not testify. Witnesses said it was too dark to see who was doing what. Bruss was acquitted.[4]

At Dixon, three men of the 13th US Colored Troops were charged with the rape of Indiana Rose. She said she was riding home on her mare, "on the pike," when Daniel Tierce, George Nelson, and Lewis Hardin stopped her and forced her to travel 200 yards off the road. "I begged on my knees to let me go. The man who threw me down and violated my person said that I would have to do a heap of things that I never expected to do." In spite of testimony of threats with knives and a cocked gun, the court asked this: "Did you use your utmost endeavors to prevent him from executing his desires, or did you simply cry out, thus yielding a tacit consent?" In the end, all three men were found guilty. Nelson was hanged, Tierce was given twelve years in prison, and Hardin got ten years.[5]

Nicholas Adams, 14th US Colored Troops, was charged with the rape of Mrs. Eliza Robb, at Kelly's Ferry, about "three miles from Lookout Creek." She told the court that several colored soldiers had come to her house where she was with her mother and two children. When the men began to break in, the women fled out the back door. In the dark, her mother fell, dropping one child, who cried, thus alerting the intruders. After several escape attempts, Eliza was captured in the cabbage patch by one soldier and raped while still holding her baby. A witness said it was very dark and "all Negroes just look alike to me." Adams was freed for lack of positive identification.[6]

At Claibourne County, John Henry, 11th Tennessee Cavalry, was charged with the theft of ten gallons of apple brandy and the rape of Mrs. David Shupe. There was no testimony about the rape. Henry got six months in prison for stealing the brandy. Henry's partners in crime fared less well. James Dixon, of Henry's regiment, was recognized by his victim, Pamela Shupe. "It was the night of December 4, 1864. They came to the door searching for Mr. Shupe. I told them he was not here. Then they rolled in a barrel of liquor and commenced on me. They told me to lay my baby down or they would knock it out of my arms. Benjamin Carroll offered me a quart of liquor to let him do as he pleased with me, then they offered me the whole barrel to let them both do as they pleased with me. They had me down two or three times, trying to put their hands under my clothes."[7]

Carroll, 11th Tennessee Cavalry, had made a fuss at another house before visiting the Shupes. His first unwilling host said that the group came to his house, singing dirty songs in the presence of young ladies. "They were set to leave and Ben Carroll said they would take my barrel of liquor. Ben said, 'By God we will freeze to it and we will fuck it.' [At this point, Carroll had mounted the barrel, making coital motions]. John Henry said he had come out to fuck and he intended to fuck. 'My prick is as stiff as a buck's horn and I intend to limber it up before daybreak.'" Dan Carroll got three years in prison, as did James Dickson.[8]

At Trenton, Lieutenant Elijah Baker of the 4th Illinois was charged with being drunk and attempting to rape Nancy Mallard, Mary Harrison, and Mary Dennis. Nancy told the court, "He said what he'd like to do, but he did no harm. He asked me to do something, which I declined." Mary Dennis told the court, "He was never improper. He did not propose me to go into a barn or a shed." Baker received a reprimand.[9]

In Rutherford County, John Dancy, 4th East Tennessee Cavalry, stole a rifle, a pistol, a silver watch, and a mule. He also killed a very valuable mule and "with force and violence had carnal knowledge of a female colored servant, the property of Allen McCord." (Witnesses said Dancy was a criminal even before the war.) The rape victim of was neither named nor invited to testify. Dancy was convicted of the thefts and sentenced to have his head shaved and spend fifteen years in prison.[10]

In Ford County, James Dalzell, 15th Indiana, was tried for the rape of pregnant Sally Ann Roberts. "When he first came to the house, he talked clever as a gentleman, then he said, 'We are far from home and the women ought to accommodate us.' He threw me down and hurt my back. My linen was very nasty from his emission." In November 1862, Dalzell got hard labor for the rest of his enlistment, wearing a ball and chain.[11]

"Father was drunk in his bed. Mother and I were in our bed. Mr. Casey took off his pants and tried to get in our bed . . . he grabbed my foot . . . Mother and I went and stayed with neighbors." This was the story told by fourteen-year-old Fredonia B. Howsley of Davidson County, during the trial of John Casey, a federal civilian employee, who got 30 days at hard labor. Tried with Casey was another Federal employee, Pierce Kane, who was drunk and in bed with the unconscious Mr. Howsley. Kane invited Fredonia to his bed, but made no actual attempt to touch her and was acquitted.[12]

John Locker, 2nd Illinois Light Artillery, was drunk and disorderly at Clarksville and attempted to rape fourteen-year-old "Rachel, a Negro girl." The location of the crime was "just south of the square . . . at a Negro shanty, known as a house of ill fame." Ann Bailey and Winnie Harvey, both residents there, described Rachel as "not grown yet and is considerably below medium-size." Locker arrived drunk and began to feel Rachel's "bosoms and under her clothes," to which she offered little objection. But when he threw her down on the floor and attempted penetration, she began to scream. The court asked Winnie what Locker was doing. The reply: "I suppose from his actions that he was trying to screw her." Ann Bailey had yet a different view: "The man said he would screw her or kill her." A member of the guard, James W. Hale, 83rd Illinois, described the scene. "From what I saw he was having sexual intercourse with her." The court asked Rachel, "Why did you not permit the accused to have carnal knowledge of you?" She told them, "Because he was not of my color." Locker was fined three months pay and spent three months in prison. General Lovell Rousseau disapproved the unusually light sentence for this "flagrant and disgusting" crime.[13]

At Guy's Gap, in June 1863, two men of the 33rd Indiana, Perry Pierson and William Lindsey, attempted the rape of two slaves, apparently sisters. Pierson chose Harriet McKinley, followed her when she jumped out of the window, threw her down, and raped her for fifteen minutes. "I was a virgin. He inserted his private parts into me. I hollered so that you might hear me for two miles." Lindsey was less successful in his assault upon Matilda McKinley. "He said he wanted a fucking. I knocked him down and then master came and run him off." Lindsey got four months at hard labor; Pierson got a year.[14]

At the "Negro corral," at Grand Junction, Sergeant Thomas Graham, 15th Michigan, was drunk and belligerent. He entered the tent of a "Negro girl," who began "hallowing and crying." When a guard interceded, Graham hit the guard; there was no testimony about the attempted rape. Graham was reduced to the ranks and given three months at hard labor with a ball and chain. "I want to marry your daughter; will you sell her to me?" George May, 81st Ohio, addressed these words to Mrs. Martha Jane Hall at Giles County, as he cursed Mrs. Hall and all her children and chased their chickens. He was given ten days at hard labor, as was his accomplice, John Southard of the same regiment. Both men were drunk.[15]

Samuel Dunwoody, 5th Ohio Cavalry, got drunk at Athens, went AWOL, robbed a William Reed and forcibly entered the home of a Mrs. Roberts, where he went into "the private bedchamber of two young ladies and proceeded to forcibly feel and examine their persons and told them that he would like to fuck them." He was sent to Dry Tortugas for eight years.[16]

At Pine Bluff, Henry Duncan, 4th US Colored Heavy Artillery, went AWOL. He threatened to burn down the house of a white widow, Elizabeth McDougal. When she let him in, preferring this to being burned alive, he raped her for half an hour in front of her thirteen-year-old son. Duncan was fined four months pay for being AWOL. There was no finding on the rape charge. Equally puzzling is the case of David Ellis, 118th Ohio, charged with theft of $85 at Estell Springs and the rape of Rebecca P. Wade, on Christmas Eve, 1864. The witnesses knew nothing. Miss Wade did not testify. The case was dismissed.[17]

Ransom Hennan, 180th Ohio, was also suspected of robbing the Wade house and of raping Miss Wade. All the testimony centered on some gold coins and greenbacks in Hennan's possession. One witness visited the Wade household on Christmas morning and noted that mother and daughter were crying and the house looked "torn up;" but the women were not called as witnesses. Hennan was acquitted.[18]

Several men were looking for forage at Salem. At a house owned by a Mr. Moore, the "white folks" were not at home. There was a colored woman who was sick in bed. Two men went to the barn, while John J. Hamilton, 36th Illinois, stayed in the house. A few minutes later, a "colored boy" ran to the barn asking the soldiers to remove Hamilton. Isaac Kemp, 3rd Indiana Cavalry, found the door was locked. "I went to a small window. The woman was on her back on the bed. The prisoner was standing on the floor, his penis was out and he was holding her legs, drawing her close to him. She was crying for help." The victim was not named, nor did she testify. Hamilton was drummed out of the army, with his head shaved.[19]

Guerrilla and former Confederate soldier Abe Hendricks escaped death through witness intimidation. In Franklin County, he and six other men robbed a Mr. Marshall of his horses, then shot him in the head. Two weeks later, they returned and raped his widow, Martha Marshall, and her sixteen-year-old niece. At the trial, the women declined to identify Hendricks and he was freed.[20]

Perry Holland, 1st Missouri, confessed to the rape of Miss Julia Anderson at Cerro Gordo and was sentenced to be shot. His confession meant that there was no testimony. The death sentence was commuted.[21]

Thomas Hooks, guerrilla and probably a former member of Company G, 14th Tennessee Cavalry (Confederate) was tried for dozens of crimes at Obion County. Robbery and murder were his usual activities, but the charges did include the rape of a 14-year-old "colored girl," Susan Brandon. He was convicted of numerous crimes; regarding Susan, he was convicted only of attempted rape. The sentence of death by hanging was commuted to life in prison.[22]

Lieutenant Alexander Hudson, 2nd Illinois Light Artillery, was so drunk at Fort Donelson that he fell into the creek, called another officer a "Goddamned Swede," and went to the room of a Mrs. Tuttle, where he removed his clothes and "attempted to have carnal knowledge of her." There was no testimony about either the nudity or the attempted rape. Hudson was reprimanded for his remark about the "Goddamned Swede."[23]

Charles C. Hunter, 7th Kentucky Cavalry, raped Mrs. Mary Kirksey, a widowed seamstress living in Lookout Valley. He bound her, gagged her with a leather strap, and "accomplished his vile purpose." Hunter did not remove either his pants or his boots during the assault. Hunter appealed his sentence of eighteen years in prison, but Holt was totally unsympathetic.[24]

Mrs. Catharina Farmer was married in 1802. Sixty-one years later, she met Lieutenant Harvey John, 49th Ohio, near Tullahoma. Harvey was straggling, picking berries, when he encountered his victim. He dragged her into the bushes, told her he would kill her if she didn't "give it to him." He tore her dress, broke her hoops, and "put his private parts into her," for which he got ten years in prison.[25]

Calvin Young, 125th Ohio, was at Blue Springs in March 1865. After dark, he entered the home of Sarah Johnson as she lay in bed, said, "I will have some," and lifted her nightie. He pleaded guilty and got a year in prison. At Camp Moorhead, James Wilson, 7th Pennsylvania Cavalry was AWOL. He entered the house of a woman who was sick in bed, and made an "indecent assault" upon her. Much of the record is missing. He was acquitted.[26]

Charles Pratt, 24th Wisconsin, was drunk at Mill Creek and terrorized the Martin family in November 1862. In addition to pillage and plunder, he was charged with trying to rape a white woman and a Negro slave. After long testimony, he was convicted only of the theft and was given fourteen days at hard labor.[27]

In Montgomery County, Richard Mitchelson, 16th US Colored Troops, was AWOL on Christmas Day. He was convicted of tearing the clothing of a Miss Bayliss and of threatening to shoot her if she did not permit him to have intercourse with her. Testimony is missing from the record. Mitchelson was given five years at hard labor in prison.[28]

At Choctaw County, Moses, "a colored citizen," tried to rape the daughter of Jonas Nenning. Moses pleaded guilty, so there was no testimony. The September 1865 trial sentenced him to a year at hard labor in prison.[29]

Henry Murphy, James Riley, and other soldiers of the 35th Indiana were looting the Sanford Plantation at Murfreesboro in January 1863. They were drunk. Riley was convicted of shooting at Negroes and given thirty days of hard labor. Murphy raped a twenty-year-old married "Negro woman," whose name is unknown. Witnesses said, "Her person was exposed . . . his pants were down . . . they were fucking . . . the Negro was frightened to death." The rape went on for two hours. Murphy was convicted and sentenced to be branded with a capital "R" in indelible ink (i.e. tattooed) in the presence of the regiment, put to hard labor for 30 days, and then drummed out.[30]

Lieutenant John S. Roberts, 22nd Indiana, was in charge of the gunboat *Silver Lake No. 2* at Gainesboro. He seems to have been a useless drunk, as he had missed two entire battles while too intoxicated to issue commands. He went to the apartment of Amanda Gaw, "colored," said, "I want a little of your cunt," and then raped her. Many witnesses confirmed the charges against him, but he was acquitted. He was honorably discharged in August 1864.[31]

At Decherd, Mary Dile, Millie Kilgore and Louisa Thomas lived in the same house. Sgt. James C. Smith, 43rd Wisconsin, was charged with entering the house, saying, "By God, I came here to get a fuck," and threatening the very pregnant Louisa with a pistol. Louisa could not be found to testify, but the other two women said that Smith was not the man who had threatened them, and he was acquitted. William Swift, 72nd Indiana, left his picket post at Alexandria, violently raped "a woman of color," and made threats of killing the lieutenant who arrested him. A surgeon examined the unnamed woman and told the court that he was "satisfied that she had been ravished." Swift was sentenced to have half his head shaved, spend five days with a ball and chain, be drummed through the brigade, spend a year at hard labor in a military prison, and then be dishonorably discharged.[32]

At Central Knob (possibly near Chattanooga) John Lewis, 16th US Colored Troops, went AWOL at night and entered the home of Mrs. Sally Benford, "colored." He demanded bread. "I told him we had not had any bread in three days." He asked her for "some skin." "Well, that's a pretty question to ask a married woman." Lewis said her husband wouldn't know about it. "If my husband would not know about it, God would, and if I had done the like I could not be depended on by my husband. I am a lady." Lewis then made offers of money, gloves, and shoes, which she refused. He got a year in prison for his behavior.[33]

Franklin Troutman, 14th US Colored Troops, left his camp at Chattanooga and went to the home of Martha Brown, where he threatened to burn down the building unless she let him in. She did so and he tried to lift up her dress and that of her friend. The two women escaped and hid in the river bottom. Both women testified. Troutman got three months at hard labor and lost six months pay. His less aggressive partner in this venture, James Wiley, received a fine of one months pay and a reprimand.[34]

An event at Elk River illustrates some Victorian concepts of morality. John Turner, 16th Illinois, assaulted, wounded, and raped Elizabeth Ann Walls. She testified against him. The court noted, "the conduct and bearing of Mrs. Walls is not refined or ladylike . . . [Her] character . . . not becoming a virtuous woman." This view of women probably accounts for the light sentence: thirty days hard labor. James Finn, 14th Michigan, convicted of aiding Turner, also received thirty days at hard labor.[35]

There were four rape cases from Nashville. Frederick Cox, 115th Ohio, was AWOL overnight. He brutally raped Mary Budget. Medical examination showed: "Her privates were torn . . . bleeding profusely . . . she suffered very much." Cox was fined two months pay. At the contraband camp, washerwoman Mary Hirdspeth was raped by Isaac Cox, 5th US Artillery, and by a second man not identified. "They said they'd fill my mouth with rocks if I hollered. They crushed my throat so I couldn't eat for a week . . . he pushed his thing into me as far as he could . . . they took turns holding me down." A character witness said that Mary was "very decent and proper." Isaac Cox was acquitted.[36]

Sergeant William Walker, 1st Ohio Light Artillery, broke into the home of Captain Hunter Brooks, provost marshal of Nashville, by climbing in the window of Brooks' two servant girls, Jenny and her daughter, Louisa. They called for help from "Bill," (Private William Llewellyn), the captain's orderly. He ordered Walker to go back out the window and behave himself. "I could see Walker was drunk. He tried to push the women into my room, saying, 'I will bloody well fuck the pair of them.'" Walker was reduced to the ranks and fined eight months pay.[37]

Rape and possible voyeurism were issues for Frank Hunter, also of the 1st Ohio Light Artillery. The same Jenny and Louisa washed and ironed for the officers. Jenny found a man in bed with Louisa, but the man was not Hunter. He was outside, looking in, watching as Sergeant Walker had sex with Louisa. Hunter was set free.[38]

A deathbed statement by the victim was the sad end of Anna Mason, age thirty-two, described as "short and heavyset." She had been seriously alcoholic for many years before the fateful night she met Hugh Burns, 108th Illinois, another drunk. In an all-night orgy of rape and drunken abuse, Burns tied her to a tree in "the orchard" and did many unspecified things, which resulted in her death two days later. Autopsy showed "bladder neck torn loose from the vulva, clothes torn and bloody." In a long dictated statement made the day before she died, she identified her attacker and told of his cruelties. An additional horror was the presence of her six-year-old daughter that night in the orchard. Burns got ten years in prison and a dishonorable discharge. Holt said he should have been hanged.[39]

On April 21, 1865, Brigadier General Richard W. Johnson wrote to Brigadier General William D. Whipple, Assistant Adjutant-General, Department of the Cumberland, complaining of three men from the 2nd Tennessee Mounted Infantry: Thomas H. Brewer, Walter F. Stutts, and Paul (or Thomas) Kiddy. Twelve days earlier, the three had gone to the home of Mrs. William Johnson, living on Sugar Creek, twenty miles southwest of Pulaski. When she could not produce the $12,000 they demanded, they hanged her and her daughter several times, then let them down. All three then raped Mrs. Johnson. The threesome then went to four other homes, where they committed murder, torture, and robbery. General Johnson urged that they be prosecuted. They were not.[40]

At Williamson County, in central Tennessee, several women were raped, although details are scanty. The same Civil War-era author also mentions rapes in Arkansas and North Carolina.[41]

Kentucky

War in the border states was especially brutal. The notorious guerrilla "One Arm Berry" (Samuel O. Berry) often rode with the murderous cross-dresser Sue

Mundy. In addition to robbing banks and murdering fourteen men, Berry was charged with the rape of two women in Spencer County, Susan Lee and a Laura, both "colored." For his numerous crimes Barry was sentenced to hang. Berry's friends showered President Andrew Johnson with petitions, describing the murderer as a fine young man. Holt derided Berry as an "atrocious character," who richly deserved to die. Johnson commuted the sentence to prison.[42]

Another of Sue Mundy's men, Henry Magruder, was charged with the murders of Jacob Winstead, James Engle, and twelve other men, as well as the rape of Mrs. Catherine Raymor, in Edmonson County. Magruder was convicted of eight of the murders, but acquitted of the rape. He was hanged October 20, 1865, at Louisville.[43]

Five "colored citizens" were tried for the rape of Miss Susan Carroll, a white woman, at Hickman County. Around midnight, on March 11, 1865, a dozen "colored men" surrounded the house of Mr. James A. Carroll. After numerous threats, they broke down the door and held Mr. Carroll at gunpoint. Two men, Dow Nailin and George Narrin, raped Carroll's daughter. She told the court, "I know Nailin. They took hold of me and mashed my mouth until the blood run out of my nose and choked me. There were four of them who forced me. The prisoner did it first. One of the four is not caught." Nailin and Narrin were hanged August 21, 1865 at Paducah. Three other men—Louis Knox, Arthur Hinton, and John Harris—were acquitted of the rape and received light sentences for being guerrillas.[44]

At Greensburg, John Linville, 54th Kentucky Cavalry, and his superior, Second Lieutenant Dudley O. Bravard, were charged with the rape of 11-year-old Biddie Lewis, "colored girl." The men came to the Lewis home March 21, 1865, at night. After threatening the adults, they pulled Biddie outdoors and under a locust tree. "They pulled up my clothes and said if I screamed they'd shoot my damned brains out. After the first man unbuttoned his clothes and laid on me, the other got on me too . . . he hurt me right smartly and caused me to bleed." Bravard was dismissed and sent to prison for five years, as was Linville.[45]

Robert E. Cropps, 2nd Maryland, was drunk on the Covington Pike near Frankfort. He was charged with robbery, horse theft, and rape, all on July 11, 1863. Two soldiers testified that Cropps was drunk and belligerent that evening and had seized Sarah, a slave belonging to citizen Lydia Howard, threw Sarah down over her protests and raped her. He was on her for about half an hour. Cropps offered to shoot anyone who came to her rescue. Afterwards, as the slave girl left, Cropps fired several shots at her. Sarah, the victim, did not testify. Cropps got five years in prison and a dishonorable discharge.[46]

Second Lieutenant Charles Helton, 39th Kentucky Mounted Infantry, was far out of line at Rockcastle Creek. He approached the wife of his captain, told her he wished to have sex with her, tore her dress open, and "thrust his hand into her bosom." He then tried something similar with the captain's daughter.

Helton was dishonorably dismissed and sent to prison for three years. Not surprisingly, he had been drunk.[47]

Second Lieutenant Robert Warnick, 41st Illinois, was a drunk and belligerent lieutenant. At Paducah, he kicked open the door of a fifty-six-year-old woman and said he wished "connection" with her sixteen-year-old daughter. The mother called the guard. Warnick and his friends beat up the guard, who returned with reinforcements and drove the malfeasants away. Later, Warnick returned and broke the windows in the home of the woman who had spurned his entreaties. In January 1862, he was dismissed from the army.[48]

On the Fourth of July, 1865, Frederick Wagner, 31st Illinois, was posted at a Louisville saloon to keep order and prevent drunkenness. He did not faithfully keep his vigil, there on 4th St between Main Street and the river. Instead, he appeared, naked, in the room of the saloonkeeper's daughter and seized her by the throat. Her screams summoned her father, who chased him away. Wagner's acquittal is a puzzle.[49]

At Camp Wickliffe, in Nelson County, the only witness to the crime was a girl who did not know her own age. George Mackley, 6th Ohio, was tried in December 1861 for the attempted rape of May Cape. The court noticed that she had the appearance of a seven-year-old and was too young to understand the nature of an oath, but decided to admit her statement, "which was given in a straightforward and intelligent manner." "I know the man . . . one day he took me up in the woods and sitting down on the log took me in his lap and put his hand under my clothes. He held me there some time." The court found her story credible. Mackley has his head shaved and was drummed out of his regiment.[50]

Sergeant John Thomas, 4th US Colored Heavy Artillery, was drunk and disorderly at Columbus. He had been assigned to guard a supply of whiskey. Instead, he drank much of it. In this condition, he shot at the corporal of the guard, escaped from arrest, and entered the house of a widow, Anice Young, and tried to rape her daughter, Maggie. In October 1865, the court sent Thomas to prison for three years, with a dishonorable discharge.[51]

Captain Horace G. Whiting, 2nd Ohio Heavy Artillery, was stationed at Bowling Green, and in March 1863 was charged with embezzlement, false recruiting, and rape. In regards to the latter, he confined Private Atwood to jail and then raped his wife, Jane Atwood. The testimony did not support the charge and Whiting was acquitted on all counts. Mrs. Atwood could not be found to testify, but a defense witness said, "She is a nymph and a frail one (i.e., prostitute), now plying her trade under the euphonious name of 'Fay'."[52]

West Virginia

At Weston, on December 11, 1863, two soldiers of the 4th West Virginia Cavalry terrorized the Skidmore family. Forty-one-year-old Mrs. Mary Skidmore testified. "John Williams and Jacob Bladner came to the door at ten at night, saying they could not get through the pickets and needed a place to spend the night. I did not want to keep them, but they said if they could sleep in front of the fire, they would behave themselves." They did not. An hour after their arrival, Bladner came to her bed and said, "I want to fuck you." She had her young son tell the men to leave. They demanded a drink of water. When it arrived, Williams threw the water into the fireplace, making the room dark, and Bladner threw Mrs. Skidmore into the bed, cracking her head on the wall, and raped her. "The emission from his person entered my person." Bladner got 15 years in prison; Williams was sentenced to eight years.[53]

Chapter 17

RAPE IN THE WEST

Louisiana

While not traditionally "Western," the Pelican State is west of the Mississippi. To further its western credentials, it borders on Texas, was contested in early struggles between Spain and the expanding United States, and bears the name of the Louisiana Purchase, by far the largest single western jump in our nation's history.

At Port Hudson, First Lieutenant Charles Wenz, 4th US Colored Cavalry, was drunk on April 21, 1865, and compelled an enlisted man to forcibly carry "an aged colored woman" to her cabin, where Wenz "forcibly and against her will, feloniously did ravish and carnally know her." The victim, Ann Booze, was not sure of her own age but thought she was about sixty. "He told me if I didn't take off my clothes, he would have the rest of his men come and do it to me. He'd made me take off my clothes, even down to my chimmy. He had me in bed half an hour and did with me as he liked. When he was tired of me, I put my clothes under my arm and ran into the woods." The lieutenant had had her husband arrested and held without charges just before the incident. Wenz was found guilty and dishonorably discharged, given five years at hard labor, and had his officers' insignia torn off in the presence of his regiment. Holt refused Wenz' appeal, perhaps after noting the victim's words while being raped: "I'm an old crippled colored woman who can't walk without a stick. I ain't no 'count. I ain't no 'count."[1]

The rules of evidence seemed to have saved Sylvester LaMotte, 4th Wisconsin Cavalry, who was on picket duty at Baton Rouge, where he abused his authority. In December 1863, civilians needed a pass and a signed oath of allegiance in order to pass the pickets. He was charged with robbing Mrs. Louisiana Jones, "a white lady," and of raping her black servant. Miss Jones submitted a signed a statement, but did not appear at court. In her statement, she claimed to have had both oath and permit ready, but LaMotte delayed her passage until dark. He then drew his pistol and took her money. "Then he cursed my black woman and made her get out of the carriage, where he violated her person." The case was dismissed because a written statement cannot be cross-examined.[2]

At Franklin, First Lieutenant William Gardner was accused of raping Martha Davis. "He walked in my house without knocking. He said he'd put me out of the house if I didn't do as he wanted. He had me sit on a trunk. He tried to put my left hand inside his pants. I refused. Then he undid his pants, took out his privates and wanted me to take them in my hands. I have rheumatism in my right hand. I told him to leave me alone. He pulled up my dress and effected an entrance." She also recalled his threat to return with a friend. Gardner's defense produced three witnesses, Edward Cooper, Isaac Trowbridge, and Dr. J. W. Lyon, who all swore that she was not of chaste character. The court "honorably acquitted" Gardner. General William Franklin ordered the term "honorably" to be dropped, since Gardner's conduct was "highly reprehensible."[3]

Fort St. Philip is on the Mississippi River, sixty miles downriver from New Orleans. There, in June 1862, Corporal William C. Chinock, 26th Massachusetts, was ordered to take twenty-three-year-old washerwoman, Mary Ellen de Riley, "Negro," to nearby Fort Jackson. "When the boat was away from the shore he told me to lie down and let him ride me. He beat me with his fists, pulled my clothes over my head and rode me—for an hour". Chinock was reduced to private and fined $10 a month for four months.[4]

At Pineville, at one in the morning, Mrs. Elizabeth Huffman was asleep in bed. Michael Barnes, 47th US Colored Troops, put his hand in the window and pulled back the bedclothes. She said that he intended to "take liberties." He said, "I was just stealing the quilt." (A quilt in August in Louisiana?) Barnes got a month at hard labor.[5]

Evan Williams was eighteen years old in 1863 and stood 5'6" in his bare feet. He was born in Greenfield, Mississippi, no doubt as a slave. When with the 48th US Colored Troops, he saw action at Coleman's Crossroads, Mississippi, and at the siege of Blakely, Alabama. On September 5, 1865, he raped Miss Georgianna Josephine Bryant, white, at Shreveport. "My parents were both sick and I was driving in the cattle. The accused came up to me and said he wanted to have to do with me. I told him I would not let him. He followed me . . . knocked me down . . . said if I made a noise he'd kill me. He was much stronger than I was and I had been sick for some time." Williams admitted having had intercourse with her, but minimized the impact. "She screamed a little but I told her to hush." He was sentenced to be shot, but escaped from prison before the date of execution.[6]

"It is the rule that black men must sleep with white women because white men have slept with black women." Thus spoke Fowler Willis, a former slave, as he and six companions invaded the plantation house of Frank M. Neff at Point Coupée. They shot and killed Neff and his son and raped the daughter, Aloysia. As the senior Neff lay dying, he asked not to be shot again, because "my first wound is mortal." In reply, Willis kicked him in the head. (This January 27, 1864 event caused great concern among other plantation owners.) Willis was hanged November 21, 1864.[7]

William H. Hilton, 16th Indiana Mounted Infantry, shot and killed a "little yellow girl" at Pelton's Plantation, Bayou du Lac. Hilton, drunk, had thrown her to the ground, saying he wanted to "ride her." She was screaming and crying and trying to get away. A colored woman begged him to stop: "She is too little and too young for a man." Hilton shot the girl in the forehead, killing her instantly. He confessed to the murder and was sentenced to be hanged. With great reluctance, General Stephen Hurlbut remitted the death sentence on a legal technicality. The details of this trial transcript are an eye opening view into race relations of that time and place, and cry out for further study.[8]

At Houma, Felix Gautreaux shot a black man with a double-barreled shotgun, wounding him severely. The shooting victim had tried to rape Gautreaux' daughter saying, "I'm the master now," as he ". . . unbuttoned all his pantaloons." Gautreaux was acquitted.[9]

Lieutenant Thomas B. Curtis, 162nd New York, was drunk at Camp Parapet. Really drunk. A few nights after Christmas 1862, he went to the guardhouse and asked if any Negroes were available. "Being answered in the negative, he went to the Negro quarters and there assaulted and beat a black woman with intent to violate her person." A few days later, during daylight hours, "He took out his privates and pursued officers with the avowed purpose of making water on them." (Avec moi, le déluge?) Not surprisingly, Curtis' further military career was quite abbreviated.[10]

At Bayou de Large, Omer Boudreaux, an officer apparently absent without leave from his Confederate regiment raped thirty-four-year-old Mrs. Artemis Verret. Boudreaux had his guerrilla companions hold Mr. Verret, while he worked his will on the wife. For this, and for other crimes, such as shooting a Union prisoner, he was sentenced to death. The appeals filed on his behalf, including pleas by the "leading citizens" of several parishes, fill hundreds of pages and, in time, his date with the noose was commuted by Andrew Johnson.[11]

Missouri

Rape in wartime Missouri was a rural affair. The metropolis of St. Louis generated no military trials for rape. While rape itself is brutal, in Missouri it seemed to be unusually vicious, perhaps reflecting the bitter partisan guerrilla warfare that burned through the state.

Private Benjamin Davis, 1st Missouri Cavalry, raped a woman at Bull Mill, a town too small to merit a post office today. She told the court: "He pushed me on the bed, tore off my clothes, made me lay the baby by my side, took me from both front and back and then a third time." Her 11-year-old brother said, "I saw him pull my sister's clothes off." After the rape, she hid in the knee-deep creek for two hours, fearing further assault. The questions of the court to her are remarkable. "Did you like it?" "Was it like with your husband?" Then the court asked the husband, "Did you beat her as she merits?" (!) They did find Davis guilty and ordered him to have his head shaved and be drummed out of the regiment to the Rogue's March. Further, if he was found near by, he was to be shot.[12]

Bull Mill was the seat of a second outrage, this one involving three generations. William Evans, 59th Illinois, and three unidentified men, came to the home of 80-year-old widow Sarah Downing, who lived with her daughter and three grandchildren. The daughter testified first. "The accused said he'd come to fuck me. He raped me standing in front of my mother and children, then the second man raped me, then Evans again. Then he raped my mother; it was all in the same room." The mother had her recollection: "He said he wanted to see if 'it' was as gray as my head. He pulled out his penis and tried to put it in my mouth and then he raped me. I resisted, but he was too strong." Evans received the same punishment as Davis.[13]

At Lebanon, James Robinson and Samuel Stewart, both of the 8th Missouri Militia Cavalry, terrorized a family. They threw Elizabeth Vernon on the floor, saying, "You must submit to our wishes," but apparently failed to complete the rape. They told her father, "We will do as we please with your daughter." In addition to the sexual offense, the men stole cash, clothes, and a watch. Robinson got three years in prison and Stewart got five. Both received a dishonorable discharge.[14]

At Pilot Knob, a courageous artist, William Hineley, saved a woman from a rape. "On March 31, 1862, I was in my room taking a portrait when I heard cries of distress. One hundred yards down the road was a woman, a part of her exposed, naked, with the soldier on top of her." Hineley described the rapist's heavy breathing, his hurried covering of his private parts, and his firing two shots at the rescuer. The victim was Nancy Willard, whose husband was away in the 12th Missouri Cavalry. The rapist was Private John Lowney of the 3rd Missouri Cavalry, who was sentenced to hard labor until the end of the war.[15]

John W. Morgan of the 1st Missouri State Militia Cavalry was a menace to two 28-year old women at Maysville. It was June 1864. Morgan, drunk, went first to the home of Martha D. Smith and asked, "How much money would it take to let me fuck you?" His next stop was at the house of Mrs. Frances Cummings. He threw her on the ground, held her down with his knees, waved a cocked revolver, and put his hand under her dress, touching her private parts, all of this witnessed by her children. The court gave Morgan a dishonorable discharge and five years in prison.[16]

Second Lieutenant Walter Purcell, 10th Iowa, was officer of the guard at Cape Girardeau in May 1862. Cynthia Shelton was held a prisoner on the third floor of the Johnson House, a "public house." One evening, Purcell came to her room and had sexual intercourse with her five times. He then left for an hour to meet a newly arrived steam boat, returned to her room, and did it again. In the hour that he was away, she made no effort to leave or to summon help. She had been visited by five other men the night before and had had coitus with each of them. Others said she was "Not a woman of virtue." The charge of rape was dropped and Purcell was set free.[17]

At Sibley, Private Frank Paul, 11th Kansas Cavalry, was charged with robbing two men at gunpoint of $15,000 (in today's money). He and another soldier, Alfred Weaver, went to a "colored house." Weaver told the court, "Paul threw Ann Rennick on the floor, pulled up her clothes and said, 'By God, I intend to screw you.'" Weaver told him to get off. The victim was not asked to testify. Paul was acquitted.[18]

At Tipton, two men of the 6th Missouri, Benjamin Wilson and Lambert Webster, entered the home of J. W. Brand at midnight. They robbed Brand of whiskey, tobacco, pants and, possibly, a pair of mules. Brand recalled, "They went then to the Negro cabins, hauled the girl out and he [Wilson] with three others ravaged her." The court record does not give her name, nor did she testify. Webster was imprisoned to the end of the war; Wilson served only one month. The other two men were not identified.[19]

In Johnson County, politics and rape were closely connected. John F. Herd, William Fisher, Thomas Estes, and Joseph Phillips (all white) went to the home of Harriet Nelson (also white) and stole clothing, carpets, and blankets, over the protests of Mrs. Nelson. Herd went into the backyard to Amelia Caroline, "colored," age 13. "He throwed me down and choked me. Then he ravaged my person." Her story was confirmed by her father, Richard Brown, and by Mrs. Nelson. Only Herd was tried; he was given fifteen years in prison. The following people wrote to Abraham Lincoln on Herd's behalf: the court clerk, the county treasurer, the assessor, two justices, and a deputy sheriff. Lincoln referred the case to Holt, who ridiculed these appeals, calling the crime "fully proven," and the sentence "minimal." Forty-nine of the men of Herd's old regiment wrote to say that he was a fine young man. A state justice and a major of the Missouri State Militia wrote, denouncing Harriet Nelson as "a rebel and a liar," claiming that she had called Herd, "a Goddamned Lincolnite and a nigger stealer." None of the correspondence mentioned the raped girl.[20]

Forty-seven-year old William Hensley, of Cedar County, was not a Union man. He refused to enlist in the Union Army and refused to take the oath of allegiance. He approached 39-year old Mary Brown, whose husband was in the Union Army, and threatened her with violence unless she submitted to his "carnal solicitations and desires." He was imprisoned at hard labor to the end of the war.[21]

Henry Fairbrother, 2nd Missouri Militia Cavalry, was accused of raping a Mrs. Harper in her home at Bloomfield. She told the court that a man broke down her door and got on her bed. When she cried out, he choked her. She was holding a baby. Her assailant ordered her 11-year old child to take the baby, and then completed "connexion" with Mrs. Harper. There was no light in the house. Fairbrother was acquitted because of a lack of visual identification.[22]

At Ironton, Thomas Finnell, 17th Illinois Cavalry, was charged with the attempted rape of Margaret Bradshaw, widow, age 26. She was at home after dark, with a neighbor Martha Willis. Finnell, drunk, came in and demanded beer. The women sent him away. He returned a few minutes later, broke down the door, threw Mrs. Bradshaw on the bed, put his knee on her breast, and choked her until she partially lost consciousness. Mrs. Willis summoned the guard, who took Finnell away. The court gave him a year at hard labor.[23]

John Estes was an 18-year-old farmer in Clay County near Holmes Creek. He had been a member of Company G, 25th Missouri, but claimed to have been discharged for "ill health." He was accused of being a guerrilla with "Joe Hart's men," and with the rape of Melinda Poage. He was acquitted of the rape charge, based on the document prepared by his counsel and signed with Estes' "X." "I have known Melinda Poage for five years. Her reputation for chastity is bad. I have known her carnally four or five times. The first time was in a tent at Camp Liberty, in the daytime. I gave her a dollar and a half. It was a fair and legitimate transaction." The couple met another time at Hamill's on the Missouri River and, more recently, when they met on the road. "She acceded to a proposition to go into the woods . . . and for the sum of one dollar have intercourse." Estes was convicted of being a bushwhacker and given five years at hard labor. His appeal to Andrew Johnson was referred to Holt, who noted Estes' reputation for being "a bad boy and thievish." Holt concluded that Estes was "a ruffian" and not deserving of clemency.[24]

Clint, "a colored citizen," tried to rape 11-year old Ellen Maroney, at Macon, in October 1863. "I was walking up the road. He was hammering a board. He asked me if I would wash a shirt for him. I told him, 'No.' He showed me a one dollar greenback. When he saw I was going to tear it up he took it back . . . He asked for some fuck. I told him I did not know what he meant. He said, 'God damn you, I'll soon show you!' He took me by the hair and dragged me down. I commenced to holler and he put his hand over my mouth. He got on top of me. Afterward, I found something like starch on my clothes." Clint was sentenced to hang and the records were sent to Lincoln, who asked Holt's opinion. In his report, Holt noted: ". . . bruised, lacerated and terrified, the little victim, when released from the clutch of her assailant, ran weeping to her home . . . An examination of her clothes and her person, made by women and by a physician disclosed all the confirmatory evidence of attempted ravishment . . . An examination of the Negro's parts by the doctor corroborated the other proof." The final note in this case reads: "Sentence approved. A. Lincoln April 14, 1864."[25]

Patrick Bolen, of the 25th Missouri, faced two charges in January 1864: attempting to force carnal intercourse on a colored woman, and habitual drunkenness. His regiment was camped near New Madrid. His intended victim, Nancy, "a contraband woman" who cooked for the drummers, told the court: "He came to my tent with his canteen of whiskey. He wanted me to take a drink. I told him I did not want any. Then he took out some money and wanted me to take it. I told him I would not and then he tried to put it in my hand and I threw it down. He tried to get in my bed, but I threw him out." Bolen was acquitted of attempted rape, but was convicted of habitual drunkenness. Several witnesses described Bolan's obsession with alcohol. One statement will suffice: "He is a very good soldier when there is no liquor about, but when he can get liquor he is no soldier at all." Bolen, with half his head shaved, was drummed out of the army.[26]

Arkansas

Little Rock was the locus of most Arkansas cases. Three civilians were tried in the attempted rape and death of "one Mrs. Smith, a colored woman," also called Aunt Harriet. Those tried were Michael Mackey, a teamster, John Johnson and H. H. Wiseman. Pompey Smith, who shared the "shanty" with his mother, said, "Mackey pulled the cover off my mother, put his hand on her breast and tried to get in bed with my mother. She was dying. My mother said, 'O! My soul.' Mackey replied, 'Ass and soul all go together.' He pestered her pretty good for half an hour." Matilda Budd, Harriet's landlady, heard the victim cry out, "Let me die in peace." Johnson's presence there was to pay Harriet two dollars owed her for laundry work. Pompey testified that Wiseman was not present during the affray. Mackey got fifteen years in prison; the two other men were acquitted.[27]

On January 29, 1864, at Little Rock, Charles Jordan, "colored," was accused of "carnally ravishing" ten-year-old Betsy Smith, "colored" to whom he gave "a certain bad and loathsome disease." Betsy's mother's employer was a captain Margraff, who told the court, "Jordan confessed the crime to me." Betsy said Jordan was guilty. His defense was that she had asked for it. "She teased me and said do me like Papa does to Mama." Jordan was acquitted.[28]

Sarah Lafave was a fourteen-year-old orphan living with her aunt, Frances Ellis, in August 1864 at Little Rock. Sarah told the court that William Powell had said, "I came for some fucking and I am going to get it." "He choked me and laid on me. It hurt when he did it." Mrs. Ellis said, "Sarah told me all about it, every detail. She was having her period." The defendant, a civilian, was sentenced to be hanged. General Frederick Steele remitted the sentence, saying the evidence was "poor."[29]

Ellen Ward, a seventeen-year-old "free women of color," was cleaning rooms at Little Rock's Anthony House Hotel. She testified that citizen John Ryan said he wanted to "crack" her, had sex with her against her will, and then threw money at her. Cross-examination elicited her prior employment at Jo Clegg's "fancy house," as well as her attempts to live "ladylike" since leaving her mother at Huntsville, Alabama. Ryan was acquitted.[30]

Anthony Lander, 113th US Colored Troops, was charged with two rapes at Little Rock, both upon the wives of soldiers in his own regiment. A. J. Jackson, husband of Elizabeth Jackson, asked Lander what he'd done to Mrs. Jackson. "I got what I wanted. I throwed her down and took it from her. I did it because I wanted to. I don't give a damn if she is your wife." Susan Washington, the other woman, described Lander's demand for sex, his slicing her with a knife, and her fleeing from him across a field. He was sentenced to hang but was remitted on a technicality.[31]

At Dardanelles, a 20-year old former laborer, born in Mississippi, Henry Jay, 57th US Colored Troops, raped "a white woman." He was tried by drumhead court-martial and executed on June 21, 1865.[32]

Also at Dardanelles, William Burden of the same regiment was charged with being AWOL and with raping two white women, Mrs. Charlotte Barnett and Miss Mary Ann Barnett. The former recalled that the night was very dark and her assailant was very black, but she was sure it was Burden. "He had carnal knowledge of me; his member entered my body." The court chose startlingly Anglo-Saxon terms in its cross examination: "Did you try to keep the prisoner from screwing you? How many times did he screw you?" The other victim, Mary Ann, recalled that there was enough moonlight to identify Burden. "He forced me to lie down and then he cracked me." One witness recalled Captain Andrew Fitch saying to Burden, "I'll have you shot tomorrow. I'm going to kill a nigger and it might as well be you." In the absence of reliable identification, Burden was convicted of being absent without leave but not of rape. He was fined $16.[33]

Pulaski County contributed two cases. Private Robert O'Brien, 3rd Missouri Cavalry, raped Sarah Dunn in early 1864. "My husband was sick and I'd gone into the woods to pick spicewood for tea. The defendant threw me down and entered me. He didn't last long; he was too far gone. When he left, he said he'd see me tomorrow. I told him I would see him in the next world." David Brinniger, of the same regiment, said he'd paid $1.25-two fifty-cent pieces and twenty-five cents in postal currency—to have intercourse with her. The court acquitted O'Brien based on Sarah's lack of virtue.[34]

Citizen John White was accused of raping eight-year-old Anna Eliza Wittkamp and murdering her father. The family lived on the Mount Ida Road in Pulaski County. Anna Eliza testified. "Mr. White was at my house. He said, 'Let's get the gourd and go down to the spring.' There he threwed me down and hurt my head. He pulled the thing out of his breeches and made the blood run out of me." Her mother told the court: "I heard her cry. She said he pulled up her clothes. I examined her and found she was hurt some in her privates but not so she wouldn't get over it. Her appearance did not indicate that her person had been entered." The family tied up White and threatened legal action, but they released him on his promise of better behavior. A few days later, he reappeared with armed companions, who shot Anna Eliza's father many times, killing him on his own front porch. White was sent to prison for three years for attempted rape, but acquitted of murder.[35]

At Helena, Private Anton Herter (or Hester), 17th Missouri, was charged with the attempted rape of six-year-old Anna Haegle. Herter was drunk on the porch of the regimental hospital. Anna was on his lap. She began crying and left. The regimental surgeon, John D. McConoughy, testified. "I was called to see her shortly afterwards. I found [her] parts swollen and tender. No injury done. Some swelling and tenderness. [Illegible] by a solution of sugar of lead. I don't believe prisoner attempted to commit rape. Same effect could be produced by feeling of the vaginal parts with the finger. No internal injury. Same effect might possibly be produced by an attempt to introduce the penis, but if an attempt had been made to enter with the penis, the parts would doubtless have been injured to a greater extent." Herter was acquitted.[36]

At Montgomery County, Friday the 13th was bad luck for John Vincent—he was hanged. This private of the 3rd US Cavalry had raped a widow, Martha E. Simpson, of Mountain Township, in the summer of 1865. "I met him on the road three miles below Cedar Glades. He took hold of my mare's bridle and led her outside the road. He pulled me off the mare and told me in the roughest way what he was going to do and he went about it with all his desire." The court asked what seemed to be an inane question. "Did you feel any part of his bare body?" "Of course I did. He had his breetches open and he lay on me." On further inquiry to the court learned that "He had his member in clear up to the body. He remained until he had satisfied his passion." Once again, a question by the court. "How do you know?" "I have been married long enough to know when he had satisfied his passion." The court was not finished. "When he pulled you off your horse what did he say he was going to do?" "He said he would fuck me and he did." The court's search for truth ended with a sentence of death for Vincent.[37]

Further West

At Drywood, Kansas, Privates William Jones and Horace Ralph were public menaces. They not only stole money and threatened arson, but these men of the 3rd Wisconsin Cavalry were charged with the rape of Mrs. Caroline Martin. Ralph held her at gunpoint, while Jones molested her. "I was not raped, but he put his hand on my bosom." Both men were sentenced to be shot. Ralph was commuted; Jones was not.[38]

At Iola, Kansas, John Bell, 2nd Kansas, raped Mrs. Elizabeth Haywood three times in her own home. A drumhead court-martial ordered that "he be hung until he is dead, dead, dead." Bell died July 11, 1862.[39]

Near Keokuk, Iowa, Private Eden Hill, 10th Missouri, had been sent to arrest a deserter who was working in the fields. He insisted on taking ten-year-old Sarah Allen McCormic, the deserter's sister, as his guide, over the protests of Sarah Allen's father. When alone in the woods, Hill raped the girl, effecting partial penetration. Medical examination showed severe bleeding, a partial tear of the hymen and severe emotional disturbance. Hill was sentenced to be shot, a decision strongly endorsed by Holt.[40]

At Camp Flat Rock Creek, Cherokee Nation, Private Henry Scott, 9th Kansas Cavalry, was charged with the rape of Peggy Pumpkinpile. She was on the way to the camp of the regiment with onions for sale, walking with her friend Betsy Dennis. Scott seized Peggy, demanding sex. She pleaded that she did not want to, that she had a husband and four children and that she was pregnant. He told her he would kill her and her unborn child, and then rape her anyway. He hit her on the head with his pistol and stood on her belly with his boots. Meanwhile, during this prolonged attempt at rape, Betsy summoned the guard. At the trial, Scott said he had given her half a dollar to have sex with him. The sentence of death was overturned on a legal technicality.[41]

At Fort Boise, Idaho, in March 1865, Lieutenant Herman Funk, 1st Washington Territory, was charged with a sexual assault upon an eight-year-old girl, Belle Dubois. The records state that the rape was not completed, but that he "mutilated her with his hands." The trial was postponed five times in a search for witnesses. None could be found and the case was dropped.[42]

Private Samuel Callan, 15th Ohio, was charged with the attempted rape of "Mary, a colored girl," who was a cook for Mr. Fenner, near Victoria, Texas. At the October 1865 trial, she told of the events: "He came through the window. He stood there a good bit, then asked for a drink of water. After he got the drink, he went out again through the window. He did not say anything out of the way. That's all." Callan was acquitted.[43]

At Edinburg, Texas, Charles Aiken, 45th US Colored Troops, "attempted to force the chastity and person of Simóna Garza." Simóna testified through an interpreter. "He uncovered my face but my mother held me close and protected me." Aiken was acquitted of attempted rape, but convicted of stealing gold jewelry and given eighteen months hard labor and a dishonorable discharge.[44]

In Texas, on the road between Clarksville and White's Ranch, citizen Charles Wright was walking with Mrs. Ann Hall. "I had known him about a year at Bagdad. He was walking with me toward Clarksville when he put his hands around me and said he wanted to do something to me. I was confident of his purpose from his expression. I screamed and as there was a buggy coming, he let me go. Then he apologized." Wright got two years in prison at Brownsville.[45]

John Smith, 1st California, was attracted to Hispanic laundresses. And to whiskey. At Fort Yuma, Arizona, in March 1862, he pled guilty to entering the quarters of Gautier de Reyes, attempting rape, and calling the corporal of the guard a "son of a bitch." A year and a half later, at Fort Craig, New Mexico, after Taps, he forced himself into the bedroom of Paula Trujillo, who recalled that, "He seemed amorously inclined." For the first incident he got seven months hard labor, and three months for the second offense.[46]

Chapter 18

RAPE UP NORTH

District of Columbia

Charles J. Bregstrom, 3rd Massachusetts Heavy Artillery, was AWOL overnight and was charged with the rape of Mary Brown, "a colored woman," at Fort Stevens. He was convicted of being AWOL, but acquitted of rape. The victim did not testify. Captain John Mara, 1st US Veteran Volunteers, was charged with assaulting Jane Northedge, wife of Sergeant William Northedge, at the corner of First and D Streets, and with the attempted rape of Margaret Mahoney, "colored," both on the same day. Both women testified. Mara claimed the women were "harlots," and was acquitted.[1]

Thomas Vanderlip, 3rd New York Artillery, was charged with the attempted rape of Miss Margaret Knowles, in January 1865. "He threw his arms around my neck and tried to make me go outside." Two other soldiers pulled him off. Vanderlip was convicted of a robbery but acquitted of attempted rape.[2]

Attempted rape was only one of many charges leveled against Sergeant Leander Davis, 1st New York Artillery, in January 1862. He was drunk, and left Camp Barry by presenting a cocked revolver at the face of the sentinel. Davis entered a citizen's home and accosted servant Barbara Shaefer. "I was at the washtub. He held a whip over me and called me a damned little whore. His pants were open and his private parts were exposed." After being arrested, Davis escaped and threatened Shaefer again. He was reduced to the ranks and sentenced to thirty days in the guardhouse.[3]

John Forrest, 3rd Massachusetts Heavy Artillery, seized a married woman, struck her in the face, and said, "Let me fuck you." Forrest received a dishonorable discharge and six years at hard labor for this January 1865 assault.[4]

Maryland

Three offenses occurred at Point Lookout, site of a large prisoner of war camp. John F. Hall, 5th New Hampshire, was a patient in the smallpox hospital. (The records frequently show contagious patients assigned to be guards or nurses.) He had been posted as a guard, but left his post and raped Mary Campbell, "colored," a 16-year-old girl in homespun, who was a patient in the same hospital. Three Confederate soldiers testified against Hall. Dr. Elias Bronson saw her the next morning. "She seemed more unwell, but I did not examine her." [He is likely the Elias Bronson who graduated from Massachusetts' Berkshire Medical College in 1859.] Hall was sentenced to three months of hard labor and lost eight months pay.[5]

In February 1865, William A. Underhill, 5th Massachusetts Cavalry, went to a citizen's home, where he beat up a man and offered money for sex to Eliza and Anne Carnes. Underhill was acquitted of attempted rape, but was fined six months pay for indecent and disorderly conduct. George Butler, who seemed to have accompanied Underhill, entered a citizen's home where a mother and her son and daughter lived. Butler forced the son to drink whiskey before beating him. He then threw the daughter on the bed, choked her and attempted to rape her, "acting the part of a dog or a hog [*coitus a tergo?*]." The mother poured a chamber pot over Butler to make him stop, whereupon Butler punched her in the head. He was sent to prison for twenty years.[6]

In Prince George's County, Thomas McIntyre, 125th New York, threw Mrs. Nancy Simms on the floor and tried twice to "violate her person." He also stole twenty cents and a hairbrush. He pleaded guilty and was given three years in the penitentiary and a dishonorable discharge for this August 1863 crime. In July 1864 at Point of Rocks, Conrad Shafer, 12th Pennsylvania Cavalry, attempted to "ravish" a Mrs. Pry. She did not testify. He pleaded guilty and received hard labor for the rest of his enlistment.[7]

In May 1865, Captain James F. Farrell, 5th New York Artillery, faced seven charges, including making false certificates, mutiny, conduct unbecoming an officer and a gentleman, and attempted rape, all at Baltimore. Ella Moore testified. "My husband Francis Moore is a private in Company H. Captain Farrell came to my house about dark. He asked me to sit on his lap . . . I refused, but he took hold of me and made me sit on his lap." The captain went on to tell her that he would keep her husband locked up for three years unless she would yield to him. She produced a revolver, which he took away from her. He then sat on the bed and "put his hands down my bosom." She told him to stop and he accused her of being "cross." The defense attempted to show that Farrell had not taken "indecent liberties" with her. He was convicted of most of the charges and was cashiered.[8]

At Bladensburg in July 1865, Charles Clark was tried for the rape of thirty-eight-year-old Nancy, "a colored woman." She was questioned on the meaning of an oath and replied that if she told a lie under oath she would be punished by God after her death. She was not sure of the date of the crime, but, "The corn had just come up and it was on a Thursday night, for I was ironing." She said that Clark chased her through the woods until she could run no more. "He said if I did not stop, he would kill me with the butt end of his whip." He threw her on the ground and overcame her attempt to hold her clothes down. He dug his fingernails into her thighs and forced them apart. He said he would kill her if she screamed. "He then did to me what men do to women. He took out his thing, that thing that God has given every man, his cock, and he put it in my thing." The court asked how far he went in. "About four inches." Then the court asked, "Did you render the prisoner any assistance during the time that he was inserting his cock into your body?" "I did not." Two defense witnesses had heard from other men that Nancy was "a whore." (A startling bit of hearsay.) Clark himself admitted intercourse with her, but said she offered hardly any resistance. He was acquitted.[9]

In June 1864, Daniel O'Keefe, 5th US Cavalry, was tried for the rape of Mary Selby, "colored," property of Thomas Hodges of Choptico, St. Mary's County. Both Hodges and 14-year-old Mary identified O'Keefe as "a big red-faced man," and Mary's mother testified that he dragged Mary out of her bed at the colored quarters and took her outside in the dark, screaming. There was prolonged testimony as to whether O'Keefe had grown a beard, and whether it made identification difficult. Mary recalled being raped by a big man who then held her down while a second man raped her. Private Andrew Kimball testified that O'Keefe was with him the entire evening, searching for smugglers. O'Keefe was acquitted.[10]

New York

There were two rape cases from Fort Schuyler, on Throg's Neck, in the Bronx. In September 1865, John Egan and Patrick Kelly, both of the 4th US Infantry, were tried for the rape of Mrs. Bridget Kilkenny. She said that the two men came to her as she was working in the fields. Kelly cut her with a sickle and held her while Egan unbuttoned his pants. An approaching wagon interrupted them and Egan returned to camp. Private Arthur Juliet testified through a German interpreter that Egan wanted to wash blood off his hands and used the coffee as wash water. Egan said he was too drunk to remember anything. He got five years in prison and a dishonorable discharge. Witnesses described Kelly inflicting a deep wound on Bridget's arm, which bled profusely, using the victim's own sickle, and confirmed his holding the victim so that Egan could unbutton his pants. Kelly was given seven years in prison and a dishonorable discharge. In

1866, he wrote from Sing Sing Prison, asking his mother to go see President Andrew Johnson and beg for a pardon.[11]

Connecticut

In a case of child molestation, Richard J. Jackson, 14th US Infantry, was tried for the attempted rape of five-year-old Caroline Stack, at Fort Trumbull. She was the daughter of the bandleader of the 3rd US Artillery. Caroline testified: "I recognize the prisoner as Jackson. He brought me up on top of the fort and took out his thing and told me to lay down . . . he made me lay down . . . he put his tongue in there (pointing to her vagina) . . . he promised to give me some candy . . . he swore Jesus Christ. He unbuttoned my pantalettes and I cried . . . he hurted me (pointing again to her vagina) . . . he said he was going to fuck me." The girl's father told the court that these were words that the girl never heard at home. Witness Caroline Keller said, "Mr. Stark sent me to look for his daughter. I went up to the fort and I saw the prisoner. As soon as he saw me, he commenced covering in front of his privates with his blouse." Jackson was given a dishonorable discharge and life in prison.[12]

Maine

In the winter of 1863, Frederick King, 17th US Infantry, offended several women near Cape Elizabeth and Fort Preble. He was absent without leave on December 14 and while absent, he "indecently exposed his person in the presence of several respectable women, in the road before the house of Mrs. Mary Thrasher," and soon thereafter assaulted her "with the intention of committing rape." A neighbor, Mrs. Hannah Kinney was hanging out clothes in her yard. "He exposed himself to me. He coughed to get my attention and I saw his pants were unfastened." Mrs. Thrasher, age 56 and the mother of eleven children, saw King in her yard with his pants unbuttoned and his privates exposed. She went into the kitchen and he followed her. "He made no attempt to touch or detain me." The defendant said he could not have committed the offense, as he was busy with assigned duties. "Besides, I have the venereal so bad as to prevent me from thinking such a thing as exposing my person." He was convicted on the exposure charge and acquitted of attempted rape. He had half his head shaved, spent a week in solitary confinement, was drummed out of the army, and was sent to prison for a year, followed by a dishonorable discharge.[13]

Illinois

Illinois was the site of five rapes tried by court-martial. At Chicago, in March 1864, Hospital Steward J. C. Webb, US Army, tried to rape Mrs. Lucy Parker, a matron at the City General Hospital. Mrs. Parker said that he had taken his dinner in the kitchen of her quarters, then tried to drag her into the bedroom. She was injured by being dragged out of her chair and against the doorway. "He said nothing. I resisted and he did not succeed in getting me into the bedroom." In cross-examination, Webb asked her, "Have I not always treated you as a lady?" Her reply: "Far from it." J. A. Jackson, surgeon in charge of the hospital, treated her for profuse bleeding from the uterus and attributed the hemorrhage to Webb's assault upon her. "I noticed she was bruised in the groin and on the left side." John Munson, 107th VRC, recalled, "She said she was sick from falling off some chairs and from marrying young." Webb said the case was contrived by a doctor who was discharged for swindling. "I was the principal witness against him." Webb received a dishonorable discharge.[14]

Another Chicago case was that of Alfred Bartholomew, 8th VRC, who was accused of sexual assault upon ten-year-old Alice McDonough in the barracks at Camp Douglas. Defense witnesses said he was the victim of persons jealous of his impending promotion, and besides, "She was a rather forward girl." Prosecution witnesses said that he had boasted of putting his finger into her private parts and that he had been seen with his hands under her clothes. "She was on Corporal Hahn's lap. The accused was standing right in front of her . . . had his hand under her clothes . . . I cannot say how far." He was acquitted.[15]

At Camp Butler, six miles east of Springfield, John Keahl, 16th Illinois Cavalry, was charged with chasing a fourteen-year-old girl with the intent of rape and with trying to break down the door of a woman living alone. The girl, Leena Young, recalled that at one in the morning Keahl and two other men threatened to break down the door unless it was opened. One of her sisters opened the door. Keahl came in smoking a cigar and waving a revolver. He announced, "If you don't do what we want, we will shoot you all." He took Leena's hand, but she jerked it away and knocked the cigar out of his mouth. "The only thing he said to me was that I should go to bed with him and that he intended to have intercourse with me." Leena's mother, her eight-year-old sister and her brothers, ages five and eleven, all asked the men to leave. John, the older boy, told the court that one of the soldiers had put his hands under the covers of his sick mother. Keahl said to Mrs. Young, "If I can't have your daughter, I'll have you." Witness George Peabody recalled, "I went by Mrs. Young's home [the next day] for a drink of water. She told me, 'Those German cavalrymen came last night, broke in the door, and said they wanted to fuck me and all the little children . . .' then she told me she didn't like to do it for money since so many of the boys had the clap. She consented to let Sergeant Peabody do it for money, provided he was clean." Another witness described Mrs. Young as "a short chunky woman, who speaks mostly German." Nik DeWald of the 16th Illinois Cavalry knew the family. "The husband is in prison. I know she has connection with men. I had it about two times myself. I paid a dollar each time." Keahl was found guilty.

He went to prison for a year, with a dishonorable discharge. Henry Bergmann, also of the 16th Illinois Cavalry, was with Keahl in the invasion of the Young household. Bergmann was convicted only of being absent without leave and was sentenced to 10 days of police duty.[16, 17]

First Lieutenant Patrick Moran of the 15th VRC was charged in August 1864 with molesting Miss N. Hosmer, an 18-year-old mulatto girl at Camp Douglas. She told the court that he chased and captured her, tearing off her clothing, stopping only when "compelled by her screams to desist." Moran was dismissed.[18]

The final Illinois rape case was that of John Marion Osborne. In 1864, he had spent two months in jail for deserting from the 6th Iowa Cavalry, en route to Fort Randall in Dakota Territory. After the war, he worked as a hired hand for Mrs. Delia Mathews, near Yates City, Illinois. In the early 1870s he raped and murdered his employer. Osborne was hanged for his crime.[19]

Research Possibilities in Civil War Rape

As Robert K. Krick pointed out, in his foreword to *The Story the Soldiers Wouldn't Tell*, the eminent authorities of a generation ago could state, "Rape, of course, was unheard of in that era." Now we know that was wrong, simply because the basic research had not been done. With the stories presented here, at least three new research possibilities suggest themselves. First, is the Southern belief in the unbridled lust of the colored man, barely held in check by the overseer's whip and the patrollers shotgun. There were roughly 180,000 men in the US Colored Troops. Were their arrests for rape disproportionate to their numbers? On a related theme—justice for non-whites—were black men more likely to be executed for rape than white men? A third related subject for study might be the rape of black women by Union soldiers, who, in our schoolbooks at least, had come to bring them freedom. The original records of Civil War misbehavior open a whole new landscape for future researchers.

A Summing Up of Rape

Rape in the Civil War can be most fairly compared with the same crime in other historical eras. We saw in Chapter 13 that in most wars, even within the most recent decade, rape was widespread, and has been seen as a soldier's prerogative, or as a means of humiliating members of a defeated culture. ("See, you are weak and cannot protect your own women. I leave her humiliated, dishonored, and pregnant with *my* seed, not yours.") The Union army discouraged rape as a prerogative by hanging rapists, at least some of them. Rape intended as geopolitical humiliation does not seem to be in these records. The roughly 250 rape cases in the Union record, out of an army of roughly 2.4 million, suggest that one out 10,000 Union soldiers committed an identified rape. While there are many unknowns in such statistics, it would appear that Union soldiers were remarkably well-behaved. Even in Sherman's much-maligned March to the Sea there is a dramatic lack of documented rape.

Certainly, critics can say, "Even one rape is too many," and of course that is true. And irrelevant. In a war that spanned an entire continent, rape was—happily—a rare event.

Chapter 19

CONFEDERATE RAPE

Rape by Confederate military personnel is in a very different category for two important reasons: the major sources of documentation are missing, and those that have survived make almost no mention of rape.

One of the mysteries of wartime military justice is the almost total absence of rape cases among the records of Confederate soldiers and officers. A glib answer would be that the armies of the South were composed of one million gentlemen, who would never stoop so low as to insult or impose upon a lady. While in theory this epidemic of chastity might be true, it seems improbable.

Since our only source of Civil War knowledge is records, we must examine the systems of providing and recording military justice. In the Union, there were two principal types of courts-martial: "general" for major crimes and "regimental" for minor crimes. The former are filed in National Archives Record Group 153; the latter are at the same archives but are scattered throughout regimental records and are much harder to locate. Summaries of the general courts-martial were gathered as "General Orders," set in type in a 4 x 6 inch format, widely distributed, and frequently bound as annual collections. The handwritten verbatim transcripts of general courts-martial, records that contain the entire testimony, were sent to the Judge Advocate General's office in the War Department and form the bulk of Record Group 153.

The men who commanded the armies of the South were graduates of West Point, just like their peers in the North. Not surprisingly, they adopted the same system of military trials and records as the North. As far as is known, the full transcripts of Confederate courts-martial were sent to Richmond for filing. At the fall of Richmond in April 1865, any pretense of record preservation went out the window—literally. While some records were moved west and survived, the vast majority fitted the following description, printed in the April 5th *Evening Whig:* ". . . official documents, pamphlets, etc., were scattered on

Monday morning. Confederate bonds, Confederate notes, bank checks, and bills flecked and whitened the street in every direction—all so worthless that the boys would not pick them up." Shortly thereafter, the Confederates set fire to their own capital and it would seem that the full texts of the Confederate courts-martial are gone forever.[1]

A set of printed general orders of the Army of Northern Virginia survives, and has been made available on microfilm, but the summaries are woefully short of details. A soldier might be charged with "conduct prejudicial to good order and military discipline," but the details are absent. Was it theft? Or drunkenness? Or assault? Or perhaps rape? A review of over five thousand of these general orders has found not a word about rape.

A diligent researcher, Jack A. Bunch, has spent decades visiting state archives throughout the South, looking for court-martial records and has found about 20,000. However, a review of his columns of names, presented alphabetically, shows no sign of rape and there is no subject index.[2]

There is a tantalizing hint of what happened to the legal records of Robert E. Lee's army. On April 10, 1884, W. H. Atkinson addressed the Beech Island Agricultural Club. This South Carolina farmers club was founded in 1856 and continues even today as a social and literary society. Atkinson told the members: "Nineteen years ago I witnessed a most melancholy incident—General Lee's surrender at Appomattox Courthouse. I'd rather expected a desperate fight then a quick surrender, for Gen. Lee about two o'clock Saturday night ordered me to burn up all the papers of the Judge Advocate General's office."[3]

Who was Atkinson? William Henry Haywood Atkinson is said to have studied law at Princeton and was age thirty-seven when the war began. He began his military career as a private in Company D, 14th South Carolina, and was assigned as a clerk in the commissary department. He was soon given more responsible duties and in October 1863 was assigned to be a clerk in the office of the Judge Advocate General of the Army of Northern Virginia, and ". . . surrendered with Lee's army in April 1865." This makes his record-burning story very plausible, but it still leaves us with a paucity of records.

Two history professors at the College of Notre Dame of Maryland, E. Susan Barber and Charles Ritter, have been pursuing the possibility that rape cases in the Army of Northern Virginia were referred to the civil authorities for prosecution, but their search in the civil records thus far has been inconclusive.[4]

Some clarification of the issue is seen in a letter from Confederate Secretary of War Judah P. Benjamin to the governor of Virginia, John Letcher. "There are in the [Confederate] Army, unfortunately, some desperate characters—men gathered from the outskirts and purlieus of large cities—who take advantage of the absence of civil authorities to commit crimes, even murder, rape, and highway robbery, on the peaceful citizens in the neighborhood of the armies. For these offenses the punishment should be inflicted by the civil authorities . . . The crimes committed by these men are not military offenses. If a soldier, rambling through the country, murders a farmer or violates the honor of his wife or daughter [i.e., rape], courts-martial cannot properly take cognizance of the offense . . ."

In the disruption of war, the Virginia state and county governments were hardly able to catch, confine, and punish these miscreant Confederate soldiers. Judah begged the Virginia state legislature for ". . . protection to Virginians." This would seem to be a major abdication of responsibility by the Confederate War Department. Judah's letter may be the key to the paucity of recorded Confederate rapes: the Confederate armies would not prosecute and the Confederate states could not prosecute. Certainly the Union punished Union soldiers for crimes against civilians, hanging and shooting dozens of Union soldiers. An example of the official Union position is seen in General Orders No. 12, from the Department of the Rappahannock on May 16th, 1862, issued by Major General Irwin McDowell. "The punishment for rape will be death; and any violence offered a female, white or colored, with the evident intent or purpose to commit a rape, will be considered as one, and punished accordingly." The Division commanders were empowered to order immediate execution by hanging—or by shooting "if hanging should not be convenient." The North hanged rapists; the South ignored them. Why the Confederacy chose to give free rein to the brutal crime of rape is a deeply disturbing mystery. If it was a manifestation of states' rights, the consequence was to protect the criminals who wore gray.[5]

Through both serendipity and diligence, we have been able to document a few cases of rape involving Confederate military personnel. We begin with Samuel Mathews Summers (Somers). A Union document dated May 30, 1862, a "List of Confederate Prisoners taken in hospital at Front Royal . . . By Gen. Shields," describes "S. M. Somers, Q.M. on Jackson's staff, left by the Rebels in jail for Rape." Confederate Special Orders 129/21, dated June 2, 1862, shows him dropped from the rolls for conduct unbecoming an officer and a gentleman. Sommers was born in Shenandoah County in 1831 and attended the University of Virginia and Washington College. He was a lawyer in Clarksburg when the war began. After his liberation from jail by the Yankees, he was exchanged three months later. His dismissal was revoked and he became an assistant quartermaster with Lee's reserve ordnance train. At Appomattox, he commanded the Army of Northern Virginia ordnance train. He returned to the practice of law after the war and died in 1872. As to the rape, an exhaustive search of the relevant records tells us nothing more.

John Duncan enlisted at Sweetwater in the 3rd Tennessee Mounted Infantry (Lillard's Regiment). General Orders No. 21 state that in late 1862, he was convicted of absence without leave, outrageous assaults on a citizen, and two attempts to commit rape. He was to be imprisoned for 25 years.[6]

Review of his sentence yielded this opinion: "If the evidence of the two women be deemed worthy of credit the finding is correct, but it appears that the character of these witnesses is not good and that ill-feeling has existed between them and the accused. The events occurred at Mr. Swallow's house, with Mrs. Swallow and her sister-in-law present. Duncan fired his musket and arrested them under pretended military authority and then tried to violate the women. Defense witnesses say the house is one of ill fame and the women are of bad character. Duncan's colonel, John Vaughn, said the women are "the outcasts of society," and that Duncan had been a good soldier. He was returned to duty.[7]

The 1861 Richmond *Dispatch* reported a rape on November 5. Near Portsmouth, four members of the Polish Brigade (13th, 14th, and 15th Louisiana Infantry) tied up a farmer and took "forceful and improper liberties with his wife." A letter to the editor on November 6 stated that the Polish Brigade no longer existed, and that the miscreants were from the 3rd Louisiana Battalion, and were not Polish. On November 11, a news article named William Cain as the ringleader. He was a soldier with the "Saint Ceraw [Ceran?] Rifles" (Co. D, 15th Louisiana Infantry) and had been shot by the arresting officer. Another man of the group was to be shot by a firing squad on November 11, and two other men were awaiting trial.

Newspapers shed some light on civilian rape in Virginia. The Richmond *Sentinel* on February 10, 1865, reported two men accused of raping Mrs. Henrietta Vance. The *Dispatch*, during July 1862, had three reports of rape. On the 17th, Frederick McSweeney and Patrick Sullivan were charged with making a "lascivious attack on an aged" colored woman. Two black slaves had attempted to rape two women near the coal pits in Chesterfield County. A Mrs. Rudd was raped, while a Mrs. Corse escaped. Rudd's assailant was sentenced to hang. The other man was "transported."

With these few cases, we close the canon of Confederate rape. Only a remarkable find will open it to reconsideration.

Chapter 20

MASTURBATION

Masturbation Antebellum

Masturbation, the activity of self-touching for sexual pleasure and release, is known by many names: self-stimulation, self-abuse, the solitary vice, secret habits, bad habits, and self-pollution, plus a wide variety of coarser terms.

It has sometimes been termed onanism, but a glance at the Bible (Genesis 38: 9) shows clearly that the crime of Onan was coitus interruptus, not masturbation. Under the levirate customs prescribed in Deuteronomy 25:5, it was Onan's duty to marry his brother's widow and to impregnate her; this he failed to do, when he spilled his seed upon the ground and was smitten dead by an angry God. (The New York *litterateur*, Dorothy Parker, called her pet bird Onan, because he spilled his seed upon the ground.)

The current teachings of the Catholic Church recognize that masturbation is "extremely common" among young men and "fairly common" among girls and women. Although this practice is common, "It has been the constant and clear teaching of the Church . . . that masturbation is a serious sin that will keep one from heaven." However, it is a mortal sin only if the act is a fully deliberate choice of what the perpetrator fully realizes is seriously evil. Masturbation with only partial realization of its import, or only "partial choice of the will" is but a venial sin. Spontaneous emissions during sleep are no sin at all. Further, masturbation as a result of "repressed conflicts," "irresistible impulses," or "neurotic compulsions" carry little or no fault. The confessor must make a correct pastoral diagnosis before prescribing pastoral treatment. The issue of diminished moral responsibility may also be seen in many of the Civil War cases to be presented here. [1]

Ellen Gould White, co-founder of the Seventh Day Adventist Church, was another who warned of the perils of masturbation, in her 1864 essay, *An Appeal to Mothers*.[2]

Other cultural traditions have had less negative views of self-stimulation. Amboyna, the capital of the Moluccas in today's Indonesia, was the center of great clove plantations. To ensure a good harvest, the men would go out at night, spilling their seed upon the plants, while crying, "More cloves!"[3]

The founding fathers of the future United States, with little interest in Moluccan traditions, were as concerned as their Judeo-Christian co-religionists in the Old World about the baleful effects of masturbation. Three hundred years ago, Samuel Terry of Springfield, Massachusetts, annoyed those in the meetinghouse by "chafing his yard to provoke lust" while the sermon was underway. Terry's oscillations were seen as intended acts of insolence, but more private masturbation was also of concern, as it denoted the corruption of fallen humanity and embodied disobedience to God's will. The clergy in the 1600's warned against masturbation because, while it was widespread and an apparently minor defect, it could be but the first step in the road to degradation. The solitary vice could lead to fornication, adultery, bestiality and finally utter damnation. Samuel Danforth, in 1671, declared that a man who practiced this "uncleanness with his own body alone," became "both . . . whore and whoremaster." Behind all these concerns was the principle that sex, in its true purpose of marital reproduction, was merely one more aspect of God's real design: the harmonious and virtuous ordering of the universe.[4]

Sometimes, harsh measures seemed necessary to maintain this harmonious ordering. In New Haven, Connecticut, in 1646, William Paine was put to death. In England, he had been a noted "sodomist;" when transplanted to the New World, "he corrupted a great part of the youth . . . by masturbations, which he had committed and provoked in others to the like of a hundred times."[5]

In the early 19th Century, Sylvester Graham, inventor of the cracker that still bears his name, lit the fires of an anti-masturbation conflagration that lasted over a hundred years. His 1834 book, *Lectures to Young Men*, went through ten editions in fifteen years. In its inflammatory pages, Graham claimed that the solitary vice led to physical decay, insanity, and suicide. Dozens of tomes echoing Graham's warnings flooded the bookshops over the succeeding decades. Surgeon John H. Kellogg, brother of the corn flake king, in his 1888 book, warned that those who committed the sin of "self-pollution" were "below the meanest brute that breathes" and "ought to be ashamed to look into the eyes of an honest dog."

An 1861 letter of Charles Noething tells of one man's anxiety over the effects of self-stimulation. He wrote to his brother, describing his current activities as a "Stud Horse," and told of his relief that his previous "vicious practice" had not impaired him.[6]

Mark Twain regarded these warnings as absurd, preferring to deem self-abuse a "majestic diversion," yet others, including the medical profession of Twain's time, were deeply influenced by the medico-religious cries of alarm.[7]

In 1853, William Young, a Philadelphia physician, published a book whose title leaves little doubt as to the book's contents: *Amativeness or the Confessional: A Treatise on Onanism and Self-Abuse, Manhood's Debilities, as Impediments to Marriage and Premature Failure of Sexual Power, to Which is Added the Confessions of Many Young and Old Men who had been Rescued from the Verge of the Grave.*

Effects of Nervous Exhaustion on Parents and Offspring.

This 1896 image, from Prof. F. C. Fowler's *Life: How to Enjoy It and How to Prolong It*, shows parents wasting away from "nervous exhaustion," while their son is dying from masturbation.

St. Elizabeth's Hospital, the Federal institution for the mentally ill, lies on a hilly expanse southeast of Washington, D.C. In the six years preceding the Civil War, twelve men were admitted to this hospital with disorders caused, according to the hospital records, by masturbation. Eight of the men were diagnosed with "dementia;" three men had "mania;" while one suffered from "melancholy." Nine were civilians, with one man each from the 2nd US Artillery, 8th US Infantry and the US Navy. The average age at admission was 25; the age range was from 20 to 36 years.

Were these mental disturbances from "masturbation" of serious consequence? Eight of the twelve died within a year of admission! The true nature of these illnesses, in terms of current medical concepts, is most mysterious. What would dement and then kill such young men? Could it be a form of encephalitis? The answer is that we do not know, but it certainly confirmed the opinions of the authorities that had been warning the youth of America.[8]

Before passing on to the subject of masturbation during the Civil War itself, it might be instructive to consider the same issue as it applied to the female sex.

There has long been a tendency to see females as less sexual than men, mainly on the basis of the absent phallus. Until recently, most physicians were men, with little real interest in the private lives of women. (The author can attest to the total lack of teaching of sexual matters at Stanford Medical School in the 1950's.)

In the 1800's, the most common diagnosis among female patients was "fever." The other leading diagnosis was "hysteria," with symptoms of anxiety, irritability, abdominal heaviness, pelvic edema, and fainting. As long ago as 1653, the Dutch physician Pieter Van Foreest noted that these symptoms were more common among widows and female religious. He recommended that the patient's genitals be massaged by a midwife until "the affected woman can be aroused to the paroxysm."

By the early 1800's, American physicians adopted a similar approach to this mysterious illness of hysteria, but noting the labor-intensive nature of these "treatments," soon turned to technology, so that the beneficial paroxysms could be produced with less direct involvement by the doctor himself. The earliest technologies used jets of water applied to the pelvic region. By 1870, a clockwork vibrator became available, but the springs tended to wind down just before the therapeutic paroxysm arrived. Next came the steam powered vibrator, marketed by Dr. George Taylor, who warned that its use should be closely supervised to prevent "overindulgence."

By 1900, commercial electricity had arrived, and proverbial Yankee ingenuity was soon evident. The Chattanooga Vibrator, with its heavy cast iron frame, arrived in 1904, followed shortly by the Carpenter Vibrator, with its long oscillating cable. By the time of the First World War, the hand-held electric vibrator, now nearly unchanged in ninety years, was featured in the Sears, Roebuck catalogue.

The remarkable aspect of this was not the availability of devices, but the medical profession's ability to regard these treatments (at least until around 1910) not as any manifestations of sexuality, much less masturbation, but as a remedy for a condition—hysteria—whose anatomy and physiology had never been defined.[9]

Two entirely opposed currents ran in medical thought on the subject of masturbation by women. The one just described saw women as largely asexual, suffering from "hysteria," which could be treated by mechanical devices. The other saw women as potentially oversexed; many doctors clearly identified clitoral stimulation as a form of masturbation, and carried out, as early as 1812, a long series of operations to remove the clitoris, thus "curing" the problem.[10]

To return to the central theme, let us now consider the issues of male self-stimulation in the years 1861-1865, and see what part it played in medical and legal thought, as revealed in the documents of the time.

During the Civil War

St. Elizabeth's Hospital continued to flourish during the war, adding medical and surgical sections to the original function of "insane asylum." Twenty soldiers were admitted to the psychiatric section during the war, with causation listed as "masturbation." None were officers. Six of the men died in the hospital; nine were listed as "recovered." Eight were foreign-born, while twelve were natives of the United States.

One relevant Confederate record has been discovered. In February 1864, a young man wrote to the superintendent of the Western Lunatic Asylum at Staunton, Virginia, "I have had some conversation with the physician who attended my brother previous to his going to the asylum and he advises me to inform you of the fact that he had learned from some of my brother's associates, who were in camp with him, that he was addicted to masturbation while in camp."[11]

Doctors and pharmacists in the Civil War were happy to oblige the young man worried about the effects of the solitary vice. Walter Powers, M.D., of 61 Franklin Street in New York City, ran a newspaper ad touting his Essence of Life. He queried his readers: "Young man, are you subject to that soul- and body-destroying disease: secret habits?" Dr. Powers promised "manhood and the vigor of youth regained in three days," including remedying the symptoms of "seminal weakness, sexual debility and nervousness . . . resulting from self-abuse."[12]

The front page of the March 31, 1863 Cincinnati *Daily Enquirer* carried a full-column ad by Dr. Raphael (no first name given) of 59 East Fifth Street. This "English botanic physician" wrote of the sad story of a young man who "had become the victim of a habit—the mere allusion to which causes a shudder—and after years of suffering and doctoring had given up all hopes of recovery." The young man wished to marry, but "dared not wed on account of the shattered state of his system." Of course, by taking Dr. Raphael's remedy, "all the bloom and vigor of youth has returned and he is now the father of a pair of bright boys."

The same paper, on April 23, 1863, carried a notice by Drs. Bonaparte and Reynolds of 132 Sycamore Street (no first names given). Not only would they cure syphilis, gonorrhea and unwanted pregnancy, but they offered unfailing success in the treatment of "nocturnal emissions, seminal weakness and impotence." On the same page, Dr. Stevens (again, no first name) of 78 Third Street guaranteed cure for those suffering from "involuntary loss of semen," as well as aiding "young men injured in body and mind from the effects of self-abuse." Nearby, at 46 East Fourth Street, Dr. W.C. Brown, also offered sure cures for "young men suffering from the effects of solitary habits."

Army doctors, too, were prepared to meet this menace, by consulting *A Manual of Instructions for Enlisting and Discharging Soldiers*, prepared by Roberts Bartholow, M.D. After outlining the telltale signs of alcoholism ("ferrety eyes . . . unsteady gait . . . tremulous tongue"), he addressed detection of the inveterate masturbator. "There is a state of cachexy or discracy produced by another vice, still more unfortunate than drunkenness—masturbation. In all of our general hospitals, there are numerous instances of men reduced to a most pitiable state of physical weakness and mental imbecility by this vice—a large proportion of them married men, separated for the first time from their wives." Dr. Bartholow enumerates the telltale signs of a masturbator: "emaciation, mental feebleness, small genitals and an elongated foreskin."

Much of his discussion hinged on a "fact," then accepted by medical authorities, that emission during intercourse was healthful and natural, while emission from self-stimulation was crippling. In a burst of prescience that set him apart from other medical men of that time, Bartholow speculated that excess masturbation might be the *result* of a disordered intellect, rather than the cause, but he let this insight, far ahead of his time, slip away.

Did the military authorities, indeed, take this matter seriously? The answer is "Yes!" The court-martial records give over a dozen examples. One case even involved the President of the United States. The central figure was Camillus Nathans of the 90th Pennsylvania. In March 1862, when he enlisted at age 23, he stood 68 inches tall and had blue eyes. He deserted at Washington, DC in September 1862. Some records say that he was arrested in December of that year, while others say late 1863. He reappears in the records as a patient in Washington, DC's Armory Square Hospital. There, in November 1864, Surgeon D.W. Bliss wrote, "I have carefully examined Private Camillus Mathews (Nathans went under several aliases) and find he has general debility and dementia, sequellae of nocturnal emissions, and I believe he is the subject of self-abuse . . . he is entirely incompetent to do military duty." This report, sent to Surgeon General Joseph K. Barnes, was, for reasons not recorded, sent on to President Lincoln, who wrote, "The name is Camillus L. Nathans. Let him be discharged. A. Lincoln Nov. 3, 1864." Nathans died in 1870 of alcoholism. His mother's request for a pension was denied.[13]

Peter Murphy, a native of Ireland, enlisted in the 2nd District of Columbia in February 1862. He was twenty-two years of age, 5'7" in height, with blue eyes. A year later, he was discharged with this note by T.J. Porter, Assistant Surgeon. "Mental incapacity and hebetude of the brain, alleged by the patient to be connected with a fall on the head, but believed to arise from long-continued and excessive masturbation, the vice and its effects antedating his enlistment."

(Hebetude, a word long out of use, means mental dullness with impairment of the special senses, such as sight and hearing.)[14]

After the Seven Days battle in June 1862, near Richmond, Virginia, Private Franklin F. Adams of the 2nd Vermont deserted and was gone over a year. At his court-martial, a letter from his family doctor was introduced as evidence for the defense. "I, Paschal Maxfield, of Vergennes, Vermont, on oath say that I am a physician and surgeon and have practiced . . . upwards of 20 years. Said Franklin Adams has always lived at home . . . except since his enlistment . . . I have always known about his condition . . . his peculiarities. For the past ten or 12 years, the effect of excessive masturbation has been very apparent . . . and for five or six years I have considered him so much affected by his indulgence in such habit that he has hardly been capable of performing half of a day's labor, and has lost more than half of his intellectual power. I know of no more serious instance of the baleful effects . . . of secret indulgence . . . he is wholly unfit . . . for the duties of a citizen or of a soldier." Private Franklin was given a dishonorable discharge.[15]

A very different story was that of Captain Moses Hagadon of the 11th New York. Ten officers of his regiment signed a petition that Hagadon should resign because he "persuaded his colored servant boy to commit the crime of masturbation." One prosecution witness, a young lieutenant, told the court, "Captain Hagadon said another officer asked the nigger how long it had been since he had been with a woman; they took the nigger in another part of the tent and made him jerk himself off, made him come his oats." There was much contradictory testimony, and in the end, Captain Hagadon was acquitted. The servant boy, Jimmy, did not testify.[16]

The gravestone of Private Weaver who, according to Federal records, died of masturbation. (Photo courtesy of A. H. Ledoux, Civil War Tombstone Project.)

Near the little Virginia village of Culpeper, the petals of the dogwood blossoms flutter down onto the grass of the National Cemetery. There, among the hundreds of other headstones, at Site 1-A-1, is the final resting place of Private John Weaver, Company C, 87th Pennsylvania. He had been a laborer before the war, was captured at Carter's Woods (a landmark in the Second Battle of Winchester, Virginia) on June 15, 1863, paroled, and sent to Camp Parole, near Annapolis, Maryland. He deserted from the camp but returned voluntarily in October 1863. He died five months later in the regimental hospital from "softening of the brain effected by onanism."[17]

Another soldier from the 87th Pennsylvania, Louis (Lewis) Holter was a twenty-one-year-old cooper, whose military career was marked by illness. He was in army hospitals at Frostburg and Baltimore (both in Maryland) and at Alexandria, Virginia. Holter was discharged twice for medical reasons. His November 1862 disability certificate notes "imbecility and general debility." Remarkably, he was allowed to rejoin the army, was hospitalized with diarrhea and was discharged a final time in May 1865. Surgeon Theodore Augustus Helwig left this note: "Incapable of duty because of general debility caused by masturbation. (An improper enlistment.)" Holter later received a pension.

Sentenced to be shot! That was the fate of William O'Brien, a private in the 131st New York, who deserted "in the face of the enemy" at Port Hudson, Louisiana. He was tried a second time because of a question of his sanity. Surgeon H.G. Bates testified. "He acts as though out of his mind . . . incoherent in speech. I don't think his intellect is sound. [The problem] is caused by masturbation and intemperance early in life . . . masturbation produces a species of indolent imbecility, and if persisted in will result in entire and complete insanity." The court rescinded the death penalty and sentenced O'Brien to five years at hard labor with a ball and chain (weight not specified), "being thus lenient because he is mentally an imbecile and not responsible for his actions."[18]

Gettysburg was the scene of many heroic moments, but not for Constantine Dickerson, a soldier with Company B of New York's 1st Long Island Regiment. On the afternoon of July 2, 1863, the regiment was ordered into the reserve line. They were not actively engaged, but a few stray bullets flew overhead. Dickerson was not seen again for two days. At his court-martial, Captain W. C. Dermady said, "Dickerson has a laxness to think and act . . . a want of mental capacity . . . he is devoid of a sense of responsibility" The judge advocate was curious as to the cause of this condition, and asked: "Are you aware of any secret habits which would injure his mental capacity?" ("Secret habits" was a term reserved for masturbation in the 1860s.) The captain did not answer the question directly, but simply added that the defendant was "a mental imbecile." He was sentenced to be shot, but was remitted on a technicality.[19]

Thomas L. Jones of the 21st Maine deserted twice, once at New York City and again at Augusta, Maine. Private William Sidelinger testified in Jones' defense. At home, he had known the defendant for eighteen years and had recently shared a jail cell with Jones while they both awaited trial. In jail, Jones "talks to himself all the time, shakes his head forward and pulls his hair. He has not eaten much until lately. He makes faces and wrings his hands." Surgeon C. Briggs gave his views. "I have seen him today and four times before. I have discovered mental weakness caused by masturbation. There is mental imbecility. He could not see [that] his practice would lead to insanity." The Court recommended dismissal from the service and is "thus lenient . . . because the appearance of the accused confirmed the testimony of the surgeon, that the accused was idiotic."[20]

The 68th Indiana had been captured and paroled at Munfordsville, Kentucky in September 1862. Private Andrew Moore, with the others, was given a brief furlough but did not return for ten months. He was tried for desertion and absence without leave. Surgeon John Wooden testified that Moore was not responsible for his actions, having become "deranged" from his addiction to "bad habits." The verdict was acquittal, based on diminished capacity.[21]

Private Jeremiah McCarthy of the 72nd New York was accused of entering his lieutenant's tent at 2:00 in the morning with the intention of robbery, while the regiment was camped along Virginia's Rappahannock River. McCarthy's strange demeanor caused him to be examined by Acting Assistant Surgeon Fred R. Simpson, who told the Court: "I found him in a state of excitement and trembling, with a rapid pulse. He would not look me in the face. I put him in the hospital so that I could judge whether . . . his was a true case of insanity." The patient escaped from the hospital twice, when recaptured, he said a young lady (who seems to have been imaginary) had brought him tea and a furlough paper. When asked his opinion on the cause of McCarthy's bizarre behavior, Dr. Simpson said, "By what I have heard from his captain and others, I believe it is self-abuse." Hospital Steward Ferdinand Wiley added that while McCarthy was in the hospital, he had left his money lying on the floor and seemed "careless" and "restless." The Court acquitted McCarthy of robbery and recommended that he be discharged as unsuitable.[22]

Private Thomas Palmer of the 1st Missouri Cavalry deserted at Elk Creek, Missouri, taking his horse with him. When captured and tried eleven months later, he pleaded guilty, but made a statement in his defense. "I have a weak mental organization and fits of depression, from the practice of self-pollution in my youth." He was sent to prison for six months, had his enlistment extended for eleven months and had $10 a month held back from his salary until he had paid for his lost horse—$136.95.[23]

Private David Aarons (his name is spelled eight different ways in the records) of Company E, 81st Pennsylvania was admitted to the post hospital at Camp Cadwallader, near Philadelphia, on July 5, 1865, with a diagnosis of "Masturbation." He died the same day.[24]

During combat at Boydton Plank Road, Virginia, Private Thomas Cresiday (Cassidy), Battery B of the 1st New Jersey Artillery, was sent for ammunition. He did not return for two months. Cresiday seems to have been unwell even before the battle: "When the firing commenced, he fell down in a fit . . . turned ghostly pale and a thick foam came out of his mouth."

During his trial, he had another fit, described in detail in the legal transcript: "His head turned over toward his right shoulder. His eyes quivered and then his eyeballs disappeared entirely under his eyelids, leaving nothing but the whites visible. He fell from the stool . . . doubled up in a heap, then he straightened out and struggled violently." This "struggle" (probably the clonic phase of a seizure, in which the body jerks rhythmically) continued about five minutes. Fifteen minutes later, the surgeon pronounced him again capable of assisting in his defense, and the trial resumed. (Most likely, Cresiday was still quite befuddled.)

Dr. B. Gesner, Surgeon in Chief, Artillery Brigade, Second Army Corps, testified at length about the difficulty of telling real from feigned epilepsy, and named the potential causes of this condition: "It usually appears in habitual drunkards, and in those addicted to masturbation . . . as well as being a hereditary disease." Testimony was followed by a lengthy opinion by the judge advocate on the definitions of legal insanity, a discussion very reminiscent of sanity issues in trials today. Cresiday was convicted, forfeited all past and future pay and was sent to a medical board for possible discharge. This 33 year-old former sailor, born in Ireland, was discharged from Carver Hospital, at Washington, DC with a diagnosis of "Epilepsy, paroxysms frequent."[25]

Private George W. Emery drove a peddler's bakery cart before he enlisted in the 17th Maine. He was on sentry duty in Washington, DC, in September 1862, when he was discovered sound asleep. Surgeon H. L. Wiggins stated that Emery was not responsible for sentry duty and gave his reasons: "His intellect is naturally low and his moral sentiments also. Either from abuse of himself or disease of the brain, he now manifests less intellect than he naturally would. I judge he is in the habit of indulging in masturbation and that is the cause of his extreme prostration of the brain. I have been a practicing physician for 15 years and have been in the habit of treating masturbation." Emery was ordered to be dismissed from the army.[26]

Twenty-one-year-old Private Levi Robbins had been a farmer before the war and was 5'5" at the time of his enlistment in the 92nd Ohio. In December 1863 he went away from the hospital in Louisville, Kentucky and when caught a month later was tried for desertion. The trial transcript notes: "He did not appear to be in a sane state of mind . . . talked foolish . . . threw himself upon the ground, rubbing his privates." Robbins had a fear of wagons and did not seem to understand the purposes of a musket. The Court urged that he be sent to "a hospital for insane soldiers."[27]

John H. W. Stuckenberg, chaplain of the 145th Pennsylvania, noted in his diary on October 12, 1862, two men in Company A, who begged his assistance in getting discharged. Both were married men, but ". . . such are the pernicious effects of the early indulgences, that now they frequently have nocturnal emissions, foul dreams, etc."[28]

First Lieutenant John M. Higgins of the 33rd Ohio faced four charges in his April 1863 trial: forging a parole certificate; advising an officer to desert; being absent without leave; and conduct unbecoming an officer and a gentleman. The fourth charge is the one most relevant to the topic under discussion. He had written a letter to a second lieutenant of the same regiment, in which Higgins stated, "I am in a bad way in regard to my eyes, which Missy says I will lose if I don't quit fucking, which I started by jacking off [which] is the sole cause of my disease." He was found guilty of three charges and acquitted on the charge of forging a parole. He was dismissed from the service.[29]

Private Herbert Daniels of the 7th Rhode Island wrote a series of passionate letters to his lover, Mrs. Salina Waterson. On September 6, 1864, his four-page missive included these thoughts: "I think of your bed and the joys of love," but he worried that such thoughts, which might lead to self-stimulation, could be carried to excess and "possibly injure my system." He promised his loved one that he would suppress his feelings until she "could have a hand in it."[30]

Masturbation in the Navy Records

Navy disciplinary records also reflect an assumed connection between masturbation and sickness.

The aptly-named USS *Restless*, while patrolling St. Andrew's Bay in Florida, put into shore in October 1864. Its skipper, Acting Volunteer Lieutenant W.R. Brown, seems to have been a wild man. In addition to assaulting his ensign, stealing soap, embezzlement, urinating overboard, and giving orders while seated on the privy, he offered a piece of medical advice that seemed to trouble the naval authorities: "Boys, there are loose women there where you're going ashore. If the doctor would recommend it, I'd let you go ashore and get your lanyards greased [have intercourse] . . . it would be better [for you] than to practice masturbation." Lieutenant Brown was dismissed from the navy.[31]

On the US Steamer *Shenandoah*, off New Inlet, North Carolina, Martin Ames, Second Class Boy, had shown poor performance in late 1863. He escaped punishment based on a report signed by three navy surgeons, Richard Dean, F.M. Dearborne and A.E. Emery. "We find him affected with adynamia from the secret vice." Their written opinion added that his condition was not service-connected.[32]

Another sick sailor fell under the same rubric. James A. North of the *Commodore Hull* was examined by two surgeons. Their opinion? "We have held a strict and careful survey upon James A. North, 19 years, first class boy. We find him very much debilitated in body and mind, this state arising, in our opinion, from the habit of self-abuse. This condition wholly unfits him for the service and we would recommend that he be discharged. The disease did not originate in line of duty. The duration is uncertain."[33]

Landsman George Brady, admitted to the hospital from the *Commodore Reed*, was given the diagnosis of "masturbation." At age eighteen, he was discharged from the navy on November 27, 1863, as "unfit."[34]

Masturbation Post-War

The Civil War was not truly over until the last veteran died, and indeed, in the hearts of many, it is not over yet. Relevant to the issue of "self-abuse," the records of the Pension Bureau contain many rejected claims, rejected on grounds of "that withering incubus," that vile "nocturnal pollution." Witness the case of veteran Joseph Batson, Co. H, 123rd Indiana Infantry, committed to the Indiana Hospital for the Insane, with a diagnosis of "mania from masturbation." His application for a government pension was initially denied because he had "caused" his own disability. After a lengthy process of appeal, he did receive his pension. Not so lucky was Civil War veteran Lewis Y. Crum, who had served in the 14th Indiana Light Artillery, and received no pension because "his disability resulted from onanism."[35]

The medical profession did not take this problem lying down. They rose to the challenge and in the 19th Century, dozens of anti-masturbation devices were patented. A typical one was the 1897 "McCormick Surgical Appliance, Patent No. 587994," a set of steel clamps and spikes, which when properly adjusted would discourage erection, much less masturbation.

In our "modern" age, are we more rational about this issue? Surgeon General Jocelyn Elders suggested that compared with careless intercourse (which produces illegitimate children, swells the welfare rolls, and transmits AIDS, syphilis, gonorrhea, Chlamydia, herpes, venereal warts, and other sexually transmitted diseases), masturbation was a relatively safe and responsible alternative. For this view, she was fired from her post in 1994.

Can masturbation be dangerous? Certainly. The author had a hospitalized mental patient, a young man in his early 20's, who, after a weekend visit home, returned with his virile member a knot of purple lumps and bruises. I quickly summoned a urologist, who took one look at the young man and simply said, "It's a typical vacuum cleaner injury." And so it was.

Forced masturbation, under observation, was used by Nazi "medical" scientists, both as dubious science, and as a way of humiliating prisoners. The same forced activity has been reported in the Balkans and in Iraq.[36]

Masturbation can even cost one a judicial career. Creek County (Oklahoma) District Judge Donald D. Thompson announced his retirement shortly before facing an ouster trial, based on a charge of indecent exposure. Court reporter Lisa Foster and bailiff Zelma Hindman both said they had seen the judge using a penis pump while presiding from the bench. Investigators were checking DNA samples from the judge's robes, his chair, and the courtroom carpet. He will receive $88,800 a year for life, unless convicted of a felony. (Subsequent news articles noted that the unusually dexterous jurist also shaved his scrotum while on the bench.)[37]

Our Civil War ancestors saw a dangerous cloud hanging over this apparently universal activity. Mark Twain's view of it, as a "majestic diversion," was shared by few authorities, whether medical, military or ecclesiastical, at the time of the Civil War.

Chapter 21

HOMOSEXUALITY

Close relationships between persons of the same sex are very much in the news in the early twenty-first century, with emphasis on committed couples and their legal rights. The possibility of legal marriage has concerned some observers to a sufficient degree that a constitutional amendment forbidding such unions is under consideration, and many states, through referenda, have banned same-sex marriages. However, the military justice cases, especially in the Civil War, involve same sex relationships that reflect abusive or disruptive activities, rather than manifestations of affection.

Homosexuality Antebellum

Sexual connection between men has a long and heavily documented history. In the most ancient recorded narrative, the tale of Gilgamesh, the hero has as his closest friend, a homosexual lover. Jumping ahead 1500 years brings us to classic Greece. It is commonplace to speak of "Greek love" when discussing pederasty, and it is widely assumed that connection between men, or between men and boys, was an everyday occurrence. After all, did not Socrates himself spend his days at the wrestling school, admiring the young naked men, their bodies glistening with olive oil? But Greek society was far more complex than today's activists and apologists might have us think, and a closer look will show us that sodomitical practices, especially the role of he who is penetrated, were widely regarded with disdain and disapproval.[1]

True, Alexander the Great was fond of young men, and Emperor Hadrian (76-138 AD), who was not averse to adultery with married women, had a special place in his heart for the boy Antinous. When his young lover drowned in the Nile, Hadrian had a city, Antinoopolis, built to mark the site and memorialize their love.

In the New World, dozens of Indian tribes had the berdache, men who dressed in women's clothes and married men. Their fellow tribesmen did not disdain the berdache, but regarded them as a third gender, one with magical and spiritual powers.[2]

The Mochica of Peru (300 BC-700 AD) produced a vast amount of pottery of remarkable artistic quality, which depicted in vivid detail every imaginable form of sexual connection, including men with men.

Detailed study of New England colonial records has revealed many tales of homoerotic behavior, such as that of Nicholas Sension of Windsor, Connecticut, who, in the mid-1600s, was widely known for attempted sodomy on many male servants and fellow citizens over a period of two generations. In 1637, John Alexander and Thomas Roberts, of Plymouth colony, were found guilty of "often spending their seed one upon another."[3,4]

Our War for Independence generated the courts-martial of Private John Anderson of the Maryland Line (convicted of attempted sodomy), and Lieutenant Gotthold Enslin of Colonel Marcum's Company, who was drummed out of the Revolutionary Army for attempted sodomy while at Valley Forge, Pennsylvania.[5]

But these men were small fry, barely known to history. Of greater note was Baron Frederich Wilhelm Ludolf Gerhard Augustin von Steuben. In addition to a brilliant (if possibly fabricated) military career in Prussia, he had been a member of the inner circle of King Frederick II, the most notorious openly homosexual ruler in Europe. In one of the ironies of history, a letter accusing von Steuben of taking liberties with young boys prompted him to accept Benjamin Franklin's offer of high rank in the Continental Army. Von Steuben's role in transforming an American rabble into a professional fighting force was crucial to American independence, and he is still justifiably remembered as providing the key to George Washington's successes.[6]

This briefest of introductions suggests that male-male connection, clearly present for over 5,000 years, might also be found in the Civil War. Indeed, such liaisons were present, but the existing records suggest that they were relatively rare. Rare or not, the cases we have discovered are both vivid and well documented.

Homosexuality in the Civil War Armies

Perhaps the most remarkable example of such transgressions was Lieutenant Colonel George Stanton Hollister of the 16th New York Cavalry. He graduated from West Point in 1860, 38th in his class of 42. He served several years with the regular army out west, in Indian Territory, Kansas, and New Mexico, and was present at the battles of Valverde and Peralta. He was first court-martialed in February 1863 while serving at Fort Union, New Mexico. Hollister had used a false authorization to obtain a six-mule government wagon, with which he hauled a load of "Mexican women of disreputable character" to a fandango in the nearby village of Loma Parda, where he danced "in common with enlisted men ... and Mexican prostitutes." In spite of damning evidence, he was acquitted. Ten months later, he was commissioned a lieutenant colonel in the volunteer service, and began his career with the 16th New York Cavalry[7]

He was soon in trouble and was court-martialed for conduct unbecoming an officer and a gentleman. The specifications included that he "did repeatedly lay hold of and in a beastly manner attempt to make use of the private parts of Captain A.L. Washburn for the purpose of gratifying a disgusting and venal appetite and ... did several times seize and manipulate the private parts of said Captain Washburn with his hand and did thrust his tongue into the said Captain Washburn's mouth while Captain Washburn was partially asleep and did endeavor repeatedly to get his mouth down to the private parts of said Captain Washburn for a most disgusting and beastly object after the manner of a dog ... all this at Fort Ethan Allen, Virginia." Hollister apparently repeated these activities at Annandale, Vienna, and Fairfax Court House, all in Virginia, in early 1864.

The record further states that Hollister approached Lieutenant William Farrell in the same manner. Apparently willing to inflict his favors upon both sexes, Hollister visited a house in Annandale "and while there, in the daytime, and in the presence of enlisted men, did take liberties with a girl, did feel of, and try to unfasten and toy with, and take out her bosom, and did take other liberties of a scandalous nature." Hollister was also charged with wild and noisy drinking parties lasting until dawn.

The records contain a sworn statement by Lieutenant George H. Grosvenor, claiming that Hollister "came into my tent ... took off most of his clothing ... placed his face near my private parts and took my penis in his hand and it appeared to me that he tried to introduce it into his mouth." Grosvenor pushed Hollister away, but "he threw himself upon my back and endeavored to thrust his penis into my anus." Grosvenor, who seems to have his own shortcomings, was dismissed from the service a few weeks after making this statement.

The lengthy transcript of the trial mainly confirms the charges listed earlier. The defense introduced a Major G.G. Horton, who said he would not believe anything said by Captain Washburn. Lieutenant Grosvenor, the same man who swore that Hollister had molested him, also said that Washburn was a liar and "a man of no honor." Lieutenant Joseph Schultz was called next and characterized Washburn as "a habitual and notorious liar." Surgeon James Horniston, also of the 16th New York Cavalry, was another who doubted Washburn, although he could give no reason for his doubts.

William Farrell, now reduced to private from his former status as lieutenant, testified that Hollister made "several attempts to unbutton my pantaloons."

After six days of trial, the record ends suddenly with a note that there was no quorum. Appended to these records is a long-overdue bill from the Metropolitan Hotel on Washington, DC's Pennsylvania Avenue, for $41.43 ($1200 in today's money) with a request that the adjutant general withhold this amount from Hollister's pay.

Although the court-martial came to no conclusion, in October 1864 Hollister was dismissed from the service—but the story is far from over.[8]

His widowed mother, Mrs. Frederick Hollister, launched a series of pleas to high officials. In her letter to Lincoln's Secretary of State, William H. Seward, she reminded him of the political favors her late husband had done for him and for the future Secretary of War, Edwin Stanton. She concluded by citing her son's service in New Mexico, where "he proved himself in many trying situations." Mrs. Hollister sent a similar letter to Thurlow Weed, a highly influential New York politician and editor, while her other son (who was secretary to the Governor of Nevada) wrote to Roscoe Conkling, asking this well-connected New York congressman to intercede in George's dismissal.

The circle of interested parties continued to widen. Fourteen officers of Hollister's cavalry regiment petitioned for his reinstatement, while seven others, including the regimental chaplain, signed a petition asking for just the opposite result. Colonel H. M. Lazelle wrote, asking for the dismissal of Hollister as well as Captain Washburn and Lieutenant Schultz. Major Horton wrote, describing Washburn as "obnoxious, odious . . . a horse thief."

In November 1865, Hollister was still out of the army and in disgrace when to his rescue came Major General John A. Dix, 67 years old now, but still functioning very well. Dix noted that Captain Washburn had been dismissed in disgrace and that Lieutenant Farrell had been in Old Capitol Prison for desertion. Thundered the old general, "No man accused of acts which degrade him to the level of the brutes should be judged guilty except on evidence of the highest credibility." In January 1866, Hollister's dismissal was revoked.[9]

In 1867, Hollister was back with his old army regiment, the 7th Infantry, serving now in Florida, where his penchant for politicking was evident in the venue of his marriage to Philoclea Fisher—they pledged their troth in the living room of the Governor of Florida. Hollister's other penchant was in evidence as well—he was convicted of being drunk on duty and was cashiered (dismissed in disgrace).[10]

Again, his mother rescued him. Although Judge Advocate General Holt noted that Hollister had falsified records to cover his misdeeds, and advised President Andrew Johnson that "Hollister's removal from the service would probably derive much benefit," Johnson responded to political pressure from John Galbraith, the Attorney General of Florida (and 246 other pillars of society) and reinstated Hollister, who served in Utah and Montana until his retirement in

1871. A decade later he died of "uremic convulsions," at the Jackson Sanitorium, at Danville, New York.[11]

What are we to make of this unusual life? Was Hollister an alcoholic bisexual satyr or simply the victim of scheming and perjured peers? A clue may lie in the 1863 obituary of his father, a Utica, New York businessman, that described a series of business expansions and collapses, spells of expansive optimism followed by enormous bankruptcies, all in spite of his "magnetic personality." This, of course, is the picture of bipolar disorder, a hereditary psychiatric condition that often manifests itself as hyper-sexuality and ill-advised ventures. Maybe Hollister's accusers were right, after all.[12]

The next case centers around a war of words, with a little scuffling. The 15th New York Engineers convened a court-martial at the Anacostia Engine House, Washington, DC, in October 1862. The defendant, Private John Conner, was charged with saying to First Lieutenant Augustus Greene, "I can lick you, you damn son of a bitch, you are a bastard and a thief" and other language "too gross to be repeated."

He was also charged with pushing Lieutenant Greene, who had been walking up the company street after his inspection of the drum corps. "Conner approached me and said, 'There goes that son of a bitch of an adjutant. Pretty boy. I'd like to fuck him.'" A few moments later, Conner allegedly added, "You are a cock sucker. I'd like to put my lips up to yours and suck them."

In cross-examination, Conner asked Greene (defendants did their own cross-examinations in many Civil War trials), "Did I not say, 'I want nothing to do with you?' Did you not rub up against me all the way to the avenue? Did I not say, 'For God's sake, go away from me,' before I used any harsh language? Did you not say that I was a big coward, a big loafer and a sucker? Did you not whisper to me, trying to get me to hit you? Did you not laugh in a sneering way?" Lieutenant Greene said, "No" in response to all these questions.

Witness Corporal George Garrett had heard Conner say to Greene, "My privates are bigger than yours," and recalled Greene following Conner up and down the street. Another witness said that Greene had "a derisive smile," while a third witness recalled the quarrel starting when Conner said, "Keep away from me. I don't want anything more to do with you."

Defense witnesses told a somewhat different story. Private John McCafferty recalled, "Lieutenant Greene kept following Conner up the street and elbowing him pretty close. The lieutenant appeared to be trying to aggravate Conner. He called Conner a blower." (The 1847 Webster's defines a blower as one who melts tin. Idiomatically, it may be related to blow hard or blow job.) Another witness told the Court that Conner said to Greene, "You have done enough to me already. I want you to leave me be. You are shook off by all your friends—even your brother has shook you off." Greene replied, "You are all mouth, all brag. You dare not hit me."

Other witnesses, who were only a few feet from the altercation, agreed that Greene seemed to be provoking Conner. "Greene came up to Conner and said, 'Why should I leave you alone? You are a pretty fellow. I like the looks of you.'" When asked directly, the witness said, "The lieutenant's reputation is bad."

Further witnesses were called. One had seen Greene come up to Conner and take Conner's arm and provoke him. "Lieutenant Greene's reputation for truth is decidedly bad. I did hear Conner say, 'I'd like to have you suck me.'" John McGuire had his say: "I saw Conner walking up the avenue talking with one of the other men. Then Greene walked up behind Conner and gave him kind of a shoulder. Conner begged Greene to leave him alone. Greene called him a coward, shouldered Conner again, then shoved him with his hands and called Conner a 'cock-sucking bastard.' I was four yards away. Then Greene whispered something which seemed to enrage Conner."

The trial concluded with the testimony of three officers, all of whom described Greene as truthful and honorable. Conner was found guilty of using insulting language toward Greene and was fined $8 a month for two months (60 percent of his pay). The record states, "The Court is thus lenient . . . in consequence of the strong provocation offered by the officer."

What are we to make of these proceedings? The 15th New York Engineers had 111 general courts-martial—an unusually unruly and turbulent regiment. (Wisconsin troops averaged 23 courts-martial per regiment; for New Yorkers, the average was 68.) The defense witnesses were nearly all enlisted men with Irish names. Was this mainly a clash of ethnic and social class differences? The petty and petulant tones of the conversations and the frequent reference to oral sex that seemed to characterize this encounter suggest something more. An apparent aura of sexual tension between the two protagonists sounds much like a lover's quarrel. An openly homosexual colleague, Jerry Graham, a former National Archives employee, viewed the transcript as "obviously a snit between two queens."[13]

The final meaning of Conner's tribulations may be forever ambiguous, but the case of Lance Corporal Thomas Rayment is not. He was a teacher at the Army Music School on Governor's Island, in New York Harbor, where the students—future fifers, drummers, and buglers—ranged from age eleven to seventeen. Rayment was charged with attempting to violate the persons of Henry Schoales, Robert McBeth, and Charles Gale, all members of Company B, Music Boys. Rayment was an old soldier with almost forty years of service. The season of Rayment's downfall was Spring 1864.

Who were these boys? When McBeth was 14 ½, his father, Robert M. McBeth, consented to his enlistment. The boy was 4'7", with a fair complexion and hazel eyes. The enlistment records of Schoales and Gale are missing.

Shoales told the Court, "The prisoner offered me a drink of beer in his room. Both of us wore only our shirts. He asked me if I would dip him off. I understand by dipping off, rubbing up and down of his private parts, the same he done to me. I told him I could not do it and had never done anything of that kind before. I succeeded in getting away from him by jumping out the window. He then followed me to my room and put his hand on my privates, but I made him go away."

McBeth told a similar story. "I went to the room of Corporal Rayment to get some stationery. He asked me to stay and write the letter in his room, then he locked the door. He put the key in his pocket. He took hold of me and rubbed my belly and attempted to do the same to my private parts, but I prevented him. He came up to me with his private parts and asked me to dub him off. He meant that I should take hold of his prick and jerk him off. I would not do it." After half an hour, Rayment let him out of the room.

Gale was the third prosecution witness. "On June 15th, 1864, he took me into his room to sleep with him. I did so. When I awoke, he was sucking my privates. He said he felt something slipping down his throat just like an egg. On the night of the Fourth of July he invited me to his room again and I drank a glass of beer with him and returned to my room. He followed me, sat on my bed and felt my private parts. I remonstrated and he left. We slept together before, but never went to extremes." Defense witness Sergeant G. Byron added an unusual observation. He had cautioned Rayment "not to place any confidence in certain noncommissioned officers of Company B, Music Boys . . . because their associations would draw him aside from the religious habits he was desirous of following." The religious aspect was curiously foreshadowed in a letter written May 4, 1837 at "Fort Ridgely, MT" [Minnesota] by Chaplain Joshua Sweet, addressed to "Any Protestant Clergyman." In this missive, Sweet wrote, "I beg leave to bring to your notice Thomas Rayment of G Company, 10th Infantry, for whose salvation I feel great solicitude. You will at once perceive that he is gentlemanly and intelligent. I commend him to you as a brother in the faith—although not a communicant—and trust you will care for his spiritual welfare."

Rayment wrote a spirited defense, blaming Gale for instigating a campaign of spite, extortion, and perjury, and denied any "evil intentions against such children." He concluded, "Gentlemen, I plead guilty to being an old drunken fool," but denied any sexual misbehavior. He was found guilty and sentenced to have his head shaved, be drummed out and spend five years in prison. The reviewing general, Lewis C. Hunt, remitted the prison portion of the sentence, in view of the defendant's long service.[14]

Rayment was not the only musical man in trouble in New York Harbor. At Fort Hamilton, in February 1864, Musician John W. Seamon of the 6th US Infantry was accused of "violating the persons" of Musicians Patrick Dixon, Thomas Downey and Henry Weitzel, "contrary to the nature and dignity of man."

Dixon, born in Brooklyn, had enlisted "to learn music," when he was age 14. The records show his occupation as "boy," and his father as giving consent. At 4'9" he was taller than the other boys. Downey was also age 14 when he enlisted in 1862; his mother, Johana Downey, gave her consent. Blue-eyed Thomas was 4'7". Weitzel's enlistment papers are missing from the files.

Principal Musician Charles Ruby testified. "Patrick Dixon, a drum boy, told me that he was afraid to sleep in his own room on account of the prisoner, who had threatened his life. I told the boy if the prisoner came near his bed to get up and strike him with anything he could get hold of and then call for me." Dixon testified, "Musician Seamon and I were sleeping in the same bed. He commenced to make a rape upon me. He commenced to jerk me off, as they call it. He caught hold of my cock. I went to another bed." Thomas Downey, the second boy, told the Court that Seamon had never made any attempt to violate him, and there Downey's testimony ended.

Weitzel's story, by contrast, alleged a serious violation. "The prisoner came to my bed, undressed, and tried to fuck me. Then he commenced to try to jerk me off. He tried to put his cock in my ass. He caught hold of my cock and rubbed it up and down. I got out of my bed and got into Downey's bed."

Two other musicians had seen Seamon going down the hall and getting into boys' beds. "The only light was the fire. It looked like Seamon had been drinking."

Seamon made his defense. "The boy Weitzel and myself had been drinking that evening in Irishtown, near the fort, in a liquor store kept by a lady by the name of Mary Jane. We got a bottle of whisky and took it into the fort with us. Back there, Weitzel had the bottle and wouldn't give me a drink. He thought I'd had enough." As a further defense, he submitted his discharge from the 1st US Artillery, where, after five years, his character had been deemed "good."

He was convicted of most of the charges, and was sentenced to prison for the rest of his enlistment. In October 1864, Seamon's lawyer wrote, claiming that the principal witness had retracted his statement. Two months later, in a letter to Lincoln, Seamon asked to be returned to duty, citing his thirteen years in the service and his being the sole support of his aged mother. John Nicolay, the president's private secretary, handled the matter by asking the opinion of Holt, often a severe man. In a rather unusual communication, Holt counseled mercy. "In view of the absence of evidence of inveterate depravity (the inference being reasonable from all the proof that his misbehavior was the result of a dissipated frolic, rather than a brutalized moral sense), it is believed that the man may return to duty without detriment to the service." Seamon resumed his military career.[15]

Far from New York Harbor, the 178th New York was camped at Chalmette, Louisiana. There, in March 1865, Private Charles Katzenstein was charged with attempted sodomy. The principal witness was John Garity, "private servant" to

Lieutenant Colonel J.B. Gandolph. "We were playing cards in the tent and I asked Katzenstein to lend me a quarter until payday. He did so, then lent me more money. Later he called me out to go down to the sutler's. I went there in my drawers and sock feet. He said he would treat me to a can of peaches. On the way to the sutler's, he made me put my hand on his tool. After he bought me the peaches, he wanted me to jerk him off. I wouldn't do it. Then he put his tool between my legs. I said I'd holler, so he let me go." Katzenstein simply denied the charges. The Court did not believe him and sentenced him to three months of hard labor.[16]

A very different story was that of William Harper, Jr., whom the records show was both an honored warrior and a swindling, sodomitical jail house lawyer. He had served as a captain with the 1st New Jersey Cavalry, where his gallant service earned him the brevet rank of major. He liked life on horseback, and applied for a commission in the regular army after the war. In July 1868, at the age of 26, he became a first lieutenant in the 6th US Cavalry. By the summer of 1876, his career was unraveling at Camp Lowell, Arizona Territory, near today's Tucson. In July, he was tried for defrauding both officers and enlisted men, from whom he had borrowed—and never repaid—large sums of money, over a period of two years. More relevant to our inquiry were the charges that he had written to Private Frank W. Morse, describing "an improper and unofficerlike intimacy," and that "he did commit the crime and act of sodomy with said Private Morse." He was acquitted of most charges and received a light sentence. The reviewing officer was apoplectic; he noted that nearly every rule of law had been broken by the court, especially when it ignored "the grave offense of an officer to seek to sleep with an enlisted man."

A second trial was based on more letters Harper had written to Morse, complaining that the private had not kept a bedtime rendezvous. By invoking the concept of double jeopardy, Harper was acquitted. Again, the reviewing officer disagreed with Harper's "legalistic quibbling."

A third court martial, in September 1876, found Harper guilty of lying about liquor in his living quarters, about his finances, and about his correspondence with Morse. The sentence of dismissal from the service was automatically appealed to the president, Ulysses S. Grant, who asked the opinion of his judge advocate general; the legal adviser noted that the departmental commander had described Harper as "untruthful" and "addicted to the crime of sodomy." The president extended no clemency.[17]

Another war hero who tarnished his own reputation was Joseph B. Rife. He began the war as a second lieutenant in the 6th US Infantry and was brevetted a captain for gallantry at the Battle of Antietam. His postwar career out West was different. In February 1872, Brigadier General William Hazen wrote to his superiors from Fort Hays, Kansas: "For all our sakes, let there be as little publicity as possible in the Rife business. God knows it is bad enough and disgraceful enough to bury it as quickly and as quietly as we can." What so concerned General Hazen? Was it what Colonel Benjamin Grierson, in 1870, called Rife's "indolence and general uselessness," or what Captain O. H. Moore observed: "Rife is always seeking a leave of absence . . . he is a shirker."? No, it was worse.

The records hold a long notarized statement by Private Oscar Bergh of the 6th US Infantry, who "deposes that Captain Joseph B. Rife did, at sundry times and places, compel, by threats and otherwise, deponent to commit with him unnatural crimes . . . such as compelling him to take his (Captain Rife's) penis in deponent's mouth & by friction of deponent's hand in order to excite and gratify his (Captain Rife's) sensual appetites." This activity continued over several years, at Fort Sill, Gypsum Creek, and Camp Supply, all in Indian Territory, as well as at Fort Dodge, Kansas. Rife used a combination of threats, whiskey, and promise of promotion to continue his use of Bergh's services. Rife's case generated considerable interest. Major General John Pope described Rife's acts as "horrible . . . criminal." Senator Simon Cameron, demonstrating once again his boundless absence of principle, wrote to the War Department, reminding them that Rife was a fellow Pennsylvanian, and that the Senator took a "warm interest" in Rife's welfare. The records end with Rife's resignation in late 1872.[18]

The 15th New York Engineers generated another trial with homoerotic overtones. The regiment was camped at Potomac Creek Bridge, Virginia, in February 1863. Several officers were drinking punch in the tent of Second Lieutenant Daniel Higgins, when First Lieutenant Daniel Curran entered, sat on Higgins' bed and placed his hand on Higgins' "person," as the Victorians euphemistically termed the genitals. Higgins told Curran to stop, not once or twice, but three times. Instead of desisting, Curran called Higgins a son of a bitch. Higgins drew a pistol; their peers calmed the situation. Curran, found guilty of conduct unbecoming an officer and a gentleman, was dismissed from the service.[19]

A possible event of homoerotic flavor is described in a letter written on May 13, 1862, by First Sergeant Alfred Lewis Wardlaw, Company B, 1st (Orr's) Rifles, South Carolina. He gave the usual news (hearing the enemy's drums, picket duty near Fredericksburg, the slave who carries his overcoat) and then describes a pair of men who don't want to share a tent because one is too "affectionate," as well as having poor personal hygiene.[20]

The Union Navy had many cases of unambiguous homosexual behavior, but before proceeding on to those stormy waters, let us consider a final dozen or so army cases that seemed to have a distinctly homoerotic overtone.

Private Joseph Rossman of the 30th Independent New York Battery clearly had too much to drink at Martinsburg, Virginia, in December 1863. In the expansive camaraderie that overcomes some drunks, he approached Lieutenant

Frank Grasse, lauded him as "the best lieutenant in the battery," and demanded that Grasse walk arm in arm with him. When the lieutenant declined this honor, Rossman's mood changed 180 degrees; he shouted to his comrades, "Lieutenant Grasse fucked me in mine arse and I swear that, by God, it is true!" This outburst put Rossman at hard labor for the rest of his enlistment. (Both the offense and the trial were conducted mainly in German.)[21]

At Murfreesboro, Tennessee, Second Lieutenant Timothy Hynes of the 36th Indiana was convicted on charges that, when very drunk, he took his blankets to the quarters of the enlisted men and said that, "he wanted to sleep with them." A few months later, in July 1863, he took three enlisted men away from camp and bought them liquor, an excursion that ended in a brawl, to "the disgrace of their company and regiment." Hynes was dismissed from the army.[22]

Private Richard Platt, 152nd New York, was absent six months at Suffolk, Virginia, and was charged with desertion. Platt told the court, "Major [George] Spalding said he had a pass for me. When he left Suffolk, he took me with him and told me I was all right. We went to his store in New York." The pass mentioned by Platt is in the file; it is a badly worn, blank marine insurance receipt, bearing a hand-written message: "This is to certify R. Platt, the bearer, is not an enlisted man & is my orderly to take care of [bringing] a horse to New York City." It seems curious that Spalding would perjure himself in order to have the use of this eighteen-year old boy for six months. The Court thought so, too, and suggested an investigation. None appears in the record. (Platt was no innocent. He received two regimental punishments for insubordination, spent time in the hospital for gonorrhea, and shirked when returned to duty.)[23]

Private William Thomason of the 15th Illinois Cavalry was at Helena, Arkansas, in July 1864, charged with murder. Prosecution witness Captain J. M. Weir described the pre-murder setting. "There was a squad of men laying on the stoop of my shanty, jesting of something with regard to myself. I got up from my bed and took a chair on the porch with nothing but my shirt on. The accused came up there as usual and he was handling my legs to some extent, making some remarks about my legs being so fat." Does Weir's statement describe normal social action in the 1860s?[24]

There are many records in which no actual sexual contact is reported, yet the wording suggests that such might have occurred. These seem worth documenting, if only to illustrate the ambiguity in old records made for one purpose and reviewed a century or more later for an entirely different purpose. Several cases reflect strange relationships (real or only implied) between officers and men. John Frick of the 5th Ohio Cavalry was drunk on the march to Charleston, Tennessee in April 1864. When stopped and searched (probably for a bottle), he called out, "Get some soap. The colonel wants to fuck me." Frick was docked four months pay. At Fort DeKalb, Virginia, Charles Bates of the 4th New York Artillery returned to camp and announced, "I'm here to fight for my country, but

I've been drunk for two nights and two days." His captain, a tolerant man, simply suggested that Bates go to bed, but Bates didn't quit while he was ahead. Not only did he call the captain a "gray-headed son of a bitch," but asked, "What are you going to do with me after I've gone to bed?" Bates' outburst June 1862 earned him a year's hard labor wearing a ball and chain.[25]

Some members of the 9th Maine were rioting at Morris Island, South Carolina in August 1863. When the colonel collared one ringleader, Private Frank Plummer, the miscreant spoke up, saying, "You are a damned pretty colonel; better take your hands off my shoulders." Plummer went off to prison and received a dishonorable discharge.[26]

Not all offenders were enlisted men. Dr. Francis Huebachmann, surgeon of the 20th Wisconsin, was drunk most of 1862, and consumed "72 bottles of liquor and seven gallons of whisky" in eight weeks. He lost—literally—three patients, including one with typhoid, who was never found. Among his offenses was calling the colonel "a queer boy." Amazingly, the doctor received only a reprimand and was returned to duty.[27]

Not all of the war was fought in the east. The 9th US Infantry was stationed at the Presidio of San Francisco, California, and on Christmas Eve, 1862, two men were drunk and disorderly at a "boarding house" at the corner of O'Farrell and Market Streets. The offenders were Second Lieutenant Joseph Marshall and a soldier, Private Edward O'Brien, with whom he was "intimately familiar." The boarding house proprietor, Catherine Kinney, told the court, "O'Brien seemed to take a deep interest in the officer and kept touching his shoulder." O'Brien said he was only trying to keep his drunken superior from being arrested. A policeman said they were both obviously drunk. The lieutenant was put at the bottom of the promotion list.[28]

In 1862, Fort Baker was located on the Eel River in California's Humboldt County. The fort was a center for operations against the Indians. There, Lieutenant William Ustick of the 3rd California composed a routine memo regarding forage. The recipient was First Lieutenant John Hanna, Jr. Tucked inside the papers was this note: "Lieutenant Hanna You are a P. Brick. I want to hug you. You good-looking guy—fascinating—wait till I see you—that's all. Ustick" The 1847 Webster's defines a brick as "an admirable good person." The meaning of "P." remains a mystery, as does the true intent of this missive.[29]

Many German men served in Union Missouri regiments. Among them was First Lieutenant Philip Dickenhoff, of Captain Winkelmaier's Pontonier Company. The lieutenant was charged with being drunk, with calling his captain "an old scoundrel" and with dancing with a Private Heinman, who wore only "a drawer and a shirt." Other witnesses added slippers to the ensemble. While men often danced with men in a womanless environment, both partners were usually fully dressed. Under rigorous cross-examination during the May 1862 trial, most of the prosecution testimony melted away and Dickenhoff was acquitted.[30]

Hundreds of thousands of men served in the US Colored Troops. In February 1865, Major Nicholas Vail of the 14th USCT was charged with numerous episodes of drunkenness in Tennessee and Alabama, including one in which he "sat in the lap of a colored soldier" and "put his arm around a colored soldier." Vail was found not guilty.[31]

Captain Willard Daggett was not so fortunate after his transgressions with the 29th USCT in August 1865. At Galveston, Texas, he was frequently drunk. When ordered to put his men aboard a steamboat, he invited them to go swimming with him instead. (In that era, no bathing suits were provided.) He also allowed them to go into town and get drunk. Daggett was soon a civilian.[32]

First Lieutenant Andrew Wall of the 1st District of Columbia was drunk and disorderly in May 1863 at Falmouth, Virginia, when he invited his drinking partner, a sergeant, to sleep in his tent. Wall was cashiered. A Pennsylvania corporal, Michael Donovan, of Captain Paul Jones' Independent Battery, was drunk and "quarreled with the sergeant over a drummer boy" in April 1862. The exact relationship of the three men is hard to determine from the records.[33]

In 1922, a former Civil War drummer boy, then age 79, applied for a pension, alleging sexual mistreatment during the Civil War. Francis Barney enlisted in the 14th US Infantry in 1861 and deserted the following year. In 1862, he reenlisted as a substitute, was found out and was sentenced to hard labor to the end of his enlistment. Later, he was reinstated and received an honorable discharge. In January 1865, he enlisted again, deserted again, and never returned. He also claimed service in the 14th Connecticut, for which there is no record. In the late 1800's, he worked on the vaudeville stage. In his 1922 pension application, he wrote, "I am a true American. I was abused by my drum major. He had me nearly crazy by pounding me so much and he wanted me to do immoral things. He threatened to kill me if I informed on him." (Were these immoral things of a sexual nature?) Barney's pension was denied, as he was still a deserter. In 1932, eight years after Barney's death, his family requested that he receive a retroactive honorable discharge. There the record ends.[34]

In some of these cases, the facts are clear. In others, the true meaning is open to interpretation, but we cannot know more than the records left by our ancestors. The war (and its records) was not designed to accommodate us, a century and a half later, but occurred in its own time and for the purposes of men then alive. What we can do, in modesty and forbearance, is to present what is saved in our nation's archives and, with a keen sense of our limitations today, present the written words and some possible meanings of those words.

Homosexuality in the Navies

Winston Churchill was the central figure in an old navy tale. In 1912, when serving as First Sea Lord, he locked horns with several admirals, one of whom accused Churchill of ignoring time-honored traditions of the Royal Navy. Churchill ended the conference with a stinging retort: "And what are [those traditions]? I shall tell you in three words. Rum, sodomy and the lash. Good morning, gentlemen."[35]

Sadly for those who relish a tart retort, the famous "three words" encounter never happened. But sodomy does occur in navies, including the United States Navy. In 1848, the navy was required to render a crime statistics report to the US Senate. Of the 5,936 case reports for 1848, less than a dozen—which bore such labels as "sodomy, indecent liberties with boys," and "improper conduct too base to mention,"—seemed to reflect homosexual behavior, accounting for much less than one percent of the cases tried. During the Civil War, the U.S. Navy conducted 1,440 general courts-martial; 39 (2.7 percent) were about sexual misbehavior between men. This is a much higher proportion than is seen in the 1848 figures. The Civil War cases reflect events on eighteen different ships.[36]

There were four cases on the *Louisville*, an ironclad center-wheel steamer built at St. Louis in 1861. Her powerful guns engaged the Confederate forces along the Mississippi, White, Yazoo, and Red Rivers. Forty-nine-year-old John Nore, Captain of the Hold, had gray eyes and a dark complexion, and was tried for sodomizing two sailors. His first victim, a 17-year old illiterate boy with the rank of landsman (the lowest rank of seaman), was Orville Crane. "On the afternoon of the 23rd of October 1863, John Nore asked me to go down to his hold. I went down and laid down on his bed. About 20 minutes later he came down and pulled off my pants and coat and buggered me. At the time I was so much under the influence of liquor that I knew no better than to submit to him." Nore's other victim was 18-year-old Peter Olson, a native of Norway. "Nore held his hand over my mouth, but I pushed his hand away and hollowed for help." This attempt on Olson's virtue was aided by Quarter Gunner Charles Brown, who held Olson's legs, while Nore attempted penetration. Later, we will hear more of Brown. Orville Crane, Nore's first victim, was convicted of "scandalous conduct" and "drunkenness" and sentenced to a year in prison. However, the court recommended clemency in view of his youth. Nore was sent to prison for seven years.[37]

Forty-year-old seaman Charles Stewart of the *Louisville* was tried for "scandalous conduct" (as well as drunkenness and attempted escape) as a result of his sexual assaults on Albert Lillie and Louis Weddieken. Lillie, a 20-year-old boy with gray eyes and a ruddy complexion, told the Court, "On or about October 1st, 1863, I was asked by the accused to come and lay down with him, which I did. During the night he did get on top of me. I got away from him." Weddieken, age 17, and only five feet, two inches in height, recalled his encounter with Stewart: "He tried to take down my drawers. I would not let him, but pushed him away three or four times. He offered me rum to drink." Stewart also participated in the attack on Olson, by trying "to unbutton his britches."

Stewart was convicted and sent to serve three years hard labor, wearing a ball and chain.[38]

Charles Brown, age twenty-four, the man who held Olson's legs, was also convicted of scandalous conduct, but received a light sentence: twenty days in solitary confinement on bread and water and loss of two month's pay. This mild sentence provoked a remarkable fulmination from the pen of Admiral David Dixon Porter, the reviewing officer.

> On the 7th day of December 1863, I ordered a court martial in the case of Charles Brown, quarter gunner, on board the USS Louisville, on charges preferred for the commission of a crime so unnatural that the laws of the Navy make no provision for punishment adequate to the offense. Never but once during my official career have I known of such beastly conduct as was proved against the above-mentioned Charles Brown and his associates, and in the case alluded to, the Court found all the parties concerned guilty and visited them with severe punishment. In the case of Charles Brown, the accused is considered by the Court only an accessory and he is awarded a milder sentence than would be given by a summary court martial for a drunken frolic, or violation of naval etiquette. I have been unable to discover, after a careful revision [review] of all the proceedings, how the Court has arrived at this conclusion. The accused deserves all the punishment or none. He has been proven guilty of the charges, according to the finding of the Court, and only proved guilty of the specifications so far as being an accessory. I can draw no distinction, in a case like this. The specification charged Charles Brown with an attempt to commit an unnatural crime, and it is clearly proven that he aided and abetted others by holding one Peter Olson down, while his companions were to perpetrate the outrage. The conduct of Charles Brown in this instance was, if possible, more brutal and disgusting than that of his associates, and I cannot see where the distinction between the cases can be drawn.
>
> Cognizance, even, of such of a crime, without an immediate report of it being made to a superior, would be a high misdemeanor, to say nothing of the guilt of being an accessory.
>
> By placing my name to a sentence so inadequate to the offense as the one awarded to Charles Brown and thereby approving it, I should be holding out a reward for crimes of this nature, and would be admitting (what I so much deprecate) that an accessory to an offense of this nature is entitled to more clemency than the principal actors.
>
> While I do not wish to influence the opinions of members of courts martial, yet when their decisions do not agree with my convictions,

I cannot confirm them, and in the present instance I disapprove entirely of the finding and sentence of the Court, as being inadequate to the crime attempted by Charles Brown, who was not even dismissed from his rank of petty officer. The object of punishment is to prevent crime. In this instance, the punishment is of so slight a nature, that it would have no effect, whatever, except that it would lead depraved characters to suppose that they might commit offenses of this kind with comparative impunity, and if many such sentences were awarded, immorality would be in the ascendant.

While I regret that the accused, Charles Brown, will escape any punishment (and he deserves as much as any of the parties implicated), I cannot permit anyone to suppose that I look lightly on this or any offense against the laws, by placing my name to the proceedings, except in the way of disapproval."[39]

One ship generated three trials of sexual misconduct. The *Pinola* was a 158-foot-long propeller-driven gunboat, built in Baltimore in early 1862, and had been struck by Confederate shot twelve times during the capture of New Orleans. In June 1865, the shooting was over, the ship was scheduled for decommissioning in a few weeks and, following an old tradition, the devil found work for idle hands, as the ship lay at Calcasieu Pass, Louisiana.

There, First Class Boy Lewis Goozoof "took down the pants of another first class boy, Joseph Machin, and attempted to commit an unnatural connexion." Goozoof, (described as "colored") pled guilty and offered this as his sole testimony: "I did not know there was any law about that." He was sent to prison for five years.[40]

The day after Goozoof's attempted connection, two other *Pinola* men were observed in the act itself, a case that seems to reflect an exploitive relationship. Cook Marion Chapman exerted a loving tyranny over Landsman Henry Harper. Chapman washed Harper, combed his hair, and caressed him. When "the boy" was on watch, Chapman would wait until they could turn in together. Chapman spoke harshly to Harper if he talked with any other man. At night, witnesses said, "Harper would cry out, 'Oh, Chapman, you hurt me!'" The fatal occasion was described vividly by one witness: "They were rolled up in a blanket, huddled together like man and wife. He had connexion [sic] with the boy several times that night." Both Chapman and Harper were sentenced to prison for ten years. The sentences were strongly endorsed by Rear Admiral Henry K. Thatcher.[41]

The *Muscoota* was anchored at Key West, Florida in September 1865. Like on the *Pinola*, post-war duties had given way to frolic and misbehavior. Ordinary Seaman William Stewart was in a drunken stupor and had been placed for safekeeping in "double irons" (hands and feet both shackled) in the aft pilothouse. Not long afterward, Seaman Henry Williams, "drunk and noisy," was also put in double irons and placed in the same pilothouse, where he was soon seen "committing sodomy upon the person of the boy Stewart," according to three witnesses. Both Williams and Stewart were sentenced to ten years in prison, although the court recommended clemency for Stewart on grounds of "youth and drunkenness." They noted Stewart's testimony that he recalled nothing of the event, and added, "The evidence for the prosecution admits that he was so drunk that he was incapable of assisting Williams to commit the crime."[42]

Confederate commerce raiders threatened Union ships bound for California via the West Indies. Sent to protect them was the *Neptune*, a wooden-hulled propeller steamer. On New Years Day, 1865, Seaman James Conley "attempted sodomy upon Joseph Morris, Landsman," who told the Court: "I was lying down on the port side of the spar deck. Conley lay down and put his hand on the flap of my pants. I got up and left. Three weeks later, on the gun deck, he slung his hammock next to mine and put his hand under my blanket. I asked what he was doing. He said to turn around. He said, 'I want to do woman fashion towards you and you could do the same to me.' I said no and left. Weeks later, I was asleep and woke up in pain. He had his penis next to mine and made a mess on my shirt." The Court gave Conley a dishonorable discharge and ordered a description of him sent to all navy recruiters, to prevent future enlistments.[43]

A month later, Seaman John Henry, also of the *Neptune*, was tried for attempting "to commit a disgraceful and scandalous act on the person of John French, Landsman, at Cape Haitien." The victim testified as follows: "I was in my hammock, asleep, when I woke up. The accused had my penis in his mouth, sucking of it. I told him of it and he said, 'Don't tell of me this time.' I said yes I will and put a stop to it." French complained to the corporal of the guard, who passed the problem, through several levels, to the captain. Henry was also convicted and received the same sentence as Conley.[44]

In March 1865, the *Osage* struck a torpedo (mine) in Alabama's Blakely River and sank. In the preceding two years, this single-turret monitor had seen action on the Black and Washita Rivers and in the assault on Mobile Bay. In the summer of 1863, a different sort of assault occupied three of her crew. The instigator appeared to be Seaman Peter Bourne, who was tried for committing sodomy with Landsman Joseph Gebo and of soliciting sodomy of Landsman George LaGrosse.[45]

The master-at-arms testified. "I saw Bourne and Gebo sleeping together, rolled up in monkey jackets." (These were short jackets, which left the legs free to climb rigging.) Gebo pled guilty to charges that included the following: "Gebo abandoned his person to the unnatural lusts of the said Bourne and allowed the latter to masturbate him and induce an emission . . . and subsequently to have complete and full unnatural intercourse . . . with an emission inside Gebo." Gebo, who spoke French, told an officer, "Now I am in a state of sin," and that after his penetration by Bourne that he had been "much chafed." Gebo was sentenced to ten years in prison at hard labor, but the court urged clemency because of his "weak mind."[46]

LaGrosse was charged with inducing Gebo "to commit the crime of sodomy" with Bourne. LaGrosse, who also spoke French, testified that, "Bourne was always after me. He kissed me like a girl, then he said, 'Take down your breeches and lie on your belly.' Then Bourne unbuttoned his own breeches and put my hand on his penis, which was erect. I told Gebo, 'You sleep with him. I don't want to.'" LaGrosse was sentenced to a year at hard labor and a dishonorable discharge. Bourne was given ten years at hard labor with no recommendation of clemency.[47]

The first cruise of the sailing frigate *Sabine* was to Paraguay in 1853, where she helped subdue an anti-American government. During the Civil War, she served along the Atlantic coast until 1864, when the *Sabine* was sent to New York and became a training ship for navy apprentices. There, Private George H. Shears, USMC, was charged with "inducing Apprentice Boy No. 187, Benjamin Herricks, into improper commerce," leading to a "disgusting, immoral act . . . destructive of the moral character of the naval apprentices of the U.S. Navy."[48]

Herricks said that Shears "asked me to let him go up my grummet. [A grommet is a small, stitched opening in a sail.] I told him that he might." Several other boys said that the group of men which included Herricks and Shears was "only telling tales," and that they had seen no such misbehavior. However, Apprentice William Moore claimed he had seen "Herricks jerking Shears off." Dr. A. Hudson examined both men and found "no evidence of sodomy having been committed on Herricks." The doctor also examined Shears' "development" and concluded that "I do not think the connexion would have been easily accomplished." The Court concluded: "the evidence of Apprentice Boy No. 187 is entirely unreliable."

They did consider the statements of Moore and those of Apprentice Richard Boerum ("Shears hugged me . . . said I was like a little girl . . . and asked for a rub"), and Apprentice Charles Wilgers ("He wanted me to touch his privates and give him a shake, but I refused."). The Court concluded "the presence of such a person on board this ship can only be destructive of moral character," and sent Shears to solitary confinement, in double irons, on bread and water, for thirty days, and recommended that he be transferred to a different ship.

The *Winooski*, a side-wheel gunboat, was not completed until June 1865 and her maritime adventures were limited to peacetime patrolling. The ship was tied up at New York City when a court-martial had to decide whether two men were just "tickling and skylarking," or were engaged in something abhorrent to the navy. Coal Heaver Gilpin Coffin and Landsman George Copelind were under a blanket. One witness said, "They were playing the same as a man and a woman." Another witness told the Court, "They were working together, as a man and a woman do in copulation . . . I saw Coffin undressed and Copelind with his pants and drawers down." A third witness said it was "just play." The court concluded it was more than play and gave both men a year in prison, to be followed by a dishonorable discharge.[49]

The *William G. Anderson* was a fast sailing barque that captured many Confederate blockade runners during her four-year career. She was tied up at Pensacola, Florida, when a sailor came up to Master-at-Arms John C. Johnson and said breathlessly, "I'll show you something." Johnson followed the sailor and, "I saw men in motion. I raised the blanket and saw what I have often heard of but never seen—two men lying together as man and wife. I let the blanket fall until they had disengaged themselves." Another witness said, "They were considerably in motion." The two men were 22-year-old Landsman George Curtis and 19-year-old First Class Boy John Matthews, who protested, "We were just talking." Both men were sentenced to ten years of hard labor at the New Orleans Parish Prison.[50]

A few dozen Chinese men served in the Union Navy. One was George Hitchings, Officer's Cook, on the *Kennebec*, a gunboat with long service along the Gulf Coast. The ship's muster roll describes Hitchings as "a Chinaman," age 24, 5'2", born in China. He was tried for "committing sodomy upon the person of George W. Libby, Coal Heaver." Both were found asleep together on a mattress with their pants down. Hitchings had his arm over Libby, and told the court, "Me no sleepee last night . . . me no sleep in hammock, me sleep alongside of boy . . . me poke him once." The findings of the court are puzzling. Libby was convicted of "immoral conduct," and ordered discharged from the navy, while Hitchings was found not guilty. The reviewing officer disapproved the acquittal.[51]

The *Roanoke* served the navy for 28 years, retrieving filibusters (American adventurers and revolutionaries) from Nicaragua, and carrying Japanese diplomats. In its final incarnation, this veteran ship became an ironclad monitor. Another veteran, this one human, was 54-year-old Quartermaster James Prince, who was tried for sodomy with 18-year-old Second Class Boy Prentiss Oscar. The forbidden act occurred in the aft gun turret. Later, Prince gave Oscar a shirt. That's not all he gave him.

The ship's surgeon testified that Oscar had "a venereal soreness around the anus . . . with an offensive discharge of pus from the rectum." This might have been rectal gonorrhea or an anal fissure with an abscess. (Both would have been difficult to cure in the days before antibiotics.) Whatever the diagnosis, Prince was sentenced to two years in prison with a ball and chain. Prentiss Oscar was not court-martialed.[52]

The gunboat *Kineo* saw much action up and down the Mississippi River. At Galveston, Texas, in November 1864, her skipper, Lieutenant Commander John Watters, wrote to Gideon Welles, Secretary of the Navy, that he had dishonorably discharged Landsman William Thomas and First Class Boy Alonzo Kneass for "a shocking crime . . . against nature, too offensive for trial before a court." Whatever his crime, 16-year old Kneass, a hazel-eyed Philadelphia native, 5 feet, 2 inches at enlistment, was out of the Navy. Rear Admiral David Farragut reviewed the correspondence and instructed Watters that in the future such cases must be tried by court-martial. Farragut also suggested that ten years in prison would be an appropriate sentence for such a crime.[53]

The *DeSoto*, W.M. Walker commanding, captured many blockade runners along the Gulf Coast. On December 30, 1861, Walker wrote to the department commander, Captain William W. McKean, that Landsman Thomas Martin, acting as a yeoman, had been reported "to me as having been guilty of such shockingly immoral practices as make him unfit . . . to remain in the naval service." The final outcome of this case has not been discovered.

In the spring of 1865, the shallow-draft gunboat *Pittsburgh* was tied up at Mound City, Illinois, undergoing repairs. The deck log contains two entries regarding Officers' Steward Prince W. Consor. "March 12: Consor is confined in double irons on charges of sodomy." "May 11: Received from Acting Volunteer Lieutenant E. Morgan, an order to release [Consor] who was confined March 12th . . . the order having been sent by Acting Admiral S. P. Lee and the charges to be withdrawn."[54]

There were other cases that were inconclusive. In May 1865, H. H. Savage, Acting Master of the *Putnam*, was at Norfolk, Virginia, where he answered charges of sodomizing a messenger boy, seventeen-year-old James Johnson. Witnesses described Johnson as frequently drunk and "perfectly useless on board the ship." Savage was acquitted.[55]

The *Vermont* had an astonishing career. She was authorized by Congress in 1816, and was sold out of the navy in 1902. In those 86 years, she survived a violent hurricane and Civil War service in the South Atlantic Blockading Squadron. While *Vermont* was anchored in New York City in December 1866, Seaman Thomas Nulty was accused of luring boys to commit sodomy with him. The evidence was scanty and he was acquitted.[56]

The *Keystone State*, a wooden side-wheel steamer, was off Philadelphia in October 1863, when 17-year-old John Ricketts, who had been found in a locker with his pants down, claimed that Seaman George Williams had tried to sodomize him. The court-martial board found no convincing evidence and acquitted both men.[57]

The *Portsmouth*, like the *Vermont*, had a long career. This wooden sloop-of-war fought in the Mexican War, suppressed the slave trade in the 1850's, captured Texas blockade runners and visited Batavia, China and France. In May 1861, Marine Corporal William Shuttleworth of the *Portsmouth* was convicted of sedition, in a conspiracy aimed at charging Ordnance Sergeant George W. Robbins with sodomy. The chief prosecution witness was Fifer J.R. Lackey.

"Corporal Shuttleworth told me to go down to Sergeant Robbins and play with his whiskers, and as soon as he got intimate to sing out." The defendant was reduced to the ranks, placed in solitary confinement for two months, and then given a dishonorable discharge.[58]

And what of the Confederate navy? Most of the records of that far-ranging and gallant body are lost forever. At least one fragment has survived, and describes an event on the CSS *Florida*. This famed commerce raider captured 37 prizes and was the center of an international incident when she, herself, was captured in Brazilian waters.

The offense recorded aboard this *Florida* (there were five Confederate vessels of the same name) included a sailor being dragged on deck by his penis. On August 23, 1864, while at sea, Ordinary Seaman Guizeppi Mastreli reached his hand under the blanket of Seaman Thomas George and felt of his "person," while murmuring, "Salvatori, Salvatori." George stayed silent. Mastreli, still thinking that George was Salvatori, climbed into the adjoining hammock and "attempted to sodomize" his beloved. The entirely unwilling and completely unItalian George leapt up, seized Mastreli's penis and "attempted to drag him on deck, but lost his hold." This failed romance was witnessed by First Class Fireman Charles Johnson, a native of Sweden. Mastreli received a dishonorable discharge and the loss of three months pay. He did receive the courtesy of an Italian translator during the trial.[59]

After the War

A few fragments from the historical record will indicate that sexual relationships between men continued to be of concern to the military. In the years between 1865 and through the Spanish-American War, the author has discovered no relevant material. World War I, with its mass mobilization, produced changes. For the first time, army regulations specifically named "sodomy" as a crime. In 1916, assault with intent to commit sodomy became a felony, while in 1919, even consensual sodomy fell under the same cloud.[60]

In World War I, prosecution of French soldiers for homoerotic activity was almost unknown. The story was much different in Germany and in the Austro-Hungarian Empire. Paragraph 175 of the German Penal Code of 1871, prohibited "an unnatural sex act committed between persons of the male sex." Many homosexual men, even exiles who had fled persecution, flocked to the German regiments in 1914. Several factors played a part, but one motivation warrants special comment: a wish to prove oneself, a desire to be seen as a brave comrade, rather than as a rejected "pervert." Many men of homosexual orientation volunteered for the most dangerous missions, sometimes in a wish to be dead, honorably dead, sometimes hoping to be accepted through heroic deeds.

The hatred and fear of homosexuality was fueled in Austria by the case of Colonel Alfred Redl, who was blackmailed by a Russian agent and from 1903 to 1913 provided the enemy with many secret documents, which led to huge casualties being inflicted upon the Austrian forces.[61]

Prosecution of homosexuals in the US Navy reached a crescendo in 1919, when an entrapment scheme at a YMCA near the Naval Training Station, Newport, Rhode Island netted many young sailors, who were convicted and sent to prison for terms as long as ten years. This operation, approved by then Assistant Secretary of the Navy Franklin D. Roosevelt, drew severe criticism.[62]

During the Nazi era, 100,000 men were arrested under the notorious Paragraph 175; 15,000 were sent to concentration camps, where most died, either from exhaustion in slave labor camps or following castration. When the author was a US Air Force psychiatrist (1961-1963), one of his duties was the examination of men accused of homosexual activity. If they were psychotic, they might be eligible for a medical discharge and veteran's benefits. (None were.) The usual outcome was a psychiatric report by me, stating that they did not need to see a psychiatrist. This group received an administrative discharge. I saw no one who seemed to be a security risk; in fact, many were men and women with superior performance reports.[63]

Between 1971 and 1992, the U.S. military discharged 28,638 men and women for homosexuality. More than half were from the Navy. Over $500 million was spent to identify and remove these persons.[64]

As of this writing, the newer policy of "Don't ask, Don't tell" has been in effect for a decade. In the year 2001, 1,273 male and female homosexuals were fired from military jobs. Whether this new policy has been successful, useful, and/or just continues to be a matter of debate.[65]

Discussion

The word "homosexuality" was introduced in 1895; other words in common use today, such as "faggot," (1910) or "gay" (1950) were introduced much later. Thus references to such activity in the 19th century used ancient terms, like "sodomy," "buggery," or "crimes against nature."

Nor was there the polarization seen today, when one "must" be heterosexual or homosexual, with only the controversial "bisexual" available as a third alternative. (Gender changes, transsexuality, and transvestism are beyond the scope of this discussion.). At the time of the Civil War, men could have intense and long-lasting friendships without much public interest in the meaning of the relationship. While there were laws against "unnatural acts" on the books of most states, only the most flagrant violations received attention. The army regulations made no specific mention of such activities, and of the two million men in the Union Army, only a handful were prosecuted for homoerotic activities. It seems unlikely that so large a group of men, over a period of four years, would be devoid of same-sex carnal connection, but the records tell us nearly nothing, and speculation would be unfruitful.

It is worth noting the difference between situational and essential homosexual activity. The former occurs in the absence of women. In prison, or on long sea voyages, men may seek each other, in preference to abstinence or masturbation. In the "essential" category, the man's principal interest is in other men. Their sight and smell excite him and may have done so from early childhood; for him, women possess little sexual allure. In the cases presented earlier, we see examples of yet a third type of sexuality: exploitive. The old soldier or old sailor attempting rape upon a boy is hardly a consensual relationship. Prosecution of men for truly consensual sexual acts is nearly absent in the approximately 90,000 court-martials that we reviewed.

The issues of non-conventional sex, whether military or civilian, are never far from public concern. The Louisiana State Appeals Court has recently upheld the two-century-old law forbidding *all* oral and anal sex. Three men were beheaded in Saudi Arabia for sodomy and for "seducing young men." Male-male connection has not only cost the Catholic Church much embarrassment and hundreds of millions of dollars, but has brought death by AIDS to hundreds of priests and at least one bishop.[66]

A rarely mentioned aspect of today's society is gay sex by avowedly heterosexual men. Among African Americans this is called "life on the down low." A similar activity by suburban white men is conducted in "T-rooms," i.e. public toilets, often as men drive home from work.[67]

Theorists today identify a major problem: we look at male-male relationships in the 1860's with the eyes of someone in the 21st Century. The intimate friendships between men during the Civil War signified entirely different things to them than they suggest to us today. Lincoln's intense friendship with Joshua Speed did not make him "gay," a category that is simply irrelevant. The opposite problem applies in our present era. If two heterosexual men today were to appear over-friendly, too simpatico, they run the risk of being seen as "queer."[68]

In brief, the cases presented here reflect the words written at the time. Their significance must be approached with much modesty on our part, since they lived in a world not so long ago in time, but very far away in underlying assumptions and understandings.

Chapter 22

SEX AT GETTYSBURG

Was there sex *during* the Battle of Gettysburg? Probably not. Both the soldiers and civilians were preoccupied with staying alive. But in all the days and all the years before and after the great conflict, sexual malfeasance—fornication, bastardy, rape, and bestiality—are well documented in local records. The tale of how those records survived is a story in itself.

Records are all that we have; without them, the past is only a sludge of myth, rumor, and legend. And records are so easily lost. The Romans burned the millions of scrolls of the library at Alexandria. Damp climate destroyed the entire corpus of Phoenician records on papyrus. Henry VIII trashed the vast libraries of the British monasteries. The British burned the Library of Congress in 1814. Carelessness burned the same library in 1851. Dozens of courthouses burned during the Civil War, and the Confederate government burned their own records in 1865. In the 1940s, the Nazis burned the great library at Louvain, and the Crusader archives at Salerno. Federal incompetence allowed nearly ten million service records from World War II to burn at St. Louis.

Less dramatic, but just as destructive, have been the decisions of hundreds of county clerks to throw out old records because of a shortage of storage space. In most jurisdictions, such records cannot be given away or sold. They are simply put out with the trash. In Texas, crates of Civil War documents were sent to the county dump. At Hartford, Connecticut, state authorities filled a dumpster with Revolutionary War documents, and about forty years ago, many Pennsylvania counties cleared out their basements and put tons of documents on the sidewalk to be hauled away as rubbish.

After the Lewis and Clark Expedition, Captain Clark became the principal agent for Indian affairs in Louisiana. His 1813-1838 correspondence filled twenty-nine volumes. After Clark's death, the bound volumes passed through several hands and, in 1883, were being sold for scrap paper when they were

219

bought for $33 by an alert newspaper editor, who found them piled on the sidewalk.[1]

Which brings us to the unsung heroes of record preservation: garbage men, policemen, ordinary citizens, and manuscript dealers. The former rescue the documents, while the latter catalog them and offer them for sale to people who will treasure them. A researcher who has paid money for a document will take good care of it and use it, while a county clerk on salary has no incentive to save old papers. It will quickly become apparent that this chapter exists only because of sharp-eyed citizens and document merchants, with no help from the uncaring civil servants who have been so quick to convert treasure into trash.

This brief ramble through the world of primary documents brings us to the search for Gettysburg—the authentic Gettysburg. Many have joined in this search. There are nearly five hundred books about the battle of Gettysburg and countless articles. Historians and park officials work to restore the land to its 1863 appearance. Re-enactors strive for accuracy in their uniforms. Writers such as Carol Reardon explore the difficulties of finding what actually happened during the days of the battle. Moviemakers attempt their own skewed brand of authenticity, climaxing in a widely praised film based a novel about a colonel who seems to have falsified his own combat records. Many Gettysburg enthusiasts cloak themselves in an aura of reverence, focusing on "sacred" sites, such as Little Round Top and the High Water Mark.

This is not meant in any way to depreciate the courage and suffering of the soldiers at those locations. The author's ancestors never made it to Gettysburg, having been killed at Fredericksburg. Nor is it meant to diminish the inspiring words spoken by Lincoln a few months later, yet our reverence and awe are to some extent modern inventions, or at least, rediscoveries. In 1899, hundreds of white folks came to witness a watermelon-eating contest at Gettysburg. All the entrants were black, eating what the newspapers called "colored people's favorite fruit." Another well-received Gettysburg amusement in the late Victorian era was throwing a baseball at the head of a "coon." The black man won if he ducked quickly enough. No hotels in that era allowed black guests. In 1925, 10,000 Ku Klux Klan members honored the site in a great rally at Gettysburg, a conclave to which veterans of the US Colored Troops were not invited.

On the other hand, Round Top Park, situated halfway between Devil's Den and Little Round Top, attracted tens of thousands of black excursionists from Baltimore, who danced, drank, and flirted in a manner denounced by the white press. Not to be outdone, white members of the Grand Army of the Republic, in their annual parade, featured transvestites and "callithumpians," all in vigorous contrast to the "authentic" reverence demanded today.[2]

Clearly, Gettysburg was and is many things to many people, and one of those enduring and truly authentic aspects is its existence as a small agricultural town, where ordinary people did ordinary things—including misbehave. For evidence of such, especially court proceedings regarding malfeasance of a carnal nature, we must thank the chain of rescuers, collectors, and dealers cited earlier.

A sampling of records from other jurisdictions and times will set the stage. At Plymouth, Massachusetts, in 1693, Sarah Wilcox of Little Compton was indicted by the Grand Inquest for "committing fornication."[3] In 1697, a grand jury concluded that Dan Throops of Massachusetts, "Got a maid with child." In 1695, at Rehoboth, Massachusetts Bay Colony, Elizabeth Savage posted bond on the charge that she "committed fornication with Joseph Haydn . . . sometime in August last." In 1698, at Taunton, Massachusetts Bay Colony, Nathaniel Smith "came before the Subscriber . . . And acknowledged to be justly indebted to our Sovereign Lord the King his heir and successor in the penal sum of 10 pounds . . . to answer for himself and his wife for their committing fornication before marriage."[4]

In 1707, the constable of Little Compton, Rhode Island, was ordered to arrest Mohittabol Dye who, the grand jury found, had "a bastard child born of her body." Two other cases from Little Compton tell us yet more of life back then. In 1712, Mary Manchester sought child support from Thomas Bugges, and in 1728, Mary Davenport, a single woman, accused William Hall, bricklayer, of "getting her with child."[5] At Rockingham County, New Hampshire, in 1792, Hannah Marshall, widow, was apprehended for buying nine quarts of stolen Indian corn from Mary Green, "a known dissolute, lewd and disorderly person belonging to the alms house."[6]

In 1761, at Kittery, Maine, Mehetable Ferguson charged that John Emery "by flattery and fond and lewd actions tempted your complainant to commit an act of Fornication with him . . . And did then and there beget her with child, with which she now goeth and which when born will be a bastard."[7] In 1793, again at Rockingham County, Oram J. Macgregore, Justice of the Peace, took the testimony of Margrette Spear, spinster, of Londonderry. She told him that on September 6, 1792, at the dwelling place of Robert Boyd, a John Beeton of Wyndham "through wheedling, flattery and promises of marriage did obtain knowledge of her body, whereby she is now pregnant and big with child and that said John Beeton, and only he, is the father of this child."

William Bradford (1755-1795) was a lawyer, a Princeton man, a life-long friend of James Madison, and a Lieutenant Colonel in George Washington's army. He was the attorney general of Pennsylvania in 1788, when he signed this document: "The Grand Inquest for the County of Bedford aforesaid upon their oaths and affirmations respectively do present that William Cowan junior late of the County aforesaid yeoman the 10th day of November in the year of our Lord 1788 at the County aforesaid and within the jurisdiction of this Court did commit fornication with a certain Eve Rippleogle and there and then did beget a bastard child on the body of said Eve contrary to the form of an act of the General Assembly in such case made and provided and against the peace and dignity of the Commonwealth of Pennsylvania."

In 1814, at Nottingham, New Hampshire, Richard Hull complained that Abigail Knight had committed a libel by claiming publicly that he had offered her nine pence "to lie with him and have carnal knowledge of her body." In 1824, at Middleton County, Connecticut, Avery Crandall and Sally Maria Mather were charged with fornication and begetting a bastard child. They settled the case by being joined in marriage on September 22nd of that year. Their legal difficulties cost them $14.33 (about $750 in today's dollars), including two dollars for being kept in custody.[8]

Gettysburg is in Adams County, Pennsylvania. Available prewar records relevant to our theme commence in 1822 with Stewart Corner, schoolmaster, who in Huntington Township "did commit fornication with a certain Rachel Myers, a single woman, and a male bastard child on the body of said Rachel Myers did beget, contrary to the form of the act of Assembly in such case made and provided, and against the peace and dignity of the Commonwealth of Pennsylvania." Also in 1822, John Sterndman, yeoman, on March third, in the township of Menallen "did commit fornication with a certain Solema Slaybaugh, spinster, a female bastard child then and there did beget."

In January 1823, Elizabeth Van Schyorck, spinster, was charged with permitting an unknown person, at Latimore Township, to get her with child, a "female bastard." In 1826, Poll, "a woman of color," spinster, of Franklin Township, committed fornication with a person unknown, thereby creating a "bastard child." In 1827, laborer Moses Muntorff of Huntington Township, committed fornication with Jane Neely. Their union created "a male bastard child." William Shaffer, yeoman, was apparently the father of a four-year-old son. In April 1832, he was charged with committing fornication "with force and arms" upon Sarah Myers, a single woman, on January 28, 1828. The term "force and arms" certainly suggests rape. David Hoffinger, "Minister of the Gospel," on June 2, 1829, with "force and arms, committed fornication with Mary Ann Sheely, a single woman, producing a female bastard child." Eight witnesses appeared in this case. The Reverend Hoffinger apparently fled Adams County when he was indicted in April 1830. (There seems to have been much forced sex in that era.) In 1834, David Kefover, yeoman, committed fornication with Lydia Ashbaugh, a single woman, producing another "female bastard child."

The Grand Inquest for Adams County found that on March 25th, 1831, John McConly [poor legibility], yeoman, "with force and arms," had committed fornication with Mary Stambaugh, thus conceiving a "male bastard child." At Menallen Township, Henry Brown, shoemaker, affirmed that on July 2, 1840, he saw Howard Yetts (Letts?) of Tyrone Township "commit buggery on a black sheep and further saith not." Buggery seemed to linger in the minds of citizens back then. In 1853, three years after the alleged event, Henry Slaybaugh was brought to justice. He was a farmer in Butler Township. The Grand Inquest concluded: "Henry Slaybaugh, late of the county aforesaid, feloniously, wickedly, diabolically, and against the order of nature, had a venereal affair with a certain mare, and then and there feloniously, wickedly, and diabolically, and against the order of nature, with the said mare did commit and perpetrate that detestable and abominable crime of buggery (not to be named among Christians) to the great displeasure of Almighty God, to the great scandal of all humankind and against the peace and dignity of the Commonwealth of Pennsylvania."

An 1834 Grand Inquest found that on August 7, 1833, Henry Saunders "by force and arms, committed fornication with Charlotte Byrum, conceiving a male bastard child." On New Years Day, 1834, Polly Lutz conceived a child, as yet unborn, by a person "unknown to the Grand Inquest." In 1836, John Duncan was taken up by the Grand Inquest for a male child conceived ten months earlier with Sarah Baltzley. Sarah Riffle committed fornication with "a person unknown to the grand inquest," on February 10, 1842, and "permitted a bastard child to be begotten."

In the April 1845 Quarter Sessions at Adams County, Thomas McCreary, student, was charged with fornication. His partner was Caroline Clark, "single woman, and a male bastard child on the body of her . . . then and there did beget . . . against the Peace and Dignity of the Commonwealth of Pennsylvania." Harvey Waddle appeared as a witness for Miss Clark.

On February 17, 1855, Justice of the Peace Henry A. Picking issued an order to Daniel March "or any constable" to apprehend William Noel. Why? Because "Eliza Stough, daughter of Adam Stough, of Hampton in said County [Adams] hath made affirmation that William Noel, blacksmith, of said town of Hampton on the 16th instant and on other days before and since . . . did commit open and gross lewdness and lascivious behaviour and did then and there lewdly and lasciviously expose his private parts in a most indecent posture and situation in the presence of said Eliza Stough with intent to excite in her mind lewd and unchaste desires and inclinations."

In 1856, the Adams County Grand Inquest took up the case of John Heagy, yeoman, and found that on April the 19th, he had committed fornication with Sarah A. Schriver, producing "a male bastard child." An unusual case was that of Worley Jones. On November 5, 1858, George E. Bringman requested that constable Solomon E. Taylor, of the Borough of Gettysburg, arrest Jones, "On the complaint of Mary Bolinger of the Township of Cumberland that she is now pregnant with a bastard child which is likely to become chargeable to said County and charging that Worley Jones, colored, did beget her with said child and is the father of it and that said defendant did have illicit connection with complainant by forcing and threatening to do her injury if she resisted."[9]

On November 21, 1860, Oliver Weller conceived a bastard daughter upon Julia Ann Eck, but she did not complain to the Grand Inquest until three years later, almost at the time that Robert E. Lee arrived at the little town and made its name immortal.

The battle of Gettysburg and the history of our carnal malfeasants converge with the story of John L. Burns, "the Old Hero of Gettysburg." Burns was born in 1793 and had served in the war of 1812 and in the Mexican War. When Lee's forces attacked at Gettysburg, Burns seized his rifle and fought the entire three days as a sharpshooter, returning to his post even after sustaining three wounds. In a somewhat less dangerous role, six years before the battle, he was serving as a constable. On June 16, 1856, Burns was ordered to apprehend William Snyder, who had begot Mary Marsden with a male child, born the preceding May 19th.

Even with war impending, the Grand Inquest for Adams County continued its work, and found that Andrew Ebert, yeoman, in January 1861, had committed fornication with Henrietta Bower, producing a "male bastard child."

Was Thompson McCosh looking for a new mother for his small children, or was he only a heartless seducer? This yeoman was charged in August 1862 with begetting a "male bastard child" upon the body of Elizabeth Tawney. The 1860 census shows 34-year-old McCosh living with his two children, Nancie, age four, and Mary, age one, and no wife. Elizabeth was a 21-year-old "domestic" living with a 45-year-old hotelkeeper, Israel Gannett [difficult legibility], who had a wife and five children. It would seem that love did not bloom for McCosh and Tawney, since Elizabeth pressed charges. The laws on fornication cut both ways. Elizabeth herself was called to the Grand Inquest to answer charges of fornication and of permitting a man to beget a "female bastard child" upon her.

In the same year as Miss Tawney's unwanted motherhood, Christian Buchen (?Bacher) was in trouble. The sheriff of Adams County was commanded to "take the body of Christian Buchen ... and him safely keep ... to answer us concerning a certain bill of indictment for fornication and bastardy." The woman was not named in this warrant.

Another 1862 case of fornication and bastardy came to an abrupt end, based upon a legal error by the Grand Inquest, an error that saved Lodusky House, who was charged with the now familiar act of fornication, in this case with Sarah M. Kuhn, who thereupon produced "a bastard child." W. H. Duncan, the district attorney, noted that the sex of the child had been omitted in the indictment, a fatal error. "I pray your Honors to quash the within bill of indictment." A final 1862 bill of indictment concerned Moses Degroff, yeoman, charged with fornication with Matilda Shaner. The couple had produced a "female bastard child."

In 1863, Maria White, spinster, was charged with fornication and the production of a "female bastard child," the father being "a person to the jurors unknown."

Love gone wrong was the continuing saga of Julia Ann Eck, daughter of John Eck of Liberty Township, and mentioned earlier. She "was delivered of a daughter (a bastard) on the 21st day of August, 1861 and that Oliver Weller, a single man of Frederick County, Maryland, was the father." They were engaged to be married, but by March 1863, Julia began to have some doubts about Oliver's good intentions, hence her visit to the Grand Inquest. Julia herself had to give $50 bond that she would appear as a witness.

The Battle of Gettysburg raged the first three days of July 1863. On the fifth day of July, "Hugh Gallagher, late of the County of Adams, soldier . . . with force and arms . . . in and on one Catharine Bishop, married woman, against the peace of God and the said state . . . violently and feloniously did make an assault . . . and forcibly and against her will did ravish and carnally know [her]." In other words, rape.[10] The indictment does not tell what us regiment he belonged to. The author reviewed the military service records of the thirteen Civil War Hugh Gallaghers from Pennsylvania; none were at the time or place to have committed this crime. The court-martial records in the National Archives make no mention of Hugh Gallagher. All we have is one sheet of paper, headed "In the Court of Oyer and Terminer, General Jail Delivery, August Session, 1863, Adams County SS."

On July 25, 1865, at Bendersville, Rovinia Cullings, a single woman of Menallen Township, appeared before a justice of the peace whose name is illegible and told her story. On several occasions in February of 1865, she had had "carnal knowledge" of a physician, William (Wilmore?, Willimer?) James, and she was now "big with a bastard child." In early 1866 an indictment was handed down, noting the "male bastard child" now extant. The record shows that the sheriff was unable to locate Dr. James.

In November 1869, a warrant was issued for the arrest of John Stall, based upon the complaint of Anna Elisa Ritter of Mount Joy Township. She swore that on October 29, just a few days earlier, he had "laid violent hands upon her person and pulled her from the gate of the house behind the bake oven with the intent to commit a rape." It seems that he held a promissory note against her son, Casper, and against her husband. "He said it would be an easy way to pay it off, if you come into the woods with me."

In April 1871, the sheriff of Adams County was ordered to arrest and jail Joseph Little, on charges of "keeping a disorderly bawdy house." Who was the keeper of this Adams County whorehouse? The 1870 census shows four Joseph Littles living in Gettysburg. Their ages were 56, 58, 70, and 73. Was it one of these men? We do not know.[11]

More than a century has passed since these passions and heartbreaks stirred the men and women of Adams County. Their troubles are over and in the words of Shakespeare's *Fidele*:

> Golden boys and girls all must,
> As chimney sweepers, come to dust.

Chapter 23

BESTIALITY

The Civil War was a cauldron of conflicts. Blue versus Gray. Cavalier versus Roundhead. Abolitionist Presbyterian versus slaveholding Presbyterian. Low tariff versus high tariff. States rights versus federalism. A further conflict, nearly invisible and confined not just to the war years, raged in those deep recesses of the human mind, sometimes termed the Collective Unconscious. Language shapes our thoughts and our minds. Without knowing it, we think with the grammar and logical construction of our language, while applying the values and moral strictures of quite different cultures and its languages. We speak in Indo-European tongues, but we think Semitic thoughts.

The Indo-European languages have their origins in the Sanskrit of ancient India, thousands of years ago, and their modern descendants include English, Irish, French, and German, languages familiar to all of us. The Semitic languages are of Middle Eastern origin, most familiar in the forms of Arabic, Hebrew, and Aramaic, and they shaped both the Old Testament and the Koran. A synthesis and turning point may have come with the Alexandrine transformation, when Greek-speaking Jews produced the Septuagint, in which Semitic thoughts in Hebrew were transformed into Greek, an Indo-European language.

What does all this have to do with charges of bestiality among Americans in the 1860s? After all, Exodus 22:19 settles the matter quite succinctly: "Whosoever lieth with a beast shall surely be put to death." Leviticus 18:23 goes a step further and enjoins both men and women from cross-species coitus. When Genesis 1:26 commands man to have dominion over the fish and the fowl and the cattle and every creeping thing, that dominion was certainly not to include sexual union. Such is the ancient Semitic tradition, and it is ours today.

But what about the Indo-Europeans? With the Vedic Indians, the ancient Greeks, and the Romans, white stallions were associated with power, virtue, virility, and kingship. And sexuality. The Irish, too, had a tradition, as we will see, that joined man and beast in sacred union. The Rig Veda, composed over 3000 years ago, describes a fertility ritual in which a consecrated stallion and a chief queen simulated intercourse, while priests chanted sacred texts.[1] In the pre-Christian Irish rituals, the King copulated with a sacred mare, that was then killed, dismembered, and cooked. The king drank of the broth and then bathed in that same equestrian consommé. Finally, the broth was distributed to the people, who shared in this sacred meal, a Celtic communion predating St. Patrick.

True, intercourse with beasts was permitted only to royalty, and only on sacred occasions, but this is so different from the utter and total proscription of Exodus, that the two are as night and day. The contrast might be enhanced by imagining Mary Todd Lincoln with the white stallion, or Jefferson Davis with the sacred mare. Not possible. Our pre-Christian Celtic origins are buried too deeply. Our 19th century offenders were judged by the ancient laws of Israel.

Before considering our boys in the War Between the States, it is worth a glance at a rich tradition of American buggery. Every schoolchild knows the story of the Mayflower and Plymouth Colony. These Puritans looked darkly at bestiality. Consider the case of seventeen-year-old Thomas Granger, sentenced to die just 24 years after the Pilgrim fathers set foot on the famous rock. Granger, after close questioning, confessed to buggery with a mare. Soon after, he told the entire court the story, and later told the crowd that had gathered for his hanging, of additional liaisons with a cow, two goats, five sheep, two calves, and a turkey. Under the law of Leviticus 20:15, the animals were also executed. The traditions of Dieudonné (literally "given to God") forbade the consumption of the convicted animals. Thus not only did Granger lose his life, and Love Brewster lose his servant, but the little community lost an important part of its agricultural wealth.

It is worth noting the exactitude with which the guilty parties were identified. Twelve sheep were rounded up, so that Granger could identify the five with whom he had had carnal connection. The other seven sheep were sent back home, spared the executioner's knife.[2]

In Massachusetts, in 1673, Benjamin Goad committed the "unnatural and horrid act of Bestiallitie on a mare," and was sentenced to be hanged. As was the custom, the mare was executed first, before Goad's very eyes, by being "Knockt on the head." Nineteen years later, in New Jersey, one Harry, described as "a Negro manservant," was convicted of "Buggering a Cow." Of course, the cow, whose degree of consent remains unknown, was executed. Harry was sentenced to be hanged, "till thy body bee dead, dead, dead."[3]

As noted earlier, in 1848, Howard Yetts of Gettysburg was indicted for buggery upon a black sheep; nearby, Henry Slaybaugh was indicted two years later for the same crime, but with a mare. Since the ancient Vedics favored horses, we will commence our Civil War cases with those of equestrian content.

William Bishop was mustered into service at Evansville in August 1861, and joined Company H, 1st Indiana Cavalry. He brought his own horse, for which he was reimbursed forty cents a day. Four months after joining, he was charged with "grossly immoral conduct," having attempted intercourse with a mare on the Caledonia Road, in Iron County, Missouri. Private George Johnston, of Bishop's company, was on night picket with Bishop. "The accused took a horse and rode down the road . . . about 700 yards. I walked up to about twelve steps from him and asked him what he was doing. He said he was fooling. He was standing about two feet behind a gray mare, buttoning up his britches with one hand. I said, 'You are played out!' because I thought he was doing something with the mare, but I did not see him doing it." Bishop was acquitted.[4]

John Byford of the 6th Illinois Cavalry was 6' 4", with blond hair and blue eyes. In an army of short men with dark complexions, he was hard to overlook, more so on the night of April 2, 1862, at Paducah, Kentucky. Thomas Blakely, of Byford's company, was feeding his horse when he heard someone crying, "Whoa!" in the stable. Blakely saw a rack of poles constructed behind the mare, with Byford standing on the poles, "going through the motions of having connection with the mare." Lion Gadon, another member of Byford's company, told his version. "I met Blakely who told me Byford was buggering a mare. I didn't believe him. We went and saw Byford going through the motions with the mare. We went and got a candle. He had a blanket over the horse's rump. When he saw us he threw the blanket down over the rump." Byford, in his defense, said that members of his unit were plotting to get rid of him. He was found guilty and sentenced to a year at hard labor, with seven days of each alternate month to be in solitary confinement on bread and water. In his review of the case, General U. S. Grant noticed that the court had been convened illegally," but the crime with which the prisoner is charged is of so heinous and revolting a nature, that he should not escape punishment." Grant, who had a long and happy association with horses, ordered a dishonorable discharge. However, Byford appears in the records in 1863 and 1865 as a "straggler and a deserter."[5]

Anthony Rasställer, a thirty-five-year-old native of Karlsruh in Baden, (now part of Germany) was 5'5", with a dark complexion and gray eyes. Before the war he had been a saddler, but in December 1863 he was serving with the 15th New York Heavy Artillery, at Fort Lyon, Virginia. He spoke only German. His unusual behavior was observed by Privates Zwanzig and Obinger. "It was about eight P.M. Accused was standing on an upside down pail behind the mare. She had raised her tail in an extraordinary manner. A man's seed was running down the genitals of the mare. The same thing was on the front of Rasställer's pants. His trousers were open. He offered us ten dollars if we would not report him.

He said, 'It will ruin me and my family.'" He was sentenced to three years at hard labor, later commuted to a dishonorable discharge.[6]

The 54th Massachusetts, a regiment of African American men, is famous for its heroic exploits, later enshrined in the movie "Glory!" Less glorious were the charges against James Riley, that at nine P.M. on November 5, 1863, he had had sexual connection with a mare in a stall at Morris Island, South Carolina. Witness John Brown heard a "fuss" in the stable, and found the mare with her head turned down. He told the court that Riley's pants were unbuttoned and that there were horsehairs on Riley's coat. A few minutes later, the regimental surgeon, Charles Briggs, examined Riley by candlelight. "His clothes were not wet. His pants were missing several buttons, so that his private parts were visible. Those parts were dry. So were the mare's private parts." Riley was acquitted.

Here, the story takes an unusual turn. Dr. Briggs, with several accomplices, appeared the next night, kidnapped Riley from his tent, took him to the doctor's tent, had him stripped, gagged, and bound down, and circumcised Riley against his will, cauterizing the bleeding wound with a hot iron. Briggs was charged with assault, but was never tried, probably protected by his Harvard friends.[7]

The chaplain of the 6th South Carolina (Jenkins' Brigade) and later the 12th South Carolina (Gregg's Brigade) wrote in his diary, "This evening just before dark a man . . . took Major Jone's [sic] mare off to the woods, and was caught in the act of sexual intercourse. Such is human nature. Oh my God deliver me from myself."[8]

Samuel Parks served with Company G, 87th Pennsylvania, and lost his left index finger at Spotsylvania. His pension application contains an interview with his wife, Lucinda. "We have 13 children . . . one son surprised Sam in the barn in the act of having connection with a hen, a common barnyard chicken. [Would Lucinda have been less offended if it had been an Aracana?] I asked him to never do that again . . . instead, he left home and never returned. He never sent support for the children or paid his debts. He was a poor provider. Our home was no better than a hog house." When Sam died in 1899, his second wife, Julia, appeared and the Pension Bureau had to unravel this tale of bigamy and chicken abuse.[9]

Stephen Hughes was a Welsh coal miner who enlisted October 10, 1864 in the 2nd California Cavalry, perhaps attracted by the $400 bounty ($12,000 in today's money.) He was age twenty-one, 5 foot 2 inches, with blue eyes and auburn hair. His career was a checkered one. On October 30, three weeks after enlisting, he deserted from Camp Union, near Sacramento, but reappeared five days later. In his brief time in camp before deserting, he was in more trouble. On the moonlit night of October 20, 1864, two soldiers observed Hughes with the camp dog, a large white bitch. He had led the dog away from the tents and was found kneeling over the dog, which he held by the collar. His pants were unbuttoned and he had thrown his blouse over the dog. Both observers testified that Hughes was "having connection with or attempting to have connection with the dog." On October 22, 1864, his company commander, Captain Thomas Barker, wrote a letter noting that Hughes had "committed a crime against nature, in illicit intercourse with a bitch dog," and requested that "this degraded wretch be dishonorably discharged." Barker's recommendation was passed from one office to another without resolution. Fourteen *months* later, Hughes was given a medical discharge, based on a badly healed leg fracture present before his enlistment.[10]

A century and a half later, fragmentary evidence suggests that such transgressions are still with us. In San Francisco, police arrested a man who was sitting in his car at night with two chickens and a 15-ounce jar of Vaseline. He was caught in the act—the very act—and the chickens were rushed to a veterinarian who examined them for signs of sexual abuse. Further south in California, police in Malibu arrested 54-year-old carrot peddler, Bruce House, on six felony counts of animal cruelty and six misdemeanor counts of having sex with a horse. The cruelty charges came from the tightly hobbled hind legs of the horse; two mares suffered from vaginal lacerations. His more recent acts of cruelty occurred while he was out on bail for other similar charges.[11]

Even in pre-Christian Ireland, Bruce House would have been excluded from the horse ceremonies. House was certainly no member of a royal family, but rather a commoner, of a cruel and evil nature.[12]

America's heartland was the scene of further transgression when, in February 2006, 34-year old Gene D. Teufert of Freeburg, Illinois was sentenced to two years of probation for "inappropriate sexual contact with his dog in the presence of a minor." In a plea bargain, prosecutors agreed to drop two felony counts of sexual contact with an animal.[13]

Chapter 24

BAD LANGUAGE

Maledictive language is either blasphemous or sexual or both. Exodus 20:7 clearly prohibits the inappropriate invocation of the Deity. Purely religious cursing is a field for theologians, and beyond the purview of this essay.

Sexual cursing is an act of sexual aggression, a rape of the ears, as it were, a communication in the phallic-intrusive mode, as attested in the psychoanalytic literature.[1] While most Civil War curses were carried away by the wind, hundreds were captured by court scribes and became part of our nation's heritage—perhaps not written in stone, but certainly recorded on good quality rag paper. (These words, harsh as they may be, could be a boon to re-enactors, novelists, and movie producers, in their constant search for authentic dialogue.)

Most of the malediction presented here falls into one of eight categories. However, many curses involved several categories in the same breath; they are arbitrarily catalogued by the dominant theme. The eight principal categories are: family relations, coital suggestions, reproductive organs, oral sex, excretory functions, prostitution, poetry and extended metaphor, and a miscellany.

Family Relations Malediction

Most such cursing centered around the alleged traits or quirks of the victim's mother, as embodied in the almost universal "son of a bitch." The meaning is obvious: "Your mother was a dog [an unclean animal in many cultures] and you are the product of a bestial, unnatural, and degraded act." In other cultures, "son of a donkey," or "son of a camel" conveys a similar message. In our review of 75,961 courts-martial, 5,460 military commissions, and 193 courts of inquiry, all from Union Army records, we found 1,740 cases in which the defendant was charged with calling someone a "son of a bitch." In the 1,550 Union Navy trials, the total number of "son of a bitch" cases was seventy-four. The following cases represent a brief sampling of this common offense.

William C. Smythe, 22nd VRC, was a badly wounded veteran of five battles. He attacked the military police patrol, because "someone in the patrol called me a son of a bitch and that means he is saying my mother is a whore." Edward MacLean, a first class fireman on the USS *Osage* was drunk and disorderly and called the assistant engineer a "black son of a bitch." A drunken US Marine Corps private at Pensacola attacked the officer of the day, pulling out part of his beard, kicking him in the groin, and calling him a "Dutch son of a bitch." Patrick Troy, 17th Massachusetts, was drunk and violent while on guard duty at Baltimore. He called his lieutenant a "damned son of a bitch and the damned son of a whore."[2]

At Camp Griffin, Virginia, George Dunn, 6th Maine, refused to speak civilly to his captain, calling him a "damned son of a bitch and the damned son of a whore." At Fort McHenry, long celebrated in "The Star Spangled Banner," Clement Kunsman, 2nd US Artillery, called a sentinel "a son of a whore," for which he was reduced to the ranks. Sidney Rogers, a seaman on the USS *Hendrick Hudson*, at Key West, was more expansive. He called his lieutenant "a son of a bitch," "a son of a whore," and "a god damned Western Ocean government robber." Such cursing could have consequences. John Carrigan of the USS *Lancaster* got a year in California's notorious San Quentin Prison for calling the master's mate "a pretty son of a whore." He was also drunk and disorderly. Seaman James Hughan of the USS *Canandaigua* was captured while deserting. He called his commander a "black-muzzled son of a bitch," and added, "May the curse of Jesus Christ rest on the brass-bound bastards." A final example of "sonship" cursing will suffice. At a trial conducted in German, but recorded in English, Peter Baumgarten, 52nd New York, was convicted of calling his superior (in German) an "incest fellow." A German friend of the author knew exactly what was said in German, but told me it was so awful she could not say the words in English.[3]

In a variation on the theme of "son of a bitch," many soldiers addressed women directly as "bitch." Captain Morris Hazard, 51st New York, addressed widow Eliza Mason as a "goddamn bitch" and asked at her doorstep in the middle of the night, "Are you a whore . . . are all your whores full?" Sergeant Henry McIntyre, 33rd US Colored Troops, knocked a laundress to the ground at Charleston, South Carolina, and said, "You are old as hell and a damned bitch." Charles Dugan, 2nd New York Light Artillery, met his match in Elizabeth Kirsten. "He called me a damned bitch and said what he would do, in language I do not care to repeat. I called him a drunken puppy."[4]

The Coital Suggestion

The "F" word. The dreaded "F" word. The word never to be uttered in the presence of parents or other figures of authority. Enshrined in our language since it emerged from Middle Dutch around 1495, the "F" word has lived a shadow life—always understood, but employed only under great duress or upon abandoning all sense of gentility. Yet a recent decade has seen a liberation, an unshackling from these bonds. A recent book—an entire book—has been published by a respected editor of the Oxford English Dictionary, and it tells us as much as any normal person would want to know about the origins and uses of the "F" word.[5]

In a historic moment, on June 25, 2004, the "F" word reached its apotheosis, when the vice president of the United States of America, the Honorable Richard Cheney, turned to United States Senator Patrick Leahy and said these immortal words: "Fuck yourself." Our humble Civil War ancestors, who never dreamed of the ennobling and exalted position of vice-president, did their best to keep the word in circulation, as it awaited its final efflorescence—its rapture, if you will—on the lips of their descendents. Cheney's ancestor, Captain Samuel Cheney, 21st Ohio, would no doubt be proud of his descendant, although the little we know of Captain Cheney is that he himself was never court-martialed. Here are a few of the contributions by those boys who saved the Last Best Hope on Earth.[6]

On Christmas Eve, 1863, John Gibbons, 24th Ohio, broke into the home of "Old Lady Enos" and said, "I came for fucking and fucking I will have." Gibbons was part of a "riotous mob" that disturbed that holy night at Alpine Coal Mines, Tennessee. Before proceeding further with our study of the sacred and the profane, a story told to me by noted manuscript archivist Stephen L. Carson, about his contact with the Civil War Turner-Baker Papers, seems relevant. "That was my very first project as a National Archives employee in 1967. I remembered gingerly handling my first original manuscripts belonging to the government. With ever so delicate care and awe I got to the file 'Threats Against the President,' or something like that, and as I opened it up, I read, 'President Johnson: you are a mother fucking son of a bitch!'"[7]

Gustav S. Hoffman, 5th New Jersey Light Artillery, was on trial for concealing a letter from a deserter. The letter, mostly in French, is in the file. One sentence reads, "Dire le bonjour de ma part à Maggie, but I don't want any fucking done there." Two drunken captains of the 5th VRC, were out for a stroll. Samuel Place said to some passing ladies, "Sis, don't you want to fuck?" To his companion, Place said, "Captain, she wants you to fuck her." At Providence, Tennessee, James Smith, 2nd Illinois Light Artillery, insulted a lady. Miss Mattie King told the court, "He said, 'I intend to fuck you.'"[8]

Colonel John Groom, commanding the 100th Ohio, was drunk at several places in Kentucky. Among his many indiscretions, he regaled his fellow officers with this remembrance of things past: "Of all my fucking scrapes, I suppose one of my first ones was the greatest. One day . . . two of my comrades came to me in great haste that a very beautiful woman had come to town to make her living by prostitution. About suppertime, my employer being gone and the store being empty, I saw her coming. She was very beautiful, with black eyes, jet black hair and a voluptuous person. I was so excited and fired up that I thought it would burst. I took her behind the counter and as I endeavored to have connection with her, I spit all over her thighs and dress."[9]

At Lookout Mountain, Tennessee, Harrison Adams, 78th Pennsylvania, was charged with making an obscene drawing (captioned "Alan Anchors fucking a cow") and posting it on the company street. Henry Ballma, 2nd Missouri Light Artillery, said of the Illinois troops camped near Memphis, "They ought to send for their wives, and if they can't pay the fare, I will, and I will fuck them, and if I can't, my dog will." A Confederate Colonel, Virginius D. Groner (Grover), commanding the 61st Virginia, was charged with a dozen offenses, including sleeping in a hotel while his troops were in the field, and with stopping the music at dress parade, so that he could finish his supper. On Christmas Day, 1862, he called his principal musician, "a damned half-fucked son of a bitch." Men of the cloth, like musicians, did not always receive respect. Around Christmas, 1862, Captain J. Edward Savery, 5th New York Heavy Artillery, called Chaplain William A. Barnes, a "fuck ass" and "a good for nothing loafer."[11]

Robert McKnight, US Marines, stationed at Folly Island, South Carolina, was ordered to fall in for inspection. His response? "What the bloody hell is wanted of me now? This is a fucked up company anyhow." The court, which sentenced him to sixty days of solitary confinement in "single irons" and two weeks on bread and water, petitioned for clemency, noting that he was "a brave man, but surly and disagreeable." The 7th New Hampshire was traveling by train in April 1864. At one stop, Henry Robbins leaned out the window and addressed a woman standing on the station platform: "I'm going to fuck you." Robbins, who was also drunk and disorderly, got three months at hard labor. At Fort Barnard, Virginia, a twenty-gun redoubt in today's Alexandria, First Lieutenant C. A. Talbot, Battery D, 1st Maryland Light Artillery, said to Lieutenant G. Smith, "You are a rascal. I did not make my money in the way that you did, your wife went afrigging. That's the way you got your money." [Frig is an ancient variation of fuck.][12]

Lieutenant Corwin Holmes, 25th New York Cavalry, borrowed very large sums from enlisted men and did not repay them. When one private asked for his money, Holmes replied, "Ask him if his wife didn't want to come through from Saratoga [New York] to Washington, to get fucked four or five times." In a letter received by Samuel Hamilton, Company L, 3rd Indiana Cavalry, written by John M. Brubaker of Halifax, Pennsylvania, in January 1865, we learn of the home front. "Every Little Miss who has fairly entered her teens considers herself pretty able to understand the nature of the passion and as a matter of course bare its fruits. To cut a long story short, fucking is the order of the day now, for nearly every woman is a soldier's widow and consequently her husband being shot or dies in Hospital, she is privileged to use her private property as she pleases and cunt being of that order, everyone must find food for it."[13]

Half a year after the shooting stopped, in December 1865, John Brown, 12th Illinois Cavalry, broke into the homes of several Houston, Texas women and threatened to shoot them if they did not submit to his desires. Mrs. Allen Flood testified, "He was very drunk, cursing me and my children. He asked me to go into the room with him." The court asked, "What were the words that he used?" "He asked me to fuck him." Brown got two years in prison. At Chattanooga, Tennessee, Second Lieutenant Joseph Smith, 44th Indiana, assaulted Nancy Owner, "colored," lifting up her clothing and saying, "I will fuck you right here." The court dismissed him, but asked for clemency, which left the reviewing general ". . . astounded and humiliated."[14]

Oram Brumley (Brumney) was a 20-year-old, blue-eyed farm boy, when he enlisted in Lillard's 3rd Tennessee Mounted Infantry (Confederate). After his capture and imprisonment at Rock Island, he decided to "galvanize" and became a soldier in the 2nd US Volunteers (Union), where he was sent west to fight Indians. At Fort Larned, Kansas, he got drunk and called his captain a "Goddamn nigger fucking son of a bitch." Sergeant George Merrill was in the 19th New York Cavalry. On August 7, 1862, he wrote home to "Friend Ira," describing the battle of Deserted Farm, near Suffolk, Virginia. After telling of artillery duels and captives, he turned to hometown matters. "You spoke about Peter fucking somebody, but you did not say who he fucked."[15]

John H. Bennett, 78th Pennsylvania, was gone overnight at Nashville and made a nuisance of himself. When arrested, he called his captain "a goddamn nigger fucking son of a bitch." Later, he pleaded for clemency, asserting, "I am the only support of a widowed mother and two fatherless sisters." In June 1865, Patrick Haffey, 19th Pennsylvania Cavalry, was incoherent with alcoholic rage and, while resisting arrest, called his sergeant "a Goddamned nigger fuck faced son of a bitch." Sixty days at hard labor may have dried out his brain.[16]

The Reproductive Organs

It is a cliché of Freudian psychology that snakes have phallic connotations in the human mind. This connection was not lost on Van B. Hall, Company D, 11th West Virginia. The charges filed against him include the following: "Private Hall . . . whilst in the ranks of said company at roll call, deliberately unbuttoned his pants and publicly drew out his penis and then did ask and say in the presence of his commanding officer and of the said company, 'How do you like that fellow?'" [and then said] "'. . . it is the biggest snake in the company.'"[17]

The serpentine Hall was not the only miscreant in the 11th West Virginia. Captain Lewis Smith, at Parkersburg, took Jenny Robinson, "a notorious whore," into his tent. A witness reported her leaving the tent at midnight, *without her bonnet*! Later, on the march through Jackson County, he shot at Mrs. Riddler's's chickens. True to her mountain heritage, she called out, "You do that again, I'll shoot your head off." Smith replied, "The head of my prick, I reckon."[18]

Joshua Chilcoat, 8th Missouri Militia Cavalry, was drunk and disorderly at Quincy, Missouri. While being arrested, he was asked by his captain, "Do you have a weapon?" Chilcoat replied, "I have my prick!" Hospital Steward Justus Rathbone was an embezzler and troublemaker at a Washington, DC hospital. One of the pieces of evidence in his trial was this note, written by Rathbone himself. "Notice. Captain Charles A. Perry. You are a damn fool. Why in hell don't to let the cooks fry the pork, you son of a bitch. [signed] T. Prick."[19]

At Chattanooga, Tennessee, Frank P. Allen, 1st Ohio, complained to his lieutenant about the lack of tents, beginning with these words: "Oh, prick, I'll be goddamn [if we have any tents.]" Cornelius F. Mowers was the Lieutenant Colonel of the 79th US Colored Troops. He was charged with, among other things, putting his hands under the dress of Lavinia, a "colored woman." Mowers was drunk most of the time and while in this condition, in the presence of other officers and of his wife, ". . . exposed his person [genitals]." When criticized for this, he replied, "It is a pity a man can't shake his old cock." Enoch Colen, 15th VRC, was on "light-duty" (apparently *very* light duty) in a saloon at Cairo, Illinois. His captain urged him to tend to his duty in a more productive manner, and Colen replied, "You make me walk too fast. My bollocks [testicles] pain me, you fuck with my bollocks."[20]

Michael P. Comber, 30th Pennsylvania, came to the attention of General George B. McClellan. Comber, when asked to do some duty, called his captain "a swell bollix," for which the 1857 Webster's dictionary gives three definitions: a bungle, a botch, and testicles. The war was only six months old and already Comber had been in the hospital twice with syphilis. He was sentenced to be drummed out. McClellan reviewed the trial and wrote, "The evidence exhibits him utterly unworthy of companionship with brave and respectable men . . . The service is well rid of him."[21]

Captain Robert Hazeltine, 6th New York, was staggering drunk when he approached a sentry at Santa Rosa Island, Florida. The sentry demanded the password. Hazeltine replied "Prick!" That was not the correct answer. In October 1864, Major General D. B. Birney issued General Orders No. 39, concerning the disposition of ambulances. Written on the back of one copy of these orders is this note: "C. Getz. Suck my nuts. A. J. Bowman, Esq." Christian Getz and

Andrew J. Bowman were both lieutenants in the 67th Ohio. R. F. Barton, 174th New York, was not a happy soldier. At Tarleton's Plantation, Louisiana, he broke the company cart, threw his musket in the fire, complained that, "There are not enough men in this shanghaied regiment," and when told to be quiet, replied, "Bite my nuts." This surly attitude earned him five years in prison.[22]

On April 26, 1865, Amos Breneman wrote to a friend, "The chief vegitable of life is cunt rum and tobacco . . . I have got a better place to sleep then I had but still not so good as against a woman's bare legs." The mortar schooner *Sophronia* was not a happy ship. Mate Henry Fuller and seventeen-year-old First Class Boy Robert Clark, had a strange relationship. Witnesses said, "Mr. Fuller used to be always fooling around with that boy." Clark called Fuller a "Goddamn boy fucking son of a bitch." Fuller, in turn, called the boy a "cunt swabber," and said, "At Washington, DC, Clark swamped whore's cunts." In his defense, Fuller said he was only cautioning the boy about the dangers of visiting prostitutes.[23]

Fellate—The Other "F" Word

Corporal George Godby, 170th New York, managed to combine sexual deviance and hatred of the British conquest of Ireland in a single verbal outburst, when, at Union Mills, Virginia, he called his sergeant "a damned old bugger, a cock sucker, and a bloody English Orangeman." Thomas Post, 14th New York Cavalry, was on a drunken rampage at Franklin, Louisiana. He lost his carbine. He lost his canteen. He kicked his sergeant, and he called his lieutenant "A Goddamn cock sucking stinking son of a bitch," and "a whore's bastard," all of which got him two years in prison.[24]

A trio of men from the 6th New York, in June 1862, at Pensacola, Florida, may have set some sort of record for foul-mouthed utterances. They refused fatigue duty, left the camp, got drunk, and resisted arrest. William Day and James Buckley called their sergeant, "A cock sucking son of a bitch." Michael Holland used the same term, while adding, "Goddamn big bloated son of a bitch, big sucker," and "Jack yourself." All three men went to prison.[25]

Three cases out West show that the fellatic word was not the sole property of Easterners. At Camp Nye, Nevada, William Mulligan, 1st Nevada, left his guard post and stole knives, beans, and brown sugar. When arrested, he called the sergeant, "A Goddamn cock sucking son of a bitch," all of which earned him a year at the prison on Alcatraz. Fort Craig, in New Mexico's southern desert, was the site of outbursts by two men of the 1st California. Sergeant Major Thomas Wrenn objected to his breakfast, calling it, "a damned cock sucking mess," and Olin Gillen said of his corporal, "A cock sucker and he is one."[26]

James Burke, 2nd New York Veteran Cavalry, a twenty-nine-year-old, blue-eyed native of Ireland, was charged with calling his sergeant a "Goddamn cock sucker," but was never brought to trial. Six more soldiers and sailors used the same words in the same contexts. Slight variations appeared in three other contexts. Edwin Manderville, 1st VRC, was drunk at Fort McHenry and exclaimed, "The sergeant cock sucked to get his position." Charles Morril, 117th Illinois, at Montgomery, Alabama, posted a "scandalous placard" on a tree. The text read, in part, ". . . looking for a nigger wench and to act as an organ sucker." The full text of the message specified that no one from the state of Maine need apply, and was captioned "Multim in Parvo," [Latin: Much in Little] suggesting an above average level of education.[27]

Jacob Mittaner, 20th New York, said to his sergeant at Camp Hamilton, Virginia, "A liar is not so bad as a sucker." Consultation with several 19th century dictionaries yielded at least three definitions of sucker: "a simpleton," "a social parasite," and "a term considered abusive and insulting." Mittaner, most likely, had the third definition in mind.[28]

Excretory Epithets

Insults involving bowel and bladder functions hark back to early childhood, in their simplicity and direct abusiveness. Many such insults center around the ritual humiliation of oral-anal contact.

General Samuel Heintzelman had little patience with the drunken Lieutenant William Stewart, 3rd Independent Battery, New York Light Artillery, who shouted "Kiss my arse," at the old West Pointer. Stewart was dismissed. Missouri officers could be earthy in their remarks. Major John McDonald and Lieutenant Colonel James Peckham, both of the 8th Missouri, had a shouting match in front of their troops, inviting each other to "Kiss my ass," among other curses. Lieutenant William Hill, 7th New Hampshire, was accused of keeping a whore at Fort Jefferson. Hill invited his accuser to "Kiss my Goddamn arse," and "Make your peace with God and speak for your coffin."[29]

Jonathan Holden, 89th Illinois, was absent without leave at Huntsville, Alabama, when he invaded a private home, stole food, called the wife "a whore," and told the husband to "Kiss my ass." Charles Munser, 4th Missouri Cavalry, rode his horse into the kitchen of "the widow Ramsey," and when she objected, he told her to "Kiss my arse." A drunken lieutenant, Thomas Gorman, 46th Pennsylvania, who was incoherently intoxicated on the steamer *New York*, and at Annapolis, issued this cryptic remark to a fellow lieutenant: "Bill Weber, you can kiss my ass or I will kiss yours." Lieutenant Joseph Lock was an officer in the 11th Louisiana, African Descent. He was intimate with a black woman named Easter, and at Snyder's Bluff, Mississippi, issued this rejoinder to one of his critics: "Tell him to shove it. Tell him to kiss my Goddamn royal star spangled jolly old arsehold."[30]

William Cronan, a captain in the 7th Vermont, was in a quarrel with his superiors, and added this to our linguistic heritage: "The colonel can kiss my royal, majestic, brown, military touch hole." Cronan was reprimanded. James Mellon, an assistant engineer on the USS *Delaware*, went ashore at New Bern, North Carolina, got roaring drunk, and refused to return to his ship. When sent word that he must return, he told the messenger, "Commander Davenport may kiss my lily white ass." That was the end of Mellon's career. Perhaps the most remarkable example of suggested procto-osculation was that made by Lewis Jones, 40th Ohio, in a letter to Captain Milton Kemper, in which Jones wrote, ". . . you may kiss my Royal Bengal, Military Cracked, Shanked, Red, Tired, Convalescent Damned Ass."[31]

Early in the war, boredom was a major enemy. The 4th New Jersey was camped in northern Virginia. One man returned from town bearing a tasteless ceramic knick-knack. Corporal John Holton looked at it and exclaimed, "It's an old woman sitting on a damned shit pot." A colonel overheard the remark and had Holton arrested. By the end of the war, this regiment had lost 266 men, and this trivial incident was long forgotten.[32]

J. G. Bassler, a lieutenant in the 4th VRC, was already a wounded, disabled veteran of the 48th Pennsylvania before he was twenty. He was tried for conduct unbecoming an officer and a gentleman, for calling another lieutenant "a Goddamn cripple," and inviting him to "suck my ass" and "fuck my shit." The court added ". . . and other expressions too vulgar to recite." One wonders what *those* might have been. George W. Scheerer, 1st Maryland Cavalry, was given a 32-pound iron ball attached to his ankle for two months, as a reminder to abstain from remarks such as this: "If I want to shit, I'd go to the lieutenant's tent and do it, and shit a big turd." Major Matthew Avery, 10th New York Cavalry, who seems to have been a horse thief, was jealous of an apparent friendship between the colonel and a lieutenant, and said to the junior officer, "You and the colonel has been sucking arses together." At the end of the war, Avery was brevetted brigadier general for "meritorious service."[33]

Charles Florence was an old salt, with nine years in naval service. On the USS *Cayuga*, where he was boatswain's mate, he seems to have overstepped the bounds of naval etiquette, when he called his skipper a "damned old shit" and a "son of a whore," while inviting him to "suck my arse." Charles Hall, 22nd Ohio, objected to some unpleasant duty and told his sergeant, "You can suck my hole." This intemperance earned him fourteen days in the guardhouse on bread and water. Acting Ensign George W. Nelson, argued with another officer at Newport News, Virginia. His opponent called him a "coward." Nelson replied, somewhat more creatively, "I advise you to have the top of your head taken off, the contents removed, and allow some sensible man to shit in it."[34]

'Sergeant George H. Bailey, 5th Maryland, insulted three officers in less than five minutes. He called the colonel a "damned dirty son of a bitch," and warned the lieutenant not to "stick your Goddamn nose up my ass." He merely threatened to beat up the major after the war was over. Lieutenant John Merklee, 158th New York, was furious that Captain J. M. Reidenbach had opened his mail; he called the captain "a goddamn Dutch old fart." Merklee was kicked out of the army in June 1863. His nemesis, Reidenbach, was thrown out of the army just a few weeks later, for his own transgressions.[35]

Michael Jordan, 2nd New York Artillery, left his guard post not just once but three times, without permission, to go and get his breakfast. On the third offense, his sergeant reprimanded him. Jordan retorted, "You can go up in my arse." A soldier of the Irish Brigade, Michael O'Rourke, 5th New York Artillery, was drunk at Relay House in Maryland when he told his captain, "You can suck my arse." This got him three months at hard labor. At Wilmington, North Carolina, Sergeant Oren Kimball, 7th New Hampshire, was too drunk at parade to stand without wobbling. When urged to behave by his captain, Kimball responded with, "Suck my arse," which lost him his sergeant's stripes.[36]

Thomas Nolan, 30th New York, left a truly cryptic remark in our nation's records: "Sam Potts or Sam Kettle, I don't care a damn which left the regiment at Rappahannock Station with a sore cock or a sore ass." At Fort Bennett, Virginia, a five-gun redoubt on Arlington Heights, Elias Gailock, 2nd New York Artillery, was locked up for drunkenness. Confinement did not prevent him from shouting to his lieutenant, "You can stop up my arse if you want to." Lieutenant Charles D. Griggs, 36th US Colored Troops, was often in conflict with authority. He frequently refused duty and insulted his colonel. The final step in his dismissal came when he announced, "The colonel doesn't know enough to command a shit house battery."[37]

Far from the fields of battle, in Los Angeles, California, at the "Coronado" saloon, civilian Charles Helms heard of the assassination at Ford's Theater. His reaction? "I would walk a thousand miles to have the pleasure of shitting on the president's grave." A military court found him guilty, but released him because, "He is an ignorant person, occupying no social position."[38]

Aqueous excretion occupies a less prominent position in these files. At New Orleans, the USS *Kensington* had captured a shipload of rum. As night follows the day, the men guarding it were soon drunk. The captain arrived and admonished the men. Charles Jones, the ship's cook, replied, "You don't impress me. I have pissed on a commodore!" Thomas Riley, of the 13th New Jersey, was drunk and disorderly, waving a knife and being insubordinate to his officers, by offering to "piss in the coffee." William Murphy, 8th Vermont, was drunk and insolent at Franklin, Louisiana, calling the sergeant a "damned piss pot." The Irish vote was important and the governor of Vermont interceded for Murphy, requesting reduction of the five-year sentence.[39]

A Taxonomy of Tarts

The conversations of soldiers included many references to prostitutes. Some such references were enough to merit a court-martial. There was almost a second Civil War in 1864, between the California troops and the Mormons of Utah. Captain Izatus Potts, 3rd California, at Camp Douglas, near Salt Lake City, said out loud, "Every house in this camp is a whorehouse." He frequently made other remarks hostile to the Latter-Day Saints. William Bond, 2nd Invalid Corps, had wounds insufficient to keep him from running through York, Pennsylvania, calling the women of the town, "Goddamn whores." Lieutenant Joseph Jennings, 111th Ohio, called his captain, "a whorehouse pimp."[40]

Major William A. Ketchum, 15th New York Engineers, when he heard that General James Wadsworth had been killed at the Wilderness, said, "Wadsworth was a whoremaster. I know he kept a whore in Washington, DC." Jacob Stippich, 9th Wisconsin, was drunk and violent at St. Louis, Missouri. He ran over a child with his horse and called the distraught mother, "a bitch and a whore." Sergeant James Lofton, 1st New York Mounted Rifles, was drunk at Yorktown, Virginia, where he called his lieutenant "a whorehouse son of a bitch." There were dozens of trials for men who had called civilian women "whores" and who called their officers "whorehouse pimps." In addition, there were variations on these themes.[41]

Family honor is especially important in Spanish families. A detachment of the 1st New Mexico Cavalry was returning from a scout near Fort Wingate, New Mexico. Desidirio Utabarri and Lorenzo Garcia were quarreling. Garcia said Utabarri's mother was a prostitute. Utabarri shot and killed Garcia.[42]

Lieutenant Frank Filley was drunk at the dress parade of the 16th New York Heavy Artillery. He was displeased with his men's appearance, and shouted, "Your company looks like a whorehouse gone to seed." He was cashiered. General Ben Butler, who reviewed the case, wrote, "While being tried, [Filley] fell senselessly drunk on the floor before the court, which forbids any possible revision of the proceedings." There was lively friction between Lieutenant Frank Doherty and his captain, both of the Missouri Engineer Regiment of the West. Doherty said, "The captain is a Goddamn whoremaster, and was after every old rotten whore at Cape Girardeau. He has tried to cover [coitally mount] cattle, horses, mules, and dogs." Captain James Clifford, 1st Missouri Cavalry, was drunk on duty at Rolla, Missouri, and tried to incite a mutiny. When his lieutenant colonel put a stop to this alcohol-fueled insurrection, Clifford called him "a whore's melt" and "a whore's pimp."[43]

Mary Ann Bauman, washerwoman for Company F, 54th New York, made complaint against James Bagley. "He came into my tent and took his pants off and wanted to give me $50 to treat me in some bad way. I called the corporal to take him away. Bagley's pants were off and he was showing everything." Bagley defended himself, saying she was a whore, who ". . . is in the habit of having sexual connection with the men in the company." Major Edward H. Bergmann, 1st New Mexico Cavalry, was accused of keeping "a whore," the wife of a soldier, in his quarters at Fort Bascom, just north of Tucumcari. An officer was sent to interview Prudentia Erwin. She stated that she had lived with Bergmann for eight months as his woman, and that he was a "bueno muchacho"[a good boy]. In 1865, Bergmann was brevetted lieutenant colonel for his mounted service.[44]

Captain George Avent, 3rd New York, got drunk at Albany, New York and approached a lieutenant's wife with a rather gauche conversational opener: "There are no whores in this town. I can't get it anywhere else, so I'll get it here." Captain Edward Henshaw, of Henshaw's Battery (Illinois), was a whirlwind of alcohol, accusations, drinking with enlisted men, political vengeance, and fascination with whores. At Loudon, Tennessee, he was happy to tell anyone who would listen: "When Lieutenant [Azro] Putnam and the doctor first came here, they went to a nigger house and caught the clap. Mrs. Putnam cured him."[45]

Poetry and Metaphor

The Library of Congress has an extensive bibliography of Civil War era songs and poetry. The small number presented here are the results of random serendipity and are mostly associated with malfeasance and the carnal life. Sergeant Francis Hause, Company K, 67th Pennsylvania, kept an extensive war diary. On April 5, 1865, he made an extended entry—"The Clipper Ship Louise—Larry's journey."

> Just listen dear messmates to one of my yarns
> Tis of big-bellied Larry who went on the Barney
> He had such an adventure as one seldom sees
> With a little Dutch gal by the name of Louise
>
> It happened one day as he lay in the ship
> He hoisted her canvas to take a short trip
> His flying jib-boom was stiff as you please
> Which brought up in the stern of the clipper Louise
>
> But how that he managed, I'm sure I can't say
> For I think his big belly would be in the way

> But no doubt it grew small when in a tight squeeze
> Like when pressed on the deck of the clipper Louise
>
> He lays my fine Lassie, I'm sure you must know
> That such a large cargo you seldom have—Oh
> The deck load is heavy but still more with ease
> You might stow in the hold of the clipper Louise.

This extended bit of doggerel goes on for eight more stanzas, and certainly seemed worthwhile to Sergeant Hause.[46]

Lee Hendrix, a soldier in Company B, 1st North Carolina Sharpshooter Battalion, and a native of Forsyth County, wrote eight letters that have been preserved. On February 17, 1863, he discussed death on the home front and the bacon ration at Port Royal, and closed with a little poem. His spelling was confusingly idiosyncratic. Converted to standard English, it tells this story:

> We are the boys that fear no noise
> Although we are far from home
> Although I had rather be a finger ring
> And on your girl's hand
> And every time she wiped her ass
> I would view the promised land.[47]

A poem, said to be written on the back of an envelope by "a lady," reads:

> Men do not kiss among themselves
> And it is well that they refrain
> The bitter dose would [kill?] them
> And they would never kiss again.
> As sometimes on poor women's lips
> Applied this nauseous lotion
> We have to kiss among ourselves
> To counter act the poison.

Like most poetry, it invokes images and suggests connotations, rather than stating clearly defined facts. One possible interpretation is the disgust of the poet with the products of fellatio.[48]

A broadside is piece of paper, usually large, printed only on one side, with a single proclamation or message. A poem entitled "The Fair Maid's Song When All Alone," to be sung to the tune of "The White Cockade," was published in 1820 as a broadside. Its message of longing is presented in occupational metaphors.

> One evening as I walked alone,
> I heard a fair maid make her moan:
> And thus she did begin her tone,
> *I can no longer lay alone!*
> I wonder what the cause can be
> The young men do not fancy me?
> I have a thing belongs to me,
> Would please a young man handsomely;
> If he be a miller that is kind,
> All in my mill I'll let him grind:
> And if his stones are even hung,
> His mill forever shall go strong:
> I'll open wide the postern gate
> And patiently for toll will wait;
> And let him come by night or day
> I'll have all things out of his way.
> If he be a sawyer by his trade,
> I have a saw-pit ready made;
> Whilst he above and I below,
> Will toss the whip-saw to and fro:
> Imagine not I'm such a fool
> That I can't understand your rule;
> Give the dimentions [sic] of your square
> And I'll set a compass to a hair.

The anonymous poet goes on for twice this length, using the trades of teamster, shoemaker, and tailor to extend the theme. In this era of mass production, television laugh tracks, and store-bought plastic merchandise, many of the allusions will lost on the contemporary reader, but it is easy to imagine the farm boys in blue and gray sitting around a campfire, amused by such humor.[49]

A hand-written Civil War era poem entitled "Fair Jenny" brings us the plaint of a new bride, disappointed by her husband's amorous accoutrements. The concluding lines tell the story of her annoyance.

> To honor you have no regard,
> You base, you perjured man!
> You swore that something was a yard
> Whereas, 'tis but a span [9 inches].[50]

The Vicksburg *Daily Times* was published briefly in 1866 during the Union occupation. The following undated clipping is preserved in a scrapbook at the Old Courthouse Museum, an historic edifice with a cannonball still imbedded in one wall. It was unusual for something so risqué to be openly published. This bit of doggerel is entitled "Volunteer Drilling."

> Sweet Amy said, with pleading eyes,
> "Dear Charley, tell me (will you?)
> The words I've heard your captain say:
> "I should so like to drill you."
>
> "What, Amy pet, *you* take command!
> Well Amy, I'm quite willing:
> In such a company as yours,
> I can't have too much drilling."
>
> "Stand over there, and sing out clear
> Like this: Squad stand at ease."
> "O Charles, you'll wake papa upstairs;
> Don't shout like that, dear, please."
>
> "I stand at ease like this, you see,
> And then I scarce need mention:
> The next command you'll have to give
> Is, "Now then Squad! Attention."
>
> "Now, Amy, smartly after me—
> You're sure, dear, it don't bore you?
> 'Forward'—'Quick March'—'Halt'
> 'Front' 'Right Dress'—
> There now, I'm close before you."
>
> "Present arms—well, it *does* look odd,
> (You don't believe I'd trifle—)
> We hold our arms straight out like this
> In drill without the rifle.
>
> "Now say, 'Salute your officer.'"
> "O Charles, for shame, how can you?
> I thought that you were at some trick,
> You horrid, cheating man, you."
>
> Charles "ordered arms" without command.
> She smoothed her rumpled hair.
> Pouted and frowned and blushed and then
> Said softly, "As you were."

If puns can be a form of poetry, this little story might qualify. After the battle at Sharpsburg, Confederate troops were marching through Shepherdstown. A large puddle occupied the middle of the street. Most men marched through it, but one soldier deviated around it. A hanky-waving Southern girl called to him, "Ain't you ashamed. Close up [ranks]." He replied, "I'd like to see you in this water with your close [clothes] up."[51]

John Pugh of the 3rd Pennsylvania Heavy Artillery observed a Confederate ram coming down the James River to attack the Union fleet. Noting that a ram was also a male sheep, Pugh wrote, "Sam, I want to tell you that the rebel ram came down the James River the other day. I guess his object was to fuck our ewe, but I guess he had to go back with a hard cock and the load in his belly yet, for the ewe was not in the right humor for fucking. I guess she was [k]nocked up already by the way she acted, for she did make one hell of a noise and it scared the old ram, so that he started back as fast as he could."[52]

Miscellany

Cursing was hardly confined to the lower ranks. John H. W. Stuckenberg, chaplain of the 145th Pennsylvania, wrote in November 1862, "Brigadier General [Winfield Scott] Hancock, now commanding our division, however brave and courageous he may be, is addicted to one very unmanly, unsoldierly vice—profanity. Day before yesterday he swore most vilely in presence of our regiment." The chaplain wrote Hancock a letter, describing his cursing as "low, unmanly and wicked" but never sent it. Hancock, both during the Civil War, and among his advocates today, was known as "Hancock the Superb" and "The Handsomest Man in America." The preceding pages suggest the wide choice of words he might have commanded as he upset the delicate ears of the Reverend Stuckenberg.[53]

Charles Rodgers (Rogers), Company I, 82nd Pennsylvania, made free use of the language in a letter to "Friend Arthur," sent from near Petersburg in January 1865. After discussing his plans to desert and go west for a high-paying job, he turned to carnal thoughts. "Oh, say, how's your machine and do you ever get it greased? My pushing pole is all hunky. Boy, I had the best fuck while in Troy that I ever had in my life. I guess you will get your gudgeon greased pretty often. Did you say those folks are on it? I would give much more to go up Susie's flue this morning than I would for a ton of coal. Oh, you dirty devil [illegible] made you do so well that you would beat your meat for 35 cents—ah, no. Ha ha ha. I would like to go up somebody's flue this morning as I have a stiff limb." He ended the letter with a somewhat pointless tale of a boy having intercourse with "an old sow."[54]

American writers and speakers of the Victorian age produced millions of noble words and high-minded sentiments. What has been less documented is the informal speech cited above—coarse, rough, and deeply scatological. The near impossibility of incorporating such talk into cinematic versions of the Civil War does not mean that it did not occur. It simply indicates a collective need to view our ancestors in a better light.

Chapter 25

A VAST MISCELLANY

In addition to the voluminous records of prostitution, rape, and venereal disease, a decade of research has turned up a wide variety of findings whose common thread is that of reproduction and/or sexual tension. These miscellaneous Civil War subjects include abortion, contraception, cross-dressing, exhibitionism, castration, tattooing, and pornography.

Abortion might seem to be a modern object of attention. History tells us otherwise. In 421 B.C., Aristophanes' play *Peace* mentions the plant pennyroyal as an abortifacient. Galen, around 150 AD, described many remedies for producing abortion.[1]

In *Every Man his Own Doctor*, printed 270 years ago, the anonymous author tells us of "a common complaint among unmarried women, namely the suppression of the courses [i.e., missing a menstrual period]" and recommended pennyroyal and Highland Flagg, to which is added a diet with mustard, horseradish, and beer. In the early 1800s, American newspapers carried advertisements for abortion clinics and medication to produce abortion, and by the time of the Civil War, twenty percent of all American pregnancies ended in intentional abortion, almost exactly the same percent as today.[2]

The key to understanding the published material on abortion in the 1860s is that the word "abortion" is never used. Instead, "obstructed menses," "suppression," "blocked menses," and "irregularities," are used as euphemisms, conveying the notion that a missed period is caused by an undefined "obstruction" rather than by early pregnancy. This terminology can be seen in many newspaper advertisements.

Dr. Powers, of 61 Franklin St. in New York City, sold drops that "are the very best thing for the purpose and will bring on the monthly sickness in case of obstruction from any cause." Radway's Regulating Pills, manufactured at 23 John St, New York City, worked fast. "Six pills suffice in the worst cases and they operate in three to six hours."[3]

The Louisville *Daily Journal* of September 10, 1861 provides several examples of advertisements promoting abortion. "Dr. Hall's American Periodical Pills," available at the Louisville Medical Infirmary, ". . . can be relied upon in all cases of Menstrual Obstructions, Irregularities, etc." Dr. Dewees' Female Monthly Regulator, available from the Galen's Head Dispensary at 314 Fifth Street, between Market and Jefferson Street, was also sold to cure "Obstructions." Madame Cafrada's [sp?] Female Monthly Pills, available from the Private Medical Dispensary at Third and Market Streets, were, once again, for "Obstructions." For those with money for a steamboat ticket, Madame Lozier's Female Monthly Pills were available from the Cincinnati Venereal Hospital.

Joshua Bridge, M.D., offered to send a booklet on treatment of "irregularities" to any woman who sent a postage stamp to No. 2 Bond St, New York City. Sir James Clark's Celebrated Female Pills claimed to "remove all obstructions." In a stroke of brilliantly hypocritical advice, the potential user was advised: "These pills should not be taken by females during the FIRST THREE MONTHS [sic] of pregnancy, as they may bring on a miscarriage." On May 16, 1864, the Richmond *Sentinel* reprinted some news from the North. A female Treasury clerk had died of an abortion, and several "high male officials have fled for parts unknown."

The trial of Private Henry Andrus, 124th Ohio, shed unexpected light on the patent medicine business. In August 1863, he was tried for disloyalty, desertion and correspondence with the enemy. The desertion was not unusual—he just left. The disloyalty charge stemmed from having raised $40,000 for the Confederacy. His correspondence was with his mail order patients in the South, people he began treating when he had offices in New Orleans and called himself Doctor Andrus. The court-martial record contains his brochure, describing "Doctor Andrus' Medicines," good for "irregularities" and "suppression," as well as nervous diseases, spinal diseases, scrofula, female weakness, fistula, piles, asthma, dyspepsia, and several other diseases. Eight letters were seized when Andrus was arrested. One was addressed to Mr. Hogan Wadsworth, Harpersville, Alabama, and promised, "You will gain so fast you will be surprised," and offered a larger supply of medicine for five dollars. Another letter is addressed to a patient in Uvalde, Texas. Andrus was sentenced to be shot. In January 1864, Lincoln commuted this to "hard labor during the war."[5]

Authentic vintage bottles of abortifacients are very rare. This modern conception conveys the hypocritical warnings given to pregnant women. (Copyright 1999 Jim M'Guinness. Originally published in *The Pharos* of Alpha Omega Alpha Honor Medical Society, Spring 1999, page 20.)

Contraception, like abortion, has an ancient history. The desire to separate the pleasure of intercourse from the responsibilities of parenthood can be traced back at least 3500 years. Plato, Socrates, and Aristotle had much to say on the subject, and the ancient Egyptian Ebers papyrus, 1000 years earlier, gave formulae for the prevention of pregnancy. The wish for birth control was no different during the Civil War than it had been in 2000 B.C.[6]

A decade before the Civil War, a printed circular told of Dr. William Young's "French Safe or Cover." Young, who had offices at 416 Spruce Street in Philadelphia, offered his condoms in India Rubber, gutta percha, and gold beater's skin. He was also the only agent in the United States for the Louis Napoleon Safe ". . . at $2.00 each, one of which will last with CARE, a lifetime." (It is hard to imagine a condom lasting forty years.)[7]

An 1863 catalog of the G. S. Haskins Company offered French ticklers, plain condoms, and condoms concealed in candy confections. Also in 1863, an enterprising Mr. DeYoung of Philadelphia sent brochures to the postmasters of hundreds of small towns, offering them franchises to sell DeYoung's condoms and ticklers. He wholesaled them at $1.50 a dozen, to be marked up to $3.00 a dozen, a clear profit to the postmaster. The same mailing contained a sample "skin," with a cuff at the open end and a pink ribbon, to facilitate its employment. A similar condom, sold to prevent unwanted children, that might become "subjects for alms houses and poor houses," was donated to the National Museum of Civil War Medicine, Frederick, Maryland, in 2002. Another brochure, whose address heading has been removed, offered "French patent safes, French ticklers, and French caps," all varieties of condoms.[8]

The early condoms were supplied in paper envelopes. The "little tin boxes," so familiar to the nervous adolescent of the 1950s, did not appear on the market until 1920. Since then, hundreds of brands of condoms have appeared in the United States alone, indeed enough to fill an entire book or two.[9]

Intra-vaginal sponges, withdrawn after coitus by means of a ribbon, were widely used in the 1860s. Such devices were still sold in the 20th century, under such brand names as Sanitary Health Sponge and the Hygienic Sponge. Indeed, contraceptive sponges have been reintroduced as of 2005, reflecting concern over long-term uses of contraceptive medications.

Non-mechanical contraceptives were widely known. Under the headline, "Glorious News for the Ladies—A Preventive to Have Children," a botanic physician, Dr. Rafael, of 59 E. 5th St, Cincinnati, told the story of a woman whose life was threatened by dangerous childbirth, a woman saved by Rafael's Botanic. Doctors Pancoast and Meiggs, at the same address, offered similar services, with this seemingly apologetic note: "To the pure, all things are pure"[10]

Venereal disease was a major problem during the Civil War. A general discussion appears in the author's *The Story the Soldiers Wouldn't Tell*. Among Union white troops there were 73,382 *reported* cases of syphilis and 109,397 *reported* cases of gonorrhea. The true numbers are higher. Reports of specialized venereal disease hospitals will appear in future publications, as well as reports of venereal disease playing a role in military justice. This book will confine itself to three images representative of the problem.

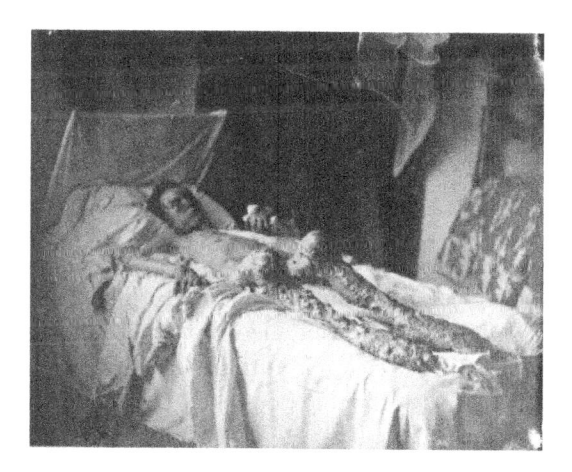

This Union soldier is dying of syphilis. His legs have become a mass of rotting sores. Syphilis before penicillin was no laughing matter. (Otis Historical Archives, National Museum of Health and Medicine.)

The Union Army medical service purchased over 100,000 penis syringes. These were used to forcefully irrigate urethras infected with gonorrhea. Lead chloride was commonly used. Most syringes were either glass or, like the one shown here, pewter. (Author's collection).

Gonorrhea infected men, north and south. Here we see John C. Calhoun, grandson and namesake of the famous senator, and captain in the 10th Battalion of South Carolina Cavalry. He was hospitalized for gonorrhea in August 1864 and seven months later was still too sick to return to service. The photo is by Quinby & Co. of Charleston, and is inscribed to Miss Sally Hampton. Students of fashion will note that he "dresses" to the left, rather prominently. (Author's collection).

Pornography

A vast pornography industry, centered in New York City, flourished during the Civil War, sending out hundreds of thousands of catalogs to the boys in blue. But long before secession, there was pornography in the army, as shown in this 1833 trial at West Point. Private Enoch Townsend, US Military Academy Detachment, stole ". . . a small volume lettered Night Thoughts, having on the title page Memoirs of a Woman of Pleasure." Townsend was put in solitary confinement for two weeks and then drummed out.[11]

The vastly expanded army thirty years later increased the pool of potential customers. A colonel of the 39th Illinois discovered a "dealer peddling obscene material to the troops aboard trains on the Pacific Railroad between St. Louis and Sedalia." Dr. William Young's *Marriage Guide—A Great Physiological Work or Everyone His Own Doctor*, was promoted as a scientific resource, but the newspaper ad also noted that, "It is a book that must be locked up and not lie around the house."[12]

Some of the naughty images purveyed to soldiers were soft porn, as seen in this carte de visite. The mother sees only the daughter's hoop skirt. On the far side we see the girl's happy beau lurking beneath the whalebone frame. (Author's collection).

Philo's Army Purchasing Agency of Brooklyn, New York, was not the first firm to imply a phony government affiliation. In spite of the title of the "army agency," its offerings tell us of unusual military goods, such as "Amours of a Quaker," "The Veil Uplifted," and "Secret Habits of the Female Sex." Altogether, twenty-seven similar titles were offered at an average purchase price of fifty cents. On September 26, 1865, New York detectives seized 5000 copies of "an obscene publication called the 'Sporting Times,' which were discovered in five packages at Harnden's and Kinsley's express offices, consigned to various parts of the city."[13]

Erotic Folk Art

The sailors on years-long whaling voyages produced erotic scrimshaw and the soldiers in World War I created "trench art," which included erotic motifs. In the long months between campaigns, Civil War soldiers seemed to feel the same artistic urges. A few examples have survived. The following suggest the range of soldiers' imaginations.

This Minié ball, dug near Fredericksburg, Virginia, was probably carved into its phallic shape by a bored Union soldier during the winter of 1862-1863. (Author's collection.)

This crude lead casting, of a coitally-engaged couple, was dug by Samuel Whitt near Bailey's Crossroads in northern Virginia. It was most likely made by melting several lead bullets. (Whitt collection).

The 1858 "Flying Eagle" penny was widely used during the Civil War. A good condition penny is shown at the right. During the 1970s, the excavation for the Washington, DC subway system unearthed a hoard of coins, including this 1858 penny, on which the eagle has turned phallic. (Whitt collection).

Another coin modification is seen on the reverse of this 1848 Coronet Head penny, on which the designation "cent" has been changed to a less tasteful word. (Anonymous collector).

Another bit of Civil War folk art (not shown) is from the collection of James C. Frasca. The unknown artist used an 1865 dime as his canvas. The obverse is worn but undisturbed. The reverse has been shaved smooth and on it is engraved a most remarkable scene. A tall wooden fence bisects the image. On the right, a soldier in uniform has unbuttoned his trousers and is urinating through a small hole in the fence. On the left, a young woman in a hoop skirt gives the event her full attention.

Some folk art imitated existing forms of uniform accoutrements. This brass shoulder belt plate, dug by Gary Cole at a Confederate camp in northwest Georgia shows a soldier, complete with kepi, about to penetrate his female partner. (Dent "Wildman" Myers collection).

An example of equestrian folk art is this two-inch-high horse brass, with a coital couple, framed by a horseshoe. (Author's collection).

The imaginings of Eros have their manifestation in the genitals, and those organs, in turn, appear in some surprising guises in the Civil War record. Richard Young, 6th US Colored Troops, a twenty-five-year-old-substitute, was noted, on his mustering-in examination, to have "two heads on penis." He was also court-martialed three times for desertion.[14] One mode of recruiting black troops was to buy them from owners willing to sell them. Levi Todd entered the 67th US Colored Troops at Saline County, Missouri, accompanied by a sworn certificate stating, in part, "I, David Todd, of Boone County, Missouri . . . for the consideration of $750 . . . sell and deliver . . . a Negro man Levi . . . aged 21 . . . who is deficient in his left hand, by the loss of three fingers, and has undergone the punishment of castration." The examining surgeon noted these defects but declared him "able-bodied and sufficiently courageous." Navy recruiters noted that thirty-two-year-old William B. Lindsey, a plasterer, had a scar on his scrotum, and that shoemaker Richard Cook, a twenty-seven-year-old man, born in Ireland, had only one testicle.[15]

Brigadier General Charles Tripler, McClellan's chief surgeon, had attended a series of lectures in the 1820s, while Tripler was a student. The speaker was Dr. Valentine Mott, the most eminent physician in the country at that time. Tripler's notes tell of a man with domestic troubles, whose penis was nearly cut off by his wife. Dr. Mott stitched it back on, "preserving it and its function."[16]

On February 7, 1862, the St. Louis *Liberty Weekly Tribune*, reported that "an officer of the 26th regiment, now quartered in this city," had gone out to arrest a number of men who had departed AWOL to attend a dance. When the officer arrived at the dance, one of the malfeasants offered him a cigar. As he lit it, the men hid under the hoop skirts of several girls."

Life was not easy for many sergeants. At the Presidio of San Francisco the drunken Patrick Sheridan, 9th US Infantry, kicked his sergeants "privates." At Fredericksburg, Virginia, William Reynolds, 1st New York Light Artillery, seized his sergeant by the neck and by the genitals. That sergeant evened the score by beating Reynolds' head with a piece of firewood.[17]

At St. Joseph, Missouri, recruit James Gardner, 51st Missouri, was tried for assault with intent to kill, in that he "willfully and maliciously made an assault upon one James, a colored child, by seizing . . . its private parts . . . mutilating the said James in a terrible manner." Post surgeon James Bruner made an examination and found the child "suffering great pain," and "the penis denuded of the scarf skin from the true skin for, I suppose, nearly 2 inches." Mrs. Elizabeth Horn said that Gardner had only grabbed the child by "the britches." Gardner got two months in jail.[18]

A. Fritz, Company F, 14th US Infantry, received a bayonet wound of the penis at Fredericksburg on February 11, 1864. Major General E. R. S. Canby was aboard the gunboat *Cricket* on November 8, 1864, when a Confederate guerrilla shot him, the ball passing through the scrotum and tearing his penis. His convalescence was marked by severe pain, fever, and purulent discharge.[19]

Cross-Dressing

Men dressed as women and women dressed as men are surprisingly frequent in the records. One of the more dramatic examples was Confederate guerrilla Jerome Clark, who dressed as a woman and was best known as Sue Munday. Sue and her comrades killed several Union soldiers. She/he was hanged in Louisville March 15, 1865. The numerous books describing these partisans include the classic photograph of her with her partner in crime, One Armed Berry.

H. C. Steel, 3rd Illinois Cavalry, had a woman dressed as a man in his tent overnight, and rode with her through Memphis. She rode "in the manner and fashion of a man." At his trial, Steel pleaded guilty and "wished to say nothing." The charges filed against Steel reflected the horror felt by Victorians at women who did not ride sidesaddle. Captain Jerome Taft, 59th New York, recruited Charles Johnson, and kept him always close at hand. Johnson was, in fact, Harriet Merrill, Taft's mistress. There was a real Charles Johnson in the 59th New York, which confuses the record. At Washington, DC, Ernest Faust, 12th Illinois Cavalry, had put on women's clothes to avoid the provost guard, however "I was detected by my pants reaching below my dress."[20]

One could receive a bounty by bringing in a recruit. Elizabeth Burley, "colored citizen," put a dress on William Vaughn, a deserter from the 37th US Colored Troops, and took him to Baltimore, to enlist him there and receive credit.

Both were caught. Lieutenant Jacob Keiser, 1st Arkansas Cavalry, tried to rob a Fayetteville store on Christmas Eve, 1863, in disguise. He blacked his face with soot and grease and wore one of his wife's dresses. He was caught, tried, convicted, and dishonorably dismissed. A kindly stranger met in a saloon should not be trusted. George W. Stevens, 93rd Indiana, was in a Memphis drinking establishment, thinking of a way to leave town without being caught. A stranger said, "I have some women's clothes. Change clothes in the saloon. I'll meet you just past the picket line and I'll return your uniform." Stevens changed clothes and went up the road in his newly acquired dress and—no stranger. He was ashamed to return to the regiment in a hoop skirt, so he stayed away three weeks. By that time his beard had grown out enough to attract the attention of even the dullest member of the provost guard. Andrew Sharp, 6th Ohio Cavalry, deserted and was gone two months. He was found dressed in women's clothing. He was branded with a red-hot iron, with the letter "D" and was sent to Dry Tortugas. His appeal to Lincoln did him no good.[21]

At Wheeling, West Virginia, Col. Joseph Darr reported the receipt of a female who was wearing male apparel. She gave the name Harry Fitzallen and told two stories: that she was a Confederate spy; and that she was a soldier in the Union 23rd Kentucky. Soon, she admitted to being Marian McKenzie. Patrick Delaney, 3rd New York Light Artillery, and a friend dressed as a woman, were "ugly drunk" one moonlit night at New Bern, North Carolina. They attempted to rob a lieutenant, who knocked them both down. Delaney got a year in prison. In a confession extracted at Prince Street Prison in Alexandria from Richard Walten, 1st New York Cavalry, we learn that he was sent to Riker's Island, New York, where he collected his $300 enlistment bounty. After two weeks, he put on a woman's dress and deserted.[22]

Mrs. Francis Louisa Clayton, a Minnesota native, told reporters that she and her husband had enlisted in a Minnesota regiment and served together until he was killed at Stones River. "She is a very tall, masculine-looking woman, bronzed by exposure to the weather, and attracted universal attention by her masculine stride in walking, her erect and soldierly carriage and generally outré appearance." Later she claimed that the two of them had served in the 13th Missouri Cavalry. A Sam Clayton served in the Minnesota infantry. I could find no Clayton in the 13th Missouri Cavalry.[23]

Provost court records for New Orleans contain the following: "#219—James F. Proctor, Co. A, 1st LA Nat. GDS,—charge—out at night dressed in woman's clothes. Reprimanded and discharged." A search of the records of this African American regiment revealed no Proctor. Most likely he had given a false name.[24]

Captain William H. Boyd, 1st New York Cavalry, faced several charges, including horse theft and selling government horses. More relevant to the present theme, it was charged that he "habitually in an open and scandalous manner cohabited with a certain female of disreputable character . . . and frequently and notoriously introduced said female dressed in masculine garb, into his tent." He also kept her/him in his berth aboard a transport vessel between Alexandria and Ship River, Virginia. The lengthy testimony centered around the gender of his companion, who Boyd usually introduced as his servant, George Weldon. The surgeon of Boyd's Regiment, Frederick Elliott, said that Weldon refused to be examined. To his eye, Weldon appeared to be "about seventeen years of age." The court asked, "Has she any masculine habits?" "She associated with the men and indulged in all their common habits." Sergeant Major Jesse Wykoff had passed by her tent. One of the sideboards was broken. "She was stooping down with her pants open, in the act of making water, of course giving me a full view of the part of her person whereby I judged her sex." Captain Boyd cross-examined the witness. "May she not have been a hermaphrodite?" Wykoff replied, "I am positive of her sex . . . I never saw a hermaphrodite." The court, in a complex and closely reasoned decision, found Boyd not guilty, but "censurable."[25]

The Richmond *Sentinel* had two cross-dressing stories in 1862. July 28: Maria Underwood had tried to enlist in the [South Carolina] Palmetto Sharpshooters in disguise. She was sent to Castle Godwin prison. Anne Williams, alias Charles Waters, made it on to the front page on September 12; a long article reprinted from the Augusta (Georgia) *Constitutionalist* told of Waters' lifelong obsession with women's clothes. "He resembles a woman in appearance very much; is about the ordinary height of a woman, has long hair, a smooth face, and a soft voice, and is almost thirty years of age." He was willing to serve the Confederacy in anyway except "soldiering," and volunteered his services as a nurse.

When the author worked at San Quentin Prison, he had a therapy group of men with multiple arrests for exhibiting their private parts to unwilling spectators, usually in a pitiful attempt to assert the exhibitor's masculinity and puissance. The most commonly used alibi was, "I needed to urinate." These men were known colloquially on the Big Yard as "flag wavers" or "weenie wavers."

In Victorian times, the word "person" was used to indicate genitals. There are many Civil War cases of men "exhibiting their persons," most usually in a state of drunken, insolent carelessness rather than as a conscious effort for status. In 1865, war veteran and West Point cadet James Batchelder was drunk on the Fourth of July and "exposed himself." He was dismissed from West Point.[26]

Robert Davis, 3rd California, offended many Latter Day Saints, by appearing drunk on the streets of Salt Lake City, exposing his "person" to both men and women, and calling out to women, "How would you like to take that?" His excuse when sober: "I was making water." At the Piedmont House, Culpeper, Virginia, Captain R. E. Clary, 2nd US Cavalry, attended a soldier's funeral while drunk and, as the deceased was laid out, "exposed himself," no doubt detracting from the solemnity of the occasion. At Jackson, Mississippi, Lieutenant J. W. Taylor, 53rd US Colored Troops was drunk and "exhibited himself." Taylor was cashiered.[27]

Alfred Benoit, 9th Veteran Volunteers, was drunk and disorderly on the streets of Washington, DC, where he assaulted his corporal, cursed his captain, and spoke disrespectfully of Abraham Lincoln. He also on "exposed his person in public." At Drum Barracks, California, Lieutenant Tebina Streeter, 1st Native California Cavalry, was drunk and "exposed himself" at the depot. He did the same again at Wilmington and was dismissed. Lieutenant James Elmsley, 35th US Colored Troops, was another man who exposed himself while drunk; this offense was at Somerville, South Carolina. At Monrovia, Virginia, Lieutenant Robert Lennox, 2nd US Cavalry, was drunk and fell out of his tent, nude. "His testicles hung out on the chair . . . he was unable to walk alone."[28]

Lieutenant Effingham Hyatt, 35th Missouri, seemed inspired by life on the river. Onboard the steamer *John Bell*, as it wound its way along the Yazoo and Tallahatchie Rivers, Hyatt not only cursed Lincoln as a "damned abolitionist," prepared inaccurate reports while drunk (and sent them by a drunk orderly) but also stripped naked in front of his enlisted men and danced nude while singing bawdy songs.[29]

Naked dancing on shipboard is seen again in the case of Major Henry Metcalf, 58th Pennsylvania, who danced in "an indecent manner" on the deck of the *Escort*, wearing only his shirt, in the presence of officers and men and one private's wife. He sealed his military fate by refusing to drink a toast to his late colonel during a testimonial dinner; instead, he blurted out, "I'm glad the old son of a bitch is dead!" On the steamer *Forest City*, Lieutenant James Doyle, 37th New York, got drunk, took off his pants and "paraded around."

Exposure by proxy might describe the drunken escapade of Captain Moses Bradly, 60th US Colored Troops, at Helena, Arkansas. He called to his tent Private Moses Woodson and, at pistol point, made Moses lie down on the captain's bed and then ordered the young man to "pull out his pecker." Woodson refused, saying that such would make him feel ashamed.[31]

The Desmarres Eye and Ear Hospital, in Chicago, was the scene of Daniel McGee's transgression. There, in a fit of disorderly drunkenness, he "indecently exposed his person before ladies." His excuse was that after he had finished waiting on the tables for Thanksgiving dinner he had drunk "some Porter." This member of the 12th Michigan was fined six months pay. On a Sabbath Day in 1864, members of the Little Rock Missionary Baptist church had gathered by the river for a baptism by total immersion. The congregation became agitated when the totally nude John Cassle, 5th Ohio Battery, swam up to the proceedings.[32]

At Tuskegee, Alabama, Woodford Miles, 8th Iowa Veteran Volunteers, "unlawfully, wickedly, and scandalously did expose to the view of said persons the body and person of him the said Woodford Miles, naked and uncovered and did otherwise act in a lewd and obscene matter." Lieutenant Cyrus Lemon, 14th Missouri, (Birge's Western Sharpshooters), was drunk himself, provided whiskey to his men who also got drunk, and showed his penis on parade. Colonel James Kerrigan, 25th New York, was dismissed for poor leadership. Not only was he frequently drunk himself, and very tolerant of brawling among his troops, he allowed his men to "parade in disarray and filth, with pants unbuttoned and persons exposed." The lobby of Vicksburg's Washington Hotel was no place for "obscene and disgusting language," much less "an indecent and shameful exposure of his person by permitting his pants to be open in the front." Yet that was exactly what Lieutenant Byron Ferris did. He quickly ceased to be an officer in the 50th US Colored Troops.[33]

Many Civil War stories do not fit neatly into a single category. James Ryan, 2nd Massachusetts Artillery, cut another private's throat with a razor. Ryan wanted his victim to let him kiss him. Clearly there was no agreement on this issue. Corporal Julius Chaillou of the Baltimore Light Infantry refused a medical examination. He did not wish to strip naked in front of the examining officers. Just before the war, I. M. Evans, then in a small Ohio town, wrote a chatty letter to a friend, in which he praised women with large breasts, and added that "Martha" had to use rags or cotton to enhance her bosom, and added "You don't like artificial titties any better than I do."[34]

The "Stanhope" is a device now out of fashion. It can be any sort of small object, such as a pen or a stickpin, which contains a tiny magnifying glass and a microscopic picture. One holds the Stanhope close to one's eye and the picture becomes visible. The 1863 pornography catalog of the G. S. Haskins Company offered "Microscopic Fancy Pictures, set in watch charms, keys, finger rings, scarf pins and pocket knives." Another catalog told of "Microscopic Photographs—Each picture is about the size of a grain of sand and is mounted on a microscopic lens magnifying five hundred times." The subjects included The Lord's Prayer, Union and Confederate generals, and "French Dancing Girls." In July 1863, Patrick Caulfield was driving a wagon to Springfield, Missouri when he was robbed at gunpoint. The stolen merchandise included three boxes of pocket knifes of ". . . a peculiar kind having three blades and in the end of the handle was a transparent picture of a female in a state of nudity."

In 1850, a Paris, Tennessee man sued his wife Virginia for divorce, claiming that she was delivered of a "child of color," and added that since he learned of her adultery that he had not had sexual intercourse with her. David Evans, 93rd Pennsylvania, was gone three months from his regiment. He said that it was not his fault; he had been in jail in Marietta, Pennsylvania, on charges of "fornication and bastardy." Lieutenant Colonel Arthur Reed, 40th US Colored Troops, had crude ideas on how to meet women. On the train to Nashville, he showed an "obscene photograph" to a lady passenger. For this, for "utter incompetence," and for seven other offences, he was cashiered. Future Union general George

W. Morgan was the attorney for the defendant in an 1852 Columbus, Ohio defamation of character case. At issue was an occasion of intercourse. ". . . the defendant then said that this man told him that he Screwed her twelve times in one night; defendant then further said I have reason to disbelieve it"[36]

At the time of the Civil War, Nantucket was still the center of American whaling. The whalers were away for years and home for a few months. A recently discovered dildo, hidden in a Nantucket wall, sheds some light on how wives tolerated the prolonged absence of their husbands in the 19th century.[37]

Twenty-year-old William Armstrong, a Kentucky-born wagoner with the 2nd California Cavalry, was stationed at Camp Conness, in a verdant valley, fifty miles southwest of Salt Lake City. There, William was charged with incest with his daughter. The case was referred to acting assistant surgeon J. V. Landerdale. "You are well aware that all the light which science can throw upon such a case as this is very feeble and by no means conclusive. Still, from my observation of the case, I am led to believe that the child has not been the victim of the father's lust and the story now in circulation, which has led to his arrest, is without foundation."[38]

The diary of Captain Charles F. Hinrichs, 10th Missouri Cavalry (Union) contains a relevant story. In Georgia, a young African American boy along the road was looking for a job as a servant to a Union officer. Hinrichs took him on. The boy was Julius Moses. The next day he looked at the boy anew and felt her chest. "There were the tittys." She was renamed Julie, and told Hinrichs that the soldiers had persuaded her to dress as a boy, as a prank.[39]

A sex witch in Washington, DC? In 1835, a Miss Penn appeared before a grand jury twice. In the first case she was charged with "maliciously intending to inflame and excite the venereal passions of a certain Henry B. Richards, Thomas I. Earhart, John [illegible] and Edward Kincaid." She fed them tea made with two ounces of cantharides (Spanish Fly). All four men were made quite sick from this concoction. Earhart was the recipient of a second attempt at erotic bewitchment. Miss Penn put "cow itch" in his bed. This irritant, derived from the pods of *Dolichos pruriens*, inflamed his skin, but not his passion.[40]

Sometimes a novel expression turns up in the records. Jerome B. Baldwin, Company D, 21st Connecticut, wrote to his friend Ellery in November 1864, about the lack of sexual opportunities in his part of Virginia. "I have not got the mitten for over two years. What do you think of that?"[41]

On March 15, 1865, the Richmond *Daily Examiner* ran this brief article: "Hustings Court of Magistrates—Richard, a slave, for associating and cohabiting with Delia Mack, a white women as his mistress and trespassing on the premises of Caroline, a sister of Delia, was ordered 39 lashes today, 39 lashes on Saturday, and 39 lashes on Wednesday next, making an aggregate of 117 lashes to be well laid on at the whipping post." It is worth noting the date of this often-fatal punishment.

Tattoos most frequently appear in the Civil War records as part of a punishment. A man might be tattooed with a "D" for desertion, or an "M" for mutiny. A few recreational tattoos have emerged from the records. Twenty-one-year-old musician John Cunningham, 15[th]US Infantry, had deserted. Records show that he had a tattoo of two females on his right forearm and the colors of the 108th New York on his left forearm. In 1871, at Fort Ontario, New York, Surgeon H. E. Brown examined an unnamed recruit, a former sailor, and reported these tattoos: on his right arm, a full length figure of Britannia with trident, a coconut tree, a dancing girl, a mermaid, a devil with horns and tail. On his left arm, an epaulet, a Goddess of Liberty, a ship, a British flag and a woman. On his thighs, a couple copulating, a dancing girl, and another Goddess of Liberty, this one astride an eagle. On his legs and feet, a total of six dancing girls, a whale, and Amphitrite in a seashell. On his back, two more women, two ships under full sail and Mazeppa on a wild horse. Finally, on his buttocks, a dog chasing two foxes, one of them shown disappearing up the anus.[42]

Sexual union between white women and black men had long been seen as a social taboo and, on occasion, grounds for lynching. A recent study based on original documents shows that before Emancipation and Reconstruction such unions were of minor concern and gained their intense opposition as part of Southern resistance to the civil rights of newly freed slaves. In this respect, African-American men had more freedom before the war than afterward. This finding would have been little comfort to "Richard," noted earlier.[43]

There is a long tradition of drug companies manufacturing new illnesses that then require treatment. Television viewers today can hardly miss the frequent urgings to "Ask your doctor." Social anxiety disorder and pre-menopausal syndrome might be good examples of non-diseases. All that's new is old again, as we see in the many remedies sold for "spermatorrhea." Dr. Rand's Specific, made at 403 Chestnut St. in Philadelphia, was said to cure spermatorrhea and "Seminal Weakness." Dr. L. J. Czapkay, on "Sacramento Street below Montgomery, San Francisco," sold Czapkay's Prophilacticum, which cured, among other things, spermatorrhea and "involuntary discharges." Since spermatorrhea is a vague term, meaning simply flow of sperm, these remedies seem to be aimed at entirely normal functions of youth, including nocturnal emissions during sleep and the slight discharge associated with abstinence.[44]

For those who suffered from simple misery, rather than from spermatorrhea, there was Hasheesh Candy, which would produce ". . . the most perfect mental cheerfulness, a thousand-fold better than quinine for chills and fever." This widely advertised comforting remedy was imported by the Gunga Wallah Company, 36 Beekman Street, New York City.

The well-documented program of army-run prostitution in Nashville produced some unusual stories. On August 22, 1863, the Medical Department of the Office of the Provost Marshal reported the results of the daily medical examinations. Examinee number seven was Frank Norris of 126 College St. Was this a male prostitute or nearly a nickname for Frances?

The ancient sport of mooning could be deadly. A boy in gray climbed out of his rifle pit, turned round, dropped his pants, exposed his buttocks, and dared a Yankee to hit him. He did not know that the 97th New York was equipped with Enfield rifles, which could carry 400 yards. One shot and he was seen no more.[45]

There are many stories, most of them apocryphal, about soldiers who were struck by bullets, but saved when the impact fell upon a pocket Bible. An unnamed soldier of the 36th Illinois was saved by a lewd booklet, which he had folded and placed in his cap.[46]

On March 14, 1863, Charlie Smith of the 170th New York wrote a long letter from Suffolk, Virginia, to a friend at home. Smith told of ". . . great times with the Darkies here . . . especially the Wenches." Charles H. Littlefield, Company K, 21st Connecticut, wrote often to his wife, with whom he seems to have shared a happy physical relationship. On December 28, 1862 he wrote to her, "I would like to bee at home prity well and get some fuck." Three months later, he wrote again of celibate military life: "What I want the wurst kind is a good fuck rite smart." Many more of his letters contains similar sentiments.[47]

It was not just the lowly privates who exercised their carnal urgings. Major General Jubal A. Early fathered four illegitimate children by Julia Annie MacNealey of Rocky Mount, Virginia. The four were Joseph Emerson, Florence Annie, Robert and Jubal, all born between 1850 and 1864. The general provided a cabin for her and visited from time to time, but never lived with her. Oral accounts of a mulatto child with Daisy Turner, and four other children by a second white mistress, are undocumented.[48]

The ever-controversial George Armstrong Custer added his bit to the never ending story. Confederate General Bryan Grimes wrote to his wife that he had captured a Yankee mailbag containing letters between George and Mrs. Custer, letters "vulgar beyond all conversation and even those from his wife would make any honest women blush for her sex." Eliza Denison Brown, an escaped slave, served as Custer's cook and camp manager. Custer's subordinate, Frederick Benteen, asserted that Custer "used to sleep with his cook." A possible confirmation of the Eliza Brown story is found in a clipping (sadly missing the source and date) from a Southern newspaper.

"Miscegenation—A good story is told by a Lynchburg soldier who was in the fight with Sheridan and Custer at Trevillian Depot [May 2, 1862?] near Louisa Court House. Hampton captured Carter's [sic] headquarters, taking therefrom his commission, a picture of the white wife he left at home, and another piece of camp equipage in the shape of a mulatto woman who was temporarily supplying the place of Mrs. Custer. The paramour was in a carriage attended by another darkey, and when our boys made the charge the black driver fled leaving Mrs.

Custer and her carriage in their hands. One of our soldiers, whose name has been given to us, mounted the carriage intending to drive it to the rear, but being hard pressed by the enemy he descended from his box, cut loose the horses, and, by the aid of some of his fellows, toppled the carriage containing the colored lady, over a precipice. They stayed long enough to enjoy the fun, and to hear the cries of her ladyship, who, shut up in the carriage, was gravitating to the depths below. Custer afterwards sent for the articles that were captured, including his wife's picture, but made no enquiry about his colored spouse. This is a veritable truth, and 'we tell the tale as it 'twas told to us.'"

Benteen also wrote that Custer lived with an Indian woman while on the frontier and claimed that "the squaw 'calved'" at the site of the present Fort Sill, Oklahoma. Benteen's implacable hatred of Custer, described by historian Robert Utley as a "monumental vindictiveness and cancerous bitterness," throws a cloud over such testimony.[49]

Union cavalry General Judson Kilpatrick was famous for always traveling with a concubine, usually a woman of "disreputable character and lewd habits." Major General Joseph Hooker had his headquarters described as "a combination barroom and brothel." General Dan Sickles' prewar adventures included serial infidelity and the murder of his wife's lover. Post-war, as US ambassador to Spain, he had a torrid affair with Queen Isabella II.[50]

Colonel Richard W. Carter, who commanded the 1st Virginia Cavalry, was a constant discipline problem when he was at Virginia Military Institute as a cadet, was tried for cowardice at Tom's Brook, and was later cashiered. His men thought him "fat" and "greasy." He was involved in a love triangle involving James Keith Boswell (one of Stonewall Jackson's engineer officers) and a preacher, who killed himself. Captain William Hazleton, 8th Illinois Cavalry, wrote, "We were able to capture Col. Carter at Upperville because one of his own mulatto children pointed him out to us."[51]

On February 3, 1882, the Louisville *Courier Journal* published an article headed "McClellan's Mistress." Mrs. Essie Warren, nee Perry, in an article republished from the Vanceburg (Kentucky) *Courier* had given an interview to a reporter, who told his readers: "When McClellan took charge of the army in Eastern Virginia, Mrs. Warren was a young and voluptuous woman, and dazzled by the epaulets of the Federal commander, his soldierly bearing, his high position and his knightly courtesy she lost her heart and yielded to him (as she alleges) that priceless jewel in a women's crown. During all the time he was in command she says they lived in sweet dalliance, doing homage to Cupid, sub rosa." This author could find no independent verification of Mrs. Warren's tale.

Colonel J. Lafayette Riker, 62nd New York, was tried on a wide variety of charges, including "creating a false muster." Riker had recruited Private Walter Harold and assigned him to Captain Albert Meek's company, but with duties confined to the colonel's headquarters. Harold seems to have been female.

Two different officers "felt of her bosoms" and a third officer remembered her as Helen Lambert from Eliza ("Black Liz") Johnson's house of prostitution in Washington, DC.[52]

On a less exalted plane, on August 22, 1865, Massachusetts soldier Charles B. Smith, wrote to a friend at home, using "Office Assistant Quartermaster" letterhead. He was very happy with his work, because it included issuing permits to young country girls coming to Chattanooga to sell apples and peaches. In fact, he was meeting more girls than he could handle. "A girl came by the office today and I was in the office door and she came up to me and caught me by the arm and said she wishes to speak to me. All right. Away I went. We walked down as far as the post office and then the war commenced. She asked me what girl that was I was riding with last Sunday." Smith had much difficulty in deflecting her jealous fears.[53]

John Robert Jones occupies a special place in the pantheon of Confederate generals. He left the field on several occasions after apparently minor injuries and was court-martialed for cowardice. His post-war career is of more relevance here. He was married twice, both times to white women. One died and the other divorced him for adultery. Around 1870, he took up with his first black mistress, Melinda Rice; they had two children. The daughter, Mary Rice, was light-skinned. General Jones acknowledged her and paid for her college. Their son, who was of a darker complexion, Jones did not acknowledge. His great-granddaughter, Carrie Allen McCray, has written a family history, published in 1998 as *Freedom's Child*. In the 1890s the general had two, or possibly three, sons by a second black woman, Louise Wells, to whom he left his estate when he died in 1901.[54]

Trawling the dark sea floors of chthonic lust and craving has netted a revealing catch. Snared fatally in the folds of metaphor, struggling and flopping as they are dumped into the iced hold of the Ship of History, these stories have been brought up one by one into the unaccustomed light of the examining room, to be filleted upon the pages of this book, a feast for scholars, history buffs, re-enactors, and voyeurs. Our ichthyology of concupiscent miscellany has found some strange creatures indeed.

Appendix A

Citations, Sources, and Abbreviations

Designations of military rank. Most of the cases involved privates. Where no rank is shown, it can be assumed that the man was a private. All other ranks, including "civilian," appear in the text.

Most of the stories presented here are from the Union army general courts-martial. These are filed in folders marked with two letters, followed by numerals, for instance NN270. A full citation would be: National Archives Record Group 153 [RG153], Records of the Judge Advocate General's Office (Army), entry 15, Court-Martial Case File, file NN270, National Archives, Washington, DC.

Several hundred of these folders are empty. These held the transcripts of men who were executed; the actual documents were removed for microfilming. These trials can be read on National Archives microfilm M1523. Summaries based on the microfilm can be found in *All Were Not Heroes*, by Edward C. Johnson, privately printed, 1997.

The Union Navy courts-martial are on microfilm, occupying dozens of rolls of 35 mm film. Each court-martial has a case file number, without letters. Each roll is marked with the case numbers of the courts-martial therein. The Civil War trials all have four digit numbers, thus a trial would be adequately described by 7365. A full citation would be: Case #7365, Records of courts-martial and courts of inquiry of the Navy Department, 1799-1867 (National Archives Microfilm Publication M272) Record Group 125, Records of the Judge Advocate General (Navy).

Records of Union soldiers and officers are called Compiled Military Service Records (CMSR). A full citation would be: Record Group 94, Compiled Military Service Record, followed by the soldier's full name and regiment. Confederate records are cited as Record Group 109, War Department Collection of Confederate Records.

OR is an abbreviation for the hundreds of volumes of *The Official Records of the Union and Confederate Armies*. RG is an abbreviation for Record Group, a subdivision of records in the National Archives. VS is Voluntary Service, a special personnel file kept on officers. G.C.M.O. is general court-martial orders, printed summaries of completed trials, usually bound by year.

Soldiers too sick for combat, but well enough for restricted duty, were placed in the IC (Invalid Corps), which later became the VRC (Veterans Reserve Corps).

Manuscript dealers and auction houses issue catalogs, usually with a closing date. Entries based on such catalogs cite the name of the firm, such as Historical Collectible Auctions or Alexander Autographs and the auction date.

The name "Holt" appears frequently in these summaries. Joseph Holt was Lincoln's judge advocate general and played a major role in formulating military justice policy and in reviewing capital cases from the courts-martial. His long career of public service has been neglected by most historians, though a recent biography by Elizabeth Leonard has partially remedied this lacuna. Holt played a positive part in military justice. He was often severe, but sometimes remarkably compassionate.

Appendix B

Seven Ways to Read This Book

1. All history is local. From the chapter headings and the index find those places near your home or near where your ancestors lived. See the local picture.
2. Read by subject. The chapter headings will guide you. Pick an area of human behavior least familiar to you, and see what some folks were up to back then. Or try the chapter headed A Vast Miscellany. It's sort of like Ripley's *Believe It or Not*, but with footnotes.
3. Try the technique many of us use with *The Readers' Digest*. Keep your copy of the book in that room where no one will disturb you, and read a few pages (or even a chapter) until you emerge, refreshed.
4. Read at random. Just close your eyes. Open the book. Start to read wherever chance takes you. Fate will guide your fingers.
5. Pick six stories that seem the most interesting; four from the army and two from the navy. Hop on Jet Blue. Stay in the suburbs and take the Metro into the Archives. (Downtown DC is expensive!). The doors open at 8:45, usually. Order the four army cases (the staff will help you). Those records will arrive in the reading room about 10 AM. While you wait, read the navy trials, which are on microfilm and immediately accessible without a wait.
6. Cross your fingers and look in the index for your own ancestor.
7. Search the index for your favorite regiment. Rewrite the regimental history.

Coda

Finally, what is this book? It is a collection of pointers, words that indicate a story, but remain as pointers; they can never *be* the story. It is snippets about statements. The Irish novelist John McGahern said, "I think that nearly all good writing is suggestion, and that all bad writing is statement. Statement kills off the reader's imagination. With suggestion, the reader takes up where the writer leaves off." Perhaps these little fragmentary stories can, in the hands of poets and novelists, and in the minds of readers, approach what life was like, at certain moments, for certain people, in that misty past that is American history, approach closely enough to hasten the breath, to tighten the fingers, to feel that drawing sensation that foreshadows the stirring of lust—mingled with fear.

Endnotes

Chapter 1

1. Nils Ringdahl: *A World History of Prostitution*. New York: Grove Press, 2004. Pages 1-50.
2. 1860 Federal census, microfilm M653, roll 1221, page 764.
3. RWA Auction Catalog, March 1999, page 73.
4. II588.
5. II636.
6. MM28.
7. MM496.
8. RG 393, IV, entry 1526, 373/943/DW.
9. NN870.
10. Miscellaneous Regimental Papers, 5th New York Infantry, National Archives.
11. LL603.
12. NN1088.
13. LL2397.
14. NN3047.
15. LL2976.
16. NN2472.
17. NN2422.
18. NN2413.
19. NN2286.
20. NN2413.
21. NN2247.
22. NN3216.
23. LL2968.
24. MM2609.
25. OO1249.

26. Thomas P. Lowry: "Ruthless Rufus." *Civil War Times*, October 2000, pages 53-62.
27. NARA file T-421 (V.S.) 1862, RG 94, entry 496, box 144; File 1391-W (AGO) 1864, on microcopy M619, roll 320; M797, Turner file 2757; letterpress copies of letters sent while provost marshal, in RG 393, Part IV, entry 1526 (#373/943/DW; compiled service records; pension files.
28. Arlington *Journal*, June 23, 1999.
29. *The Ensign: A Newsletter Devoted to the Union and Confederate Navies.* March/April 1998, pages 5-6; National Archives microfilm M273, reel 112, trial 3335.
30. James G. Barber: *Alexandria in the Civil War.* H. E. Howard: Lynchburg, VA, 1988. Pages 27 and 100.
31. E. Susan Barber: "Depraved and Abandoned Women—Prostitution in Richmond, Virginia Across the Civil War," in *Neither Lady Nor Slave: Working Women of the Old South.* Edited by Susanna Delfino and Michelle Gillespie, pages 155-173. University of North Carolina Press: Chapel Hill, 2002.
32. Thomas P. Lowry: *The Story the Soldiers Wouldn't Tell.* Stackpole Books: Mechanicsburg, PA, 1998. Page 70.
33. Robert E. L. Krick has undertaken the Herculean task of reading all the Richmond newspapers from the Civil War, and is preparing an index to salient features. His estimated completion date is 2010. He has generously let me use his findings of sexual misbehavior. Readers wishing to read the original will find the cited dates sufficient unto the task.
34. John A. Smith Papers, Duke University, 1862-1865 folder, courtesy of Lee Sherrill.
35. *Confederate Reminiscences and Letters*, Georgia United Daughters of the Confederacy, Vol. 15, 2000, pages 202-211.
36. MM2779.
37. National Archives microfilm M331, roll 6.
38. Gilder-Lehrman Collection, GLC 4558, Item 98.
39. LL2883.
40. LL2883.
41. NN2543.
42. NN496.
43. LL530, folder 2.
44. NN502.
45. RG 393, Part 4, Entry 697, Volume 272/697.
46. OO663.
47. MM1711.
48. LL1844.
49. RG 105, Entry 4139, Volume 211.
50. MM3610.

51. Shelby Foote (ed.): *The Night Before Chancellorsville and Other Civil War Stories.* Signet Books: New York.
52. LL1649.
53. Remember When auction catalog, No. 6, July 10, 1999, item 117.
54. RG 343, Part I, Entry 4075, Miscellaneous Lists of the Provost Marshal General, September 1862-April 1865.
55. M395, Roll 11.
56. OO1197.
57. II679.
58. RG 105, Entry 3959, Volume I.
59. II914.
60. KK51, LL654.
61. KK215.
62. *OR.* Series II, Volume 5, Page 627.
63. Typescript in the possession of Robert K. Krick, Fredericksburg, VA.
64. J. Gregory Acken (ed.): *Inside the Army of the Potomac.* Stackpole: Mechanicsburg, PA, Page 353.
65. LL1866.
66. OO84.
67. LL1956, NN593.
68. NN2617.
69. LL2938.
70. LL2791.
71. MM3003.
72. MM3022.

Chapter 2

1. MM3180.
2. MM3929.
3. MM3226.
4. MM3910.
5. KK49.
6. MM2413.
7. MM3114.
8. 4136; also author's article in *Civil War Times,* August 2002, pages 31-35.
9. 4135.
10. 4106.
11. 4322.
12. MM3235.

13. MM3007.
14. NN3488.
15. MM3334.
16. OO1088.
17. MM2700.
18. OO1032.
19. MM2914.
20. MM3171.
21. MM3287.
22. NN2724.
23. MM3304.

Chapter 3

1. LL316.
2. LL1672.
3. LL1089.
4. NN1942.
5. LL2229.
6. NN3090.
7. NN3186,
8. OO817, OO917.
9. OO917.
10. OO918.
11. OO1312.
12. MM3676.
13. OO1314.
14. MM2449.
15. Washington *Post*, June 3, 2002, page A3.
16. *Op. cit.*, page A3.
17. OO556.
18. Harnett T. Kane: *Natchez*. William Morrow: New York, 1947, pages 125-143; author's personal visit.
19. MM3325.
20. RG 110, Reports of Scouts, Guides, Spies, and Detectives, 1861-1866. Box 1, Entry 36.
21. Vicksburg *Sunday Post*, March 15, 1987, page B2.
22. Peter F. Walker: *Vicksburg: A People At War*. University of North Carolina: Chapel Hill, 1960, pages 40-41.
23. MM3691.
24. LL2774.
25. MM3267.

Sexual Misbehavior in the Civil War

26. MM3483.
27. KK226.
28. OO112, OO108.
29. Letter at Old Courthouse Museum, Vicksburg, courtesy of Gordon Cotton.
30. MM3321.
31. MM3780.
32. NN1619.
33. Historical Collectible Auctions, March 11, 2004.
34. NN3452.
35. NN3093.
36. San Francisco *Chronicle*, March 2, 1996.

Chapter 4

1. NN3067.
2. NN2566.
3. KK6987.
4. MM649, NN111.
5. MM7.
6. MM1447.
7. LL3154.
8. NN2525.
9. H. E. Matheny: *Wood County, West Virginia, in Civil War Times*. Trans-Allegheny Books: Parkersburg, 1987, pages 190-193.\
10. Courtesy of Gerard W. Swick.
11. NN861.
12. Typescript at Fredericksburg National Military Park.
13. Alexander Autographs, item 669, November 19, 2002.
14. Courtesy of Suzanne Snook.
15. LL952.
16. II638.

Chapter 5

1. Roy P. Basler: *The Collected Works of Abraham Lincoln*. Volume 4. Rutgers University Press: New Brunswick, NJ, 1953, page 532.
2. LL2709.
3. NN2919.
4. OO1176.
5. NN2119.
6. NN237.
7. OO1102, MM226.

8. OO789.
9. LL602.
10. NN2076.
11. LL2855.
12. LL2896.
13. LL453.
14. Roger D. Hunt: *Brevet Brigadier Generals in Blue*. Olde Soldier Books: Gaithersburg, MD, 1990, page 35.
15. The pamphlet is reprinted in full in: Thomas P. Lowry: *The Civil War Bawdy Houses of Washington, DC*. Sgt. Kirkland's Press: Fredericksburg, 1998.
16. Washington *Post*, August 31, 1997, page A3.

Chapter 6

1. LL2878, LL2881.
2. LL807.
3. NN176.
4. LL812.
5. LL780.
6. MM2502.
7. LL2889.
8. LL2562.
9. LL1972.
10. LL2346.
11. OO111.
12. NN1040.
13. Thomas P. Lowry: *The Story the Soldiers Wouldn't Tell. Loc. cit.*
14. Amador *Dispatch* (Jackson, CA). April 29, 1865, front page.
15. LL2598.
16. "Scraps from old letters." State Historical Society of Wisconsin.
17. RG 110, *op. cit.* Courtesy of Michael P. Musick.
18. "Memphis' Nymphs du Pave: The Most Abandoned Women in the World," *West Tennessee Historical Society Papers*. Volume 50 (1996), pages 58-69.
19. "The Enemy Among Us: Venereal Disease Among Union Soldiers in the Far West," *Civil War History*. Volume 31, No. 3, 1985, pages 257-269.
20. David Kaser: "Nashville's Women of Pleasure in 1860," *Tennessee Historical Quarterly*. Volume 23, December 1964, pages 379-382.
21. Thomas P. Lowry: *The Story the Soldiers Wouldn't Tell, Loc cit.*, page 76.
22. NN1926.
23. LL2716.
24. NN2933.

25. KK568, KK570.
26. LL278.
27. KK226.
28. MM2212.
29. OO873.
30. NN2497.
31. OO879.
32. OO904.
33. NN2872.
34. OO602.
35. MM3879.
36. MM3864.
37. Scott J. Winslow auction, June 21, 2000.
38. MM3843.
39. LL3224.
40. NN13.
41. LL2055.
42. LL3055.
43. Author's collection.
44. OO868.
45. NN3113.
46. OO544.
47. MM1898.
48. NN88.
49. MM2900.
50. LL2845.
51. LL2717.
52. NN1698.
53. LL2859.
54. Museum of the Confederacy, file hardee 27.
55. RG 109, Chapter 2, Volume 52 ½, G.O 8, August 28, 1862, Army of Kentucky.
56. N. C. Hughes (ed.): *The Civil War Memoir of Philip D. Stephenson, DD*. University of Central Arkansas Press: Conway, 1995, page 18.
57. N. J. Bond (ed.): *The South Carolinians: Colonel Asbury Coward's Memoirs*. Vantage Press: New York, 1968, pages 92-93.
58. LL2351, LL2353.
59. NN2933.
60. NN2610.
61. NN187.
62. MM2646.
63. MM656.

64. LL2740.
65. LL1531.
66. *OR*. Series I, Volume 49, Part 11, page 1109.

Chapter 7

1. NN2081.
2. LL1265.
3. MM1781.
4. LL1737.
5. LL1737.
6. LL1975.
7. NN1426.
8. NN2096.
9. NN2081, OO699, NN1766.
10. MM994.
11. RG 393, Entry 1154, Part 4, Volume 428, Volume 1 of 2, Miscellaneous Records, Volume 1 of 2, Nos. 428/1074/107A and 424/1073DMo.
12. St. Louis *Home Magazine*, October 1985, Pages 35-36; Duane R. Snedekker: "The Great Experiment," *Gateway Heritage*, Fall 1990, Pages 20-47.
13. MM2071.
14. LL1019.
15. Samuel Newitt Wood Papers, State Historical Society of Kansas, Topeka. Courtesy of John Bradbury.
16. District of Rolla, Special Order 92.
17. RG 393, Part 2, Entry 3424, General Orders of District of Southwest Missouri, G.O. 36.
18. RG 393, Entry 1764, Volume 668/1638, 1639, 1704, 1707, DMo.
19. RG 393, Part 2, Entry 3333, Volume 297, Page 245.
20. OO827.
21. RG 393, Volume 741/1864, DMo.
22. MM1965, OO490.
23. NN2738.
24. LL2275.
25. LL2087, NN1932.
26. NN3812.
27. NN1813.
28. William E. Connelley: *Quantrill and the Border Wars*. Pageant Books: New York, 1956; Albert Castel: *William Clarke Quantrill*. Frederick Fell: New York, 1962.
29. With thanks to Jason D. Stratman, Missouri Historical Society.

Chapter 8

1. OO1118.
2. MM2128.
3. MM429.
4. NN3230.
5. LL2018.
6. KK466.
7. NN243.
8. 3862, 3641.
9. MM2768.
10. LL3069.
11. OO994.
12. OO592.
13. Letter courtesy of Budge Weidman, Civil War Conservation Corps, and NN2208.
14. NN3311.
15. NN790, NN1852.
16. RG 94, Entry 496, file M-297, box 7.
17. Pension file 378,936.
18. OO1083.
19. LL2170.
20. Articles courtesy of Robert Norland.
21. NN3723.
22. OO405.
23. OO1329.
24. MM3750.
25. MM2541.
26. LL1867.

Chapter 9

1. Cindy L. Baker: "Sacramento's Sophisticated Ladies." *Golden Notes* (Sacramento County Historical Society). Volume 41, No. 2, Summer 1995, pages 1-38.
2. Washington *Post*. July 3, 2005.
3. MM67.
4. LL678, LL1038.
5. LL1210.
6. General Court-martial Orders 84.
7. Ann F. Crawford (ed.): *The Eagle: The Autobiography of Santa Anna*. Pemberton Press, Austin, 1967, page 265.

8. Arthur Woodward: *The Great Western*. Pamphlet published by Yerba Buena Chapter, E. Clampus Vitus, 1961.
9. Smith's Compiled Military Service Record.
10. LL1999, MM3154.

Chapter 10

1. Thomas P. Lowry: *The Story the Soldiers Wouldn't Tell*. Op. cit. pages 61-65.
2. Courtesy of Richard Wilson.
3. James O. Hall: *The Surratt Family and John Wilkes Booth*. The Surratt Society: Clinton, MD, 1997, Page 13.
4. LL2127.
5. LL653.
6. NN2216.
7. NN2509.
8. NN2223.
9. MM2007.
10. NN18.
11. II751.
12. NN515.
13. II751.
14. LL3148.
15. NN1192.
16. MM2215.
17. LL2681
18. MM2513.
19. MM2513.
20. MM2074.
21. MM2018.
22. MM1289.
23. LL937.
24. LL2975, LL2983.
25. KK319.
26. NN1464.
27. NN343.
28. OO1383.
29. NN2618.
30. II607.
31. Alexander Autographs. March 29, 2003.
32. NN2340.
33. New York *Times*. April 17, 1999, front page.

34. Paul H. Bergeron (ed.): *The Papers of Andrew Johnson*, Volume 10. University of Tennessee Press: Knoxville, 1992, page 609.
35. Washington Post *Magazine*. October 29, 1995, page 20.
36. *Op. cit.* November 6, 199, page B3.
37. *Op. cit.* December 13, 1997, page P4.
38. *Op. cit.* February 23, 2001.

Chapter 11

1. MM1356.
2. OO1135.
3. OO386.
4. OO522.
5. II837.
6. OO954.
7. The Historical Shop, Spring 2005 catalog.
8. MM3130.
9. II909.
10. II995.
11. LL2746.
12. MM1779, OO504.
13. II645.
14. Washington *Post*. November 25, 2000, March 2, 2001, and March 20, 2001.
15. Americana catalog. Abraham Lincoln Bookshop, Chicago. October 2000.
16. MM2150.
17. Typescript at Richmond National Battlefield Park, courtesy of R. E. L. Krick and Harriet Kocher.
18. William J. Miller: *The Training of an Army*. White Mane Press: Shippensburg, PA, 1990. Pages 22 and 221.
19. MM3272.
20. NN626.

Chapter 12

1. Tyler Anbinder: *Five Points*. Plume Publishers, New York, 2002; Anonymous: *Vices of a Big City*. J. E. Clark: New York, 1890.
2. MM1168.
3. MM1955, MM2073.
4. Courtesy of Benedict Maryniak, Buffalo, NY.
5. NN2220.
6. 3101.

7. NN3308.
8. Nate D. Sanders catalog.
9. LL1778.
10. LL2806.
11. MM1849, OO1221.
12. MM3100.

Chapter 13

1. Trevor Bryce: *Life and Society in the Hittite World.* Oxford University Press: New York, New York, 2002, page 128.
2. Lynn Meskell: *Private Life in New Kingdom Egypt.* Princeton University Press: Princeton, 2002, page 104.
3. Rosanna Omitowoju: "Regulating Rape," in Susan Deacy and Karen F. Pierce (eds.): *Rape in Antiquity: Sexual Violence in the Greek and Roman Worlds.* Classical Press of Wales: London, 1997, pages 1-17.
4. Daniel Ogden, in Deacy and Pierce, *op. cit.*, page 27.
5. James A. Arieti, in Deacy and Pierce, *op. cit.*, page 209.
6. Corinne J. Saunders, in Deacy and Pierce, *op. cit.*, page 243.
7. David McCullough: *1776.* Simon & Schuster: New York, pages 142, 261.
8. Mary Beth Norton: *Liberty's Daughters.* Scott, Foresman, Boston, 1980, page 203.
9. London *News-Telegraph.* October 25, 2004; Washington *Post.* December 14, 2004.
10. NN20.
11. MM2593.
12. II819.
13. MM1984.
14. MM3050.
15. OO1320.
16. MM2639.
17. OO217, OO204, MM2748.
18. MM1481, Typescript of Jackson Crossley at Petersburg National Battlefield, manuscript of Captain James C. Hamilton, 110th Pennsylvania, Civil War Library, Philadelphia, Chapter 17.
19. NN2998.
20. LL1377.
21. KK383, MM1089, NN3066.
22. MM2161.
23. NN2308.
24. MM3009.
25. NN3993.
26. NN714.

Sexual Misbehavior in the Civil War | 283

27. OO886, OO1022.
28. NN2099.
29. OO175.
30. NN116.
31. KK207, Thomas P. Lowry: "Sperryville Outrage," *Civil War Times*, March 1999, pages 24-26.
32. RG 94,G737-849, Box 56.
33. MM1651.
34. II869.
35. NN2449.
36. NN3372.
37. NN3927.
38. OO654.
39. NN529.
40. NN561.
41. MM2711.
42. II773.
43. MM1525.
44. 3362.
45. Microfilm M1523.
46. NN3756.
47. MM2478.
48. MM1470.
49. LL556.
50. OO1340.
51. LL310.
52. LL2552, NN2468.
53. John W. Haley: *The Rebel Yell and the Yankee Hurrah*. Down East Books: Camden, ME, 1985, page. 226.

Chapter 14

1. NN118.
2. MM987.
3. MM3140.
4. NN2254.
5. MM3112.
6. 6. MM2106
7. MM3906.
8. MM2243.
9. OO1056.
10. MM2133.

11. OO1232.
12. MM3175.
13. Microfilm M1523, MM3937.
14. MM2320.
15. MM2511.
16. NN136.
17. MM1917.
18. OO945.
19. LL1933.
20. MM2031.
21. NN375.
22. OO1086.
23. OO1232.
24. General Orders No. 13; *OR*. Series I, Volume 49, Part II, page 669 (report of Col. Chauncey Hawley, 1st Ohio Heavy Artillery); Microfilm M1523; Papers of Lt. Edward F. Browne, Pacific Book Auction Galleries, October 15, 2001.
25. MM3806.
26. MM3827.
27. MM3023.
28. LL2227, NN2812, LL2193.
29. II780.
30. LL1562.
31. OO102.
32. MM3184, MM3197.
33. MM2318.
34. MM3937.
35. NN624.
36. KK259.
37. LL2665.
38. MM3893, MM2827.
39. MM1054.

Chapter 15

1. MM3057.
2. OO1313.
3. LL3253.
4. LL3253.
5. MM2815.
6. MM2758.
7. LL382.
8. NN1937.

9. NN3272.
10. NN184.
11. MM2534.
12. OO1017.
13. Microfilm M1523.
14. 4078.
15. MM2241; RG 45, Naval Records Collection: 1789: Squadron Letters, West Gulf Blockading Squadron, Volume 199.
16. LL1097.
17. 4175, 3572.
18. OO1292.
19. MM3494.
20. LL3172.
21. 4205.
22. NN3283.
23. MM3171, MM3682.
24. MM3192.
25. MM2825.
26. LL2688.
27. OO1421.
28. LL3150.
29. NN4013.
30. MM2368.
31. NN2165.
32. LL2737.
33. OO220.
34. Clarence Poe (ed.): *True Tales of the South at War*. Dover Books: New York, 1996 reprint, page 70.

Chapter 16

1. LL2449, NN2760.
2. LL2449.
3. MM2819, Microfilm M1523, NN478.
4. LL963.
5. NN2168, NN3007.
6. OO556.
7. OO208.
8. OO1066.
9. OO541.
10. LL2723.
11. MM287.

12. LL2758.
13. OO857.
14. MM746.
15. LL269, LL1687.
16. LL1782.
17. MM2547, NN3940.
18. NN3953.
19. NN103.
20. MM2900.
21. MM1170.
22. MM3553.
23. OO238.
24. NN1921.
25. MM742.
26. OO785, NN88.
27. NN85.
28. LL2263.
29. MM3126.
30. LL298.
31. LL2041.
32. OO1278, LL380.
33. MM2774.
34. MM2805.
35. LL693.
36. MM2806, LL2755.
37. NN3107.
38. LL2719.
39. NN3205.
40. *OR*. Series I, Volume 49, Part 2, Serial No. 104, pages 427-428.
41. H. W. R. Jackson: *The Southern Women of the Second American Revolution*. Publisher unknown: Atlanta, 1863.
42. MM3528.
43. MM2958.
44. MM2571, OO1319.
45. OO927.
46. NN432.
47. LL2695.
48. KK201.
49. MM2915.
50. II575.
51. MM3380.

Sexual Misbehavior in the Civil War | 287

52. NN3097.
53. NN2227.

Chapter 17

1. MM2780.
2. LL1108.
3. LL1505.
4. LL192.
5. MM2635.
6. OO1416, CMSR.
7. LL2820, LL2816.
8. LL3201.
9. MM3021.
10. MM434.
11. MM2802.
12. KK72.
13. KK76.
14. MM1444, NN1779.
15. LL553.
16. LL2275.
17. II928.
18. OO142.
19. II999.
20. NN2140.
21. LL289.
22. OO136.
23. OO484.
24. NN2672.
25. NN3848.
26. NN1230.
27. OO965.
28. LL1746.
29. LL2743.
30. LL3182.
31. MM3169.
32. Microfilm M1523.
33. MM3730.
34. LL1746.
35. NN2215.
36. NN3809.

37. MM3032.
38. NN2113, LL3132.
39. Microfilm M1523.
40. MM660.
41. NN3857.
42. MM2226.
43. MM3264.
44. MM3144.
45. MM3815.
46. KK22, LL1210.

Chapter 18

1. MM2044, MM2868.
2. MM1678.
3. II596.
4. MM1510.
5. MM1909.
6. MM1940, MM1981.
7. LL880, LL2405.
8. NN3498.
9. OO1428.
10. OO153.
11. MM2953.
12. MM2644.
13. NN2223.
14. NN2406.
15. LL2655.
16. NN106.
17. LL664.
18. LL2880.
19. A. M. Swan: *Life, Trial, Conviction, Confession and Execution of John M. Osborne.* National Democratic Publishing: Peoria, 1873.

Chapter 19

1. Nelson Lankford: *Richmond Burning.* Penguin: New York, 2002, page 184.
2. Jack A. Bunch: *Roster of the Courts-martial in the Confederate States Armies.* White Mane Press: Shippensburg, PA, 2001.
3. WPA Project 65-33-118, copy at the University of South Carolina library.
4. Personal communication, 2004.
5. *OR.* Series I, Volume 51, Part 2, pages 386-387, courtesy Patrice Aillot.

6. RG 109, Confederate Adjutant and Inspector General records, G.O. 21, General Orders 1863-1864, Chapter 1, Volume 3, page 252.
7. RG 109, *op. cit.*, General Orders 139, October 28, 1863.

Chapter 20

1. *The New Catholic Encyclopedia.* Catholic University of America: Washington, DC, 1967. Volume IX, page 438.
2. *Encyclopedia of Religion.* Macmillan: New York, 1987. Volume 15, page 378.
3. James G. Frazer: *The Golden Bough.* Macmillan: New York, 1922, 1996 reprint from Touchstone/Simon & Schuster: New York, 1996, page 137.
4. Godbeer, Richard: *Sexual Revolution in Early America.* Johns Hopkins Press: Baltimore, 2002, pages 64, 83, 88.
5. Friedman, Lawrence M.: *Crime and Punishment in American History.* Basic Books: New York, 1993, page 34.
6. Historical Collectible Auctions, May 8, 2003.
7. Thomas P. Lowry: *The Story the Soldiers Wouldn't Tell. op. cit.* pages 20-23.
8. RG 48, Entry 64, Volume I, Record of St. Elizabeth's Hospital.
9. Rachel P. Maines: *The Technology of Orgasm.* Johns Hopkins Press: Baltimore, 1999.
10. Thomas P. Lowry: *The Clitoris.* Warren H. Green: St. Louis, 1976, page 126.
11. Historical Collectible Auctions, May 17, 2001.
12. NN1922.
13. RG 94, Entry 409, File PPR-793 (EB).
14. CMSR.
15. NN549.
16. KK850.
17. Pension Records.
18. LL1672.
19. LL898.
20. LL764.
21. OO1165.
22. NN3869.
23. LL2535.
24. CMSR.
25. MM1837.
26. KK261.
27. LL1405, folder 1.
28. David T. Hedrick and Gordon Barry Davis (eds.): *I'm Surrounded by Methodists . . .* Thomas Publications, Gettysburg, 2000.
29. LL309.
30. War Between the States Auctions, Gettysburg.
31. 3786.

32. RG 52, Entry 31, Volume 16, page 364.
33. RG 52, Entry 31, Volume 14.
34. RG 52, Entry 24, Box 01.
35. Eric T. Dean, Jr.: *Shook Over Hell: Post-Traumatic Stress in Vietnam and the Civil War.* Harvard University: Cambridge, 1997, page 150.
36. Office of the Americas *Bulletin,* June 2004, Volume 21, Number 2.
37. *The Oklahoman,* January 20, 2005, page 1.

Chapter 21

1. Bruce S. Thornton: *Eros: The Myth of Greek Sexuality.* Westview Press: Boulder, CO, 1997, pages 99-120.
2. Walter L. Williams: *The Spirit and the Flesh.* Beacon Press: Boston, 1992, pages 17-22.
3. Richard Godbeer: *op. cit.,* pages 45-50.
4. James Deetz and Patricia Scott Deetz: *The Times of Their Lives: Life, Love and Death in Plymouth Colony.* Anchor Books: New York, 2000, page 134.
5. Microfilm M853, Roll 9, Volume 58, and Roll 3, Volume 21, Valley Forge.
6. Randy Shilts: *Conduct Unbecoming: Gays and Lesbians in the U.S. Military.* St. Martin's: New York, 1993, page 7. Steuben scholar Thomas Fleming makes no mention of homosexuality in his analysis of the general's career. *American Heritage,* February/March 2006, pages 58-65.
7. LL317.
8. NN2326.
9. RG 94, file W-2442, V.S. 1864, box 655.
10. OO2903.
11. Pension records.
12. Utica *Morning Herald,* December 18, 1863.
13. KK367.
14. LL2223.
15. NN1381.
16. OO633.
17. RG 94, file 4276, V.S. 1872, and G.C.M.O. 28.
18. CMSR.
19. LL185.
20. Brian & Maria Green summer 2005 auction catalog.
21. LL1084.
22. NN556.
23. OO55, CMSR.
24. NN3801.
25. LL1782, II984.
26. NN376.

27. KK734.
28. LL190.
29. CMSR of Captain John Staples, 3rd California Infantry.
30. KK111.
31. OO458.
32. MM3067.
33. LL677, KK111.
34. OO130.
35. Robert K. Massie: *Dreadnought*. Ballantine Books: New York, 1991, page 778.
36. *Finest Hour*, July-September 1994, page 14; Harold D. Langley: *Social Reform in the United States Navy: 1798-1862*. University of Illinois Press: Urbana, 1967, page 172.
37. 3425, 3427.
38. 3423.
39. 3425.
40. 4100.
41. 4093, RG 45, microfilm M89, roll 196.
42. 4184, 4185.
43. 3901.
44. 3898.
45. 3348.
46. 3347.
47. 3349.
48. Courtesy of Prof. Joseph Reidy.
49. 4192, 4201.
50. 3622, 3809.
51. 3431, 3436.
52. 3386.
53. RG 45, M89, Roll 194, Dispatch No. 423-4.
54. RG 24, Volume January-July 1865.
55. 4343.
56. 4509.
57. 3476, 3480.
58. 3078.
59. RG 76, microfilm T-716, Volume 3, courtesy of Terry Foenander.
60. Shilts, *op. cit.* page 17.
61. Magnus Hirschfeld: *The Sexual History of the World War*. Panurge Press, New York, 1932, pages 124-141.
62. Shilts, *op. cit.* page 16.
63. Washington *Post*, October 19, 2000, page C2.
64. *USA TODAY*, July 19, 1993, page 5A.
65. Washington *Post*, November 30, 2003, page B6.

66. Washington *Post*, November 23, 2002, page A24; January 2, 2002; and January 31, 2000.
67. J. L. King: *On the Down Low: A Journey Into the Lives of "Straight" Black Men Who Sleep with Men*. Broadway Books: New York, 2004; Laud Humphreys: *Tearoom Trade: Impersonal Sex in Public Places*. Aldine Press: Chicago, 1970.
68. Jonathan Ned Katz: *Love Stories: Sex Between Men Before Homosexuality*. University Chicago: Chicago, 2001.

Chapter 22

1. Jay H. Buckley: "The Price of Paper." *We Proceeded On*. Volume 27, Number 1, February 2001, pages 7-9.
2. James P. Weeks: "A Different View of Gettysburg." *Civil War History*. Volume L, Number 2, 2004, pages 175-191.
3. EAC Gallery, January 29, 2004.
4. Historical Collectible Auctions, September 19, 2002.
5. Historical Collectible Auctions, January 24, 2002.
6. Unless otherwise noted, all documents are from the author's collection.
7. Historical Collectible Auctions, September 14, 2004.
8. Alexander Autographs.
9. Historical Collectible Auctions, June 19, 2003.
10. Historical Collectible Auctions, January 27, 2005.
11. Microfilm M593, Roll 1289, pages 84, 95, 98, and 99.

Chapter 23

1. *Encyclopedia of Religion*. Macmillan: New York, 1987. Volume 6, pages 463-467.
2. James Deetz: *op. cit.* pages 134-139.
3. Lawrence Friedman: *op. cit.* pages 34-35.
4. KK132.
5. KK445.
6. LL1532.
7. LL3130.
8. Robert W. Patton, Sr. (ed.): *The Civil War Diary of the Rev. Charles Bowen Betts, DD*. Privately published. Rock Hill, SC, 1995.
9. Pension record 694 509 541 583.
10. CMSR.
11. San Francisco *Chronicle*. November 16, 2003.
12. *www.salon.com/health/sex/urge/world/2000/02/24/horse*.
13. St. Louis *Post Dispatch*. February 6, 2006.

Chapter 24

1. Raymond Hollander: "Compulsive Cursing," *Psychiatric Quarterly*. Volume 34, Number 1, pages 599-622.
2. OO604, 3777, 3528, II802.
3. II672, OO1135, 3210, 3568, 4299, NN302.
4. II909, MM3393, OO141.
5. Jesse Sheidlower: *The F Word*. Second Edition. Random House: New York, 1995.
6. Washington *Post*. June 26, 2004.
7. NN1290, Personal communication, 2001.
8. LL1375, LL2305, LL2859.
9. NN3790.
10. OO217, MM1545.
11. Museum of the Confederacy, OS, Box 9, page 8, LL194.
12. 3401, NN2330, NN2417.
13. NN2871, Courtesy of Marcus S. McLemore.
14. MM3259, MM3126.
15. OO1218, Olde Soldier Books catalog, July 2000.
16. OO1276, OO1270.
17. NN445.
18. NN445.
19. OO417, NN3536.
20. NN3618, NN2289, MM3179.
21. II657.
22. II901, Courtesy of George Loess, NN514.
23. Amon Breneman Papers, US Army Military History Institute, Carlisle Barracks, PA, 3923,3959.
24. NN1662, NN1803.
25. KK251.
26. OO518, OO46.
27. CMSR, MM3221, MM2629.
28. II485.
29. II791, II929, KK161.
30. OO686, MM586, LL171, NN1742.
31. LL315, 3308, Historical Collectible Auctions March 24, 2005.
32. II658.
33. OO1121, KK66, MM1094.
34. 3250, KK478, 3241.
35. KK159, LL702.
36. LL1156, KK354, OO1056.

37. LL58, OO141, OO153.
38. RG 109, Entry 213, Provost Marshal file, various states, bonds, miscellaneous amnesty papers, 1862-1864, box 14.
39. 3282, KK583, LL1679.
40. NN1649, LL1291, MM75.
41. LL2473, NN320, NN497.
42. OO715.
43. NN1667, KK127, KK170.
44. NN2479, MM2883.
45. MM2875, OO1303.
46. Diary of Sergeant Hause, Pottsville (PA) Historical Society.
47. Virginia Tech Library, Special Collections, Civil War manuscripts.
48. Courtesy Marcus S. McLemore.
49. Author's collection.
50. Historical Collectible Auctions, May 8, 2003.
51. William McWillie notebooks, Robert K. Krick collection. eBay item, 413 231 698.
52. David T. Hedrick, *op. cit.*
53. Author's collection.

Chapter 25

1. John M. Riddle: *Contraception and Abortion from the Ancient World to the Renaissance.* Harvard University: Cambridge, 1992, pages 59, 85.
2. Thomas P. Lowry: *The Story the Soldiers Wouldn't Tell, op. cit.* page 96.
3. Franklin (TN) *Western Weekly Review,* April 4, 1861.
4. Wheeling (WV) *Intelligencer.* December 22, 1863.
5. NN670.
6. Riddle, *op. cit.* pages 18, 68.
7. Historical Collectible Auctions, May 8, 2003.
8. Author's collection.
9. Gabriele Haefs: *Johnny Come Lately: A Short History of the Condom.* Journeyman Press: London, 1987; G. K. Elliott, George Goehring, and Dennis O'Brien: *Remember Your Rubbers!.* Schiffer Publishing: Atglen, PA, 1998.
10. Cincinnati *Daily Inquirer.* June 11, 1862.
11. Thomas P. Lowry: *The Story the Soldiers Wouldn't Tell op. cit.* page 55; Order No. 22, Headquarters of the Army, March 26, 1833.
12. Chicago *Tribune.* January 15, page 2; Raleigh (NC) *Weekly North Carolina Standard.* February 21, 1866.
13. Historical Collectible Auctions, November 18, 2004; Philadelphia *Public Ledger.* September 27, 1865, front page.
14. NN1259, CMSR.

15. CMSR, RG 24, Volume 42, Navy Rendezvous Books, Chicago.
16. Historical Collectible Auctions, November 7, 2002.
17. KK429, II998.
18. OO827.
19. *Medical & Surgical History of the War of the Rebellion.* Part 2, Volume 2, Chapter 7, page 344; Jack D. Welsh: *Medical Histories of Union Generals.* Kent State University Press: Kent OH, 1996, page 53.
20. LL2547, II704, LL2983.
21. MM2748, NN1578, LL1755, LL1567, LL2063.
22. *OR.* Series II, Volume 5, Serial No. 118, Prisoners of War. NN133, OO618.
23. *Fincher's Trades Review.* November 21, 1863, page 100, and October 10, 1863, page 7.
24. RG 393, Department of the Gulf, Volume 241 DG, page 189.
25. NN3925.
26. MM2642.
27. LL2625, LL1367, MM3126.
28. LL2681, LL2780, 3193, MM3225.
29. MM988.
30. NN1458, KK393.
31. OO324.
32. OO327, KK2482.
33. OO1446, KK226, II680, NN3588.
34. OO637, KK52, Alexander Autographs, February 22, 2005.
35. James C. Frasca collection; MicrofilmM345, Roll 48; and Jeanne M. Harald: "Have You Checked Your Pocketknife Lately," *Cultural Resource Management* Volume 19, Number 7, 1996, pages 15-16.
36. Remember When Auctions, June 19, 2002; NN2433; OO1302; Historical Collectible Auctions, May 8, 2003.
37. Nathaniel Philbrick: *In the Heart of the Sea.* Penguin: New York, 2000, page 17.
38. CMSR.
39. Western Manuscript Collection, University of Missouri at Rolla, E467.1.H47, c.2.
40. District of Columbia court records.
41. *The Railsplitter* catalog, September 4, 2003.
42. OO1389; RG 94, Entry 629, Box 1, "Special Scientific Reports, 1860-1880."
43. Martha Hodes: *White Women, Black Men.* Yale University: New Haven, 1997.
44. Indianapolis *Daily Journal*, October 12, 1864; June 8, 1863 (newspaper name is missing from the clipping.)
45. Howard Thomas: *Boys in Blue from the Adirondack Foothills.* Prospect Books: Prospect, NY, 1960, page 221.
46. Victor Hicken: *Illinois in the Civil War.* University of Illinois: Urbana, 1996, page 47.
47. Courtesy George C. Esker III; Connecticut Historical Society.
48. Gary Gallagher, personal communication, 2004.

[49] T. Harrell Allen: *Lee's Last Major General: Bryan Grimes of North Carolina*. Savas Books: Mason City, IA, 1999, page 220; Evan S. Connell: *Son of the Morning Star*. North Point Press: San Francisco, 1984, page 201; Jeffry D. Wert: *Custer*. Simon & Schuster: New York, 1996, page 106.

[50] Thomas P. Lowry: *The Story the Soldiers Wouldn't Tell, op. cit.*, pages 143-151.

[51] Robert K. Krick: *The Smoothbore Volley That Doomed the Confederacy*. Louisiana State: Baton Rouge, 2002.

[52] Thomas P. Lowry: *Tarnished Eagles: the Courts-Martial of Fifty Union Colonels*. Stackpole: Mechanicsburg, PA, 1997, pages 111-115.

[53] Author's collection.

[54] Dale Harter, personal communication, 2005.

INDEX

A

Aapahty, 114
Aarons, David, 192
abortion, 248-250
Abraham Lincoln and Military Justice (Lowry), 12
Accomack County, 39
Adams County, 222-225
Adams, Franklin, 189
Adams, Harrison, 234
Adams, Nicholas, 151
Adams, William, 88
Adolph Hugel, 23
Aiken, Charles, 170
Albany County Penitentiary, 97
Alberts, Charles, 134
Alcorn, Alonzo, 52
Alexander Autographs, 268
Alexander the Great, 196
Alexander, John, 197
All Were Not Heroes (Johnson), 267
Allen, Frank P., 236
Allen, Nicy, 133
Allenberg, George, 124
Alley, Bates, 100
Allison, Sarah, 55, 144
Alpine Coal Mines, 233

Amativeness or the Confessional: A Treatise on Onanism and Self-Abuse, Manhood's Debilities, as Impediments to Marriage and Premature Failure of Sexual Power, to Which Is Added the Confessions of Many Young and Old Men who had been Rescued from the Verge of the Grave (Young), 185
Amelia County, 120
Ames, Martin, 193
Amours of a Quaker, 253
An Appeal to Mothers (White), 184
Anacostia Engine House, 200
Ananias Woods, William, 51
Anderson, Francis P., 34
Anderson, Georgia, 65
Anderson, John, 197
Anderson, Julia, 154
Andrews, Caroline, 141
Andrews, James, 81
Andrews, Maggie, 33
Andrus, Henry, 249
Angus, Dora, 145
Anthony House Hotel, 168
Anthony, E. V., 44
Antinoopolis, 196
Antinous, 196

Aphrodite, 15
Appomattox, 181
Appomattox Courthouse, 180
Aquia Creek, 41
Arbuckle, John, 146
Arcade House, 20
Archer, Albert, 66
Archey, Nancy, 36
Aristophanes
  Peace, 248
Aristotle, 250
Armory Square Hospital, 188
Armstrong, William, 262
Army of Northern Virginia, 181
Arndt, George W., 100
Ashbaugh, Lydia, 222
Ashley, Alice, 30
Astarte, 15
Athens, 15
Atkins, Lucy, 127
Atkinson, William Henry Haywood, 180
Atlantic Ocean, 35
Atwater, Charles, 124
Atwell, James W., 24
Atwood, Jane, 159
Augustus, Theodore, 190
Ausbon, Reuben Y., 78
Austin, Sarah, 98, 99
Autry, 147
Avent, George, 242
Avery, Matthew, 239
Ayres, Gideon, 73

B

Bacon, Orlando, 59
Bagley, James, 242
Bagwell, Ann, 131
Bailey, Ann, 152
Bailey, George H., 240
Baker, Elijah, 152
Baker, Lafayette C., 41
Baker, Patrick, 89
Baker, Wallace, 143
Baker's Alley, 33
Baldwin, Jerome B., 262
Balfour Army Hospital, 37
Ballard, Gabriel, 149
Ballma, Henry, 234
Baltimore Light Infantry, 261
Baltzley, Sarah, 223
Balyou, J. H., 85
Bancroft, Alfred L., 59
Banister, Leander, 150
Bankister, Mary, 143
Banks, Deborah, 47
Barber, E. Susan, 25, 180
Barker, Thomas, 230
Barnes, Grace, 128
Barnes, Joseph K., 188
Barnes, Michael, 162
Barnes, William A., 234
Barnett, Charlotte, 168
Barnett, Mary Ann, 168
Barney, Francis, 208
Barnum, P. T., 100
Barnwell, Jesse, 137
Barry, Harry W., 66
Barston, Hanna, 36
Bartholomew, Alfred, 176
Bartholow, Roberts, 188
  Manual of Instructions for Enlisting and Discharging Soldiers, A, 188
Barton, R. F., 237
Bass, John, 149
Bassford, W.S., 31
Bassler, J. G., 239
Bastide, Libby, 58
Batchelder, James, 259
Bates, Charles, 206
Bates, Emma, 41
Bates, H. G., 190
Baton Rouge, 50, 161
Batson, Joseph, 194

Battle of Antietam, 18
Battle of Fredericksburg, 18, 120, 125
Battle of Gettysburg, 219, 224, 225
Battle of San Jacinto, 96
Bauman, Mary Ann, 242
Baumgarten, Peter, 232
Baxter, Emanuel, 131
Bayne, Mary Jane, 33
Bayou de Large, 163
Beal, Sara, 36
Beals, Martha, 36
Beamer, Mary, 136
Beasly, Ann, 28
Beast of St. Asaph's Street, 22
Beauregard, Pierre G. T., 16
Beazley, Ann, 29
Beck, Franklin, 77
Beckwith, Aston, 132
Bedard, Louise, 132
Beech Island Agricultural Club, 180
Beecher, Thomas K., 110
Beeton, John, 221
Bell, John, 170
Bell, Samuel, 52
Belle Isle, 121
Beloit, Lizzie, 39
Belsford, Anna, 70
Benford, Sally, 156
Benjamin, Judah P., 180
Bennett, John H., 235
Benoit, Alfred, 260
Bentheim, Levi, 117
Benton, Ada Belle, 44
Bergh, Oscar, 205
Bergmann, Edward H., 242
Bergmann, Henry, 177
Bergoon, William, 82
Bernard, James, 144
Berry, Caroline, 37
Berry, Joseph, 77
Berry, Samuel O., 157
bestiality, 226-230

Betts, Eliza, 133
Betty, Edward, 53, 72
Big Black River, 56
Big Yard, 259
Biles, Edwin R., 129
Billingsly, Charles, 148
Billips, Sarah, 16
Birge's Western Sharpshooters, 261
Birney, D. B., 236
Bishop, Catharine, 225
Bishop, Ellen, 91
Bishop, William, 228
Bixby, George, 23
Black, Sid, 67
Bladen, Richard, 73
Bladner, Jacob, 160
Blake, Alfred H., 84
Blake, Mary, 16, 103
Blakely, Thomas, 228
Blankenship, Catherine, 33, 34
Blankenship, Mary, 34
Bliss, D.W., 188
Boasman, Lucy, 30
Bodine, Martha, 64
Bodkin, Catherine, 16
Boerum, Richard, 213
Bohannon, Mildred, 33
Boirs, Charles H., 110
Boisseaux, Virginia, 34
Bolen, Patrick, 167
Bolinger, Mary, 223
Bolivar Heights, 59
Boller, I. M., 106
Bolling Air Force Base, 59
Bond, Thomas B., 124
Bond, William, 241
Bonham, Milledge, 16
Boone, William H., 80
Booth, John Wilkes, 98
Booth, Lizzie, 72
Bordan, Eliza, 36
Boskirk, James Van, 24

Boswell, James Keith, 265
Boudreaux, Omer, 163
Bourne, Joshua, 71
Bourne, Peter, 212
Bower of Beauty, 83
Bower, Henrietta, 224
Bowles, John, 46
Bowling Green, 159
Bowman, Andrew J., 237
Bowman, Sarah, 96
Boyce, Amanda, 120
Boyd, Robert, 221
Boyd, Thomas, 101
Boyd, William H., 258
Boyden, John, 44
Boykin, J. M., 32
Boyle, Felix, 109
Bradburn, James, 148
Bradford, William, 93, 221
Bradly, Moses, 260
Bradshaw, Margaret, 166
Brady, E. H., 59
Brady, George, 194
Bram, Ella, 29
Brandon, Susan, 154
Brannon, Ann, 31
Brannon, Patrick, 31
Branson, Anna Maria, 97
Bravard, Dudley O., 158
Bregstrom, Charles J., 172
Breneman, Amos, 237
Brennan, Ann, 31
Brennan, John, 128
Brewer, Thomas H., 157
Bridge, Joshua, 249
Briggs, Charles, 191, 229
Bright, Robert, 18
Brinniger, David, 168
Brittian, Columbus, 85
Brittingham, William, 37
Brock, Darla, 72
Bronson, Elias, 173

Brooks, Dandridge, 118
Brooks, Hunter, 157
Brooks, Joseph, 41
Brown, Annie, 52
Brown, Calvin, 145
Brown, Charles, 209, 210-211
Brown, Charles F., 44
Brown, Charles H., 88
Brown, Eliza Denison, 264
Brown, H. E., 263
Brown, Henry, 222
Brown, John, 66, 229, 235
Brown, John W., 98
Brown, Josephine, 69
Brown, Martha, 156
Brown, Mary, 29, 165, 172
Brown, Richard, 165
Brown, W. R., 193
Browning, Orville H., 64
Brownson, James T., 102
Brumley (Brumney), Oram, 235
Bruner, James, 257
Bruss, Francis, 151
Bryant, Georgianna Josephine, 162
Bryant, Lewis, 57
Bryant, Lily, 36
Bryte, Levi, 61
Buchannon, Louisa, 29
Buchen, Christian, 224
Bucklew, Sarah, 146
Buckley, James, 237
Budd, Matilda, 167
Budget, Mary, 156
Bugges, Thomas, 221
Bull Mill, 164
Bunch, Jack A., 180
Bunch, Molly, 54
Bundy, Nancy, 40
Bundy, Sally, 40
Burden, William, 168
Burke, James, 237
Burley, Elizabeth, 257

Burnap, Edward C., 111
Burnham, Lissie, 35
Burns, Hugh, 157
Burns, John L., 224
Burns, Thomas, 51
Burnside Barracks, 89
Burson, William, 48
Bussey, Sarah, 42
Butler, Benjamin, 35, 38, 43, 122, 241
Butler, George, 173
Butt, Ann, 37
Byford, John, 228
Byrd, Delia, 29
Byron, G., 202
Byrum, Charlotte, 223
Bywater, George, 65

C

Cahill, William, 128
Cain, William, 182
Cairo, 89
Caldwell, Alexander, 135
Calhoun, John C., 252
Callan, Samuel, 170
Cam, Maria, 29
Cambridge, Sissy, 136
Cameron, Donaldina, 95
Cameron, Simon, 205
Camp Barry, 102, 172
Camp Butler, 89, 126, 176
Camp Cadwallader, 192
Camp Conness, 262
Camp Curtin, 109
Camp Dawson, 143
Camp Distribution, 19, 20
Camp Douglas, 90, 176, 177, 241
Camp Flat Rock Creek, 170
Camp Floyd, 95
Camp Griffin, 232
Camp Hamilton, 121, 238
Camp Liberty, 166

Camp Lowell, 204
Camp Moore, 99
Camp Moorhead, 155
Camp Nelson, 65
Camp of Contrabands, 132
Camp Parapet, 51, 163
Camp Parole, 190
Camp Piatt, 58, 59
Camp Sheridan, 127
Camp Stoneman, 58, 59, 101
Camp Supply, 205
Camp Union, 94, 229
Camp Wickliffe, 159
Camp Wilkes, 39
Camp, Lawson, 151
Campbell, Mary, 173
Campbell, Sylvia, 147
Campbell, William, 112
Canby, E. R. S., 110, 257
Canterberry Girls, 24
Cape Elizabeth, 175
Cape Fear River, 132
Cape Girardeau, 165
Capps, William, 85
Capron, John, 51
Carey, James, 125
Carnes, Anne, 173
Carnes, Eliza, 173
Carpenter, Franklin, 90
Carrigan, John, 232
Carrington, Henry, 88
Carroll, Benjamin, 151
Carroll, James A., 158
Carroll, Susan, 158
Carson, Joseph, 52
Carson, Stephen L., 233
Carson, William, 29
Carson, William D., 21
Carter, Ann, 28
Carter, Charles, 77
Carter, Eli, 37
Carter, Richard W., 265

Carter's Woods, 190
Casey, John, 152
Cassle, John, 260
Castle Godwin, 259
Castle Thunder, 33, 34
Catholic Church, 183, 218
Catoosa County, 148
Caulfield, Patrick, 261
Cavano, Ann, 97
Cedar County, 165
Cedar Creek, 120
Central Knob, 156
Cephas, Albertine, 33
Cerow, Eli, 112
Chaillou, Julius, 261
Champlin, Thomas, 36
Chaplin, Prince, 139
Chapman, Marion, 211
Charles, Gertrude, 47
Charters, William, 147
Chase, Lucy, 36
Chattanooga, 156, 236, 266
Chattanooga Vibrator, 186
Chaucer, 115
Cheney, Richard, 233
Cheney, Samuel, 233
Chesapeake Bay, 35
Chilcoat, Joshua, 236
Childers, Josh, 141
Chinock, William C., 162
Choctaw County, 155
Christian, Emeline, 118
Christiansburg, 42
Churchill, Winston, 208
Cincinnati Venereal Hospital, 249
City of Cleveland, 90
Civil War, 11
  abortion, 248-250
  erotic folk art, 254-257
  malediction, 231-247
  pornography, 252-254
  sexual behavior, 11-14
  bestiality, 226-230
  contraception, 250-251
  cross-dressing, 257-259
  homosexuality, 197-208
  masturbation, 187-193
  prostitution, 15-113
  rape, 114-182
  venereal diseases, 251-252
  tattooing, 263
Clague, John T., 59
Claibourne County, 151
Clark, Caroline, 223
Clark, Charles, 125, 174
Clark, D. M., 78
Clark, Frances, 45
Clark, George R., 95
Clark, Jerome (Sue Munday), 257
Clark, Kelly, 140
Clark, Mollie, 64
Clark, Robert, 150, 237
Clark, Samuel, 120
Clark, Till, 111
Clary, R. E., 259
Clary, Richard, 146
Clay County, 166
Clay, Peter, 120
Clayton, Francis Louisa, 258
Clayton, Sam, 258
Clegg, Jo, 168
Clickner, Isaac, 93
Cliff, Zeno, 151
Clifford, James, 241
Clinton, Kate, 29
Clipper Ship Louise—Larry's journey, The (Hause), 242-243
Cloud's Mill, 40, 119
Cockburn, George, 116
Coddington, William, 100
Coffin, Gilpin, 213
Cohron, Elizabeth, 145
Colburn, Leah, 40
Cole, Gary, 255

Coleman, Clara, 28
Coleman, Mildred, 28
Coleman, William, 51
Colen, Enoch, 236
College of Notre Dame of Maryland, 180
Collins, Charles, 37
Collins, Ellen, 136
Collins, George W., 137
Collins, James, 90
Comber, Michael P., 236
Commodore Hull, 194
Commodore Reed, 194
Commodore's Pump, 145
Compiled Military Service Records (CMSR), 267
Compton, Sarah Ann, 117
Concordia Grocery, 85
Confederate States Military Prison, 30
Confederate States of America, 25
Confederate Troops
　Alabama
　　4th Reserves, 32
　　9th Infantry, 27, 78
　Arkansas
　　1st Riflemen, 79
　Mississippi
　　5th Infantry, 57
　North Carolina
　　1st Sharpshooters, 243
　　57th Infantry, 30
　South Carolina
　　10th Cavalry, 252
　　12th Infantry, 229
　　14th Infantry, 180
　　6th Infantry, 229
　　Palmetto Sharpshooters, 38, 259
　Tennessee
　　14th Cavalry, 154
　　3rd Mounted Infantry (Lillard's Regiment), 56, 181, 235
　Virginia
　　1st Cavalry, 265
　　10th Battalion Heavy Artillery, 33
　　Richmond Fayette Artillery, 30
　　59th Infantry, 34
Confederate War Department, 181
Conine, William, 82
Conkling, Roscoe, 199
Conley, James, 212
Conner, John, 200
Connerton, Margaret, 25
Connor, Arthur, 21
Connors, Ritter, 144
Consor, Prince W., 215
Constitutionalist, 259
contraception, 250-251
Cook, Charles, 131
Cook, George M., 45
Cook, John, 143
Cook, Richard, 256
Cooney, James M., 90
Cooper, Clara, 36
Cooper, Edward, 162
Cooper, Owen, 128
Copeland, Jenny, 36
Copelind, George, 213
Cordrey, Francis, 63
Core, William, 91
Corey, Robert, 137
Corner, Stewart, 222
Cornett, John, 27
Cornish, John, 131
Corypheus, 51
Cotzenberger, John, 146
Couch, Marvin, 57
Courier Journal, 265
Covington Pike, 158
Cowan, William, 221
Cowdrey, Samuel, 147
Cowing, John, 137
Cox, Frederick, 156
Cox, Isaac, 156
Cox, James J., 29
Cox, John C., 65

Cradle, Rebecca Ann, 130
Craft, Letitia, 132
Crandall, Avery, 222
Crane, Orville, 209
Craney Island, 116
Crawford, Fanny, 118
Craycroft, Thomas, 77
Cresiday, Thomas, 192
Cricket, 257
Crocker, Lemuel C., 41
Cronan, William, 239
Crook, George, 59
Cropps, Robert E., 158
Crosier, Martin, 78
cross-dressing, 257-259
Crow, John, 74
Croxen, Jerry, 119
Crozier, Robert, 137
Crum, Lewis Y., 194
CSS *Florida*, 216
Culp, Benjamin, 98
Culpeper, 41
Cumberland Gap, 77
Cummings, Emma, 33
Cummings, Frances, 164
Cummings, George G., 98
Cummings, Green, 142
Cummings, Mary A., 142
Cunningham, John, 263
Cunningham, R. M., 74
Curran, Daniel, 205
Curren, Owen, 128
Currituck County, 132
Curtis, George, 214
Curtis, Thomas B., 163
Custer, George Armstrong, 264
Cutlett, Alfred, 135
Cutsinger, William, 148
Czapkay, L. J., 263

D

Daggett, Willard, 208
Daily Advertiser, 110
Daily Constitutional Union, 97
Daily Enquirer, 187
Daily Examiner, 262
Daily Journal, 249
Daily Times, 244
Daily Whig, 26, 27, 30-31, 33-34, 34
Daley, E. J., 109
Daly, Owen, 41
Dalzell, James, 152
Dancy, John, 152
Danforth, Samuel, 184
Daniels, Edward S., 140
Daniels, Herbert, 193
Daniels, Jabez, 99
Darr, Joseph, 258
Daughters of Union Veterans, 42
Davenport, Mary, 33, 221
Davidson County, 152
Davis, Benjamin, 164
Davis, Burke
  The Civil War: Strange and Fascinating Facts, 119
Davis, David, 95
Davis, H. D., 17
Davis, Henry, 138
Davis, Jefferson, 227
Davis, Jenny, 88
Davis, John, 137
Davis, Leander, 172
Davis, Martha, 162
Davis, Robert, 259
Davy, Peter B., 91
Dawson, John C., 32
Dawson, Thomas, 127
Day, A. F., 90

Day, Mary Ann, 84
Day, Robert, 37
Day, William, 237
Dean, Bessie, 67
Dean, Julia, 98, 99
Dean, Richard, 193
Dearborne, F.M., 193
Declute, Chauncey, 45
Deep Run Road, 117
Deery, James, 141
Degroff, Moses, 224
Deir el Medina, 114
Delaney, Patrick, 258
Delta Queen, 53
DeMerritt, Josephine, 25, 29, 30
Democrat, 83
Dennis, Betsy, 170
Dennis, Eli, 52
Dennis, Mary, 152
Denton, Sarah Ann, 46
Dermady, W. C., 190
Desmarres Eye and Ear Hospital, 260
DeSoto, 215
Devall's Bluff, 93
Devil's Den, 220
Devlin, William, 117
Devore, Warren, 66
Dew Drop Inn, 34
DeWald, Nik, 176
Dickenhoff, Philip, 207
Dickerson, Constantine, 190
Dickerson, John, 148
Dickerson, Louisa, 148
Dickson, James, 152
Dietz, Pauline, 84
Dieudonné, 227
Dile, Mary, 155
Dispatch, 25, 26-30, 182
Dix, John A., 199

Dixon, Howard, 138
Dixon, James, 151
Dixon, M., 82
Dixon, Nellie, 84
Dixon, Patrick, 202, 203
Dobson, Ann, 27
Dobson, Thomas, 27
Doctor Andrus' Medicines, 249
Dodd County, 47
Doe, Robert J., 99
Doherty, Frank, 241
Dole, John, 102
Donahoe, Mary, 31
Donaldson, Frank A., 41
Donovan, Michael, 208
Dorn, William Van, 35
Dosier, Willson, 132
Doubleday, C. S., 137
Douglas, Harriet, 47
Douglas, Mary, 74
Dowd, Daniel, 111
Downey, Johana, 203
Downey, Thomas, 202, 203
Downing, Sarah, 164
Doxie, James W., 100
Doyle, James, 260
Doyle, John, 144
Doyle, Mary, 47
Doyle, Sara, 47
Dr. Dewees' Female Monthly Regulator, 249
Dr. Hall's American Periodical Pills, 249
Drake, Rebecca, 132
Drew, J. R., 16
Drewry's Bluff, 39
Driscoll, Mary, 30
Drum Barracks, 260
Drummondtown, 39
Drummondtown Jail, 40
Dry Tortugas, 19, 143, 145, 153, 258

Dubois, Belle, 170
Dudley, John, 107
Dudley, Joseph, 19
Dugan, Charles, 232
Dugger, Mary E., 149
Duncan, Henry, 153
Duncan, John, 181, 223
Duncan, W. H., 224
Dunham, Gideon H., 64
Dunn, George, 232
Dunn, Molly, 57
Dunn, Sarah, 168
Dunning, Edward H., 51
Dunwoody, Samuel, 153
Dye, Mohittabol, 221

E

E. Clampus Vitus, 94
Eagle Bar Room, 85
Earhart, Thomas I., 262
Earnshaw, Charles, 73
Ebert, Andrew, 224
Eck, John, 224
Eck, Julia Ann, 223, 224
Edmonson County, 158
Edwards, Ann, 34
Edwards, Lot, 125
Edwards, Martha, 31
Egan, John, 174
Elders, Jocelyn, 194
Elephant Butte Reservoir, 95
Elizabeth City County, 37
Elking, Joseph, 74
Ellenbeck, Robert E., 40
Elliott, Frederick, 259
Ellis, David, 153
Ellis, Frances, 167
Ellis, James H., 45
Elmsley, James, 260
Elting, Alexander, 50
Elwell, E. G., 128

Emery, A. E., 193
Emery, George W., 192
Emery, John, 221
Enger, Frank, 143
Engle, James, 158
Englebrecht, Ferdinand, 69
English, E. B., 108
Ennis, Laura, 125
Ennis, Thomas, 134
Enquirer, 26, 27
Enright, Honora, 29
Enright, Nora, 29
Enslin, Gotthold, 197
erotic folk art, 254-257
Erwin, Prudentia, 242
Escort, 37, 260
Espey, Louisa, 29
Estes, John, 166
Estes, Thomas, 165
Etheredge, Mary, 36
Eustace, John, 101
Evans, David, 261
Evans, Henry, 66
Evans, I. M., 261
Evans, William, 164
Evening Whig, 179
Every Man His Own Doctor, 248
Ewing, Ida, 73
Examiner, 26, 31, 34, 39

F

Failey, Frank, 130
Fair Jenny, 244
Fair Maid's Song When All Alone, The, 243-244
Fairbrother, Henry, 166
Fairfax County, 119
Fairfax Seminary, 42
Falkenberg, Hermann, 42
Farara, Lana, 43
Farmer, Catharina, 155

Farragut, David, 215
Farrell, James F., 173
Farrell, William, 198
Faust, Ernest, 257
Fears, Louisa, 121
Federal Triangle, 98
Federal Troops
  Other Federal Units
    1st U.S. Veteran Volunteers, 172
    2nd U.S. Volunteers, 235
    9th U.S. Veteran Volunteers, 260
  Regular Army
    2nd U.S. Dragoons, 95
    2nd U.S. Cavalry, 259, 260
    3rd U.S. Cavalry, 95, 169
    4th U.S. Cavalry, 146
    5th U.S. Cavalry, 75, 174
    6th U.S. Cavalry, 204
    1st U.S. Artillery, 19
    2nd U.S. Artillery, 185, 232
    3rd U.S. Artillery, 44, 175
    4th U.S. Artillery, 69
    5th U.S. Artillery, 128, 156
    1st U.S. Infantry, 51
    4th U.S. Infantry, 174
    6th U.S. Infantry, 202, 204
    8th U.S. Infantry, 110, 185
    9th U.S. Infantry, 207, 257
    11th U.S. Infantry, 89
    13th U.S. Infantry, 74, 76
    14th U.S. Infantry, 111, 175, 208, 257
    15th U.S. Infantry, 95, 263
    16th U.S. Infantry, 75, 76, 146
    17th U.S. Infantry, 175
    19th U.S. Infantry, 49, 88
  State Regiments
    Alabama
      1st Cavalry, 135
    Arkansas
      1st Cavalry, 258
    California
      2nd Cavalry, 96, 229, 262

      1st Native Cavalry, 260
      1st Infantry, 95, 171, 237
      3rd Infantry, 96, 207, 241, 259
    Connecticut
      1st Cavalry, 105
      1st Light Artillery, 17
      8th Infantry, 37, 121
      9th Infantry, 50
      11th Infantry, 42
      14th Infantry, 20
      21st Infantry, 262, 264
    Delaware
      1st Infantry, 109
    District of Columbia
      1st Cavalry, 121
      1st Infantry, 18, 24
      2nd Infantry, 21, 39, 42
    Illinois
      2nd Cavalry, 65, 81
      6th Cavalry, 228
      7th Cavalry, 71
      8th Cavalry, 265
      10th Cavalry, 51
      12th Cavalry, 235, 257
      14th Cavalry, 82
      15th Cavalry, 206
      16th Cavalry, 52, 176
      17th Cavalry, 166
      2nd Light Artillery, 152, 154, 233
      Henshaw's Battery, 242
      4th Infantry, 152
      10th Infantry, 138
      12th Infantry, 56, 74, 151
      16th Infantry, 76, 156
      19th Infantry, 74
      21st Infantry, 64
      28th Infantry, 80
      31st Infantry, 159
      32nd Infantry, 70
      36th Infantry, 154, 264
      37th Infantry, 84
      39th Infantry, 253

41st Infantry, 159
43rd Infantry, 93
48th Infantry, 149
52nd Infantry, 48
58th Infantry, 56
59th Infantry, 164
82nd Infantry, 146
83rd Infantry, 78, 153
89th Infantry, 238
108th Infantry, 157
117th Infantry, 238
124th Infantry, 56
146th Infantry, 89
149th Infantry, 48
155th Infantry, 77
9th Mounted Infantry, 133
33rd Veteran Volunteers, 55

Indiana
  1st Cavalry (Stewart's Cavalry), 63, 228
  3rd Cavalry, 154, 234
  7th Cavalry, 71
  13th Cavalry, 88
  1st Heavy Artillery, 106
  7th Light Artillery, 148
  12th Light Artillery, 73
  14th Light Artillery, 194
  22nd Infantry, 155
  33rd Infantry, 80, 153
  35th Infantry, 77, 155
  36th Infantry, 206
  44th Infantry, 235
  52nd Infantry, 141
  68th Infantry, 191
  71st Infantry, 89
  72nd Infantry, 156
  90th Infantry, 88
  93rd Infantry, 258
  120th Infantry, 44
  123rd Infantry, 194
  145th Infantry, 49, 148, 150

  153rd Infantry, 87
  16th Mounted Infantry, 163

Iowa
  2nd Cavalry, 72
  3rd Cavalry, 148
  6th Cavalry, 177
  7th Cavalry, 95
  8th Cavalry, 65
  6th Infantry, 134
  10th Infantry, 165
  12th Infantry, 69
  19th Infantry, 52
  8th Veteran Volunteers, 260

Kansas
  9th Cavalry, 170
  11th Cavalry, 165
  1st Infantry, 56
  2nd Infantry, 170
  10th Infantry, 81, 82

Kentucky
  2nd Cavalry, 147
  6th Cavalry, 67
  7th Cavalry, 154
  54th Cavalry, 158
  9th Infantry, 80
  10th Infantry, 66
  48th Infantry, 66
  39th Mounted Infantry, 158
  40th Mounted Infantry, 66

Louisiana
  1st Cavalry, 141, 143
  2nd Cavalry, 51
  11th African Descent Infantry, 238

Maine
  6th Infantry, 232
  8th Infantry, 118, 137
  9th Infantry, 207
  15th Infantry, 144
  17th Infantry, 129, 192
  19th Infantry, 23
  21st Infantry, 191

30th Infantry, 63
1st Veteran Volunteers, 106
Maryland
1st Cavalry, 42, 239
1st Light Artillery, 234
Baltimore Light Infantry, 261
2nd Infantry, 130, 158
5th Infantry, 240
Massachusetts
2nd Cavalry, 106
4th Cavalry, 118
5th Cavalry, 173
2nd Heavy Artillery, 261
3rd Heavy Artillery, 101, 172
17th Infantry, 232
20th Infantry, 127
23rd Infantry, 46
26th Infantry, 162
27th Infantry, 37
54th Infantry, 229
55th Infantry, 143
57th Infantry, 111
Michigan
1st Cavalry, 99
2nd Cavalry, 91
3rd Cavalry, 96
6th Cavalry, 126
11th Cavalry, 66
1st Light Artillery, 77
1st Infantry, 106
4th Infantry, 90
5th Infantry, 90
7th Infantry, 121
12th Infantry, 93, 260
14th Infantry, 156
15th Infantry, 153
18th Infantry, 76
20th Infantry, 65
26th Infantry, 117
27th Infantry, 100
28th Infantry, 45

12th Veteran Volunteers, 93
16th Veteran Volunteers, 120
Minnesota
2nd Cavalry, 91
6th Infantry, 92
10th Infantry, 82
Mississippi
1st Mounted Rifles, 71
Missouri
1st Cavalry, 70, 93, 164, 191, 241
3rd Cavalry, 93, 164, 168
4th Cavalry, 238
9th Cavalry, 85
11th Cavalry, 81
12th Cavalry, 82, 164
13th Cavalry, 83, 258
1st State Militia Cavalry, 164
2nd State Militia Cavalry, 166
4th State Militia Cavalry, 85
8th State Militia Cavalry, 164, 236
9th State Militia Cavalry, 84, 85
2nd Light Artillery, 234
1st Infantry, 154
6th Infantry, 165
7th Infantry, 71
8th Infantry, 238
10th Infantry, 49, 170
14th Infantry (Birge's Western Sharpshooters), 261
17th Infantry, 169
23rd Infantry, 84
24th Infantry, 86
25th Infantry, 166, 167
35th Infantry, 260
40th Infantry, 143
41st Infantry, 81
51st Infantry, 257
Winkelmaier's Pontonier Company, 207
Nevada
1st Infantry, 237

New Hampshire
  2nd Infantry, 119
  5th Infantry, 173
  7th Infantry, 234, 238, 240
  8th Infantry, 111
  10th Infantry, 123
  14th Infantry, 98
  8th Veteran Volunteers, 141
New Jersey
  1st Cavalry, 204
  2nd Cavalry, 71
  1st Light Artillery, 42, 192
  4th Light Artillery, 37
  5th Light Artillery, 99, 233
  4th Infantry, 239
  7th Infantry, 20
  10th Infantry, 19
  11th Infantry, 20
  13th Infantry, 240
  33rd Infantry, 132
New Mexico
  1st Cavalry, 241, 242
New York
  1st Cavalry, 258
  2nd Cavalry, 67, 121
  3rd Cavalry, 131, 133
  4th Cavalry, 98, 127
  5th Cavalry, 124
  6th Cavalry, 40
  10th Cavalry, 107, 239
  13th Cavalry, 119
  14th Cavalry, 237
  16th Cavalry, 197, 198
  19th Cavalry, 235
  20th Cavalry, 35, 123, 125, 128
  25th Cavalry, 234
  1st Cavalry Veteran Volunteers, 58
  2nd Cavalry Veteran Volunteers, 237
  1st Heavy Artillery, 172
  2nd Heavy Artillery, 240
  3rd Heavy Artillery, 172
  4th Heavy Artillery, 206
  5th Heavy Artillery, 20, 234
  9th Heavy Artillery, 101
  10th Heavy Artillery, 19
  13th Heavy Artillery, 36
  15th Heavy Artillery, 228
  16th Heavy Artillery, 38, 241
  1st Light Artillery, 123, 257
  2nd Light Artillery, 232
  3rd Light Artillery, 258
  33rd Light Artillery, 124
  3rd Independent Battery (New York Light Artillery), 238
  5th Independent Battery (New York Light Artillery), 102
  30th Independent Battery (New York Light Artillery), 205
  Independent Battery (New York Light Artillery), 140
  1st Engineers, 122
  15th Engineers, 200, 201, 205, 241
  2nd Infantry, 126
  3rd Infantry, 133, 242
  6th Infantry, 236, 237
  9th Infantry, 98
  11th Infantry, 189
  12th Infantry, 98, 132
  18th Infantry, 16
  20th Infantry, 238
  25th Infantry, 261
  30th Infantry, 240
  31st Infantry, 16
  37th Infantry, 260
  39th Infantry, 41
  42nd Infantry, 20
  51st Infantry, 107, 232
  52nd Infantry, 232
  53rd Infantry, 17
  54th Infantry, 242
  56th Infantry, 103, 137
  58th Infantry, 103
  59th Infantry, 257
  62nd Infantry, 265

72nd Infantry, 119, 191
76th Infantry, 38
79th Infantry, 21, 137
89th Infantry, 35
95th Infantry, 111
97th Infantry, 117, 264
99th Infantry, 35
104th Infantry, 125
112th Infantry, 111
117th Infantry, 21
125th Infantry, 173
128th Infantry, 50
131st Infantry, 190
141st Infantry, 110
143rd Infantry, 149
146th Infantry, 103
148th Infantry, 41
152nd Infantry, 206
158th Infantry, 130, 240
159th Infantry, 48
162nd Infantry, 147, 163
170th Infantry, 237, 264
174th Infantry, 237
178th Infantry, 203
5th Veteran Volunteers, 19
54th Veteran Volunteers, 47, 138
90th Veteran Volunteers, 127
1st Mounted Rifles (Infantry), 241
20th State Militia (Infantry), 122

New York
  12th Cavalry, 134

Ohio
  3rd Cavalry, 80
  4th Cavalry, 91
  5th Cavalry, 46, 135, 153, 206
  6th Cavalry, 258
  7th Cavalry, 65
  10th Cavalry, 79
  2nd Heavy Artillery, 159
  1st Light Artillery, 157
  5th Light Artillery, 260
  16th Light Artillery, 51

1st Infantry, 91
6th Infantry, 159
9th Infantry, 142
10th Infantry, 74, 79
12th Infantry, 62
15th Infantry, 170
18th Infantry, 49
22nd Infantry, 71, 239
33rd Infantry, 193
40th Infantry, 239
49th Infantry, 155
58th Infantry, 55
59th Infantry, 64
61st Infantry, 146
62nd Infantry, 34
66th Infantry, 22
67th Infantry, 237
68th Infantry, 89
78th Infantry, 138
81st Infantry, 153
100th Infantry, 234
102nd Infantry, 73
111th Infantry, 66, 241
115th Infantry, 156
118th Infantry, 153
124th Infantry, 249
125th Infantry, 155
126th Infantry, 63
180th Infantry, 154
194th Infantry, 102
5th Veteran Volunteers, 134
78th Veteran Volunteers, 138
80th Veteran Volunteers, 142

Pennsylvania
  1st Provisional Cavalry, 119
  3rd Provisional Cavalry, 109
  5th Cavalry, 122
  7th Cavalry, 155
  8th Cavalry, 127
  11th Cavalry, 36, 122
  12th Cavalry, 173
  19th Cavalry, 235

21st Cavalry, 39
55th Infantry, 137
2nd Heavy Artillery, 100
3rd Heavy Artillery, 121, 128, 246
5th Heavy Artillery, 117
Paul Jones's Independent Battery, 208
3rd Reserves, 17
5th Reserves, 40
7th Reserves, 18, 117
9th Reserves, 124
28th Infantry, 61
29th Infantry, 48
30th Infantry, 99, 236
45th Infantry, 21
46th Infantry, 108, 238
48th Infantry, 239
55th Infantry, 37, 138, 139
56th Infantry, 98
58th Infantry, 260
62nd Infantry, 120
67th Infantry, 242
74th Infantry, 63
78th Infantry, 234, 235
81st Infantry, 192
82nd Infantry, 246
87th Infantry, 190
90th Infantry, 188
93rd Infantry, 261
99th Infantry, 129
105th Infantry, 126
107th Infantry, 128
115th Infantry, 99
118th Infantry, 41
145th Infantry, 193, 246
148th Infantry, 21
194th Infantry, 107
199th Infantry, 109
201st Infantry, 21
213th Infantry, 107
United States Colored Troops
4th Colored Cavalry, 161
6th Colored Cavalry, 65
1st Colored Heavy Artillery, 135
4th Colored Heavy Artillery, 153, 159
6th Colored Heavy Artillery, 53
7th Colored Heavy Artillery, 51
8th Colored Heavy Artillery, 66
4th Colored Infantry, 132
5th Colored Infantry, 130
6th Colored Infantry, 256
13th Colored Infantry, 150, 151
14th Colored Infantry, 151, 156, 208
16th Colored Infantry, 155, 156
17th Colored Infantry, 73
20th Colored Infantry, 52
25th Colored Infantry, 57
28th Colored Infantry, 89
29th Colored Infantry, 208
30th Colored Infantry, 131
33rd Colored Infantry, 232
35th Colored Infantry, 57, 140, 260
36th Colored Infantry, 240
37th Colored Infantry, 44, 134, 257
38th Colored Infantry, 117
40th Colored Infantry, 261
45th Colored Infantry, 170
46th Colored Infantry, 52
47th Colored Infantry, 162
48th Colored Infantry, 162
50th Colored Infantry, 261
53rd Colored Infantry, 260
55th Colored Infantry, 151
57th Colored Infantry, 168
60th Colored Infantry, 260
66th Colored Infantry, 55
67th Colored Infantry, 256
74th Colored Infantry, 141
79th Colored Infantry, 236
82nd Colored Infantry, 145
84th Colored Infantry, 52
93rd Colored Infantry, 52
104th Colored Infantry, 138
108th Colored Infantry, 55
113th Colored Infantry, 168

123rd Colored Infantry, 64
128th Colored Infantry, 47
137th Colored Infantry, 49
Veteran's Reserve Corps
  1st Veteran's Reserve Corps, 238
  2nd Veteran's Reserve Corps, 21
  4th Veteran's Reserve Corps, 239
  5th Veteran's Reserve Corps, 42, 87, 88
  6th Veteran's Reserve Corps, 100
  7th Veteran's Reserve Corps, 100, 101
  8th Veteran's Reserve Corps, 176
  11th Veteran's Reserve Corps, 98, 105
  13th Veteran's Reserve Corps, 110, 111
  15th Veteran's Reserve Corps, 90, 177, 236
  17th Veteran's Reserve Corps, 87
  19th Veteran's Reserve Corps, 100
  22nd Veteran's Reserve Corps, 232
  23rd Veteran's Reserve Corps, 92
  107th Veteran's Reserve Corps, 176
  2nd Invalid Corps, 137, 241
Fentress Field, 128
Ferguson, Amanda, 28
Ferguson, John, 88
Ferguson, Mehetable, 221
Ferris, Byron, 261
Fessenden, Francis P., 63
Fessenden, William, 22
Fidele (Shakespeare), 225
Fielding, George, 105
Filley, Frank, 241
Finn, James, 156
Finnegan, William, 47
Finnell, Thomas, 166
Fish, William S., 105
Fisher, Ella, 33
Fisher, Philoclea, 199
Fisher, William, 56, 74, 165
Fitch, Andrew, 168
Fitch, Samuel, 65
Fitzallen, Harry, 258
Fitzgerald, Edward, 111
Fitzgerald, F. Scott, 38
Fitzgerald, William, 126
Fitzpatrick, Rose, 29
flag wavers, 259
Flashman, Harry, 66
Flash for Freedom (Flashman), 66
Fletcher, Michael, 101
Fletcher's Chapel, 128
Flood, Allen, 235
Florence, Charles, 239
Flying Eagle, 255
Folly Island, 140
Ford County, 152
Ford, Catherine, 18
Ford, Edward J., 110
Ford's Theater, 240
Foreest, Pieter Van, 186
Forest City, 260
Forrest Hall, 98
Forrest, John, 172
Fort Baker, 207
Fort Bascom, 242
Fort Bayard, 95
Fort Boise, 170
Fort Brown, 96
Fort Campbell, 67
Fort Churchill, 96
Fort Craig, 171, 237
Fort Dodge, 205
Fort Donelson, 154
Fort Federal Hill, 106
Fort Harrison, 122
Fort Hays, 204
Fort Jackson, 162
Fort Lyon, 19, 228
Fort McHenry, 105
Fort McRae, 95
Fort Monroe, 37, 43, 121, 128
Fort Powhatan, 38
Fort Preble, 175
Fort Randall, 177
Fort Ridgely, 202

Fort Rosecrans, 77
Fort Schuyler, 174
Fort Sill, 205
Fort St. Philip, 162
Fort Trumbull, 175
Fort Wingate, 241
Fort Yuma, 171
Fossard, George, 103
Foster, Harriet Ann, 121
Foster, Lisa, 195
Foster, Robert, 102
Fouts, Thomas F., 65
Fowler, Elizabeth, 57
Fowler, F. C.
  Life: How to Enjoy It and How to Prolong It, 185
Fowler, George, 150
Francis, Jenny, 36
Franklin County, 135, 154
Franklin, Benjamin, 197
Franklin, William, 162
Frasca, James C., 255
Fraser, George MacDonald, 66
Frazier, Fanton, 125
Frazier, John, 125
Frederick County, 127
Frederick II (king), 197
Freedom's Child (McCray), 266
Freeman, Adam, 74
French Safe or Cover (Young), 250
French, John, 212
French, Jospehine, 16
Frick, John, 206
Frisby, John, 52
Fritchie, Barbara, 108
Fritz, A., 257
Frossard, Eugene, 19
Fuller, Henry, 237
Funk, Herman, 170

G

G. S. Haskins Company, 250, 261
Gadon, Lion, 228
Gaffney, George, 96
Gailock, Elias, 240
Galbraith, John, 199
Gale, Charles, 201
Gale, Rollin, 23
Galen's Head Dispensary, 249
Gallagher, Hugh, 130, 225
Gallagher, Thomas, 137
Galloupe, Jerry, 148
Gandolph, J. B., 204
Garcia, Lorenzo, 241
Gardner, James, 257
Gardner, William, 162
Garfield, James A., 67
Garity, John, 203
Garrett, George, 200
Garrick, Pat, 33
Garrison, O., 135
Gates, David C., 91
Gates, Horatio, 121
Gautreaux, Felix, 163
Gavican, Michael F., 144
Gaw, Amanda, 155
Geary, Daniel, 119
Gee, George, 72
General Court-Martial Orders (GCMO), 268
Geoghean, William, 124
George, Enoch, 134
George, Thomas, 216
Gepner, Peter, 79
Gerard, Benjamin, 104
Gesner, B., 192
Gettysburg, 190
  sex at, 219-225
Getz, Christian, 236

Gibbons, John, 233
Giddens, Benjamin C., 56
Giesboro Point, 59
Gilchrist, Sarah, 124
Giles County, 153
Gilgamesh, 196
Gillen, Olin, 237
Gillham, Harry J., 92
Gilman, Charlotte, 29
Githens, William H., 75
Gladson, Betsy, 137
Glass, Luckey, 136
Gleason, Mary, 27
Glenn, Millie, 71
Glorious News for the Ladies—A Preventive to Have Children (Rafael), 251
Goad, Benjamin, 227
Godby, George, 237
Godford, Mary Ann, 36
gonorrhea, 252
Goodrich, Eliza, 69
Goodrich, Farrier Germain, 133
Goodwin, John, 147
Goozoof, Lewis, 211
Gordon, Fieldings, 53
Gorman, Thomas, 238
Govro, George, 48
Graham, Jerry, 201
Graham, Michael, 106
Graham, Sylvester
  Lectures to Young Men, 184
Graham, Thomas, 153
Granger, Thomas, 227
Grannan Joseph C., 91
Grant, Ulysses S., 81, 204, 228
Granville County, 135
Grasse, Frank, 206
Gray, Fanny, 33

Gray, John, 126
Gray, Patrick, 50
Green, Jenny, 122
Green, Mary, 221
Green, Molly, 87, 88
Green, Nathanael, 116
Greene, Augustus, 200
Greenwood, Kate, 36
Greenwood, William, 19
Greer, Clara, 141
Gregg, Elias, 79
Gregg's Brigade, 229
Gresham, Richard, 77
Grierson, Benjamin, 205
Griffiths, Mary Jane, 136
Griggs, Charles D., 240
Grimes, Alexander, 69
Grimes, Bryan, 264
Grimes, Nisa, 134
Grippen, James, 138
Grogan, Sarah, 146
Groner (Grover), Virginius D., 234
Groom, John, 234
Grosvenor, George H., 198
Grover, Daniel E., 66
Gunga Wallah Company, 263
Gunter, Agnes Ann, 40
Guy's Gap, 153
Gwynne, William M., 22
Gypsum Creek, 205

H

Hackenberry, Amos, 63
Hadrian (emperor), 196
Haegle, Anna, 169
Haffey, Patrick, 235
Hagadon, Moses, 189
Haire, T. Hamilton, 16

Hakes, George, 126
Hale, Benjamin P., 144
Hale, James W., 153
Haley, John W., 129
Hall, Ann, 171
Hall, C. A., 27
Hall, Catharine, 31
Hall, Charles, 239
Hall, George A., 112
Hall, James F., 122
Hall, John F., 173
Hall, Martha Jane, 153
Hall, Mary Ann, 103
Hall, Van B., 235
Hall, William, 106, 221
Hallion, James, 128
Hamblin, William, 21
Hamilton, John J., 154
Hamilton, Samuel, 234
Hammond, Sarah, 143
Hammond, William, 20
Hammurabi, 114
Hampton County, 37
Hampton Roads, 35
Hampton, Sally, 252
Hanam, Sarah, 57
Hancock, Alvina Ann, 145
Hancock, Winfield Scott, 246
Handy, Maria, 40
Hanley, Lydia, 123
Hanna, John, Jr., 207
Hannel, Eugène, 130
Hanvey, Sarah, 122
Hard Labor Prison, 125
Hardeman, Elizabeth, 30
Hardgrove, Alice, 33
Hardin, 151
Hardley, William, 30
Hardy, James, 33
Hargrove, Alice, 25, 29

Harkins, Hugh, 17
Harmon, C. D., 75
Harnett County, 46
Harold, Walter, 265
Harper, Henry, 211
Harper, William, Jr., 204
Harper's Ferry, 19, 22, 61
Harrington, Anna, 35
Harris, Hannah, 36
Harris, John, 158
Harrison, Frank, 140
Harrison, Mary, 152
Harslett, Michael, 96
Hart, John D., 109
Hart, Sir Basil Liddell, 7
Hart, William, 127
Harvey, Mary, 127
Harvey, Winnie, 152
Hasheesh Candy, 263
Hatfield, Gloucester, 57
Hathaway, Jeanie, 69
Hause, Francis
 Clipper Ship Louise—Larry's Journey,
   The, 242
Havre de Grace, 107
Hawkins, Edward, 106
Hawkins, Fountain B., 66
Hawley, Joseph R., 132
Hawthorne, Aldus, 101
Hayes, Rutherford B., 67
Haywood, Elizabeth, 170
Hazard, Morris, 107, 232
Hazeltine, Robert, 236
Hazen, William, 204
Hazleton, William, 265
Head, George E., 37
Heagy, John, 223
Heape, Euselia, 138
Heape, Mary, 138
Heintzelman, Samuel, 102, 238

Heizer, Louis, 142
Helms, Charles, 240
Helton, Charles, 158
Hemhoffer, George, 100
Henderson, John, 20
Hendricks, Abe, 154
Hendrix, Lee, 243
Hennan, Ransom, 154
Henning, Elizabeth, 91
Henry VIII, 219
Henry, John, 151, 152, 212
Henry, Margaret, 109
Henshaw, Edward, 242
Hensley, William, 165
Henson, Jim, 41
Hepburn, William P., 72
Herbert, Sally Ann, 35
Herd, John F., 165
Herricks, Benjamin, 213
Herter, Anton, 169
Hickey, Patrick, 133
Hickey, Timothy, 84
Hickman County, 158
Hickman, James, 117
Higgins, Daniel, 205
Higgins, John M., 193
High Water Mark, 220
Hill, Eden, 170
Hill, George, 119
Hill, William, 238
Hilton, William H., 163
Hindman, Zelma, 195
Hineley, William, 164
Hinkley, Noah, 21
Hinrichs, Charles F., 262
Hinrichs, Oscar, 41
Hinton, Arthur, 158
Hirdspeth, Mary, 156
Historical Collectible Auctions, 268
Hitchcock, Henry, 34

Hitchings, George, 214
Hobbes, Thomas, 13
Hodges, Thomas, 174
Hoffinger, David, 222
Hoffman, Gustav S., 233
Hogden, James, 126
Holden, Jonathan, 238
Holesworth, R., 32
Holland, Michael, 237
Holland, Perry, 154
Hollister, Frederick, 199
Hollister, George Stanton, 197
Holmes, Corwin, 234
Holmes, William, 98
Holroyed, Joseph, 143
Holt, Joseph, 59, 268
Holter, Louis (Lewis), 190
Holton, John, 239
Hommes, Jacob, 49
homosexuality, 196-218
    discussion, 217-218
    exploitive, 218
    in the Civil War Armies, 197-208
    in the Navy, 208-216
    post-War, 216-217
    pre-Civil War, 196-197
    situational versus essential, 218
Hooker, Annie, 146
Hooker, Joseph, 90, 265
Hooker's Division, 104
Hooks, Thomas, 154
Hoopengamer, G., 141
Hopkins, George, 18
Horn, Elizabeth, 257
Horne, Mary, 29
Horniston, James, 198
Horton, G. G., 198
Hosmer, A. A., 88
Hosmer, N., 177
Hotey, James, 99

Houache, Eugène, 100
Houlihan, Margaret, 150
Houlihan, Susan, 150
House of Prostitution, 16
House, Bruce, 230
Houston, John, 111
Howard, Abbey, 33
Howard, Clarence, 111
Howard, Lydia, 158
Howard, Nellie, 36
Howard. Charles F., 17
Howe, Marshall, 95
Howsley, Fredonia B., 152
Hoyt, Isaac, 74
Hubbard, Thomas, 63
Hudson, Alexander, 154
Huebachmann, Francis, 207
Huffman, Elizabeth, 162
Hughan, James, 232
Hughes, Anne T., 27
Hughes, Robert H., 127
Hughes, Stephen, 229
Hull, Richard, 222
Humboldt County, 207
Humphrey, Albert, 46
Hunt, Lewis C., 202
Hunt, Thomas, 128
Hunter, Charles C., 154
Hunter, Frank, 157
Hunter, Joseph, 147
Hurlbut, Stephen, 51, 163
Hurley, Edward, 145
Hurley, Mattie, 75
Huston, David, 78
Huston, Ormsby H., 69
Hutchins, Catherine, 16
Hutchinson, Ella, 36
Hyatt, Effingham, 260
Hygienic Sponge, 251
Hynes, Timothy, 206

I

Il Porto, 23
Ingram, William, 80
Invalid Corps, 268
Ireland, Robert, 130
Iron Clad, 69, 70
Iron Mountain, 86
Isabella II (queen), 265
Ishtar, 15

J

Jackson County, 236
Jackson Sanitorium, 200
Jackson, A. J., 168
Jackson, Anna, 33
Jackson, Elizabeth, 168
Jackson, J. A., 176
Jackson, James, 137
Jackson, Richard J., 175
Jackson, Stonewall, 265
Jackson, Susan, 119
Jackson, Thomas, 36
Jackson, Washington, 135
Jackson, William, 118
James River, 35, 246
James, Ellen, 27
James, Mary Ann, 66
James, Patsy, 36
James, Sarah, 91
Jamieson, Andrew, 23
Jane, Mary, 203
Jarcke, Geraldine Ann, 136
Jay, Henry, 168
Jeff Davis, 48
Jeffers, George, 19
Jefferson, Thomas, 15
Jenkins, Daniel, 107
Jenkins, David F., 55

Jenkins's Brigade, 229
Jennings, Joseph, 241
Jennison, Julia, 132
Jenny Lind, 41
Jessamine County, 65
John Bell, 260
John, Harvey, 155
Johnson County, 165
Johnson, Andrew, 74, 75, 80, 131, 138, 158, 163, 175, 199
Johnson, Charles, 216, 257
Johnson, Edward, 41
Johnson, Edward C.
  All Were Not Heroes, 267
Johnson, Eliza, 266
Johnson, Ella, 31
Johnson, Henry, 74
Johnson, Jacob, 60
Johnson, James, 27, 45, 215
Johnson, John, 167
Johnson, John C., 214
Johnson, Lizzie, 36
Johnson, Richard W., 78, 157
Johnson, Sarah, 155
Johnson, Sylvester, 143
Johnson, Thomas, 95
Johnson, William, 157
Johnston, George, 228
Johnston, Rachel, 117
Jones, Belle, 30
Jones, Bessa, 37
Jones, Betsey, 135
Jones, Chancey, 36
Jones, Charles, 240
Jones, Dilsey, 131
Jones, Ellen, 27
Jones, Henry, 76
Jones, Henry B., 82
Jones, James E., 61
Jones, Jane, 30

Jones, John H., 89
Jones, John Robert, 266
Jones, Lewis, 239
Jones, Louisiana, 161
Jones, Marcellus, 37
Jones, Martha, 135
Jones, Mary, 145
Jones, Sarah E., 32
Jones, Thomas L., 191
Jones, William, 169
Jones, Worley, 223
Jordan, Charles, 167
Jordan, M. C., 27
Jordan, Michael, 240
Jordan, Thomas, 16
Josephine Bixby-White-Plum-Gwynne, 22-23
Juliet, Arthur, 174
Jusco, Emsa, 42

K

Kanawha County, 58
Kane, John D., 119
Kane, Nicholas, 128
Kane, Patrick, 75
Kane, Pierce, 152
Kane, William, 125
Katzenstein, Charles, 203
Keahl, John, 176
Keck, Truman, 17
Keeling, Martha, 36
Kefover, David, 222
Keiser, Jacob, 258
Keith, Samuel, 150
Keller, Caroline, 175
Keller, James, 29
Kellogg, John H., 184
Kelly, Maria, 103
Kelly, Patrick, 174

Kemp, Isaac, 154
Kemper, Milton, 239
Kennebec, 214
Kennedy, Anna, 45
Kennedy, Eliza, 46
Kennedy, Richard, 137
Kent, Josiah, 56
Kerone, Henry B., 143
Kerr, John, 75
Kerr, Thomas, 75
Kerrigan, James, 261
Ketchum, William A., 241
Keystone State, 215
Khan, Genghis, 114
Kiddy, Paul (or Thomas), 157
Kilgore, Millie, 155
Killain, H. P., 137
Killian, Lucinda, 47
Killian, Susan, 47
Killingsworth House, 62
Kilmer, Washington, 22
Kilpatrick, Judson, 265
Kilpatrick, W. H., 57
Kimball, Andrew, 174
Kimball, Oren, 240
Kimberly, Charles, 111
Kincaid, Edward, 262
Kineo, 214
King, Frederick, 175
King, Georgianna, 33
King, John, 19
King, Kate, 86
King, Mattie, 233
King, Nancy, 76
Kingston, Sarah, 47
Kinney, Catherine, 207
Kinney, Hannah, 175
Kirby, Eliza, 55
Kirksey, Mary, 154
Kirsten, Elizabeth, 232
Kiser, John, 51
Kither, Matilda, 131

Kittler, G. H., 145
Klimmer, Rosine, 75
Kneass, Alonzo, 215
Knight, Abigail, 222
Knight, Thomas, 49
Knight, William, 64
Knowles, Margaret, 172
Knox, Louis, 158
Koerner, Louisa, 100
Korneday, John, 133
Kottman, Mary Jane, 124
Krause, Andrew J., 55
Krick, Julie, 26
Krick, Robert K., 177
Ku Klux Klan, 220
Kunsman, Clement, 232
Kyper, Pocahontas, 33

L

La Fonda Hotel, 18
La Reine Hortense, 51
Lackey, J. R., 215
Lacy, John, 78
Lady Adams Building, 95
Lafave, Sarah, 167
LaGrosse, George, 212
Lake Pontchartrain, 51
Lambert, Helen, 266
Lambert, T. J., 89
Lamond, John W., 71
LaMotte, Sylvester, 161
Lamper, John M., 81
Lamphier, R. M., 47
Lander, Anthony, 168
Landerdal, J. V., 262
Lane, Albert, 148
Lane, Harriet, 126
Lane, Sims, 70
Langford, Charles, 31
LaPointe, George, 121
Lauer, Charles F., 138

Lawler, Thomas G., 67
Lawton, George P., 135
Lazelle, H. M., 199
lead chloride, 252
Leahy, Patrick, 233
Lectures to Young Men (Graham), 184
Ledman, Sara Jane, 124
Lee, Elizabeth, 84
Lee, Harry, 69
Lee, Hattie (a.k.a. Emma Williams), 55
Lee, James, 132, 135
Lee, Mary, 52, 136
Lee, Pocahontas, 34
Lee, Robert E., 52, 180, 224
Lee, S. P., 215
Lee, Sarah, 140
Lee, Susan, 158
Leiber, William, 31
Lemon, Cyrus, 261
Lemon, Levi, 123
Lennox, Robert, 260
Leo, Henry, 99
Leonard, Elizabeth, 268
Letcher, John, 180
Levison, Edward B., 82
Lewis and Clark Expedition, 219
Lewis, Anna, 29
Lewis, Biddie, 158
Lewis, Doras, 93
Lewis, Earle S., 38
Lewis, Emma, 36
Lewis, John, 21, 156
Lewis, Judah, 119
Libby Prison, 30
Libby, George W., 214
Liberty Weekly Tribune, 256
Library of Congress, 219, 242
Lichtenheim, Theodore, 103
Life of Johnny Reb (Wiley), 12
Life: How to Enjoy It and How to Prolong It (Fowler), 185
Liggins, Timpy, 37

Liggon, Elizabeth, 33
Lightfoot, William, 123
Lighthouse Point, 121, 144
Lillard's Regiment, 181
Lillie, Albert, 209
Lincoln, Abraham, 7, 22, 59, 66, 72, 90, 120, 122, 165
Lincoln, Mary Todd, 227
Lindell Gardens, 82
Lindsey, William, 153
Lindsey, William B., 256
Linville, John, 158
Little Compton, 221
Little Hotel, 44
Little River Turnpike, Virginia, 16
Little Rock, 167, 168
Little Rock Missionary Baptist Church, 260
Little Round Top, 220
Little, John, 95
Little, Thomas, 143
Littlefield, Charles H., 264
Livingstone, Charles E., 38
Llewellyn, William, 157
Lock, Joseph, 238
Locker, John, 152
Locust Alley, 28
Lodusky House, 224
Lofton, James, 241
Logan, Amanda, 32
Looby, Thomas A., 46
Lookout Mountain, 234
Loughran, Robert, 122
Louie, Jew, 67
Louis Napoleon Safe, 250
Louis XIV, 53
Louisiana State Appeals Court, 218
Louisville, 209
Louisville Medical Infirmary, 249
Louisville, Kentucky Insane Asylum, 69
Lowney, John, 164
Lowry, Joseph, 100

Lowry, Thomas P.
　　Abraham Lincoln and Military Justice, 12
　　Story the Soldiers Wouldn't Tell, The, 12, 251
Loyd, Elizabeth, 33
Lucretia, 115
Ludlow, William H., 41
Lutz, Polly, 223
Lynch, Amanda, 36
Lynch, Lavinia, 36
Lyon, J. W., 162
Lyons, John, 51
Lyons, Lottie, 92

M

Macgregore, Oram J., 221
Machin, Joseph, 211
Mackey, Michael, 167
Mackley, George, 159
MacLean, Edward, 232
MacNealey, Julia Annie, 264
Madame Cafrada's Female Monthly Pills, 249
Madame Lozier's Female Monthly Pills, 249
Madison County, 143
Madison, James, 221
Madsen, Jacob, 138
Magruder, Henry, 158
Maguire, Joseph, 107
Maguire, Mary, 68
Mahoney, Margaret, 172
Maier, Jeanette, 53
Maitland, William, 16
malediction, 231-247
　　coital suggestion, 233-235
　　excretory epithets, 238-241
　　family relations malediction, 231-233
　　fellate, 237-238
　　miscellany, 246-247
　　poetry and metaphor, 242-246
　　reproductive organs, 235-237
Maley, James, 120
Mallard, Nancy, 152

Malloy, Peter, 119
Manassas Junction, 124
Manchester, Mary, 221
Manderville, Edwin, 238
Manly, Charles, 133
Manning, Patrick, 141
Manokyan, Matild, 104
Manson, Mudgy, 30
Manual of Instructions for Enlisting and Discharging Soldiers, A (Bartholow), 188
Mara, John, 172
March to the Sea, 149
March, Daniel, 223
Marcum's Company, 197
Maria Denning, 55
Market House, 92
Maroney, Ellen, 166
Marriage Guide—A Great Physiological Work or Everyone His Own Doctor (Young), 253
Marsden, Mary, 224
Marsh, Emma, 29
Marshal, Mary, 36
Marshall, Hannah, 221
Marshall, Joseph, 207
Marshall, Martha, 154
Martin, Blanche, 27
Martin, Caroline, 170
Martin, Catharine, 36
Martin, John, 119
Martin, Thomas, 71, 215
Martin, W. L., 57
Martindale, John, 98
Maryland Heights, 62
Maryland Line, 197
Mason, Anna, 157
Mason, Clark, 145
Mason, Eliza, 107
Mason, Lizzie, 92
Mason's Hill, 16
Mastreli, Guizeppi, 216

masturbation, 183-195
  in the Navy, 193-194
  post-War, 194-195
Mather, Sally Maria, 222
Mathews, Camillus, 188
Mathews, Delia, 177
Mathews, Lizzie, 49
Matthew, George, 71
Matthews, Daniel, 107
Matthews, John, 214
Maxfield, Paschal, 189
Maxwell, Fanny, 92
May, George, 153
McAdams, John, 78
McAllister, Lorenzo, 87
McBain, Remus, 85
McBeth, Robert, 201
McBeth, Robert M., 201
McCabe, Maggie, 31
McCafferty, John, 200
McCarthy, Delia, 33
McCarthy, Jeremiah, 191
McCarthy, Patrick, 99
McCarty, Arthur, 138
McClellan's Mistress, 265
McClellan, George B., 22, 236
McCloskey, Joseph, 148
McClune, Hugh, 101
McConly, John, 222
McConoughy, John D., 169
McCord, Allen, 152
McCormic, Sarah Allen, 170
McCormic, William, 91
McCormick Surgical Appliance, 194
McCosh, Thompson, 224
McCoy, Pricey, 123
McCray, Carrie Allen
  Freedom's Child, 266
McCreary, Julius, 107
McCreary, Thomas, 223
McCue, Mary, 126
McCullough, George, 121

McCurdy, Abram, 79
McDonald, John, 238
McDonald, John S., 62
McDonald, Mary, 71
McDonald, Mary E., 71
McDonald, Michael, 21
McDonald, William, 48
McDonough, Alice, 176
McDougal, Elizabeth, 153
McDowell, Irvin, 96
McDowell, Irwin, 181
McFaden, Virginia, 29
McGahern, John, 269
McGee, Daniel, 260
McGee, Edward, 37
McGill, Dennis, 118
McGill, James, 62
McGill, John, 35
McGiven, Millie, 46
McGuire, John, 201
McGuire, Peter, 137
McIntyre, Henry, 232
McIntyre, Thomas, 173
McKean, William W., 215
McKenzie, Marian, 258
McKinley, 153
McKinley, Harriet, 153
McKnight, Robert, 234
McLaughlin, John, 56
McMannus, Jane, 84
McMannus, Robert, 84
McManus, William, 132
McNutt, Joseph, 48
McPhersonville, 138
McSweeney, Frederick, 182
McTier, Mary, 138
Mead, F. J., 53
Mear, Martha, 91
Mecklenburg County, 131
Meek, Albert, 265
Meeker, Daniel, 65
Mehalic III, John, 104

Mellon, James, 239
Melton, Lucy, 31
Melton, Martha, 31
Mendelsohn, Oscar, 138
Meoliff, James, 137
Merklee, John, 240
Merricle, Rufus, 84
Merrill, George, 235
Merrill, Harriet, 257
Merrill, Robert L., 121
Merrimack (renamed the CSS *Virginia*), 35
Metcalf, Henry, 260
Metropolitan Hotel, 199
Metta, Anthony, 76
Mew, Emily, 138
Mexican War, 215
Meyers, Mary, 36
Michael, William, 91
Michener, Alice, 132
Middleton, Hugh, 87
Migrath, John W., 57
Miles, Woodford, 260
Milgate, Edwin, 90
military trials, 12
　general courts-martial, 12
　regimental courts-martial, 12
Millar, Mary, 136
Miller, Elizabeth, 29, 132
Miller, John, 82
Miller, Martha, 36
Miller, Martha Jane, 29
Miller, Maurice, 121
Miller, President, 140
Millman, Henry, 84
Mills, Daisy, 67
Mills, Richard D., 120
Millsparr, Lafayette, 46
Minié ball, 254
Mississippi River, 53
Mitchell, Belle, 43
Mitchell, Emma, 43

Mitchell, Thomas, 122
Mitchelson, Richard, 155
Mittaner, Jacob, 238
Mochica, 197
Monagan, John, 40
Monitor, 35
Montgomery County, 155, 169
Moodie, Maggie, 70
Moon, John, 63
mooning, 264
Moore, Andrew, 191
Moore, Belle, 92
Moore, Ella, 173
Moore, Francis, 173
Moore, George E., 42
Moore, Jackson, 92
Moore, James, 27
Moore, O. H., 205
Moore, Thomas J., 39
Moore, William I., 145
Moran, Patrick, 177
Morgan, E., 215
Morgan, Emily, 96
Morgan, George W., 262
Morgan, John W., 164
Morgan, Martha, 29
Morril, Charles, 238
Morris Island, 207
Morris, Ann, 97
Morris, Catherine, 87
Morris, Delia, 47
Morris, Dick, 104
Morris, John, 81
Morris, Joseph, 212
Morrison, G. F., 36
Morse, Frank W., 204
Morse, Lydia, 36
Mortars, Jerome, 60
Morton, Emma, 105
Moses, Julius, 262
Mott, Valentine, 256

Mountcastle, Mary Ann, 27
Mowers, Cornelius F., 236
Mulby, William J., 107
Mulligan, William, 237
Mullins, David, 46
Mundy, Sue, 158
Munro, William, 96
Munser, Charles, 238
Munson, John, 176
Muntorff, Moses, 222
Murder Bay, 104
Murphreys, Mary, 16
Murphy, Henry, 155
Murphy, Lawrence, 72
Murphy, Martin, 31
Murphy, Peter, 188
Murphy, William, 240
Murray, Henry A., 52
Murray, John, 131
Muscoota, 211
Myers, Dent Wildman, 256
Myers, Eliza, 36
Myers, Rachel, 222
Myers, Sarah, 222
Mytinger, Daniel, 71

N

Nailin, Dow, 158
Nantz, Richard, 30
Narrin, George, 158
Natchez-Under-the-Hill, 53
Natchez-on-the-Hill, 53
Nathans, Camillus, 188
Nathans, Camillus L., 188
National Museum of Civil War Medicine, 250
Neal, Caroline, 134
Nebraska Territory, 69
Needham, Catherine, 27
Needham, Mike, 27
Neely, Elizabeth, 49

Neely, Jane, 222
Neff, Frank M., 163
Nelson County, 159
Nelson, Amelia Caroline, 165
Nelson, Annie, 120
Nelson, Catherine, 16
Nelson, George, 151
Nelson, George W., 239
Nelson, Harriet, 165
Nelson, James K., 119
Nenning, Jonas, 155
Neptune, 212
Nesbitt, William, 90
Neville, Frederick A., 111
New Market Mills, 122
New Orleans Parish Prison, 214
New York, 238
New York City, 252
New York Hotel, 23
New York Independent Battery, 140
Newman, T. A., 89
Newsom, Nancy, 148
Newton, William, 120
Nicholas, David, 107
Nicolay, John, 203
Noah's Ark, 30
Noel, William, 223
Noell, Christian, 47
Noething, Charles, 184
Nolan, Thomas, 240
Nolan, William, 20
Noonan, Patrick, 120
Nore, John, 209
Norris, Frank, 264
North, James A., 194
Northedge, Jane, 172
Northedge, William, 172
Novel, Delia, 31
Nulty, Thomas, 215
Nussbaum, Abram, 103
Nye, William, 75

O

O'Brian, William, 70
O'Brien, Edward, 207
O'Brien, Robert, 168
O'Brien, William, 33, 190
O'Conner, John, 41
O'Donnell, Mary, 31
O'Hanlon, Terrence, 49
O'Keefe, Daniel, 174
O'Murphy, Patrick, 99
O'Neil, Thomas, 76
O'Rourke, Michael, 240
Oakley, Sarah, 36
Occoquan Creek, 124
Official Records of the Union and Confederate Armies, The, 268
Oglesby, T. A., 48
Ohio, 111
Old Courthouse Museum, 245
Old Hero of Gettysburg, 224
Olive Branch, 89
Olson, Peter, 209
onanism, 183
One-Armed Berry, 157, 257
101 Airborne Division, 67
100th Regiment Ohio Volunteers, 148
Orchard, Johnson, 45
Orchard, Pete, 45
Osage, 212
Osborne, Bunkum P., 147
Osborne, John Marion, 177
Oscar, Prentiss, 214
Owens, Lemuel, 110
Oxford English Dictionary, 233

P

Paducah, 159
Paine, Mathew, 17
Paine, William, 184
Palmer, Lewick, 22, 23
Palmer, Thomas, 191
Palmetto Hotel, 44
Palmiter, Elizabeth, 29
Pamunkey River, 126
Paneb, 114
Park Barracks, 65
Parker, Charles, 43
Parker, Charlotte, 36
Parker, Dorothy, 183
Parker, Emma, 45
Parker, John, 98
Parker, Lucy, 51, 175
Parks, Samuel, 229
Pate, Mary Elizabeth, 65
Patrick, Marsena, 38
Paul Jones' Independent Battery, 208
Paul, Private Frank, 165
Peabody, George, 176
Peace (Aristophanes), 248
Pearson, Clara, 46
Pebedy, Frederick, 20
Peckham, James, 238
Peixotto, Grace, 47
Pendergast, Sally, 29
Pendergrast, Susan, 30
penis syringes, 252
Penrose, William H., 99
Perdue, Milton W., 88
Perkins, B. W., 78
Perkins, Henry, 69
Perkins, Lawson, 125
Perry County, 142
Perry, Charles A., 236
Petersburg House, 38
Pettit, Rufus, 22
Pettus, Mary, 27
Petty, Priscilla, 69
Pfister, Joseph, 21
Phelan, Margaret, 28
Philadelphia House, 20
Phillips, James, 29
Phillips, Joseph, 165

Phillips, Sophia, 37
Philo's Army Purchasing Agency, 253
Pickett, A. T., 59
Pickett, Edward, 128
Picking, Henry A., 223
Pierman, Virginia, 122
Pierson, Perry, 153
Piexotto, Grace, 47
Pillson, Samuel, 21
Pilot Knob, 164
Pinckney, Rosina, 139
Pine Bluff, 153
Piner, Elizabeth, 45
Pinion, Elizabeth, 80
Pinola, 211
Pioneer, 92
Pitkins, Edward P., 65
Pittsburgh, 215
Place, Samuel, 233
Plato, 250
Platt, Richard, 206
Plummer, Frank, 207
Poage, Melinda, 166
Pocahontas, 125, 151
Poe, Clarence, 149
Poffy, Margaret, 29
Point Lookout, 173
Point of Rocks, 173
Poor House, 38
Pope, John, 92, 205
pornography, 252–254
Port Hudson, 89, 161
Port Royal, 47, 243
Port Royal Island, 138
Porter, David Dixon, 210
Porter, T. J., 188
Portsmouth, 215
Post, Thomas, 237
Potomac River, 16
Potter, Angelika, 108
Potts, Izatus, 241
Potts, Nixon, 60

Powell, William, 107, 167
Powers, Walter, 187
Poynton, William H., 17
Pratt, Charles, 155
Pratt, Emory F., 111
Preble, James, 132
Prentiss, William, 16
Price, James A., 71
Price, John, 119
Price, John G., 150
Price, Sarah, 84
Prince George's County, 173
Prince Street Prison, 258
Prince William County, 124
Prince, James, 214
Princess Anne County, 123
Princeton, 180
Private Medical Dispensary, 249
Proctor, James F., 258
Proctor, Samuel, 20
Prophilacticum, 263
Prossen, George, 75
prostitution, 13, 15–113
  Deep South, 50–57
    Alabama, 56–57
    Mississippi, 53–56
  District of Columbia, 97–104
  Georgia and the Carolinas, 44–49
    Georgia, 47–49
    North Carolina, 44–46
    South Carolina, 46–47
  houses of
    other terms for, 24–25
  Kentucky, 64–67
  Mid-Atlantic States, 105–109
  Missouri, 81–86
    Rolla, 83–84
    Springfield, 84–86
  other terms for prostitutes, 24–25
  Renaissance Europe, 15
  Roman times, 15
  Sumerian, 15

summary, 112-113
Tennessee, 68-80
  Memphis, 68-73
  Nashville, 73-77
The Heartland, 87-93
  Illinois, 89-91
  Ohio, 91-93
Up North, 110-113
Virginia, 15-43
  Alexandria, 15-25
  Norfolk and Portsmouth, 35-38
  Richmond, 25-35
    red light districts, 25
Way Out West, 94-96
West Virginia, 58-63
Pugh, John, 246
Pulaski County, 168, 169
Pumpkinpile, Peggy, 170
Pungo (Pongo) Bridge, 128
Purcell, Lieutenant Walter, 165
Putnam, 215
Putnam, Azro, 242

Q

Quantrill, William Clarke, 86
Quatles, Virginia, 121
Quinby & Co., 252
Quinn, Samuel, 92

R

Raccoon Ford, 127
Radcliff, Thomas, 16
Radway's Regulating Pills, 249
Rafael's Botanic, 251
Ragan, Harriet, 151
Railroad House, 73
Ralph, Horace, 169
Randolph County, 63
Ransom, Casey, 134
Ransom, Gordon, 119

Raoul, Alfred, 136
rape, 114-182
  Confederate, 179-182
  research possibilities, 177
  summary, 177-178
  Tennessee, 150-160
    Kentucky, 157-159
    West Virginia, 159
  The Carolinas, 130-140
    North Carolina, 130-135
    South Carolina, 135-140
  The Deep South, 141-149
    Alabama, 141-143
    Florida, 143-146
    Georgia, 146-149
    Mississippi, 141
  The West, 161-171
    Arkansas, 167-169
    further West, 169-171
    Louisiana, 161-163
    Missouri, 163-167
  Up North, 172-178
    Connecticut, 175
    District of Columbia, 172-173
    Illinois, 175-177
    Maine, 175
    Maryland, 173-174
    New York, 174-175
  Virginia, 114-129
    Alexandria, 117
    Richmond, 117-119
Rape, John, 79
Raper, John, 89
Rasställer, Anthony, 228
Rathbone, Justus, 236
Raucher, Peter, 122
Ravencraft, Rezin, 60
Rawdon, Lord, 116
Ray, Catherine, 57
Rayburn, Anna, 66
Rayment, Thomas, 201, 202
Raymor, Catherine, 158

Read, Jenny, 28
Reardon, Carol, 220
Rebestok, John M., 49
Record Group, 268
Red Gate, 88
Redding, Benjamin, 138
Redford, Anderson, 57
Redl, Alfred, 217
Redmond, Joseph, 125
Reed, Arthur, 261
Reed, William, 153
Reice, Lizzie, 51
Reidenbach, J. M., 240
Rennick, Ann, 165
Reserve House, 91
Reynolds, John. F., 40
Reynolds, William, 257
Rice, Mary, 144, 266
Rice, Melinda, 266
Richards, Henry B., 262
Richards, James C., 73
Richardson, Agnes, 29
Richardson, Gabriel, 138
Richmond County, 119
Richmond, Kate, 70
Ricketts, John, 215
Riddle, Mary, 27
Ridebok, Albert H., 101
Ridgely, Hibbard, 73
Rife, Joseph B., 204, 205
Riffle, Sarah, 223
Rig Veda, 227
Riker, J. Lafayette, 265
Riker's Island, 258
Riley, James, 82, 155, 229
Riley, John, 142
Riley, John E., 119
Riley, Mary Ellen de, 162
Riley, Thomas, 240
Ripon, Lucy, 35
Rippleogle, Eve, 221
Risley, James S., 70

Ritchey, William G., 76
Ritter, Anna Elisa, 225
Ritter, Charles, 180
Ritter, John F., 70
Rivers, Florence, 33
Rivers, Kate, 20
Rix, Isabella, 31
Roanoke, 214
Robb, Eliza, 151
Robbins, George W., 215
Robbins, Henry, 234
Robbins, Levi, 192
Roberts, John S., 155
Roberts, Sally Ann, 152
Roberts, Thomas, 197
Robertson County, 79
Robinson, Cornelius, 126
Robinson, Elizabeth, 48
Robinson, James, 52, 164
Robinson, Jenny, 236
Robinson, John, 101
Robinson, Kate, 27
Robinson, Virginia, 60
Rock Island, 235
Rockcastle Creek, 158
Rockwell, John W., 78
Rodgers (Rogers), Charles, 246
Rogers, Charles C., 123
Rogers, Sidney, 232
Roland, Martha Delia, 144
Rolin, H., 17
Rollings, Julia, 16
Romulus, 115
Roosevelt, Franklin D., 217
Rose, 151
Rose, Madison, 69
Rose, Sara Jane, 33
Ross, J. A., 88
Ross, Richard, 111
Rossman, Joseph, 205
Round Hill, 120
Round Top Park, 220

Rousseau, Lovell, 153
Rowe's Pump, 138
Rowlands, Sherry, 104
Ruby, Charles, 203
Russell, Elizabeth, 131
Rutherford County, 152
Ryan, James, 261
Ryan, John, 168
Ryan, William, 119

S

Sabine, 213
Sacramento, 94
Sadawhite, Irene Ann, 125
Salazar, Monica, 95
Saline County, 256
Salt Hay Wharf, 21
Salt Lake City, 241, 259, 262
San Francisco National Cemetery, 96
San Quentin Prison, 13, 232, 259
Sanborn, John, 85
Sanderson, Lucy, 75
Sandy Point, 124
Sanford Plantation, 155
Sanitary Health Sponge, 251
Santa Anna, Antonio Lopez de, 96
Santa Rosa Island, 236
Sappington, Lewis, 141
Saunders, Henry, 223
Savage, E. J., 41
Savage, Elizabeth, 221
Savery, J. Edward, 234
Saxton, Rufus, 139
Sayler, John H., 34
Scheerer, George W., 239
Schiffer, William, 131
Schmidt, Frederick, 91
Schoales, Henry, 201
Schoenemann, Rudolph, 92
Schriver, Sarah A., 223
Schroeder, Henry, 93

Schulenberg, Margaret, 127
Schultz, Joseph, 198
Schuster, Minnie, 22
Schyorck, Elizabeth Van, 222
Scott, Henry, 170
Scott, Henry W., 58
Scott, Jenny, 83
Scott, William E., 88
Scranton, Edwin J., 47
Seamon, John W., 202
Sears, John, 83
Second Battle of Winchester, 190
Secret Habits of the Female Sex, 253
Selden, Julia, 29
Self, 54
Sension, Nicholas, 197
Sentinel, 26, 31-33, 34-35, 182, 249, 259
Sergeant, Elijah, 147
Sergeant, Philip E., 64
Seventh Day Adventist Church, 184
Seward, William H., 199
Sewell, John, 67
Shadix, Matilda, 48
Shadrick, Delilah, 79
Shafer, Conrad, 173
Shaffer, William, 222
Shakespeare house, 38
Shakespeare, William
  Fidele, 225
Shannahan, Michael, 27
Sharp, Andrew, 258
Sharp, Catherine, 118
Shearrer, Clementina (Gentle Annie), 95
Shears, George H., 213
Sheely, Mary Ann, 222
Shehan, Michael, 118
Sheldon, Thomas, 49
Shelton, Cynthia, 165
Shenandoah County, 181
Sheppard, John, 117
Sheppard, Thomas, 80
Sheridan, Patrick, 257

Sheridan, Philip, 39
Sherman, William T., 22
Sherriger, Barrent, 50
Shields, Maria, 36
Ship Island, 141
Shirley House, 55
Shirley, W. H., 87
Shoe, N., 93
Shoemaker, Eliza, 41
Shook, James B., 30
Short, Reuben, 80
Shuck, Elizabeth, 64
Shupe, David, 151
Shupe, Pamela, 151
Shuttleworth, William, 215
Sibley, Henry Hastings, 91
Sibley, James, 150
Sickles Barracks, 21
Sickles, Dan, 265
Sidelinger, William, 191
Sievers, Max, 102
Silver City, 95
Silver Lake No. 2, 155
Simmons, Charles, 43
Simms, Nancy, 173
Simms, Samuel A., 88
Simpson, Fanny, 132
Simpson, Fred R., 191
Simpson, George L., 55
Simpson, Martha E., 169
Sinclair, Madeline, 69
Sing Sing Prison, 136
Singleton, Ann, 36
Sipes, Alexander, 92
Sir James Clark's Celebrated Female Pills, 249
Skidmore, Mary, 159
Skipper, I. G., 145
Slabtown, 37
Slaybaugh, Henry, 222, 227
Slaybaugh, Solema, 222
Sloan, Barnett, 16

Slocum, Henry W., 134
Slough, John P., 17, 18
Small, Peter, 141
Smart, Jerome, 86
Smith, A. C., 85
Smith, Alex, 121
Smith, Andrew, 122
Smith, Asa G., 117
Smith, Betsy, 167
Smith, Cecillia, 30
Smith, Charles, 74
Smith, Charles B., 266
Smith, Charlie, 264
Smith, G., 234
Smith, George H., 67
Smith, Georgianna, 36
Smith, Gustavus, 77
Smith, Hampton, 145
Smith, Henry, 117
Smith, James, 148, 233
Smith, James C., 155
Smith, John, 75, 107, 171
Smith, John A., 30
Smith, John M., 143
Smith, John W., 63
Smith, Joseph, 235
Smith, Lena, 52
Smith, Lewis, 236
Smith, Lucy, 29
Smith, Martha D., 164
Smith, Martin B., 62
Smith, Mary J., 31
Smith, Nancy Ann, 145
Smith, Nathaniel, 221
Smith, Pompey, 167
Smith, Rebecca, 103, 139
Smith, Samuel P., 96
Smith, William H., 146
Smith, Willie Ann, 25
Smythe, William C., 232
Snow, Henry, 89, 126
Snyder, Charles, 99

Snyder, William, 224
Snyder's Bluff, 238
Social Evil Registration Law, 83
Socrates, 196, 250
Soldier's Rest, 20, 21
Solomon, Edward, 146
Somers, Mary, 60
Sophronia, 237
Sorg, Lewis, 123
Southern Confederacy, 38
Southwick, John, 128
Spades, Jerry, 123
Spanish fly (cantharides), 262
Sparks, George, 36
Sparks, P. J., 79
Spear, Margrette, 221
Spectator, 43
Spencer County, 158
Spencer, Lloyd, 143
spermatorrhea, 263
Sperry, Charles, 119
Sporting Times, 253
Spurgeon, Franklin, 88
St. Elizabeth's Hospital, 185, 187
St. Helena Island, 139
St. Patrick, 227
Stableford, Alexander, 49
Stack, Caroline, 175
Stafford, 145
Stambaugh, Mary, 222
Stanford, Hannah, 36
Stanhope, 261
Stanton, Edwin, 199
Star, 97
Star, Ellen Nellie, 98
Starks, Austin, 147
Staten Island, 116
Stearns, Fidelia, 99
Steel, H. C., 257
Steele, Joseph M., 76
Stephens, Henry, 44

Steuben, Baron Frederich Wilhelm Ludolf Gerhard Augustin von, 197
Stevens, Abner, 150
Stevens, Elizabeth, 74
Stevens, George W., 258
Stevens, Mary, 30
Stevensburg, 41
Steward, Jeannie, 47
Stewart, Charles, 209
Stewart, Elizabeth, 62
Stewart, Fannie, 36
Stewart, Frederick, 35
Stewart, H. Clay, 35
Stewart, Mary, 37
Stewart, Samuel, 164
Stewart, William, 211, 238
Stewart's Cavalry, 63
Stiles, Mary, 119
Stippich, Jacob, 241
Stoddard, George R., 89
Stoerker House, 63
Stone, Peter, 128
Stones River, 258
Stopples, Charles, 55
Story the Soldiers Wouldn't Tell, The (Lowry), 12, 251
Stough, Adam, 223
Stough, Eliza, 223
Strauss, Peter, 98
Streeter, Tebina, 260
Strickler, Wilson, 39
Stubbs, Ann, 45
Stuckenberg, John H. W., 193
Stuckenberg, ohn H. W., 246
Stutts, Walter F., 157
Sugar Hill, 37
Sullivan, John, 27
Sullivan, Patrick, 182
Sullivan, Sarah, 27
Sullivan, Thomas, 123
Summers (Somers), Samuel Mathews, 181

Surriver, Henry, 128
Swann House, 62
Sweet, Joshua, 202
Swellenhas, Henry, 51
Swift, Silas, 111
Swift, William, 156
syphilis, 251

T

Taber, Martha, 135
Taft, Jerome, 257
Taggart, John H., 66
Talbot, C. A., 234
Taliaferro, William Booth, 123
Tapley, F., 20
Tarleton's Plantation, 237
tattooing, 263
Tawney, Elizabeth, 224
Taylor, Charles F. Fletch, 86
Taylor, Clorinda, 121
Taylor, Eliza, 98
Taylor, Frances, 29
Taylor, George, 186
Taylor, J. W., 260
Taylor, John, 29
Taylor, Mary, 34
Taylor, Robert F., 58
Taylor, Solomon E., 223
Temple, Samuel, 70
Terry, Samuel, 184
Teufert, Gene D., 230
Thatcher, Henry K., 211
The Civil War: Strange and Fascinating Facts (Davis), 119
The Land Shark, 78
The Lubricator, 62
The First Rhode Island Battery, 18
The Vineyard, 105
Thistleton, George, 42
Thomas, 105

Thomas (son of Sarah Billips), 16
Thomas, Alice, 33
Thomas, Ann, 30, 33
Thomas, Catherine, 122
Thomas, Eliza, 35
Thomas, George, 80
Thomas, George H., 67
Thomas, John, 159
Thomas, Julia, 128
Thomas, Louisa, 155
Thomas, Lucy E., 123
Thomas, William, 215
Thomas, William R., 108
Thomason, William, 206
Thompson, Ann, 31
Thompson, David, 42
Thompson, Donald D., 195
Thompson, James M., 64
Thompson, Robert, 42
Thompson, Sue, 45
Thrasher, Mary, 175
Throg's Neck, 174
Throops, Dan, 221
Tibbals, Horatio, 62
Tierce, Daniel, 151
Tiffany, John W., 100
Tillotson, George W., 35
Timmons, Lucy, 31
Titus, John, 20
Tivoli Gardens, 136
Todd, David, 256
Todd, Levi, 256
Tolson, Bretty, 131
Tomlinson, T. C., 82
Townsend, Enoch, 253
Trail, Jane, 76
Travers, Annette, 105
trench art, 254
Trent, Lavinia, 27
Trevillian Depot, 264
Tribune, 73

Tripler, Charles, 256
Trost, Lewis, 123
Trout, Dollie Ann, 36
Trout, William, 35
Troutman, Franklin, 156
Trowbridge, Isaac, 162
Troy, Patrick, 232
Trujillo, Paula, 171
Tryon, J. R., 144
Tucker, Emeline, 134
Tulley, Mark, 141
Tully, John, 119
Tully, Patrick, 134
Tungkahotara, Chanida, 104
Turner, Charles, 135
Turner, Daisy, 264
Turner, Joe, 45
Turner, John, 156
Twain, Mark, 185, 195
Tweety, Sarah, 84
Tyler, Erastus B., 22
Tyree, Willianna, 30

U

U.S. Army Signal Corps, 130
U.S. Marines, 234
U.S. Military Academy Detachment, 253
U.S. Navy, 185, 217
U.S. Secret Service, 41
Ulch, George W., 119
Ulman, Hezekiah C., 40
Underhill, William A., 173
Underwood, David, 128
Underwood, Julia, 128
Underwood, Maria, 259
Union Army, 16, 50
Union Wharf, 119
University of Missouri, 83
University of Virginia, 181
Urquhart, Samuel, 59
USS *Canandaigua*, 232

USS *Cayuga*, 239
USS *Cimarron*, 144
USS *Delaware*, 239
USS *Great Western*, 89
USS *Hendrick Hudson*, 232
USS *Kensington*, 240
USS *Lancaster*, 232
USS *Muscoota*, 145
USS *Osage*, 232
USS *Restless*, 193
USS *Sagamore*, 144
USS *Shenandoah*, 193
USS *Squando*, 46
Ustick, William, 207
Utabarri, Desidirio, 241
Utley, Robert, 265

V

Vail, Herbert, 91
Vail, Nicholas, 208
Van Auken, Elijah, 81
Van Zant, James R., 86
Vance, Henrietta, 182
Vanderbogart, Allen, 59
Vanderhorst, R. H., 135
Vanderlip, Mary E., 32, 33
Vanderlip, Thomas, 172
Vaughn, John, 182
Vaughn, Johnson J., 88
Vaughn, William, 257
Veil Uplifted, The, 253
Veitch, James, 98
venereal diseases, 251-252
Verginia, 115
Vermont, 215
Vernon, Elizabeth, 164
Verret, Artemis, 163
Veteran's Reserve Corps, 75
Veterans Reserve Corps, 268
Vincent, Fanny, 31
Vincent, John, 169

Virginia Beach, 123
Virginia Military Institute, 265
Virginia Tech, 42
Vogdes, Israel, 140
Voluntary Service, 268
Volunteer Drilling, 245-246

W

Waddle, Frances, 25
Waddle, Harvey, 223
Wade, Maria, 118
Wade, Rebecca P., 153
Wadsworth, Hogan, 249
Wadsworth, James, 241
Wagner, Frederick, 159
Wald, Paul, 53
Walder, Mary, 29
Waldron, Mary, 30
Walker, Polly, 123
Walker, W. M., 215
Walker, William, 138, 157
Wall, Andrew, 208
Wallenus, François, 140
Walls, Elizabeth Ann, 156
Walten, Richard, 258
Walters, William W., 128
War Department Collection of Confederate Records, 267
Ward, Ellen, 168
Ward, William, 74
Wardlaw, Alfred Lewis, 205
Warner, A. C., 133
Warnick, Robert, 159
Washburn, A. L., 198
Washington College, 181
Washington Post, 104
Washington, George, 197
Washington, Susan, 168
Waterbury, David A., 47
Waterfield, Elizabeth, 37
Waterson, Salina, 193

Watkins, W. C., 82
Watters, John, 214
Waxey, Alfred, 127
Weatherby, Albert, 77
Weaver, Alfred, 165
Weaver, John, 190
Webb, J. C., 175
Webster, Elizabeth, 147
Webster, Lambert, 165
Weddieken, Louis, 209
Weed, Thurlow, 199
weenie wavers, 259
Weir, J. M., 206
Weitzel, Henry, 202
Weldon, George, 259
Weller, Oliver, 223, 225
Welles, Gideon, 214
Wells, Charles V., 128
Wells, Frederick B., 127
Wells, H. H., 17
Wells, Louise, 266
Wentworth Publishing House, 67
Wenz, Charles, 161
West Point, 98, 179, 197, 238, 253, 259
West, Frances, 127
Western Lunatic Asylum, 187
Whaley Hotel, 85
Whaley, James D., 85
Wheeler, Annie, 107
Whipple, William D., 157
Whitbeck, James, 56
White Oak Church, 125
White, Ellen Gould
   An Appeal to Mothers, 184
White, Frances, 37
White, James, 134
White, John, 168
White, Lewis M., 87
White, Maria, 224
White, Richard, 139
White, Samuel, 80
White, V. A., 76

Whitias, Lizzie, 69
Whiting, Horace G., 159
Whitress, Lizzie, 70
Whitt, Samuel, 254
Wiggins, H. L., 192
Wilcox, Indiana, 36
Wilcox, Sarah, 221
Wiley, Bell Irvin
　Life of Johnny Reb, 12
Wiley, Ferdinand, 191
Wiley, James, 156
Wilgers, Charles, 213
Willard, Ella, 28
Willard, Frank, 99
Willard, Nancy, 164
Willet, Anna, 28
William G. Anderson, 214
William Land Park, 94
William, Lucy, 119
Williams, Anne, 34
Williams, Anne (a.k.a. Charles Waters), 259
Williams, Annie, 34
Williams, Delia, 27
Williams, Edward, 56
Williams, Emma, 36
Williams, Evan, 162
Williams, Frances, 36
Williams, Henry, 211
Williams, Henry R., 106
Williams, James, 52, 144
Williams, James E., 59
Williams, John, 160
Williams, Joseph, 38
Williams, Lewis, 145
Williams, Lidia, 60
Williams, Mary, 68, 79
Williams, Sue, 88
Williamson County, 157
Williamson, J. H., 142
Williamson, Peter, 52
Williamson, Sarah, 142
Willis, Fowler, 162

Willis, Martha, 166
Wilson, Annie, 70
Wilson, Benjamin, 165
Wilson, Edward W., 82
Wilson, George, 20
Wilson, James, 155
Wilson, Joshua, 79
Wilson, Mary, 20, 27, 37
Wingold, Evert, 37
Winkelmaier's Pontonier Company, 207
Winn, Lizzie, 27
Winne, Patsey, 27
Winooski, 213
Winstead, Jacob, 158
Winter, Henry, 49
Wiseman, H. H., 167
Wittenham, Emma, 27
Wittkamp, Anna Eliza, 168
Wolferton, Elza, 82
Wood, 109
Wood, Moll, 33
Wood, Samuel, 48
Wood, William H., 143
Wooden, John, 191
Woodham, Martha, 144
Woods, Daniel, 50
Woods, Kate, 71
Woods, Samuel, 91
Woodson, Eliza H., 118
Woodson, Moses, 260
Woodward, Emma, 33
Woodward, William, 61
Woolf, Clarence, 136
Woolf, Hamilton, 136
Workman, Commodore, 79
Wrenn, Thomas, 237
Wright, Charles, 171
Wright, Charles D., 85
Wright, Fanny, 66
Wright, Lizzie, 48
Wright, Mahaly, 123
Wykoff, Jesse, 259

X

Xenophon, 15

Y

Yance, Anna, 45
Yarbroth, Nancy, 148
Yarbrough, Jenny, 56
Yardley, Jonathan, 7
Yetts, Howard, 222, 227
Yokum, Catherine, 84
Yorktown, 41
Young, Abner, 124
Young, Anice, 159
Young, C. B., 38
Young, Calvin, 155
Young, Leena, 176
Young, Maggie, 159
Young, Richard, 256
Young, William
  Amativeness or the Confessional: A Treatise on Onanism and Self-Abuse, Manhood's Debilities, as Impediments to Marriage and Premature Failure of Sexual Power, to Which Is Added the Confessions of Many Young and Old Men who had been Rescued from the Verge of the Grave., 185
  French Safe or Cover, 250
  Marriage Guide—A Great Physiological Work or Everyone His Own Doctor, 253

Z

Zizeciak, John, 18

Made in the USA
Middletown, DE
10 April 2025